THE NEW POLITICAL GEOGRAPHY
OF
EASTERN EUROPE

THE NEW POLITICAL GEOGRAPHY
OF
EASTERN EUROPE

edited by

John O'Loughlin and
Herman van der Wusten

Belhaven Press
London and New York

Co-published in the Americas by Halsted Press,
an imprint of John Wiley & Sons, Inc.

Belhaven Press
(a division of Pinter Publishers)
25 Floral Street, Covent Garden, London, WC2E 9DS, United Kingdom

First published in 1993

Co-published in the Americas by Halsted Press, an imprint of
John Wiley & Sons, Inc., 605 Third Avenue, New York, NY 10158-0012

British Library Cataloguing in Publication Data
A CIP catalogue record for this book is available from the British Library

ISBN 1 85293 259 7

Library of Congress Cataloguing-in-Publication Data
The new political geography of Eastern Europe / edited by John O' Loughlin
  and Herman van der Wusten.
     p. cm.
  "Co-published in the Americas by Halsted Press, an imprint of John
Wiley & Sons, Inc."
  Includes bibliographical references and index.
  ISBN 1–85293–259–7. – ISBN 0–470–21933–5 (U.S.)
  1. Europe, Eastern – Politics and government – 1989–
I. O' Loughlin, John V. (John Vianney) II. Wusten, Herman van der.
DJK51.N49 1993
947.085' – dc20   92–36085
                                                                          CIP

ISBN 0 470 219 33 5 (in the Americas only)

Typeset by PanTek Arts
Printed and bound in Great Britain by Biddles Ltd., Guildford and King's Lynn

Contents

List of contributors   vii

Preface   ix

Part I Introduction

1. The new political geography of Eastern Europe   1
    John O'Loughlin and Herman van der Wusten

2. The transition to democracy   9
    Jiri Musil

Part II Geopolitical shifts

3. Breaking the Cold War mould in Europe: a geopolitical tale of gradual   15
    change and sharp snaps
    Jan Nijman and Herman van der Wusten

4. Precursor of crisis: political and economic relations of the   31
    Soviet Union, 1960–90
    John O'Loughlin

5. Geopolitical transitions in agriculture: the changing role of   53
    American food policyin Eastern Europe, 1955–91
    Janet E. Kodras

6. Post-Cold War security in the new Europe   71
    Simon Dalby

Part III Social and political transformations

7. Ethno-national aspirations in the Soviet Union and its successor regimes: 89
    juggling with options
    Petr Dostál

8. Pluralist mobilization as a catalyst for the dismemberment of Yugoslavia   115
    Snjezana Mrdjen

9. Gypsies in Czechoslavakia: demographic developments and policy perspectives 133
    Kveta Kalibova, Tomas Haisman and Jitka Gjuricova

10. The stolen revolution: minorities in Romania after Ceausescu   145
    Leo Paul

11. Environmental politics, democracy and economic restructuring in Bulgaria   167
  John Pickles and the Bourgas Group

Part IV   New electoral geographies

12. The electoral geography of the former Soviet Union, 1989–91:   189
  retrospective comparisons and theoretical issues
  Vladimir Kolossov

13. Democratic elections and political restructuring in Poland, 1989–91   217
  Joanna Regulska

14. Czechoslovak parliamentary elections 1990: old patterns,   235
  new trends and lots of surprises
  Petr Jehlicka, Tomás Kostelecky and Ludek Sykora

15. The political geography of Hungarian parliamentary   255
  elections, 1989
  Zoltán Kovacs

Index   274

List of contributors

Simon Dalby
Centre for International Studies, Simon Fraser University, Burnaby BC V5A 1S6, Canada

Petr Dostál
Instituut voor Sociale Geografie, Universiteit van Amsterdam, Nieuwe Prinsengracht 130, 1018 VZ Amsterdam, Netherlands.

Tomas Haisman
Department of Human Rights and Humanitarian Issues, Office of the Government, Czech and Slovak Federative Republic, Prague, Czechoslovakia.

Jitka Gjuricova
Department of Human Rights and Humanitarian Issues, Office of the Government, Czech and Slovak Federative Republic, Prague, Czechoslovakia.

Petr Jehlicka
Insitute of Demography, Faculty of Science, Charles University, Albertov 6, 12643 Prague, Czechoslovakia.

Kveta Kalibova
Department of Demography and Geodemography, Faculty of Science, Charles University, Albertov 6, 12643 Prague, Czechoslovakia.

Janet E. Kodras
Department of Geography, Florida State University, 358 Bellamy Building, Tallahassee, FL. 32306-2050, USA.

Vladimir Kolossov
Laboratory for Global Geographical Problems, Russian Academy of Sciences, Staromonetsky próspekt 29, Moscow 109017, Russia.

Tomás Kostelecky
Czechoslovak Academy of Sciences, Jilska 1, 110 00 Praha 1, Czech and Slovak, Federative Republic (CSFR).

Zoltán Kovacs
Magyar Tudomanyos Akadememia, Andrassy UT 62 Postbox 64, Budapest VI, Hungary.

Snjezana Mrdjen
Bureau des stagiares, Institut National des Etudes Démographiques, 27 rue du Commandeur, 75675 Paris 14, France.

Jiri Musil
Institute of Sociology, Czechoslovak Academy of Sciences, Jilska 1, 110 00 Praha 1, Czechoslovakia.

Jan Nijman
Department of Geography, University of Miami, Box 248152, Coral Gables, FL., 33124-8152, USA.

John O'Loughlin
Institute of Behavioral Science, University of Colorado, Campus Box 487, Boulder, CO. 80309-0487, USA.

Leo Paul
Geografisch Instituut, Universiteit van Utrecht, Postbox 80115, 3508 TC Utrecht, Netherlands.

John Pickles
Department of Geography, University of Kentucky, 1457 Patterson Office Tower, Lexington, KY 40506-0027, USA.

Joanna Regulska
Department of Geography, Rutgers University, New Brunswick, NJ 08903, USA.

Luděk Sýkora
Czechoslovak Academy of Sciences, Jilska 1, 110 00 Praha 1, Czech and Slovak Federative Republic (CSFR).

Herman van der Wusten
Instituut voor Sociale Geografie, Universiteit van Amsterdam, Nieuwe Prinsengracht 130, 1018 VZ Amsterdam, Netherlands.

Preface

The idea for a conference of geographers concerned with the sea-changes taking place in 'Eastern Europe' occurred to Stanley Brunn in late 1989, as the icy structures that had so long held Eastern Europe were collapsing. David Knight, chair of the Commission on the World Political Map of the International Geographical Union quickly accepted the idea of organizing the conference as part of the Commission's working programme and a very informal committee was set up to get the conference underway. Our thanks are due to the Commission for their sponsorship and encouragement. Since it was started at a meeting in Oxford in 1983, this Commission has been very active in bringing political geographers together from many different countries and ideologies at meetings in all parts of the world.

This book is one product of the week-long conference on the political changes in 'Eastern Europe' held in Prague in late August 1991. The conference programme was put together by Stanley Brunn, Jiri Musil, John O'Loughlin and Herman van der Wusten while the day-to-day organization and conference facilities were superbly handled by Tomas Kucera of the Institute of Demography, Charles University, Prague, where the conference was held. The success of the conference was due in large measure to the sincerity, organizational work and friendliness of the Czech hosts. Participants from North America, East and Central Europe and Israel got a glimpse of the ongoing problems of political and economic transformation by field-trips to the old industrial areas in Northern Bohemia, with one of the worst cases of water, land and air pollution in Europe. A week in Prague and a cursory tour along the spas of the same Northern Bohemia provided some additional thoughts on the enamouring parts of an even longer tradition that, inevitably, is already being touched by the current transformations.

The conference occurred just days after the failed coup in Moscow that touched off the final stages in the demise of the Soviet Union. This underlined the volatile nature of the subject participants discussed, if they needed any reminder, and was the subject of lengthy discussion in the paper sessions and in the breaks. Forty people from fifteen countries turned up to report on the current changes in all parts of what used to be called Eastern Europe, including the then-Soviet Union. The title of the conference copied the theme of a famous issue of the journal *Daedalus* (Vol. 1991, no. 1 1990) that pointed in a direction, set out a programme, and expressed some uncertainty: 'Eastern Europe . . . Central Europe . . . Europe.'

From the thirty-five papers presented at the conference, the editors selected thirteen and commissioned two additional chapters to fill obvious gaps. The fifteen chapters in this book have been written by authors currently living in seven but born in nine different countries. This results from migration but additional changes of address are looming as countries unravel and the world political map is re-drawn. These collected papers are presented as a first shot (no serious violence intended) at the new political geography of the territory that used to be called Eastern Europe, including the Soviet

Union; it does not shy away from discussing the Asian part of that former state. Momentous changes are obviously still underway in the region. We cannot hope to make any definitive statements at this juncture. We do hope that we have provided some useful background and perspectives that can be profitably applied in the interpretation of history as it, quite unpredictably, unfolds still further. There is no end in sight yet.

Part I
Introduction

1 The new political geography of Eastern Europe

John O'Loughlin and Herman van der Wusten

'We only travelled with our fingers on the map' the woman said as she was pouring the breakfast tea. We were the guests in a house on a vast housing estate on the outskirts of Prague at the end of the summer of 1991 discussing the old times. The times before 1989 that is, when civil society came to life and the discredited regimes all over Eastern Europe were toppled, finally leading to the demise of the Soviet Union, the state that had embodied one side of the Cold War order. It had discouraged free travel apart from a moving finger on a map. Now that map was being redrawn.

Not only are the features of a fairly longstanding map in jeopardy but the geographical notions that go with it are looked at anew, reinterpreted, and deconstructed. The notion of Europe has for a time been partially captured by Community Europe, the Europe of the 6 (now 12), Europe for short. This was always disputed to some extent not only by those who maintained that Europe was more than this fragment of the traditional continent. It was also challenged by views that held an Atlantic Community as the primordial unit of allegiance for Europeans (it was never quite clear to whom that applied precisely) so that any European identity was on the verge of extinction.

This capture of the notion of Europe as a designation of a fragment did not prevent the term 'Eastern Europe' from remaining common parlance. After the Cold War had frozen the border between East and the rest, its western edge was hardly in doubt. The discussion on the location of 'Mitteleuropa' (Schultz, 1989) that had occupied geographers of the pre-World War II generation had well-nigh disappeared along with the whole concept of an area in the middle. In the East, the question of where Eastern Europe ended was never satisfactorily resolved. Depending on political views and historical precedent, it might be one of the historical Polish–Russian borders, it might be the undistinguished Ural mountains, or the 'Europeanness' could diminish asymptotically as one entered the endlessness of Siberia. Clearly the seemingly insignificant peninsula at the margin of the Asian continent was divided but how far Europe extended, or to what region it should primarily belong, was less unanimously perceived.

The events of 1989 have produced a watershed in the recent history and geography of Europe. Eastern Europe has opened up at its western side and there is another round of discussion on Mitteleuropa. Community Europe's position is much discussed, no longer self-evidently part of an Atlantic Community, extending its own influence in all directions but now a contested identity. European history has reached uncharted waters. In this book, we explore some of the major issues arising from the explosion of post-World War II Eastern Europe. We analyse some of the reasons why these transformative processes occurred and why they did when they did. We encounter new political geographies that evolve from the revolutionary changes that are underway. The new political geography of Eastern Europe will possibly become a partial political geography of Europe but it will take time before this is the case. In the meantime, highly distinctive processes of transformation are underway; they are the research agenda for this book.

A geopolitical shift of major significance broke the moorings of the post-World War II order in 1989. The rumblings could be heard before and the shift did not occur overnight. It took some years before it was completed. After Mikhail Gorbachev came to power in 1985 as Secretary-General of the Communist Party of the Soviet Union, the changes that had been stalled and the old structures that had been shored up for so long became unlocked by deliberate acts of political leadership. This was initially aimed at the improvement of East–West relations. Once under way, it had to be extended towards Eastern Europe in loosening the intimate links with the local 'stadtholders' in order to keep the momentum of East–West *détente* intact.

In 1988/89, Poland and Hungary started their revolutions where reform was preached and sought and revolutionary change got underway. The roundtable discussions saw new political actors cast in major roles on the scenes of those countries. Semi-free elections in Poland showed the illegitimacy of the Communist superstructure. In the autumn of 1989, East German crowds forced the retreat of the regime, the opening of the Berlin Wall. In a week of fairly soft but sustained pressure, the 'velvet revolution' of Czechoslovakia brought the communist regime there to an end. In the meantime, the Bulgarian communists were trying to compromise with the opposition forces as best they could by removing the old leadership. In an unforgettable moment seen on the world television screens, President Ceaucescu was shouted down while addressing a crowd that had so often been forced into humble applause for his deeds. The ensuing revolt led to his death and an extremely confused situation that has not yet been clarified.

The dynamics of change in East Germany implicated the West German state at once and in turn, their common fate touched the raw nerves of the East–West relationship. In a daring move, the West Germans took the initiative (pushed by circumstances or attracted by the opportunities or both) and kept it during a year that ended in German reunification at the end of 1990. The newly-constructed Germany was then certified by the four victorious Allies of World War II in Paris, finally bringing that war to a closure.

The Yugoslav experiment, seriously in trouble ever since President Josef Broz Tito's death in 1980, during 1989 became confronted with more threatening gestures of secession, as pluralism was allowed in the northern republics, resulting in the still-temporary drawing of new international boundaries and the creating of new states. Finally, even the communist regime in little, poor, marginal and extremely isolated Albania had to adjust and open up to the world, showing a level of distress that had been hard to imagine.

The Soviet domino, standing after the 1989 wave had subsided, fell two years later after ever-increasing ethnic unrest and efforts from various sides to leave the Union. The economy progressively deteriorated through mismanagement and a series of half-hearted efforts at reform. The Soviet Union not only was no longer but it fell apart in fragments of uncertain size that were entering into patterns of unpredictable mutual relations.

In this book, the way the old pattern broke is discussed from different perspectives. There is an overall discussion of the slowly changing geopolitical forces, power distributions and relational networks in extended Europe. The decline of the Soviet economy as a conditioning factor of change is analysed. There is also an insight into one of the major instruments used by the US to drive its foreign policy preferences home: food aid. These topics relate to the whole issue of the renewal of security relations in Europe now that a bipolar world is no longer a viable proposition, and that only therefore has its potentially fatal attraction subsided. Again very much on its own, the European world has to look for the maintenance of durable peace, a duty it has occasionally neglected in the past.

As processes of internal transformation, external reorientation and possible territorial rearrangement in the former Soviet Union, former Yugoslavia and elsewhere started, some of the old problems of the Balkans and Eastern Europe showed up as if they had never been away, especially issues of competing nationalities on the same territory. Other issues are novel as they result from regimes that harshly tried to imprint certain characteristics on societies that resisted but could not escape from all the pressure that was mounted against them. Foremost among the legacies are dependent attitudes towards the state and the anomie that results from its demise, the destruction of entrepreneurial skills, the death of respect for the rule of law and the unlearning of the necessity of contract compliance. The combination of these resurfaced problems and the more recent ethno-territorial problems gives rise to the new political geography of Eastern Europe.

Geography has to do with the specificity of place. Political geography is concerned with the way in which societies resolve their basic problems. For former eastern Europe, how they handle the differences of orientation resulting from nationalism in their state structures, and how they make policy depending on local circumstances, are major problems. An over-arching issue is how they cope with the great difficulties that transformation out of communism and towards liberal democracy and a market economy implies, given local tradition, experience and opportunities and constraints that result from the cumulative experience of earlier economic development.

This book discusses the ethno-territorial drive and its destructive result for the two major cases of Eastern Europe (the then Soviet Union and Yugoslavia) and analyses the problem of one of the most enduring, mobile, and difficult minority problems, that of the Gypsies. It charts the efforts of post-communist states to adapt their state structures to the new circumstances, taking Poland as an example. It also sketches the way the environmental issue plays its part in the transformative processes underway in the region. The book does not directly touch upon the ways governments struggle with the central problem of transforming the economy from an etatist socialist to a free market economy with all the problems of small and big privatization, monetary policy and social policy that are implied.

There is a major section on the electoral fortunes of parties and politicians in the former eastern countries of Czechoslovakia, Hungary, Poland, and Soviet Union/Russia. The way mock elections have been transformed into free and secret ballots, how populations have reacted in terms of turnout, and what sort of political forces they have favoured is all part of these chapters.

The chapters in this book are not stereotypical, that is, they do not focus on the relations between states or the sea-changes brought about by the events of the late 1980s in East/Central Europe. Neither do they deal solely with the changing political life *sensu stricto* of the former East European countries. Instead, each author broadens the discussion to incorporate elements of a changing world: social, economic, political, cultural and even spiritual. About half of the authors are political geographers and about half were born in the former Eastern Europe. This blending of backgrounds and perspectives offers a rare chance of evaluating a major geopolitical transition in both its international context and its impacts on the daily lives of individuals in the affected states.

In the following chapter, Jiri Musil, a sociologist from Prague, offers a penetrating analysis of the kinds of differences that often go unnoticed between democracy and authoritarianism. He treats the chasm in beliefs that separates the two systems and notes how hard it is to leap that chasm after indoctrination in one belief or the other. He compares the diffusion of democracy in the former East European communist states to developments in the Third World and views the revolutions of 1989–1991 as part of a global process. There remains one salient difference, however; some East European countries had well-developed democratic structures before 1948 (Czechoslovakia, (East) Germany, Poland and Hungary). The prospects for a smooth transition to democracy and material prosperity for the states of Eastern Europe are still uncertain and depend in part on the success of entrepreneur capitalism, the ability to mould a national consensus on democratic processes, the acceptance of pluralism and the protection of minority rights. The tensions produced by multi-nationalism and the presence of sizeable numbers of minorities in all the states east of the Elbe will complicate the consensus-building process but will stand as an indicator of the level of liberal democratic principles.

In the section on the wider international geopolitical setting of the revolutions in former Eastern Europe, four chapters deal respectively with the evolving relations between the two major geopolitical blocs and the individual developments of the superpowers towards changing political and economic events in Europe. Jan Nijman and Herman van der Wusten treat 1989 as a year of geopolitical transition, a development that we can only construe as happening a couple of times earlier in this century, 1945 and 1907 (Taylor, 1993). Though the Cold War (1945–1989) had the appearance of ossified forms and an unbending rigidity of the blocs, both internally and externally, these two authors show how the United States and the former Soviet Union, having organized their respective blocs, allowed their bilateral relations to ebb and flow over time. Within the NATO bloc, especially, there was an easing away from the US hegemony over time by the West European states, foremost among them, West Germany and its Ostpolitik. Because of the national umbilical cord to East Germany, the Federal Republic could never turn its back on its eastern neighbours and tried, at times seemingly in vain, to maintain the bridge to the east. In one interpretation, the 1989 events were a vindication of 'Ostpolitik'. NATO and its US command was essentially a bystander to the developments surrounding the Gorbachev whirlwind. While the former Eastern bloc has changed utterly, the Western bloc has not yet reformulated a new geostrategy for a new age.

It was obvious from the beginning of the post-war era that Soviet policy would be instrumental in determining events in Eastern Europe. In his chapter, John O'Loughlin examines the economic background to the Soviet change of course in the 1980s. By the time of the accession to power of Mikhail Gorbachev in 1985, the economic crisis was already well developed in the USSR and O'Loughlin, in a world-systems interpretation, looks at the basis for the crisis for which there was only one escape, after the autarkic door was nailed shut. The Soviet Union had to integrate its economy with that of the capitalist world rather than pursuing the resource economy route that had led to rapidly-falling export earnings in the 1980s. For the integration to occur, a diminution of the ideological Cold War and military tension was an essential first step. The Soviet Union could no longer afford the relative costs of the Cold War in the absence of perceived benefits to the quality of everyday life in the country.

The United States, though taken by surprise by the events of 1989 (as was almost every observer), had been instrumental in codifying the Cold War and setting the terms of interaction by the allies of the West. Though accepting the geopolitical fault-line down the middle of Europe as fixed, while at the same time stating that it was unacceptable (Cox, 1990; Kaldor, 1990), the US tried to make use of its food surplus to wean two East European states, Poland and Yugoslavia, from the Soviet alliance. Janet Kodras shows how the development of US aid policy to the six countries of the Soviet bloc and to Yugoslavia was predicated on political relations between the super-powers, on developments in the individual East European countries and on domestic American political pressures, as a political fillip to both the surplus-producing US farmers and the immigrant Polish and Yugoslav voting interests. After 1989, the 'food as foreign policy competition' with the Soviet Union changed to a 'food as influence competition' with the US core allies of the European Community, another food sur-plus producer. Though the Bush Administration has consistently stated that the US will not be excluded from influence in the post-1989 Eastern Europe, budgetary limi-tations preclude another Marshall Plan and the US is reduced to a food weapon for generating influence. The limitations of that policy can be seen by the probable under-mining of food production in Eastern Europe and the restrictions placed on East European food exporters by the European Community and the US. Food dumping is not the kind of investment assistance that the new capitalists of Eastern Europe envi-sioned from the West.

The final chapter in this section, by Simon Dalby, poses the most difficult ques-tions of all since it concerns the notion of security in the post-Cold War world. This is not just a question for the former East, which has disbanded the Warsaw Pact; there have already been discussions of some eastern states, especially Czechoslovakia, joining NATO. It also constitutes a challenge to the former West. Dalby believes that the aims of END (European Nuclear Disarmament) were achieved by the Gorbachev initiatives and assisted by the close links of END leaders in London with the dissidents of central Europe, in Prague and Budapest especially. One of the major rallying-cries of END was to go beyond the blocs, to rid Europe of the two military pacts. One is now gone, can the other be far behind?

The second section of the book begins with a discussion of the nationalities ques-tion in the former Soviet Union by Petr Dostál. The dismantling of the state was along the lines of the fifteen republics which in turn were based on the notion of titular groups, that is, the groups that have a legal claim to territory as defined in the consti-tution. In effect, they constituted the majorities in each of the republics that are now independent, but also there are other groups who are titular with respect to sub-areas of the Russian state. Whether or not this titular right is converted into territorial sov-ereignty now is still an open question and may lead to further boundary re-makings in the independent states. Dostal examines the relations between the titular and non-titu-lar groups in the various regions of the former Soviet Union and evaluates the possibil-ities for further ethnic/territorial strife in each region. He ends his chapter with a con-sideration of the extent to which the nationalities question is temporarily or perma-nently resolved and the effects of this perplexing spatial intermingling of often-antago-nistic groups on the country and the east/central European space.

The contemporary war in Yugoslavia is the result of the territorial decisions made earlier in this century by the ethnic groups and the outside powers. Snjezana Mrdjen shows clearly the power of the Serbian group in the new state formed after the first World War and how the careful ethnic balance was tipped over in the aftermath of the death of Josef Tito and the end of the Cold War in 1989. The post-1989 elections showed a bifurcation between the Serbian regions which continue to choose communists and the non-Serbian regions which preferred non-communist independence-minded reformers. Thus, ideology and nationalism became interchangeable in the Yugoslav federal republic and the problems of the double minorities (e.g. Croats in Bosnia-Hercegovina) and ethno-territorial irredentism (e.g., the Serbian Krajina in Croatia) became the daily staple of the nightly news. Whether the Yugoslav model will become the norm for the other multi-national states of the former eastern Europe is still an open and frightening question.

The chapter by Kveta Kalibova, Tomas Haisman and Jitka Gjuricova also treats an ethnic minority but, unlike the groups that form the basis for the discussion of the previous two chapters, the Gypsy minority is not fixed to a territorial base. The couple of million Gypsies are found in all the countries of central Europe and are especially numerous in Czechoslovakia, Rumania, and Yugoslavia with scattered communities now in western Europe. Does the absence of a territorial claim make the settlement of a minority's demands easier? The evidence from eastern Europe so far has to be no. Efforts to 'absorb' the Gypsies have so far failed miserably, as the results of the urban settlement policy in Czechoslovakia show. Always the most marginal social group in the countries where they live, it is expected that Gypsies will bear the brunt of any economic failures of the proto-capitalist societies now developing in post-communist Eastern Europe. The attempted mass migration of the Romany population to western Europe, where they will receive a very cold shoulder, is likely to result from any large increase in discrimination and racially-motivated attacks in the eastern countries.

Rumania provides a nice test case of whether an authoritarian regimes like the one that existed in the Ceausescu years is significantly different from the post-repression societies. Rumania is usually not viewed as a multi-national society but as Leo Paul shows, there are large numbers of Hungarians, Germans, Jews and Gypsies that find themselves in a continued precarious state under a regime that is the least affected by the events of 1989. In fact, ethnic tensions are in many ways now more dangerous than they were under the Ceausescu regime. The present regime in Rumania is more xenophobic than its predecessor. The tension with Hungary about the status of ethnic Hungarians in Rumania is the most likely to result in conflict but by 'voting with their feet' and moving to Germany, where they have a constitutional right to settle, the German minority has indicated that they hold little hope for improvement of their status. If one had to rank the former communist states on the scale of social turmoil, Rumania would be in the top rank with the multi-national and territorially complex former states of Yugoslavia and the Soviet Union.

The environmental damage caused by the communist regimes in their industrial drives is, by now, well known. In an provocative essay on Bulgaria, John Pickles takes the theme of environmentalism as his framework for a wider discussion of how a post-communist transformation can be sidelined. The opposition found the environmental damage to be a strong rallying-cry to unite all sorts of groups who otherwise would have little in common. After they managed to oust the Zhivkov regime, they themselves were unable to push the environmental platform in the face of major economic problems, the fact that Bulgaria is still dependent on its heavy industry and does not have the resources to carry out a major environmental clean-up. Environmentalism was detoured into economic redevelopment to such an extent that the Greens were unable to win any seats in the free elections of October 1990.

The third section of the book offers a comparative analysis of the geographic and legislative outcomes of the post-1989 elections. Each of the authors explains the main voting coalitions, the social, economic and geographic basis of their support and documents the governmental outcomes on the basis of the voter support. Thus, the reader can see the similarities and differences between the four countries, the Soviet Union, Poland, Czechoslovakia and Hungary. Vladimir Kolossov has written the first detailed analysis of recent Soviet elections (Kolossov et al., 1990) and in his chapter in this book, he continues this innovative work with an interesting comparison of the rapidly-evolving electoral scene in the Soviet Union in the 'year of great changes', 1989–90. He treats the respective campaigns, party choices, electoral appeals, geographic bases of support and abstention as a form of protest in two key referenda, the Russian Presidential election of 1990 and the earlier 1989 election to the Congress of Peoples Deputies. In a particularly interesting account, he traces the local electoral campaign in a Central Asian locality near the Aral sea and shows how the former communists were able to stay in power under different labels until swept aside by Kazahk nationalists.

In her treatment of the complex restructuring of the legislative and local administrative composition of Poland, Joanna Regulska demonstrates clearly that the process of building democracy is a long hard road. Poland has seen an amazing variety of political positions and parties consequent on the splintering of the longtime opposition, Solidarity, after 1990. Since Poland has been a leader of sorts in many aspects of the revolutions in Eastern Europe (Garton Ash, 1989, 1990), its experiences with elections, government-building, state- and civil society-making, and changing hats from non-governmental opposition to governing will be instructive for the other countries.

A very interesting feature of the paper by the Czech researchers, Petr Jehlička, Tomáš Kostelecký and Luděk Sýkora, is the comparison of the patterns of voting choices in the 1990 election to the patterns that existed in the last election before the communists came to power in 1948. The traditional core areas of support did not change much and though the party names might have changed, the regional appeals remain similar despite the intervening four decades of repression. In the neighbouring country of Hungary, which has had so many elections in the past three years that the turnout in the recent local elections was only seven per cent, a growing disillusionment with politicians and parties can already be detected. Party choices are crystallizing over time but the continued core-periphery within the country will remain visible in the voting choices. Hungarian politics is perhaps the most 'developed' in the sense of closely emulating the Western democratic model but the early euphoria at free elections has vanished in the harsh light of the continued economic distress and increasing unemployment.

In Poland, Czechoslovakia, the former Soviet Union, Bulgaria, and in Hungary, moderately conservative free market parties have achieved most success so far as the newly-enfranchised electorates have opted for the fast track to economic development and capitalism. But in all countries, there remains some loyalty to the former communists (though the names have changed, the voters know who is who and these parties received between one-third of the votes in Bulgaria and about 10 per cent in Poland

and in Czechoslovakia). If the economic situation does not improve soon, we can expect major electoral shifts in the absence yet of stable party politics and the growing attraction of autonomous movements.

References

Cox, M., 1990, 'From the Truman Doctrine to the second superpower detente: the rise and fall of the Cold War', *Journal of Peace Research*, **27** (1): 25–41.

Garton Ash, T., 1989, *The uses of adversity*, Random House, New York.

Garton Ash, T., 1990, *The magic lantern: the revolutions of 1989 witnessed in Berlin, Prague, Budapest and Warsaw*, Random House, New York.

Kaldor, M., 1990, *The imaginary war: understanding the East-West conflict*, Basil Blackwell, Oxford.

Kolossov V.A., Petrov N.V., and Smirniagin L.V. (eds), 1990, *BECHA 89 (Spring 89: the geography and the anatomy of parliamentary elections)*. Progress Publishers, Moscow, 1990 (in Russian).

Schultz, H-D., 1989, 'Fantasies of Mitte, Mittellage and Mitteleuropa in German geographical discussion in the 19th and 20th centuries', *Political Geography Quarterly* **8**, (4):315–39.

Taylor, P.J., 1993, 'Geopolitical orders', In P.J. Taylor (ed.) *Political Geography of the Twentieth Century*, Belhaven Press, London, forthcoming.

2 The transition to democracy

Jiri Musil

The extent of changes which the countries of Central and Eastern Europe are passing through at present can be compared to that after the French revolution or after the two World Wars in our century. These changes, as it is well known, are composed of four interacting processes:

1. The collapse of the great social utopian project of communism; this also includes the disintegration of political, economic as well as cultural institutions derived from Marxism–Leninism;
2. The substitution of old institutions by new ones, which is, in fact, the building-up of new states on the principle of pluralistic democracy, market economy and civil society. In some countries, such as Czechoslovakia, this means a return to the developmental trajectory which was interrupted by World War II and by some forty years of communist rule;
3. In most countries concerned, however, the political transformations are rather a kind of 'postponed' liberal revolutions. In effect, this is an attempt to catch up with Western European countries, which had partly started their liberal transformation in the 17th century and partly after the French Revolution of 1789; and
4. The disintegration of the COMECON and of the Warsaw Pact Alliance, associations dominated by the Soviet Union.

The full geopolitical impact of the internal changes which the aforementioned countries are still undergoing cannot as yet be assessed. On the one hand, these changes are as yet not finished (this applies mainly to economic transformations); on the other hand, it is not clear what will be the most probable outcomes of the internal transformations on mutual relationships between post-communist countries and between these countries and Western Europe and the world in general.

In spite of the fact that almost all parts of these Eastern and Central European countries are as yet not stabilized and structured, it is possible to describe with relative accuracy the basic patterns of the internal changes as well as to estimate the risks connected with the transformation. Since geopolitical processes are, to a large extent, always affected by internal political and economic processes in individual countries, it is necessary, if we want to understand the international effects of the 1989 revolutions, to devote attention in this introduction to the most important part of the ongoing political transformations, that is, to the transition to democracy.

The attention given to this part of the transformation of post-communist societies is also important for another reason. After the first euphoric phase of the 1989 East European revolutions, it became evident that the collapse of the communist regimes does not lead automatically to liberal democracy. The heritage of the past forty years, and in the former Soviet Union of more than seventy years, created barriers which can be overcome only with the utmost effort. Among the positive elements influencing the East European transformation was the world-wide process of democratization and the deep dissatisfaction of people with the dictatorial regimes of different orientations, left and right.

The transition to democracy, therefore, is composed of positive stimuli, as well as of barriers and dangers. Both sides of the process are described in the following theses.

1. Transition to democracy. There is a global process in progress as we can see democracy expanding on all continents. The processes of democracy-building in one part of the world stimulate democratic transformation of societies in other parts. The collapse of authoritarian regimes in Spain and Portugal influenced the developments in Latin America and similarly, the end of so-called real socialism in central European countries had a political impact on countries in other parts of Europe, especially in the former Soviet Union.

2. The wide and internally diversified current of changes, which can rightfully be called a democratic revolution, is an expression of a universal trend. This is so despite all the differences, due to the diverse cultures, economies and policies of individual countries. This universal trend is the wish of peoples, regardless of their nationality, race, religion, class and occupation, to live in dignity, to influence and control governments, and not to be exposed to uncontrolled individual or group power and arbitrariness. They also wish not to become the subject of utopian political philosophies. The more it is expressed in the spirit of the individual great world cultures and economic macroregions, the stronger the universalist base of democracy becomes.

3. The failures of almost all authoritarian, non-democratic regimes should be mentioned among the important causes of the contemporary democratic revolutions. Socialism, which liked to define itself as a higher form of democracy, was unable to create either a society emancipating and liberating humans or a society with a more efficient economy than the capitalist one. Neither was socialism more considerate towards the environment. However, its main failure was in the human sphere. Socialism was not able to form a cooperative society without fear, poverty and social conflicts. On the other side, right-wing, fascist and military regimes not only curtailed human rights but they were also unable to achieve the specific goals by which they usually legitimized themselves, among them, stability, prosperity, restriction of social conflicts, and national unity.

4. The expansion of the market economy, even if modified regionally and in other ways, contributes to the rise of democracy. This view is best expressed by a South African author, 'Who is in favour of the market economy, cannot be in favour of chains'. A market economy can however co-exist for some time with authoritarian political regimes, whereas political democracy cannot exist in combination with a centrally planned economy. A market economy is an indispensable, but not a sufficient, condition for democracy. A robust democracy needs other, mainly political, institutions as well.

5. Democratic revolution and transition to democracy in Central Europe are linked to the end of several great projects of modern European history, not only to the end of socialism, but also to the end of utopias. Other grand constructions are also in deep

crisis, specially technocratic authoritarianism and the belief in big projects in general. There exists a distrust towards the state in post-communist societies and stress is laid on civil society, on self-government and on decentralization. Democracy is conceived less ideologically and more pragmatically as well as ethically.

6. The transition to democracy is not necessarily a process that has economic or social causes. Its core in Central Europe is political. Its aim is to observe human rights, restore human dignity and civil liberties, to control the state and to achieve political and cultural pluralism. In this respect, the transition to democracy lacks the 'pathos of novelty' (Hannah Arendt) and is rather a 'rectifying revolution' (Jürgen Habermas). It can also be said that in some countries, such as Czechoslovakia, it is a restoration of old political and economic institutions and ideas. At a time when Western Europe is supposedly heading towards post-modernity, Central and Eastern Europe must first restore and apply some of the modernist concepts such as universalist value orientations, enlightenment, human rights, civil society and contracts.

In Eastern Europe, as well as in other continents, there are countries where the term 'return to democracy' is, of course, not realistic. These countries (Russia, Ukraine, Bulgaria or Rumania) have to introduce democracy as a new form of government and a new form of life. For them, the collapse of communist regimes gave them the chance for starting to build a genuine democracy for the first time in history. The experience of countries which had traditionally been democratic, then went through a period of dictatorial regime and then returned to democracy (e.g. Chile, Czechoslovakia, Spain) can enrich the philosophy of democracy by new approaches. In the first place, they offer an understanding of democracy as a certain form of life (not only as a form of government); in the second place, there is what Vaclav Havel has called 'antipolitical politics', as a result of the anti-utopian, disenchanting experience of Central Europe; and in the third place, there is a deeper anchoring of democracy in ethical principles.

7. After a short period of unity and consensus, formed by the protest against the *anciens régimes*, the transitions to democracy are often complicated by crises of a structural, functional and value nature. The syndrome of popular mobilization is relatively soon substituted by political instability. Very often the crisis in the transformation processes of post-communist societies is caused by the lack of constitutional agreements, by the lack of well-defined state identities and to a large extent it is also due to the overwhelming number of decisions which have to be taken under the pressure of time and without a chance to think about the possible effects of the decisions made. The structural crisis is caused by the parallel existence of old and new institutions. In post-communist societies, for example, the existence of state and private enterprises alongside state regulations and market mechanisms in the economy cause a lot of problems. This is closely connected with the parallel existence of different roles regulating the functioning of institutions or with the non-existence of needed rules. In this phase of hybrid rules and syncretic value systems there is a growing danger of chaos.

Another strong element of destabilization can be the changes in people's consciousness. The following phases can be discerned. First is a stage of euphoria after the collapse of the hated regime; second, there is the discovery of one's inexperience *vis à vis* the immense extent of necessary changes; third, next comes a differentiation and splitting of political attitudes and loss of consensus; fourth, we can discern either a disintegration of the original coalition attitude, a formation of stable democratic attitudes or apathy or the development of mistrust, dissatisfaction and opposition attitudes often nourished by disillusion with the market economy; lastly, new mobilization and structuration of attitudes loyal to democracy happens or instead we may get disintegration of democratic beliefs and acceptance of new authoritarian ideology. Very often, this last option is accompanied by nationalisms, regionalisms and populism. The danger of developments in this direction in some post-communist countries is growing.

8. The actors of the transition to democracy quickly change according to the revolutionary phases listed above. The volatility of structural actors in Central and Eastern European transitions is caused by the specific nature of the democratic revolutions in this region. A non-existant propertied middle class, as initiators of revolutionary movements, was substituted by a coalition of intellectuals, professionals, students, skilled workers, and administrative workers. Some reform communist politicians also took part. The 1989 revolutions were thus not traditional class conflict revolutions, nor were they social rebellions. They were mainly a political conflict between those in power and the powerless who, at the beginning, were organized predominantly in civic movements composed of many different streams. Later on, in most countries of Central Europe, new separate political parties or movements began to form and this process of fragmentation is still going on.

9. Casting aside external forces, the main political options in the future in most Central and East European countries will be determined by two interdependent factors. First, the outcome of the economic reforms will matter. Will these countries fail or be successful in transforming the existing economies into free market economies and what will be the consequences of the intended or unintended social effects such as high unemployment, high living costs, growing and more widespread poverty than expected? It must be noted that some countries are still hesitating in starting the reforms, some are postponing them while others (Hungary, Poland, Czechoslovakia) are in the middle. Second, there are the unknown outcomes of the elections which are planned in some of the countries concerned. They include local elections in Poland in 1991, elections in Rumania in early 1992, elections in Bulgaria in 1992 and general elections in Czechoslovakia in June 1992. The elections can lead to new situations, different power structures at the top and in the local communities or conflicts between governments of federated states. The danger of fragmentation is growing.

The possible effects of the interaction between these two factors are manifold. It seems however that, in the Central and Eastern European post-communist societies, the following ones are the most probable: (a) the formation of a pluralist system, based predominantly on the coalition of parliamentary political parties; (b) the emergence of a neo-corporatist system based on the consensus of the state, the employers and the trade unions; or (c) the formation of new nationalist and populist regimes with weak parliaments and a strong presidency or government. These three possible political scenarios will be most probably correlated with the current geopolitical trends. The first political scenario above will be accompanied by an evolutionary extension of the European Community to Eastern Europe, the second will result from a compromise of creating a region called 'In-between-Europe' ('Zwischeneuropa'), and the third would likely result in a new division of Europe.

Part II
Geopolitical shifts

3 Breaking the Cold War mould in Europe: a geopolitical tale of gradual change and sharp snaps

Jan Nijman and Herman van der Wusten

For about forty years, Europe knew one fairly stable geopolitical order. There can hardly be any doubt that this bipolar system came to an end in 1989. We are interested in the questions how, through the deterioration of what elements and why, induced by what processes and factors, this final change came about. By no means do we imply that this final change was inevitable in this form or at this juncture. We do argue, however, that the system's stability was in large part based on a set of rules or structures that for a long time overcame all types of disequilibrating forces. And, while the final demise occurred through a series of highly visible and deliberate acts of political leaders (Hoffmann, 1990), these structural properties of the system including re-equilibrating tendencies had already been steadily undermined by the mid-eighties.

While our empirical concern is with the sweeping changes across Europe, our theoretical aim is to anchor the concepts of geopolitical order, disorder, and transition, in an emerging political geography perspective. The rapidly increasing usage of these terms (e.g., Taylor, 1990) is, in our view, characterized by a severe lack of theory and, as a consequence, remains on a rather colloquial level. In the following section, we will make an effort to provide a theoretical context for this purpose, derived from neo-realism and structuration theory. In the process, we will elaborate our definitions of geopolitical order, disorder, and transition.

In order to understand the astonishing events of recent years, as well as the no less amazing longevity of the post-war geopolitical order, we first have to give an analytical description of that order as it stood. We have to indicate its basic tenets before we can confidently state that it no longer operates. The third section gives an overview of the conditions that kept the bipolar order alive and well for so long: its structural underpinnings and the forces that moved it back in position when challenges arose.

Geopolitical orders are in a sense like living creatures, they are born, they flourish and they die. They may collapse as a consequence of chance factors, long-term trends undermining their structural underpinnings, or both. The fourth section explains the tendencies that eventually broke the system's re-equilibrating mechanisms.

The final section discusses the current geopolitical transition in wider perspective. The crisis of 1989 was not the only one of its kind, but it was evidently the most severe crisis the bipolar order had seen. It turned out to be terminal. We compare our explanations to other arguments that have been put forward and we compare earlier crises with the break in 1989. We finally characterize the current policies of transition and look for clues concerning the order that may eventually emerge.

Geopolitical order, disorder, and transition

The political geography of international relations forms part of research traditions in the field of international relations at large. The main tradition of political geography ('geopolitics') falls squarely in the 'realist' paradigm. In unreformed realism, states are unified actors, parts of a set of members of the same species, locked in a situation of continuous insecurity as anarchy thrives. They are therefore in the last resort dependent on military power that in turn poses a threat to others. Realism has been reformed to neo-realism (Keohane and Nye, 1989), questioning the empirical standing of states as unified actors, accepting the importance of networks of existing relations for predicting future events instead of looking to power capabilities as single predictors, and cautiously exploring the possibility of long term stability. Nonetheless, the connection between the state and its power position remains the privileged, initial, entry to the subject. We adopt this view in our analysis of the 'high politics' of security in Europe. Security matters have been affected only marginally by West Europe's integration which was itself, by and large, predicated on the stability of Europe's geopolitical bipolar order. The real testcase of 'complex interdependence' still lies ahead. During the last few years of transition, notwithstanding strong efforts to accelerate European Community integration, the main players have acted in a strikingly conventional fashion when it came to security issues.

In the structuration approach to social reality as developed by Giddens (1979) and others, the reciprocal relations between agency and structure are central to an understanding of the continuities and changes in social life. Structure is the set of rules that guides agencies in their behaviour towards each other. These rules form the basis of mutual expectations that can be reinforced by compatible behaviour patterns. Sometimes, however, they are not and the agency that deviates from the rules may by its very behaviour assist in changing the rules and therefore the structure. Of course, deviating behaviour does by no means always result in a (permanent) change of structure: it may constitute only a marginal disturbance of the system or the deviating agency may be brought back in line. Agencies are very often individuals in this kind of approach but there is no reason why states cannot perform this role. The structuration approach implies a distinction and interrelationship between different geographic scales (Agnew, 1987): the set of rules and structures applies to a wider geographic area in reach of the great powers, but is subject to the recreating or modifying impact of 'smaller' agencies in places within this area.

Although geopolitical orders in some respects resemble living creatures, in others they do not. They do not in so far as creatures have an unequivocal, concrete existence and predictable life-span, whereas geopolitical orders are a construct of the mind. They picture a state of affairs where intentional actors follow rules that coordinate their behaviour, either through voluntary acceptance or by force. Analytical descriptions will have to provide debatable distinctions, and all we can do is to be as clear about operational definitions as we can possibly be in the field of essentially contested concepts.

'Geopolitical order' is a concept sometimes used in common parlance for the way in which a set of adjoining states interacts, anywhere between a contiguous pair and the world as a whole. A more respectable definition emphasizes the security function in these relationships, where the meaning of security transcends mere military capabilities. It also grants that this pattern of relations needs some stability over time to be recognized as such. This implies that at a time of geopolitical order, *structure prevails over contingency*. Deviation from the rules by the agencies involved is limited and/or ineffective in creating change. Thus, a geopolitical order consists of a set of more or less established and compatible geopolitical codes adhered to by individual states that prescribe norms, rules, and expectations that guide mutual behaviours.

States that are salient to each other in terms of security tend to cluster geographically. A few major powers in the system may form the exception due to a less stringent 'loss of strength gradient' (Boulding, 1962), but even they do not dismiss geographic proximity altogether. Further, geopolitical codes reflect the perception of the specific territorial nature of the state and its environment. Thus, the geo- in geopolitical makes sense in that the location of states matters in this type of order. As a consequence, geopolitical order requires analysis against the background of real space – not theoretical space as in the billiard ball model in international relations as proposed by traditional realist authors.

The mirror image of geopolitical order refers to geopolitical voids and geopolitical disorders. In a period of disorder, the agencies are in search of new geopolitical codes as the old ones are no longer compatible. Perceptions of the political environment have changed as a result of either personal or impersonal forces, and demand a change in behaviour. Hence, at a time of disorder, *agency prevails over structure* in the sense that behaviours have not been sufficiently consistent and/or compatible to realize institutionalization of a new set of rules. Disorder may be viewed as a transitory period from one geopolitical order to another (Taylor, 1990). But this is not self-evident. Alternatively, order may be seen as the transitory stage from disorder to disorder depending on the period we study, e.g. seventeenth-century Europe (the peace of Westphalia as a temporary interruption of a long drawn out process of volatile state formation). While it would appear that in the world of states since the seventeenth-century order has become increasingly more common than disorder, there is no way of knowing how long a period of disorder might last, if it has only just begun. Indeed, a period of transition can be recognized as such only in hindsight.

Genesis, structure and stabilizers of the bipolar system

Europe was an integral part of the bipolar, segmented system that for long characterized post-war international relations. This bipolar bloc system was the most important geopolitical order of the post-war world as it encapsulated the large majority of world power and was directly significant to all outsiders. The division of Europe, Germany, and Berlin epitomized the distinction between East and West more than anything else. Only in Europe was simultaneous and permanent superpower involvement so intense that it resulted in the formation of blocs (Weede, 1975). The existence of the blocs was predicated on the subordination of the bloc-provinces (although the nature of this subordination was different in the two blocs) to the respective superpowers. In effect, the bloc-provinces renounced part of their sovereignty in the realm of defence policy. While this did not apply to all bloc-provinces to the same extent, cross-bloc divisions prevailed overwhelmingly. The neutral states that were not part of either bloc, instead of undermining the system, contributed to its stability. Austria's neutrality was created for precisely that purpose. As buffers and intermediaries, the neutral states facilitated and smoothed the functioning of the bipolar system in Europe.

This European security arrangement did not arise overnight. In rudimentary form, the structures of the post-war security arrangement emerged in the second half of the 1940s. But back then they were far from stable, nor were they comprehensive. The first major adjustment concerned the subjugation of the German problem to the East–West conflict and the incorporation of the German statelets into the two blocs. The German problem (how to end the last war) was effectively overshadowed by the new East–West conflict. Europe was the region where one crisis in East–West relations followed another, accompanied by high risks of a devastating nuclear war. It became the most militarized zone in the world and the most likely theatre for a Third World War. It was increasingly recognized that superpower competition had potentially disastrous outcomes, while possible political gains were relatively small. During the 1960s, superpower competition shifted from Europe to the Third World (Halliday, 1983; Nijman, 1991), where spheres of influence were less clearly delineated, let alone recognized. Here the risks of conflict were smaller, while possible gains were perceived to be greater. This shift has also been attributed to the Soviet acquisition of long-range power projection capabilities enabling overseas interference, as well as to the process of decolonization which provided an opportunity for superpower involvement. If there has been a 'long peace' (Gaddis, 1987), it was confined to Europe.

The achievement (and mutual recognition) of nuclear parity and the consolidation of the two blocs as superpower spheres of influence gradually brought stability. The erection of the Berlin Wall in 1961 formed a turning point. Whereas the preceding period was extremely turbulent, the period after 1961 showed maturation of the bipolar order. Despite outrage in the West over the Berlin Wall, it became evident that East and West Europe had become accepted spheres of influence. Willy Brandt starts his memoirs with the building of the wall, clearly a pivotal point in his career. As the mayor of West Berlin he saw at first hand that the Americans were merely interested in the situation of West Berlin. They, in fact, renounced any direct involvement in the situation of East Berlin despite the mandate based on formal inter-allied rights at the time (Brandt, 1990, pp. 10-11). The *de facto* acceptance of spheres of influence was further illustrated by Western reactions to the Soviet intervention in Czechoslovakia in 1968, which were quite subdued compared with the outcry that followed the Soviet intervention in Hungary twelve years earlier. The 1960s were for the most part a prelude to the *détente* of the early 1970s. The Helsinki process constituted a culmination of these developments as it implied a formalization of the bipolar European order.

The bipolar, segmented order in Europe was, by no means, the necessary outcome of long term historical processes. It was one out of a few probable options given the military situation in 1945 and the ideological differences between the superpowers. The East bloc countries, for sure, were part of an 'empire by force'. But for West Europe too, the American 'empire by invitation' (Lundestad, 1986), was a no-choice option, as the political leadership of the time saw it. Arguably, maintenance of the European bipolar order served the interests of both superpowers for a variety of reasons, from empire-building to domestic legitimation. Wallerstein (1991) considers the Cold War an essential and integral part of the Pax Americana. According to Cox (1990, p. 31), '. . . the Cold War was more of a carefully controlled game with commonly agreed rules than a contest where there could be clear winners and losers'. Nonetheless, Western military cooperation was far more broadly accepted and considered legitimate than military cooperation in the East, where it was only agreed with regimes that mustered shallow allegiance. Another important difference between the two blocs was power disparity between member states. In the Western bloc, former great powers like Britain and France and, eventually also, Germany and even Italy, mitigated the gap in power resources that so obviously existed among the countries of the Eastern bloc. As a consequence, decision-making was swift and decisive once the bloc leader had made up his mind in the East, whereas in the West decision-making processes could take a long time and even then showed more signs of compromise. The latter is perhaps best exemplified by the debates inside NATO about the 'modernization' of intermediate nuclear forces in the late 1970s and early 1980s.

The bipolar system was fairly stable for a considerable period of time. Stability does not imply, however, that the system was static (see also De Porte, 1979). Since geopolitical orders may constantly be challenged, effective stabilizing factors are needed to maintain the pattern of positions and relations that make up the system. Disequilibrating forces may result from leadership personality clashes, wrong assessments or disrupting secular trends in conditioning factors. As long as stabilizers prevail, dynamics are cyclical or take the shape of temporary disturbances. Countervailing factors are supposed to take effect when some parameter in the system deviates too far from the normal state of affairs.

One of these countervailing powers is a very general one: in the state system of the post-war period, most states tend most of the time to prefer the status quo. They tend to avoid escalatory processes in a cooperative as well as in a conflictual direction. Obviously, that policy option occasionally fails or is felt not to be available. Consequently, states to some extent compensate distinctly cooperative gestures with conflictual acts in different policy sectors at the same time or sequentially. In this way, foreign policy behaviour is equilibrated and does not induce abrupt change (Faber, 1991).

More specifically, in the bipolar system of which Europe was such an important part, two kinds of processes operated as stabilizers. The role of the superpowers as separate poles was stabilized in bilateral processes of cooperation and conflict following the mechanism just mentioned, with the additional fear of nuclear war as a potential consequence of escalated conflict. As regards the bloc-provinces, the predominance of vertical links with the protector state and the avoidance of cross-segmental relations was dependent on the evolution of bilateral superpower relations and the other way around.

On the whole, the superpowers tended to be in conflict, but deviating too strongly from a posture of fairly serious conflict proved to be a self-defeating configuration. It resulted in unusual levels of tension or *détente* that tended to undermine the premises on which the deviation rested (Stevenson, 1985). In periods of growing tension, as the risks of (nuclear) war increased, the superpowers became more inclined to accommodate and cooperate, thus reducing tension and gradually paving the way for better relations. But as tension eased and the risk of war declined, the temptation to 'defect' from cooperation and pursue their own interests increased for both superpowers. Defection by one superpower resulted in a similar response by the other, thus returning the system once again to a state of increased tension and Cold War.

This 'game', however, was complicated by the role of the superpower allies. Intra-bloc and inter-bloc developments were intricately intertwined (Goldmann, 1974). The relaxation of intra-bloc discipline that usually occurred during periods of *détente*, allowing some degree of cross-border links and a diminishing segmentation, was often perceived by the superpowers as a force undermining their status, while at the same time inducing opportunistic ventures by the other side. An increase in tension between superpowers is thus also a way to restore order. At the same time, tightening control by the superpowers of intra-bloc relations, characteristic of periods of tension, contributed to a gradual swing toward depolarization and *détente*. As order was apparently realized and superpower status unchallenged, the cast of tension diminished.

As a consequence of the differences between the Eastern and the Western blocs, their respective answers to disruptive developments also differed. In the East, tight control ensured in most cases that even small deviations were quickly corrected from the centre. Occasionally, such small deviations could escalate into all-encompassing threats to the viability of the system at large (e.g., Hungary 1956, Czechoslovakia 1968, Poland 1980). Severe repression had in these cases to be put into effect. In the West, policy swings of bloc provinces may have been larger as a consequence of less disparity in power position and greater legitimacy of the overall arrangement. But, there too, the superpower held deviations in check, and should be viewed as the most critical agency in the maintenance of the system.

The erosion of re-equilibrating forces

Despite its apparent stability, the bipolar order was not there to stay. Secular and cyclical trends in the system eventually combined to provide the necessary (if not sufficient) conditions for a geopolitical transition. On a fundamental level, the system was gradually undermined by the decreasing ability of the superpowers to control their blocs. The relative decline of American hegemony is by now a well documented story, although debates about its severity and future prospects continue (see Nye, 1990). From conservatives to radicals, there is considerable consensus that the cycle of American world leadership has reached the downturn (Calleo, 1987; Modelski, 1987; Goldstein, 1988; Kennedy, 1987; Wallerstein, 1984). The loss of military pre-eminence around 1960 due to the achievement of nuclear parity by the Soviet Union was followed by an economic decline that became manifest in the early 1970s. American productivity did not keep up with that of other developed countries, a large trade deficit was built up, and in international finance, the dollar lost its strong position while American banks gradually disappeared from the list of the world's leading financial institutions. All in all, the ability of the United States to dominate effectively and control its spheres of influence decreased.

But while most eyes were focused on the United States because of its hegemonic status, the Soviet Union was losing its imperial grip even faster. Soviet superpower had been confined to the military sphere. To achieve this status, immense sacrifices had been made which found their simplest expression in the exorbitantly high Soviet military expenditures in relation to its national product. If the proposition that military build-up constitutes a drain on economic performance has validity at all, it applies first and foremost to the Soviet Union. In a similar vein, the notion of 'imperial overstretch' (Kennedy, 1988) was without doubt most evident in the former Soviet empire. The decline of the Soviet Union became clear to its leaders in the 1970s, at a time of intensified contacts with the West, and it was realized that this superpower 'could not afford another Cuba'. For example, the shattered economy of Mozambique was not granted access to the CMEA in 1980. The invasion into

Afghanistan was not considered imperial expansion but a necessary action to safeguard a vital security interest at the Soviet border (O'Loughlin, 1989). Overall, in the 1980s the Soviets started to reduce their empire building efforts (Nijman, 1990). With the rise to power of Mikhail Gorbachev came the decisive realization that the Soviet Union needed a restructuring that was long overdue.

The decline of the superpowers is mirrored in what Cohen (1982) termed the rise of second order powers and what Väyrynen (1984, 1988) called the rise of regionalism. Abstractly, this means that regional developments are increasingly determined at the regional rather than the global level. Where a reduction of superpower control goes hand in hand with increased power of regional actors, this shift is most evident. The decline of the superpowers was also mirrored in the rise of the European Community and, especially, West Germany as global economic powers. On the other side, the Soviets could not even keep pace with economic growth in some of the East European bloc provinces, especially East Germany. Ironically, these theoretical constructs did not lead observers to reconsider the situation in the European region. Cohen directed attention mainly to new regional powers in the Third World, and Väyrynen (1984) pointed especially to the Middle East as a region where the waning influence of the superpowers was manifest. In hindsight, however, it was to be expected that the consequences of the rise of regionalism would be most spectacular where superpower involvement used to be most intense. In Europe, the imposition of the bipolar structure became less forceful and increasingly subject to modification or evasion by the European actors.

In the Atlantic Alliance, these developments were reflected in discussions since the early seventies about a so-called two-pillar NATO, in which the European allies would be provided with a less subordinate and more responsible role. This discussion was fuelled both by American desires to shift the cost of defence to the allies and by European discontent about American dominance in European security matters. The main reason that a two-pillar NATO did not materialize was the inability of the European allies to form one single pillar. In the United States, calls for the withdrawal of American troops and a shift of the defence burden to the Europeans have only grown stronger through the years. Thus, while the debate lingered on, the alliance continued to exist in its old form. Indeed, the fact that West Germany by the 1980s had most clearly outgrown its role of 'bloc province' was at least in part concealed by its tight integration in NATO's military structure. As a matter of appearance, West Germany's constrained position in the military sphere helped to sustain the image of NATO as an organization that was still up-to-date and suitable for its purpose to maintain long-term security in Europe. This discrepancy between economic and military power relations was reaching the limits of elasticity and was going to require some major readjustments.

The dynamic of the bipolar order was not confined to these secular trends. We have already seen that alternations between tension and *détente* caused an almost continuous movement of the system between equilibrium and disequilibrium. As will be explained, these cyclical and secular tendencies combined to result in an overall improvement in East–West relations, but not in a linear fashion: oscillations between cold war and *détente* remained, but levels of *détente* became higher over time and the duration of *détente* tended to increase (Nijman, 1990). This is shown in Figure 3.1.

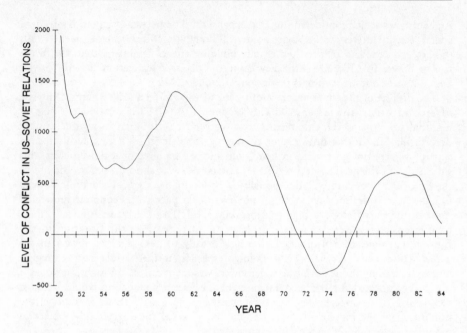

Figure 3.1 Oscillations between cold war and *détente*: the level of conflict in US-Soviet relations, 1948–1986 (5-year moving averages).

Source: Nijman 1990, based on event data from the Conflict and Peace Data Bank (1948–1978), supplemented with data provided by Dieter Ruloff, University of Zürich (1979–1986).

The growing waves of cooperation can be partly attributed to the learning process in which the superpowers were involved. The mere passing of time and the trial-and-error nature of the relationship made peaceful coexistence easier (Waltz, 1979). A good example of learning is the installation of the 'hotline' after the Cuban missile crisis. Another explanation lies in the institutionalization of cooperation, in the form of summits, state visits, treaties and agreements, and so on. The number of treaties in force provides a good indicator of the extent to which *détente* is institutionalized (Figure 3.2). This is not to suggest that treaties are always observed or that treaties do not permit the involved parties some elbow room. But the number of treaties in force does limit the possibility to 'defect'. Treaties and agreements create expectations at home and abroad and as such serve to stabilize policies of *détente* (Goldmann, 1982). In a way, they provide a safety net that prevents a full return to cold war at the previous intensity level.

For our purpose, however, the most important explanation lies in the role of the European allies. Feelings of 'abandonment' that sometimes plagued the West European allies should not be played down (Sharp, 1982, 1987) but it is important to emphasize that for the Europeans the gains during a period of *détente* were greater and more diverse than for the Americans. These were not confined to a mere reduced chance of war. In periods of *détente*, depolarization usually went hand in hand with a relaxation of superpower control of the bloc provinces. This provided the (West) Europeans with a temporary escape from their subjugation and a partial return to a more 'natural'

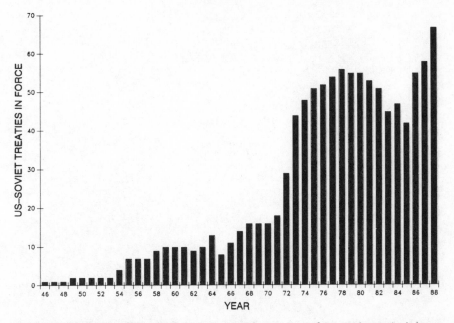

Figure 3.2   The number of bilateral US–Soviet treaties and agreements in force, 1956–1988 (includes amendments and extensions). Treaties signed before 1946 are excluded.

Sources: United States Treaties and Other International Agreements, 1950–1954; Treaties in Force, 1955–1989. For the sake of comparability with the other data presented in this chapter, the scores for each year are shifted one year to the left on the horizontal axis. For example, in the graph the year 1988 has a score of 68: this is in fact the number of treaties in force on January 1, 1989.

relationship with the European countries on the other side of the divide. This applied especially to Germany and was expressed in its Ostpolitik since the early 1970s. The difference in outlook between the United States and the European allies was particularly evident at times of renewed US–Soviet hostilities that occurred after a period of intensified cooperation and bridge-building between West and East Europe. The extension of political, cultural, and economic relations made it harder for the Europeans to return to a fully-fledged Cold War.

With the relative decline of the superpowers and the rise of regionalism in Europe, the potential to resist a renewal of cold war increased. The European allies could gradually afford to become more assertive while the superpowers' ability to control their blocs lingered. The other way around, periods of *détente* provided the bloc provinces with the opportunity to assert themselves *vis-à-vis* the superpowers. In this way, the growing waves of cooperation brought out and further stimulated the shifts in power differentials and the rise of regionalism. Hence, the two processes that were at the basis of the dynamic properties of the bipolar system reinforced each other and worked together to undermine it. Eventually, their combined progressive impact was bound to lead the system to a point of no return to equilibrium.

This conjuncture was reached in the 1980s. On a number of earlier occasions, an increase in tension primarily between the superpowers had resulted in a return to

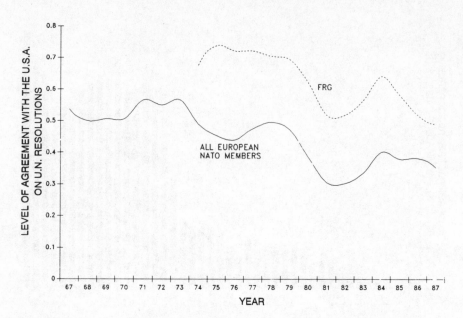

Figure 3.3   The level of agreement in terms of voting behaviour in the General Assembly of the U.N. between the United States and the European NATO members, 1966–1988, and the United States and West Germany, 1973–1988 (3-year moving averages).

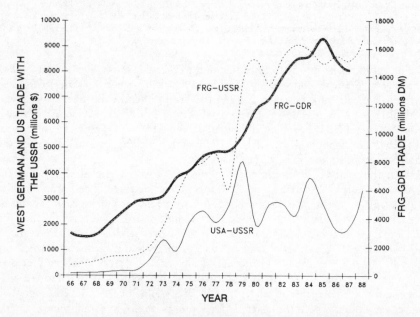

Figure 3.4   The value of trade between the United States and the Soviet Union, West Germany and the Soviet Union, and West Germany and East Germany, 1966–1988.

Sources: The Statesmen's Yearbook, 1968–1990; Nawrocki 1988.

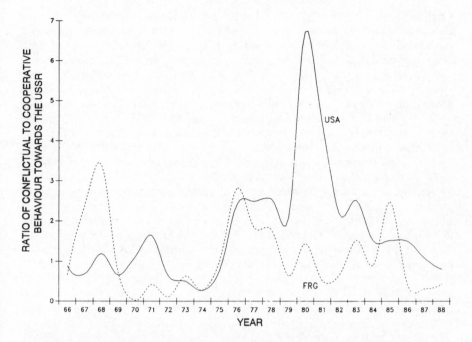

Figure 3.5 United States' and West German policies toward the Soviet Union: the ratio of conflictual to cooperative behaviour, 1966–1988.

Source: World Event Interaction survey.

clearly-demarcated spheres of influence and minimal cross-bloc links. However, when Brezhnev and Reagan undertook a new phase of the Cold War, there was some retraction from earlier engagements across the East–West divide in Europe, but by no means a return to the sharp separation accompanying earlier lows in the superpower relationship. President Reagan's rhetoric clashed markedly with prevailing opinions in West Europe, where the peace movements were successful in generating considerable support and acquired distinctly anti-American overtones. This time, the bloc provinces resisted the clarion calls of allegiance sent out by the bloc leaders. This was expressed, for example, in relatively high levels of disagreement in the United Nations in the early 1980s (Figure 3.3). Diverging preferences were also manifest in American–West European debates concerning technology transfers and other issues with regard to East West trade. The Germans in particular hung on to their renewed trading networks and political understandings in East Europe. As Helmut Kohl stated in 1984: 'Wir wollen das Erreichte bewahren und ausbauen'. (We want to preserve and expand what we have achieved) (Nawrocki, 1988, p. 66). As Figure 3.4 shows, West German–Soviet trade was much less affected than US–Soviet trade and intra-German trade continued its steep rise as if nothing had changed (see also Seppain, 1990). Figure 3.5 indicates that, in the last Cold War, the West Germans maintained a much less hostile attitude towards the Soviet Union than did the Americans.

In the East bloc, the interrelationship between depolarization and dealignment was less direct. It was mostly through the initiatives by West Germany, France and the smaller West European countries that the East European countries became differentially involved and acquired an interest in continuation of *détente*. Indeed, for the East Europeans this became a matter of sheer urgency in the light of their economic problems. The Poles, despite temporary martial law and an ailing economy, and the Hungarians, burdened with debts and dwindling expectations of further economic progress, kept as many links to the West as they possibly could. In the process, they were only half-heartedly hindered by the Soviets who were themselves unable to make any step forward in economic terms without Western assistance. The East German regime could only survive on a diet of ideological warfare and handouts from West Germany. The 'innere Emigration' of the thinking part of the populace had by 1980 already reached immense proportions. People drowned out the sound of slogans with the music of Bach (Garton Ash, 1990).

Veering back to a strict pattern of bipolarity could under the circumstances only be a surface phenomenon at best. The mechanism in the bipolar system, where an increase in tension between the superpowers normally resulted in realignment inside the two blocs, had been broken. The fact that the bloc provinces were already capable to extend their elbow room so significantly during a period of Cold War, contained a promise of things to come with the arrival of Gorbachev.

After the strings had snapped: the politics of disorder

As structure came apart and equilibrating mechanisms no longer functioned properly, contingency superseded structure in guiding the behaviour of statesmen. The quality of leadership reasserted itself as a prime factor in further breaking away from set patterns. Political leadership, to be sure, had in fact broken the spell of the bipolar, segmented order. It was the German leadership after all that had not given up its links to the East to the extent traditional rules required. And after the deployment of intermediate missiles had been accepted over much public resistance, the German political leadership stubbornly refused to accept the American requirement for the modernization of short-range missiles.

Germany's foreign minister Hans-Dietrich Genscher's slowly developing policy from an emphasis on deterrence to one on cooperation, in fact denying the possibility of actual defence for Germans, is perhaps best seen as a reflection of the evolving power relations in the Western alliance. 'Genscherism' (Meiers and Tanner, 1990) was firmly grounded in the disequilibrating forces undermining the bipolar order. It was not so much driven by attributes of leadership *per se*. In the same vein, the superpowers' acceptance not to push their preponderant roles to the limit (as they could have done by, for example, forcing Poland and Hungary back in line and pressing the West Europeans to full compliance with East–West trade policy) is best considered as an expression of diminished leverage. Once this had happened, leadership had to a far greater extent to manoeuvre in uncharted territory. As predictability diminished, the politics of transition got underway. It is the contention of this paper that 'impersonal forces' pushed the bipolar, segmented, order of the post-war era so far out of its normal position that traditional re-equilibrating forces were no longer able to restore stability. Subsequently, leadership acted upon these newly created circumstances. This point of view may be disputed from two fronts.

On the one hand, there are those (Atlanticist conservatives) who maintain that the

United States outspent the Soviet Union in the arms race and that the Soviet Union had to give up. As a consequence, the bipolar segmented order collapsed. Apart from the question mark over the effects of the arms race for the future status of the United States (Kennedy, 1987), this point of view does not explain why it is that an American technological lead in the arms race broke the Soviet Union this time, whereas such a lead had characterized the arms race for most of the time between 1945 and the early 1970s. Others view the end of the Cold War as an achievement of the East bloc by its own initiative, be it Gorbachev's or the opposition's or a combination of these two. Obviously there are earlier examples as well: Khrushchev's aborted attempts at reform in the Soviet Union and various efforts in the satellite countries, particularly in Poland, Hungary and Czechoslovakia. Apparently though, the time was not ripe. To know when it is, we have to look at the balance of forces that hold the order in check versus those who push the order towards a new position. That balance, we hold, had definitely shifted in the direction of change by the early 1980s (see also Chapter 4 in this volume).

In our view, Gorbachev entered the international political scene as the politics of transition were underway. Of course, his impact on the politics of transition was immense. The Gorbachev team was, from the outset, keen on exploring the room for new policies. Gorbachev engaged in daring proposals overstepping the rules of expected behaviour. Examples abound in the field of arms negotiations but also in efforts to install more business-like relations with satellite countries. Gorbachev's repeated initiatives after a while got a more positive response from the United States (see Goldstein and Freeman, 1990 for an analysis of these action/reaction patterns). The eventual result was a formal deconstruction of the bipolar system on both sides, since one side could not exist without the other. The dissolution of the Warsaw Pact in 1991 created an instant identity crisis for NATO. The hegemonic role of the United States in West Europe had been fading already for more than a decade but now found an honourable exit. The American presence in Europe is likely to be felt for some time but its days of hegemony are over.

The contingencies created by Gorbachev's policy innovations invited others to break away from their old geopolitical codes. This of course also happened in his own segment where the granting of increased autonomy quickly uncovered the entirely illegitimate character of the bloc-provincial authorities. As these regimes were pushed aside in the extraordinarily peaceful revolutions of 1989, the leadership of the Bundesrepublik, pressed by popular demand in East Germany, seized the momentum to restore national unity, not in the pre-war boundaries but in effect by incorporating the East in the Bundesrepublik. The bold German policy (foreign and intra-German) from late 1989 to late 1990 epitomizes the politics of transition after the Cold War in more ways than one. The Germans, in effect, set the pace of reunification and were instrumental in bringing it about. While the Americans acquiesced and France and Britain muttered, the Germans on their demand made the important deals with the Soviet Union. Legitimated through the 2 + 4 talks, the two German states and the four powers that had originally occupied Germany concluded a treaty that was finalized in later all-European agreements, in November 1990 in Paris. This finally ended the long drawn out process of postponed peace after World War II. The peace congress that, in earlier cases, had quickly concluded a global conflagration now took nearly a half century to occur (Leurdijk, 1991). That no peace/no war situation with different contenders was the geopolitical order of the Cold War. It was also a very unusual peace congress in that the party originally defeated, took the lead in bringing it about. This, especially, shows the politics of a new transition already at work.

The principal German role in the process of reunification had been in the making for several years and is likely to foreshadow the shape of the order to come. This Germany will be an all-European power: its links to the eastern part of the continent are inherently more direct and more intense than those of any other West European state, let alone the United States (Mead, 1990; Markovits and Reich, 1991). A poignant illustration of this was presented when Gorbachev was temporarily unseated in August 1991, and the Frankfurt stock exchange showed the sharpest downfall of all major bourses. The German-Soviet treaty of 1990 on 'Good-Neighbourliness, Partnership, and Cooperation' in effect restored a critical link in the European geopolitical landscape (Smyser, 1991). The Soviet role in this relationship is likely to be taken up almost entirely by the new Russia. It seems that the relative dominance of the new German state in the East, unhindered by the United States, will be even more impressive now that the Soviet Union has ceased to exist and has fragmented into smaller parts.

As Germany remoulds its geopolitical code, others will reorient theirs. During the politics of transition, such codes will be poorly coordinated, but if the events so far are any indication of the order that will eventually crystallize, the German code will set the tone. With external interference greatly diminished, European politics will be re-centred to its middle ground.

References

Agnew, J., 1987, *Place and politics: the geographical mediation of state and society*, Allen and Unwin, Boston.

Axelrod, R., 1984, *The evolution of cooperation*, Basic Books, New York.

Brandt, W., 1990, *Herinneringen*, Veen, Amsterdam.

Boulding, K., 1962, *Conflict and defence: a general theory*, Harper, New York.

Calleo, D.P., 1987, *Beyond American hegemony: the future of the Western Alliance*, Basic Books, New York.

Cohen, S.B., 1982, 'A new map of global geopolitical equilibrium: a developmental approach', *Political Geography Quarterly* **1** (2): 223–242.

Cox, M., 1990, 'From the Truman Doctrine to the second superpower détente: the rise and fall of the Cold War', *Journal of Peace Research* **27** (1): 25–41.

De Porte, A., 1979, *Europe between the superpowers: the enduring balance*, Yale University Press, New Haven CT.

Faber, J., 1991, 'Cooperation and conflict among nations: an application of multi-sample   confirmatory factor analysis', *Statistica Neerlandica* **45**:195–206.

Gaddis, J.L., 1987, *The long peace. Inquiries into the history of the cold war*, Oxford University Press, New York.

Garton Ash, T., 1989, *The uses of adversity. Essays on the fate of Central Europe*, Random House, New York.

Garton Ash, T., 1990, 'Mitteleuropa?', *Daedalus* **119** (1): 1–22.

Giddens, A., 1979, *Central problems in social theory: action, structure and contradiction in social analysis*, Macmillan, London.

Goldmann, K., 1974, *Tension and détente in bipolar Europe*, Esselte Studium, Stockholm.

Goldmann, K., 1982, 'Change and stability in foreign policy: détente as a problem of stabilization', *World Politics* **35** (2): 230–266.

Goldmann, K., 1984, *Détente: domestic politics as a stabilizer of foreign policy*, Centre of International Studies, Research Monograph 38, Princeton University.

Goldstein, J.S., 1988, *Long cycles. Prosperity and war in the modern Age*, Yale University Press, New Haven.

Goldstein, J.S., Freeman, J.R., 1990, *Threeway-street: strategies for US–Soviet–Chinese co-operation*, University of Chicago Press, Chicago.

Halliday, F., 1983, *The making of the second Cold War*, Verso, London.

Hoffmann, S., 1990, 'The case for leadership' *Foreign Policy*, **84** (1): 20–38.

Kennedy, P., 1987, *The rise and fall of the Great Powers*, Random House, New York.

Keohane, R.O., Nye, J.S., 1989, *Power and interdependence: world politics in transition*, 2nd edition, Little, Brown, Boston.

Krell, G., 1991, 'West German Ostpolitik and the German Question' *Journal of Peace Research* **28** (3): 311–324.

Leurdijk, J.H., 1991, 'The Allied Powers and the peace with Germany after the Second World War', Paper for a conference entitled 'The Great Peace Congresses'. Utrecht, 16–17 August 1991.

Lundestad, G., 1986, 'Empire by invitation? The United States and Western Europe, 1945–1952', *Journal of Peace Research* **23** (3): 263–277.

Markovits A.S., Reich, S., 1991, 'Should Europe fear the Germans?', *German Politics and Society* **23** (1): 1–20.

Mead, W.R., 1990, 'The once and future Reich', *World Policy Journal* **7** (4): 593–638.

Meiers, F.J., Tanner, F., 1990, 'Genscherism, the modernization of SNF and the future of NATO', Paper presented at the annual conference of the International Studies Association, Washington DC, April 10–14, 1990.

Modelski, G., 1987, *Long cycles in world politics*, University of Washington Press, Seattle.

Nawrocki, J., 1988, *Die Beziehungen zwischen den beiden Staaten in Deutschland*, Verlag Gebruder Holzapfel, Berlin.

Nijman, J., 1990, 'The political geography of US–Soviet relations. A geographical perspective on the evolution of superpower competition, 1948–1988'. Unpublished Ph.D. dissertation, University of Colorado at Boulder.

Nijman, J., 1991, 'The dynamics of superpower spheres of influence: US and Soviet military activities, 1948–1978'. *International Interactions* **17** (1): 63–91.

Nye, J.S., 1990, *Bound to Lead: the changing nature of American power*, Basic Books, New York.

O'Loughlin, J., 1989, 'World power competition and local conflicts in the Third World', in: R.J. Johnston and P.J. Taylor (eds), *A world in crisis? Geographical perpectives*, 2nd edition, Basil Blackwell, Oxford. pp. 289–332.

Seppain, H., 1990, 'The divided West: contrasting German and US attitudes to Soviet trade', *The Political Quarterly* **61** (1): 51–65.

Sharp, J.M.O., 1982, 'Nuclear weapons and alliance cohesion', *The Bulletin of the Atomic Scientists* 1982: 33–36.

Sharp, J.M.O., 1987, 'NATO's security dilemma', *The Bulletin of the Atomic Scientists* 1987: 42–44.

Smyser, W.R., 1991, 'USSR–Germany: a link restored', *Foreign Policy* **84** (1):125–141.

Stevenson, R.W., 1985, *The rise and fall of détente. Relaxations of tension in US–Soviet relations, 1953–1984*, University of Illinois Press, Urbana, IL.

Taylor, P.J., 1990, *Britain and Cold War: 1945 as a geopolitical transition*, Pinter, London.

Väyrynen, R., 1984, 'Regional conflict formations: an intractable problem of international relations', *Journal of Peace Research* **21** (3): 337–353.

Väyrynen, R., 1988, 'East–West rivalry and regional conflicts in the Third World', in: B. Hettne (ed.), *Europe: dimensions of peace*, The United Nations University Studies on Peace and Regional Security, Zed Books Ltd, London, pp. 101–126.

Wallerstein, I., 1984, *The politics of the world-economy*, Cambridge University Press, New York.

Wallerstein, I., 1991, *Geopolitics and geoculture. Essays on the changing world-system*, Cambridge University Press, New York.

Waltz, K.N., 1979, *Theory of international politics*, Random House, New York.

Weede, E., 1975, *Weltpolitik und Kriegsursachen im 20. Jahrhundert: Eine quantitativ-empirische Studie*, Oldenbourg Verlag, München.

4 Precursor of crisis: political and economic relations of the Soviet Union, 1960–90*

John O'Loughlin

Since the collapse and eventual disappearance of Eastern Europe in the past two years, numerous explanations have been proffered for the surprising development. Virtually no one anticipated the demise of one side of the post-war geopolitical arrangement. The term 'Eastern Europe' had a clear and unmistakable significance for people in the West. It meant a group of countries sharing communist regimes, having competitive and antagonistic relations with the capitalist bloc headed by the United States, perpetual shortages of consumer goods and surfeits of military hardware, repression of political rights and liberties, and a perception that the region was destined to remain outside the pale of Western influence. The world system was, in effect, two systems that overlapped to some extent while mutually co-existing. The communist bloc developed more economic relations with the capitalist world-system over time, while maintaining its separate ideological identity. State socialism at home was paired with tentative and highly-regulated trade links with selected Western industrial and some Third World states. It was an ideological schizophrenia that lasted for over twenty years.

The collapse of the East European communist world has been greeted with all kinds of reactions. One view from the left is that it will make the US role as leader of the Western bloc obsolete, since the rationale for that role has been removed with the disappearance of the Soviet threat and will, in effect, hasten American decline (Wallerstein, 1991). The more conventional view is that the West, led and managed by the US, won the Cold War through steady pressure on the Soviet Union and its allies, by maintaining large military expenditures, and by opposing Soviet attempts to wean countries from the Western bloc. In between are all sorts of other reactions but common among them is the surprise that the course of events wrecked the East Europe world so completely and that the various regimes were so thoroughly rejected by the populations in all eight (including Yugoslavia) countries of the region. Though former communists managed to regain or remain in power in specific places (Rumania, Serbia, Bulgaria, Slovakia), in general, the ex-communists received about 15–20 per cent in the elections that marked the end of the communist era in Eastern Europe.

*This research was supported by a National Science Foundation grant from the Political Science and Geography and Regional Science Programs. I thank Sven Holdar for help in data collection and Michael Shin for the maps. Mike Ward of the Institute of Behavioural Science, University of Colorado, provided the WEIS data on international cooperation and conflict.

Of the reasons discussed for the sudden collapse of the Soviet Union, and by extension, of Eastern Europe, four seem to be most in evidence after the failed August 1991 Soviet putsch. The 'Gorbachev factor' is most forcibly expressed by Ellman and Kontorovich (1992). They see the events in the Soviet Union as a revolution from the top without a clear path to the post-communist or even a reform-communist model. Gorbachev is viewed as the last of the reformers who tried to generate more output from a system that was incapable of doing so. Many of the authors in the Ellman and Kontorovich book, such as Khanin (1992), on the other hand subscribe to the view that the Soviet Union contained the seeds of its own destruction. In this view, collapse was inevitable, the only question being when the balancing act would fail.

A third view promoted by the Western establishment is that the loss of the Cold War ended whatever role the Soviet Union had as leader of the anti-systemic world. The costs of fighting the Cold War were so great that the country could not stay in the arms race after the Reagan Administration stepped up the pace in the 1980s, while, at the same time, further isolating the Soviet Union and its allies in the world economic and political arenas. A fourth view is that it was the Soviet Union's own gradual incorporation into the capitalist world economy, especially as a resource economy, that led to its demise. With the global downturn after about 1970, vulnerable states like the Soviet Union were unable to cope with the changed nature of the international division of labour and so suffered the consequences of all failed enterprises: it collapsed since the state and the economy were inseparable (Boswell and Peters, 1990). It is this fourth view that will constitute the theoretical perspective of this chapter.

The purpose of this chapter is to try to understand the nature of Soviet trade and political relations in a part of the Cold War period. Though countless books have been written on this subject, few have attempted to do so from a world-systems perspective. Mikhail Gorbachev himself, quoted in Ellman and Kontorovich (1992, p. 17), noted the compelling influence of the outside world on internal developments in the Soviet Union. The authors note (Ellman and Kontorovich, 1992, p. 17) that 'the 1980s was a decade in which Soviet economic policy came under the international demonstration effect of the world-wide successes of capitalism'. Though the Soviet Union maintained an ideological position that was antithetical to capitalism, it had increasingly been drawn into the capitalist world since the reforms of Khrushchev in the late 1950s. Trade was a way of acquiring the consumer goods that the country did not produce in sufficient quantity to meet the demands generated by the reformers who broke with the Stalinist model of autarky and internal military hegemony. While on the one hand, the Soviet Union was engaged in an ideological and political competition with the West, particularly for influence in the newly-independent Third World states (O'Loughlin, 1989), on the other hand, it needed consumer goods, food, and technology from its political adversaries. In exchange, the Soviet Union offered hard currency earned through its export of oil and gas at prices that soared after the OPEC oil shocks of 1973 and 1979.

The central thesis of this chapter is that the dependence on Western goods in exchange for the oil rents was jeopardized by the sharp drop in oil and gas prices after 1986. Oil dropped from about $40 per barrel to $18 in the course of a few months and Soviet export earnings dropped by a third in that year (Chadwick, et al., 1987). The resultant crisis in the Soviet Union could possibly have been weathered through a policy of discipline, like that pursued by Yuri Andropov in the early 1980s or symbolized by Stalin for his decades of rule. By choosing the reform over the repression route, Gorbachev chose the riskier strategy in hopes that the Soviet Union could compare favourably to the West in the quality of life for its citizens. We can now see clearly that the strategy was doomed to failure, but between 1986 and 1990 perestroika and glasnost became the codewords for reform communism, a concept that, in hindsight, turned out to be an oxymoron. A major question in this chapter is the accuracy of the axiom that Soviet trade and political relations were inseparable in the years of the Cold War because of the effective control of the global trade system by the United States and its Western allies. That would mean the dependence of Soviet trade on the state of East–West relations and the development of trade links that flew in the face of the rationale of the usual economic models of trade relations.

The Soviet Union in the world economy

The nature of Soviet economic relations with the capitalist world economy generated two perspectives, whether one or two world systems existed. Szymanski (1982), like Stalin, claimed that the Soviet Union was the core of a separate world socialist system. He based this claim on the grounds that the Soviet trade ratio (trade divided by total output) was very low, that Soviet trade was not run by corporations for profit and that the Soviets tended to sell and buy in the international markets well below their domestic prices, implying a subsidy for export-orientated industries and a tax on import-orientated industries. On the nature of the specific Soviet trade relations with the capitalist West, Szymanski claims that they did not depend on integration with the Western economies but that instead commodities were imported to cover shortfalls in Soviet production while technology was imported to accelerate the pace of Soviet output. Finally, he noted that there was little time-series correlation of Western and Soviet GNP growth rates and that this constituted further evidence that the two worlds were autonomous. He concluded that an historical parallel was appropriate because 'the economic linkages between the USSR and the West are comparable to those between simultaneously existing world systems such as those of the Arabs, Ottomans, China and medieval Europe' (Szymanski, 1982, p. 81).

From a world-systems perspective, Szymanski's view is clearly a minority one. The specific nature of the Soviet imports and exports, cited by Szymanski, provides further evidence for Wallerstein's (1979, p. 14) position that the Soviet Union occupied a very specific position in the world economy, engaging in trade only for 'essential exchanges'. The Soviet Union stepped up its involvement with the capitalist world economy after the death of Stalin and of the autarky that motivated his economic relations. Central planning was reformed by Khrushchev and his successors to allow imports of goods produced in insufficient quantities in the Soviet Union. Reintegration into the capitalist world economy was made necessary, in effect, by the shortages and contradictions of the Soviet model of development.

The evidence that the Soviet Union was part of the world economy, however reluctantly, is more convincing than the alternative interpretation. For Boswell and Peters (1990), Wallerstein (1991) and Chase-Dunn (1982), the Soviet Union and Eastern Europe constituted a semi-periphery. In world systems terms, this concept is applied to regions with a mix of core and peripheral processes. A core process is commodity production with high-wage, skilled workers in capital-intensive industries and is typically found in advanced industrialized countries, while peripheral production is low-wage, unskilled and labour-intensive and typically found in Third World countries. Wallerstein (1991, p. 88) dates Russia's (Soviet Union's) semi-peripheral status back to 1914, seeing it as the weakest power of the then-core or the strongest power of the then-periphery. Like contemporary revolutions (Boswell, 1989; Chase-Dunn, 1990), whose incidence appears to be more frequent in semi-peripheral states, the Russian Revolution occurred in one also. The reasons for this are that in semi-periphery states, the core-periphery dimension exacerbates rather than cross-cuts class antagonisms (Chase-Dunn, 1982, p. 27). Wallerstein interprets the 1917 Revolution as a revolt against further European core penetration.

The fervour of the debate over whether the Soviet Union was part of the capitalist world economy was generated, in part, by the issue of how socialist were post-revolutionary states. Condemned as 'Quislings' by Taylor (1991), most retained socialism as state ideology and instituted domestic relations that enshrined non-capitalist beliefs, while maintaining trade relations with the states of the capitalist world economy. Though the socialist states may have been models of resistance to capitalism and may have sponsored anti-systemic movements elsewhere, by their continued adherence to the world economy, they effectively undercut whatever authority and power they possessed to re-order the world system. A socialist mode of production could never be solidified in the small number of states that had successful anti-systemic movements. When the anti-communist revolutions began in Eastern Europe, the regimes subsequently fell like a house of cards.

The Soviet regime was a 'state capitalist' one at home, with state power used by a bureaucratic class to exploit Soviet workers and to compete for power and economic advantage in the larger world economy (Chase-Dunn, 1982). The world system is characterized by an integrated logic in which the political power of states is harnessed to the economic power of the national capitalists to generate advantage for the respective 'factions of capital'. The Soviet Union operated in a manner that mimicked the actions of the capitalist national bourgeoisies. Like the other large communist power, China, the USSR reduced its links to the world economy after its revolution (the West was most concerned to isolate the Soviet Union after 1917) but it re-entered the capitalist world as a 'resource economy', through (in Frank's 1980 phrase) 'transideological enterprise'. (See also Blank, 1991.) The result was that socialist states challenged 'the cultural hegemony of capital but not very effectively because their political ideals and institutions reflect their defensive position in the capitalist world economy' (Chase-Dunn, 1982, p. 48).

To classify the Soviet Union and its former allies as semi-peripheral is not to place them in a uniform category. There are at least four kinds of semi-peripheral states (poor peripheral Europe, the Latin American type, the New Industrializing Countries of East Asia, and Eastern Europe). While they had different trajectories, they all shared a mix of core and peripheral processes and strong state involvement in economic activities (Martin, 1990). The Soviet Union built its economy after the Revolution along Stalinist principles of production for use, rather than for exchange, with a central planning agency responsible for all regulation of commodity prices, purchasing a substantial part of the products of the national economy and allocating the raw materials, labour and capital investment.

The best-known mechanism of central planning was the series of five-year plans developed in consultation with the Central Committee of the Communist Party (Chase-Dunn, 1982, p. 35). One of the key elements of these plans that determined in large part the involvement of the Soviet Union in the world economy was the balance between consumer and national industrial goods and the nature and extent of the hard currency to be used in the purchase of foreign foods, industrial products and technologies. With increasing standards of living promoted by Khrushchev and his successors after 1955, there was no turning back to the Stalinist autarky model because it was clear that the Soviet Union could simply not produce these products domestically. Its exports to the West had low levels of processing (Firebaugh and Bullock, 1986), a characteristic of peripheral states; its exports to the CMEA (Council of Mutual Economic Assistance) countries were composed of resources like oil, as well as heavy manufactured goods. At the same time, its imports reflected the unmet needs of the Soviet citizenry and regime with foodstuffs and high technology products highly represented.

It has already been noted that autarky was the economic strategy of much of the Soviet Union's history. Faced with an initial Western attack on the new socialist state and economic crises at home, Lenin had promoted a New Economic Policy (NEP) that eased the pressure to nationalize the agriculture sector. Stalin reversed this policy, induced chaotic conditions and famine in agriculture and pursued a policy of rapid heavy industrial growth from the 1930s, all within a framework of separation from the capitalist world economy (Nove, 1982). The period 1935–1955 were years of very rapid growth rates propelled by the heavy industry that increasingly provided the military–industrial base of the Soviet Union. After the establishment of the Cold War lines, Stalin took the opportunity to enforce the intimate economic relations with the countries of the buffer zone in Eastern Europe, while retreating from the wartime dependence on the United States for key products. 'In practice, resources were concentrated in heavy industry and military production at the expense of light industry consumer production, a practice reified politically by the Party "line"' (Boswell and Peters, 1990, p. 14). The industrial base of the Soviet Union was quota-dep-endent, strongly regulated, characterized by assembly line production, and targeted to the perceived needs of the state rather than to those of the population.

After Stalin's death, Khrushchev was able to begin the allocation of resources to non-state needs. The 1950s and 1960s were boom decades for the Soviet Union with growth rates (yearly average of 4.9 per cent) ahead of all other countries except Japan (Boswell and Peters, 1990, p. 7). The country also had strong rates of increase in national income, which averaged over 11 per cent in the period 1932–37, 6 per cent 1940–50, 7 per cent 1950-60, 6 per cent 1960–65 and 4 per cent 1965–70. Though the rate of Soviet income growth fell consistently from the late 1930s peak, the percentages exceeded the rates of the Western capitalist countries (Nove, 1982). But by the 1970s, the Soviet growth rates had fallen behind all regions, including its political allies in Eastern Europe. In the 1980s, Soviet growth rates dropped again but remained higher than the stagnant Western and Eastern European economies.

Leonid Brezhnev was in power from 1964–1982 and the major feature of these years was the fusion of political and economic realms in the Soviet system, as a more complex economy was matched with a more demanding society and a residue of conflict left over from the Khrushchev years. In Wallerstein's (1991, p. 94) view, Khrushchev made the fatal error of reforming a little bit with political liberalization spurring consumer demand. Brezhnev tried to stuff the genie back into the bottle but failed. Some Western firms started joint enterprises with the USSR (Levinson, 1978). Demand for consumer goods was still present when Gorbachev came to power in

1985. The Soviet Union began to end its trade isolation with the West by signing agreements in the late 1960s years of *détente*. In this instance, trade relations followed political developments. The Soviet Union recognized that 'developed socialism needed developed capitalism, for political, as well as economic, reasons' (Bunce, 1983, p. 147: Brada, 1988).

The international trade ideology of the Soviet Union was initially determined by its national political ideology. Since Khrushchev, the Communist Party came to see exports as a way of paying for needed imports under a general policy of balanced trade. Once the terms of the relationships were established with the various trading partners, they remained stable despite Gorbachev's three-sided policy of increased merchandise trade with the Western world, more balanced trade with the CMEA states to ease Soviet subsidies and more commercial trade and less aid for the less-developed countries (Hardt and Boone, 1988). Hardt and Boone (1988, p. 330) conclude that external factors (good harvests, drop in global oil prices, etc.) appear to affect Soviet trade more than its foreign trade policies or those of its neighbours. In the Brezhnev years too, the costs of empire rose dramatically so that both Eastern Europe and the Third World socialist states allied to the Soviet Union began to drain heavily the limited foreign aid and economic support of the USSR (Bunce, 1985). By 1986, the Soviet Union began to try to cut its Third World losses (Kanet, 1986: Fritsche, 1989).

The Soviet Union was always in a weak position in the development of its international trade, a fact that did not go unnoticed to Soviet observers. Soviet imports and exports were controlled by 'strategic lists' drawn up by the US and its allies and the preponderance of fuels and resources among Soviet exports made the country vulnerable to price fluctuations and alternative sources (Ivanov, 1987). Despite this vulnerability, Marxist principles still underlay the Soviet position. Starting from the comparative advantage position of the neo-classical school, Grote and Kühn (1988) theorize the implications for socialist states motivated by principles of non-profitability. They quote Marx to the effect that a socialist country can obtain goods more cheaply than it can produce them itself through participation in the international division of labour because these advantages will be materialized in a savings on social labour. They further maintained that the entire system of foreign trade could be managed and planned to help the socialist country and further that the socialist world should not take advantage of its competitive advantage with less developed countries. Despite the changed rationale for trade after Stalin, the weakness of the Soviet economy in the new international division of labour undermined whatever principles governed Soviet trade and left the country permanently vulnerable to global forces beyond its control.

The research on the benefits to the Soviet economy produced mixed results. Early work (McMillan, 1973) examined the 1959 Soviet input–output table and used a two-factor model of labour and capital to conclude that Soviet imports were relatively intensive with the developing sub-group of both the capitalist and socialist worlds and more capital-intensive with the developed capitalist and socialist countries. This pattern of trade is what trade theory would predict. Hewitt (1984), after looking at the changing terms of trade for the Soviet Union from 1970, noted that the terms of trade for the Western (hard currency) countries fell rapidly after the 1973 oil-shock and that of the Eastern Europe countries fell less rapidly. It was no wonder then that 'given the development in relative terms of trade between oil and grain, and gas and grain on the world market and within the Soviet economy, (that) it is hardly surprising to see that the Soviets have opted for long-term dependence on grain imports from the West. In fact, *what is surprising is that the Soviet Union imports so little grain given the extremely unfavourable domestic tradeoff between additional output of oil or gas, and grain* (original emphasis) (Vanous, 1984, p. 101).

The gain for the Soviet Union from trade varied significantly between the world's regions. In trade relations, the Soviet economists always claimed that while the West exploited the South, the Soviet Union did not because they had unfavourable terms of trade with that region. The ratio of Soviet imports and exports with the developing world always remained below 16 per cent of the totals. The exchange was mostly Soviet manufactured goods, expecially arms, for Southern raw materials (Jackson, 1985). Becker (1986) believed that the arms trade was the principal instrument through which the Soviet Union obtained entry into Third World economies and Liefert (1990) estimated that the Soviet gain from trade with the West was so diluted from its relations with the South and with Eastern Europe that the net effect was no effective gain for the USSR. Attempts by the Soviets to increase manufacturing exports since 1960 failed so that their share of total exports fell from 27 per cent in 1970 to 15 per cent in 1986 (Gardner, 1988).

The specific trade relations of the USSR with less-developed countries (LDCs) were carefully examined by Wolf (1985). Bilateral clearing agreements (BCA) with many LDC and CMEA countries provided the basis for the trade, with the Soviets discriminating in price in favour of the partners. Soviet relations were stable and gaining in volume with these BCA countries in the 1970s and although the LDCs had deteriorating terms of trade with the USSR, the relationships were net losses for the Soviet Union with no obvious compensation in political terms. Frank (1980, p. 194) argued that though the Soviet Union exchanged manufactured goods for raw materials with the Third World, this does not constitute *prima facie* evidence of exploitation because of evident unequal exchange. Instead, he stated that exploitation means the exchange of commodities that benefit the dominant partner and that here the evidence was mixed. In the West, there was a clear bifurcation in exports to the Soviet Union with the West European countries and Japan exporting manufactured goods, with a large ratio of high-technology manufacturing, and the US, Canada, and Australia exporting mostly grain and food products (Martens, 1984). On coming into office and seeing these stable relationships that had developed over the previous two decades, Gorbachev tried to increase merchandize trade with the developed West, balance hard goods trade with the CMEA countries and put the trade with the LDCs on a more commercial basis with less foreign aid (Hardt and Boone, 1988). The basis of Soviet trade was not the usual combination of distance, price, comparative advantage and reciprocity but instead was strongly influenced by the peculiar nature of the Soviet incorporation into the world economy and the state of political relations with its opponents in the West.

The Soviet economic crisis, 1986–1991

The collapse of the Soviet political and economic system in a couple of years was the culmination of decades of increasingly severe difficulties. Because the economy, the government and the party were inseparable in the minds of the Soviet citizenry (96 per cent of all industrial production was state-generated: *Economist* April 28, 1990), it effectively meant that the economic crisis became a magnified political crisis (Dipalma, 1991). The ideology of the state, Marxism–Leninism, was lost as a result. Since 1989, all commentators seem agreed on the essential weaknesses and structural problems of the Soviet system: the precise timing of the collapse is attributed to the futile attempts of Gorbachev to reform the system through undermining of the central role of the Communist Party without the provision of an alternative (Ellman and Kontorovich, 1992; Draper, 1992; Kuran, 1991).

In this 'declinist' interpretation of the events leading up to the 1989–91 crisis, there is an implicit assumption of consistent and increasingly severe economic difficulties. Yet, a review of Soviet economic statistics does not show such clear developments. Until the 1960s, the USSR had positive and significant growth in output. In the 1980s, not only economic, but all indicators of the quality of Soviet life, moved into negative figures. Overall, between 1960 and 1989, the Soviet business sector grew at an average annual rate of 3.1 per cent, the same as the United States and 0.5 per cent less than the OECD average (Pitzer and Baukel, 1991).

When we examine the components of the overall growth indices by time period, the picture becomes a bit clearer. The business sector growth rate dropped from an average growth of 4.3 per cent in the period 1961–75 to 1.7 per cent between 1976–82, the industrial average growth dropped from 6.0 to 2.1 in the same period, and non-farm business dropped from 6.0 to 2.1 at the same time (Pitzer and Baukel, 1991). Worse from the Soviet perspective, the values of total factor productivity actually reached negative figures after 1973. The average growth rate of business factor productivity went from 0.7 per cent in 1961–75 to –1.0 in the 1976–82 period, while the values for industrial (1.3 per cent to –0.9 per cent), agricultural (–0.6 to –1.2) and non-farm business (1.2 to –1.0) also show the same decline trend. (Data from Pitzer and Baukel, 1991.) The crisis of Soviet productivity after 1975 is blamed on a new economic policy by Pitzer and Baukel (1991, p. 80) but as Schroeder (1985) showed, the problem was more fundamental than a policy shift. She attributed the Soviet slowdown in the 1970s, despite the rent generated by the OPEC oil-price rises after 1973, to the inability of the Soviet economy to generate sufficient total factor productivity growth to offset the declining contribution of factor growth.

Why should the Soviet economy enter a decline phase at the same time as the external earnings from oil were growing rapidly? Khanin (1992) reflects the views of many by following the 'exhaustion of resources' thesis. In this view, the Soviet Union had been 'depleting its inherited environment', not only the natural resources that were increasingly accessible but Khanin also extends the argument to the 1920s/1930s industrial base and the genetic composition of the population. Though, like Ellman and Kontorovich (1992), we can reject the genetic depletion argument for lack of supportive evidence, we must pay particular attention to the industrial base argument. The Soviet industrial base was built up in the Stalinist boom years of the 1930s and 1940s. Characterized by military-driven, heavy industrial-led growth, the Soviet industrial base was highly inefficient with high levels of labour intensity. In the years of the Kondratieff IVA, 1945–1973, the world economy grew strongly and led to growth in all countries, including the Soviet Union and its CMEA allies. Further, the timing of the economic downturn corresponded with the exhaustion of the model of 'extensive industrialization' adopted by Stalin in the late 1920s:

which depended on the availability of ever new supplies of labor power and raw materials to maintain a satisfactory rate of growth. As the sources of these new supplies dried up – which of course was bound to happen sooner or later – the growth rate lagged at the expense of living standards and the provision of social services. And this occurred at the same time that the Reagan Administration in the United States was stepping up the external pressures on the Soviets through a greatly increased arms program (Sweezy, 1991, p. 3).

The argument that the global economic downturn after 1970 generated the Soviet economic crisis rests on the assumption of Soviet integration of the world economy, in the semi-peripheral mode described by Chase-Dunn (1982) and Boswell and Peters (1990). Though the Soviet economy was quite isolated in world economic terms, there seems little doubt that the level and duration of world economic growth would have positive effects even there. The validity of the argument is challenged by the question of why the economies of Eastern Europe should be more affected by the downturn than the advanced capitalist economies of the West. The reason is attributed to the more flexible nature of the Western economies, with many more organizational and political procedures, and the military style conformity of state socialism. 'Centralized and militaristic Stalinism was the exact opposite of flexible production. Rather than a harbinger of a communist future, state socialism was stuck in the past' (Boswell and Paters, 1990, p. 16). In a sense, perestroika and glasnost was a belated attempt to provide a political response by the Soviet state to the conjuctural crisis of the 1970s, just as all governments had to deal with similar negative impacts (Wallerstein, 1991, p. 95).

The enormous oil rents received from OPEC-driven revenues covered up the structural problems of the economy and allowed the Soviet Union to import significantly increased amounts while delaying recognition of the fundamental need for reforms (Pitzer and Baukel, 1991; Moe, 1991). The one-third drop in revenues in 1986 reduced the imports, making daily life even more difficult and adding to the accumulated net debt of the country. By 1990, this burden had reached between 65 and 68 billion dollars (McAuley, 1991). The Soviet economy switched from low positive growth rates to 1989 to a negative increase of 5 per cent in 1990 and a further drop of 15 per cent in 1991. An improvement of the economy is not expected for another five years.

It is a central concern of this chapter that the economic fortunes of the Soviet Union were tied to political developments at home and to the state of the central post-war relationship with the United States abroad. There seems little doubt that the collapse of the Soviet economy was tied to its militaristic nature. In fact, the Soviet Union provides the best evidence of the 'Kennedy thesis' (Kennedy, 1987), which argues that the government spending demanded by a large military diverts revenues from rebuilding the economic base and eventually reduces the domestic economy to shreds. Tilly (1990) documents how previous dramatic political changes in modern Europe were preceded by external wars:

All of Europe's great revolutions, and many of its lesser ones, began with the strains imposed by war. The English Revolution began with the efforts of Charles I to bypass Parliament in acquiring revenues for war on the continent and in Scotland and Ireland. The debt accumulated by the French monarchy during the Seven Years War and the War of American Independence precipitated the struggles of the French Revolution. Russian losses in World War I discredited tsarist rule, encouraged military defections, and made the state's vulnerability patent: the revolution of 1917 followed (Tilly, 1990, p. 186).

The enormous costs of the Cold War 1945–90 added to the structural problems of the inefficient Soviet state generated by the global downturn of the Kondratieff IVA.

Trade and the Flag: the Soviet experience.

The vast majority of work on international trade ignores non-economic factors that determine trade. Indeed, researchers appear to believe that the state of political relations has an insignificant effect on the level of trade between two states. Polachek (1980) and Gasiorowski (1986) showed how incorrect this approach is by demonstrating a relationship between the state of conflict or cooperation and the level of trade, arguing that the flag follows trade. An increase in interdependence of economic relations gradually produced a reduction in tension and improved political relations. Later work by Pollins (1989a, b) confirmed the significance of political relations in addition to economic factors in international trade but he claimed that the causal arrow ran from the flag to trade, in other words, trade followed the flag. Given the frequent ebb and flow of conflict between the West and the Soviet Union, it was only to be expected that this relationship would be examined most closely.

Gasiorowski and Polachek (1982) advanced two hypotheses on the nature of East–West trade relations, that the incentives to reduce conflict are related to the desire to protect the benefits of the interaction and that the assymmetric interdependence can lead to linkage diplomacy and to greater conflict reduction from one side than the other. Looking at quarterly time-series data from 1967–78, they demonstrated that there is a strong inverse relationship between trade and conflict and that trade causes greater reduction in Warsaw Pact conflict than in US conflict. 'Trade had a much stronger effect in moderating Soviet and Warsaw Pact behavior than US behavior . . . Incentives to reduce hostilities are stronger for the country that benefits more from the interaction' (Gasiorowski and Polachek, 1982, p. 721). The better fit of a hyperbolic curve to the data showed that the percentage increase in trade was associated with a proportional decline in conflict. The results of the study are weakened by questions about the number of cases in the Granger causality that purported to show the direction of the causal relationship but there seems little doubt that the trade of the Soviet Union with the West had a greater effect on Soviet behaviour in subsequent years than US trade had on US political behaviour towards the East.

While it might be expected that the trade relationships between East and West would be strongly influenced by the political state of affairs, a more controversial claim is that Soviet trade has been purposefully used by the Soviet governments to induce Third World regimes to follow the Soviet line in world affairs and to tie their economies to the Soviet one. This position was first advanced by Goldman (1967) who saw Soviet foreign military and economic aid as a device to induce trade dependence on the Soviet Union, which was then used to produce political compliance. Roeder (1985) followed this theme and using data from sixty-two Third World states, he argued that the Soviet Union fostered dependence by the LDCs and generated high costs to them of breaking the relationship and substituting a new one. His data show that LDC trade dependence on the USSR actually decreased in the 1970s and that the putative Soviet attempt to generate dependence backfired. He agreed with the Valkenier (1979) assertion that the Soviet Union was trying to link itself to the world economy through building stronger links to the Third World states since the direct trade paths to the Western nations were frequently blocked by the poor state of political relations with the US and its allies.

The Roeder study results are suspect because of the effect of geography. As Zhukov (1990), among many others has shown, the Soviet Union generated most of its trade with the bordering socialist states, both in eastern Europe and in Asia. We know from international trade theory that distance is the most important single determinant of the level of trade between two states. All of the bordering states of the Soviet Union were socialist (Afghanistan was a possible exception till 1979) and it is very hard to separate the effects of contiguity from ideology in the examination of Soviet trade ratios. Specific examples of enormous change in trade direction after a political event are not much better so that the fall in Eygptian exports to the USSR after the 1972 ejection of Soviet advisors by Anwar Sadat from 39.7 per cent of the total to 4.2 percent in 1980 is not surprising, nor is the close link between supportive UN votes and receipt of Soviet foreign aid (Roeder, 1985).

There developed a significant difference among the Western bloc in trade relations with the Soviet Union in the early 1980s, the time of the second Cold War. The Reagan Administration in the US tried to isolate the USSR both politically and economically and told the US companies not to take part in the construction of the Siberian gas pipeline. After pressure from the companies involved and the European NATO allies, the US administration backed down. However, in the direct trade relations with the Soviet Union, the US behaviour was more purposeful. A grain embargo was imposed after the Soviet invasion of Afghanistan in 1980 and not lifted till political relations improved in the mid-1980s. By contrast, the relations of Germany and other European states were more stable; Seppain (1990) interprets the growing strength of trade relations between Eastern and Western Europe as another attempt to use trade to improve political relations by the Europeans. The Germans especially were concerned not to isolate or alienate the Soviet state but, as an element of 'Ostpolitik', to gradually reduce the political gaps between East and West. Another important state in this gap-bridging was Finland, which acted as a gateway to and from the Soviet Union during the long years of the Cold War (Liebowitz, 1983). As a result, the Finnish economy was the most severely dislocated of the Western states after the demise of the Soviet economy.

The Soviet Union in the world system, 1960–90

Many voices, from both left and right, have stated that the demise of the Soviet Union in the late 1980s was caused by the weakening position of that country in the world system over the previous quarter-century (Franklin, 1988). In order to see if these opinions merit consideration, an examination of the Soviet trade position, composition and trading partners is necessary. Additionally, the relationship of the political and trade links of the Soviet Union is expected to be of large significance, given the ebb and flow of the superpower dyadic flows of cooperation and conflict.

Data on Soviet trade were collected from two sources. The International Monetary Fund's *Direction of Trade Statistics*, published yearly, reports total imports and exports. However, because flows between the CMEA countries were not reported by the IMF,

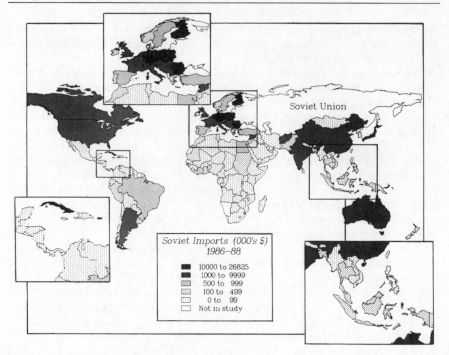

Figure 4.1   Geographical distribution of Soviet imports, 1986-88. Data sources are IMF Direction of trade statistics and Vienna Center data.

recourse was necessary to the Vienna Center for Comparative Economic Analysis annual report on the economies of the Soviet Union and Eastern Europe. This latter volume gives both the general composition of trade into and from the CMEA countries (commodity group) and the flows of these commodities to the major world economic blocs (western capitalist, LDCs, CMEA and other socialist countries). For political relations, though many indicators are available (UN voting alignments, agreements signed, etc.), a very useful indicator is a measure of total conflict that can be computed from the events data bank, WEIS (World Events Interaction Survey). Using the events reported in the New York Times, researchers recorded dyadic relations on cooperative and conflict scales, with weights assigned according to the significance of the event. Thus, a diplomatic protest note would receive a relatively low weight while a declaration or act of war would receive the highest conflict score. By taking the sum of the weighted conflict events for the years under study, 1966-88, (both to and from the Soviet Union), we can measure the general state of tension in a dyadic relationship and compare the pattern across years or between dyads. The WEIS conflict score, then, provides a useful measure of political relations and can be correlated with the volume of trade to see if political and trade relations are mutually affected.

The values of Soviet imports from all countries for the three-year period, 1986–88, are shown in Figure 4.1. Values over $1 billion were confined to the CMEA countries of Eastern Europe, the major grain exporters to the Soviet Union

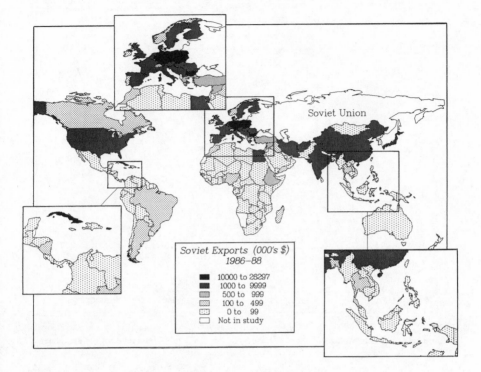

Figure 4.2   Geographical distribution of Soviet exports, 1986-88. Data sources are IMF Direction of trade statistics and Vienna Center data.

(US, Canada, Australia and Argentina), the largest western trading countries (West Germany, France, Japan, etc.) and to the two largest LDCs, China and India. Sizeable trade with other LDCs is notable by its absence. The map of Soviet exports (Figure 4.2) is similar, with only six countries (East Germany, West Germany, Finland, Poland, Bulgaria and Czechoslovakia) receiving more than $10 billion. The peculiar role of Finland as the gateway to the Soviet Union during the Cold War years has already been noted and the small amount and ratio of exports (about 10 per cent of total Soviet output) is not too surprising, given the special nature of Soviet trade, on Western terms, on the ideological basis of supporting CMEA and other socialist states, and on a tangible reluctance to leave a neo-autarkic position. When it is considered that the other superpower, the US, also has a low rate of exports of about 10 per cent, the Soviet figures are not *prima facie* evidence of autarky.

Graphs of Soviet imports and exports since the early 1960s (not shown) indicate similar trends. Soviet trade with the CMEA partners rose strongly for a quarter-century, even during the years of Soviet economic difficulty in the late 1970s and late 1980s. The value of imports from the CMEA states was about $2 billion in 1980, climbing to $4 billion by 1988, and that of exports to the same countries was also $2 billion in 1980, rising to $4.5 billion in 1988. By comparison, trade with the West, the LDCs and the other (Third World) socialist states rose more gradually to the

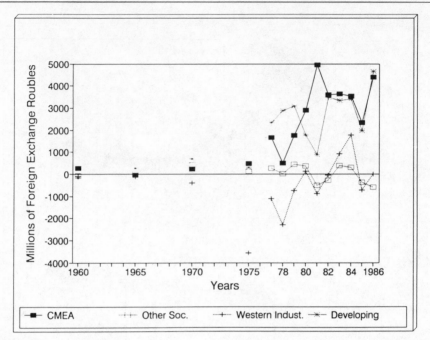

Figure 4.3 Trends in the Soviet balance of trade by region, 1960-1986. Data source is Vienna Center.

mid-1980s and then fell. During years of difficulty, when Soviet export earnings were not capable of paying for the expensive food and consumer goods that these states provided, the country fell back on its reliable partners in Eastern Europe. Though the Soviet Union continued to experience negative terms of trade with Eastern Europe, the relationship was mutually beneficial.

The yearly balance of Soviet trade with the major economic blocs is shown on Figure 4.3. In this and succeeding graphs, the balance is computed as exports minus imports, so that values below the line indicate a negative balance. The consistently positive balance with the CMEA states is a distinguishing feature of the graph, as is the near-balanced trade with the other socialist and LDC blocs. With the Western industrial states, however, the picture is less clear. Until 1982, the Soviet Union had a negative balance with these countries, but after the Andropov reforms the balance is positive, with the exception of 1985. A large amount of the fluctuations in the Western trade with the USSR can be attributed to the contractural nature of the trade agreements, which tended to run for a specified period (often five years) and therefore undermine any steady growth or decline trend. The overall picture, however, is that the Soviet Union consistently benefited from international trade. The country not only acquired badly-needed goods (food, high-technology industrial products and consumer goods) but also managed to secure steady markets for its own resource and industrial products. The latter would have been uncompetitive in world markets and the economic bailiwicks of the CMEA offered a trade safety valve.

The balances of trade by commodity group, using the Vienna Center classifi- cation and data, are graphed in Figure 4.4. The picture confirms previous studies of the

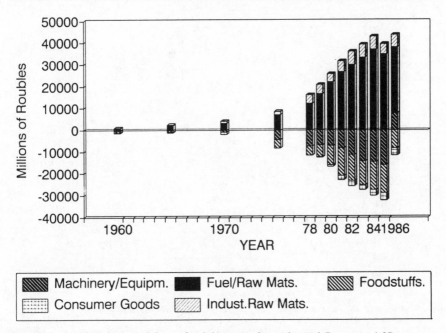

Figure 4.4   Trends in the Soviet balance of trade by commodity, 1960-1986. Data source is Vienna Center.

commodity-specific nature of Soviet trade. The USSR was a consistent net importer of machinery and equipment, food and consumer goods, though the latter group accounted for only a very small ratio of Soviet imports. The net negative balances of these groups of imports grew consistently over the past few decades till 1986, when there was a sharp decline consistent with the USSR cutting back on its imports as a result of the drastic price cuts in its main export, oil. By contrast, the oil/fuel/raw materials (including wood and forest products, another major Soviet resource) group accounted for almost all of the net Soviet exports (Figure 4.4). This net export grew substantially from about 15 billion foreign-exchange roubles in 1978 to about 30 billion roubles in 1986. The Soviet Union increasingly became a resource economy at the same time as other semi-peripheral states were reducing their dependence on raw materials exports during the post-Fordist restructuring years of the 1970s and 1980s.

In a recent study, O'Lear (1992) has computed the country by country commodity import and export trade of the Soviet Union. Using a different classification scheme than the one developed by the Vienna Center, one based instead on the level of processing and value-added (Smith and White, 1987), she shows that in the 1987–89 period the biggest importers of Soviet extractive products were Yugoslavia, Finland, Italy, West Germany, France and Austria. These same states and Egypt also imported the largest volumes of Soviet manufacturing goods, outside the CMEA bloc. Many of the same set of states (West Germany, Italy, Finland, Yugoslavia and France) provided the largest share of the Western high-technology goods reaching the Soviet Union while the US, Canada, and the U.K. joined this set in the export of simple extractive goods (mainly grain and foodstuffs) to the Soviet Union.

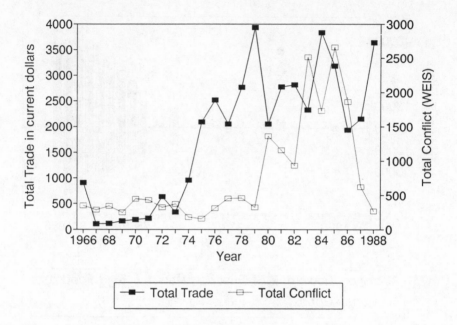

Figure 4.5   Trade and political conflict in the US-Soviet relationship, 1966-88. Data sources are IMF Direction of trade statistics, Vienna Center data and WEIS databank.

The connections between trade and political relations are shown in Figures 4.5 to 4.7. Only Western industrial states were examined because the trade relationship of the CMEA states was predetermined by their special ideological relationship to the USSR. The Western bloc is quite diverse and not all Western states, or even the NATO states, followed the US lead closely after the Reagan presidency began in 1981. Consequently, the wealthy capitalist bloc is divided into three groups, the US, the NATO states of Europe (West Germany, the UK., France, Italy, etc) and the non-NATO members of the OECD (Sweden, Finland, Yugoslavia, Austria, Ireland, Australia, New Zealand, Japan, etc). The specific interest is in the relative strength, consistency and direction of the flag-trade correlation between the Soviet Union and the three Western blocs.

If one did not know that the US was the main Soviet political adversary in the past quarter-century, the graphs in Figure 4.5 would not indicate it. A simple correlation of +0.42 suggests that as trade increased, so did the level of US–Soviet conflict (conflict sent and conflict received). (For our purposes, it does not matter which variable is dependent: it suffices to show a consistent relationship). The level of US–Soviet trade was low till the *détente* years of the early 1970s and the subsequent grain agreements. Thereafter, the level of US trade grew (most of the trade was from the US to the Soviet Union) till the beginning of the second Cold War in 1980, after the Soviet invasion of Afghanistan. American grain exports began again in the early 1980s. The oscillatory nature of the trade is due to the specific contracts that regulated it. Meanwhile, the state of Soviet–US conflict ebbed and flowed, independent of the year to year pattern of their trade. However, the events of 1972 and 1980 showed how much

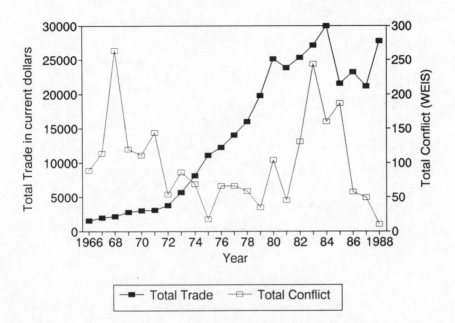

Figure 4.6   Trade and political conflict in the NATO Europe-Soviet relationship, 1966-88. Data sources are IMF Direction of trade statistics, Vienna Center data and WEIS databank.

this eventually depended on the long-term political relationship. The ability to withhold grain from the Soviet market, despite opposition from American farmers and many allies, and its marginal interest in Soviet exports, showed that the US was in the driver's seat in the trade negotiations.

There is no relationship between the level of conflict of the NATO states in Europe with the Soviet Union and their total trade (Figure 4.6). A correlation coefficient of –0.05 confirms this. Trade from Western Europe rose consistently during the study period till the Soviet ability to pay hard currency for the European products dropped in 1985 as a result of falling oil rents. At the same time, the overall NATO (minus US)/Soviet political relationship shows classic Cold War I–*détente* I-Cold War II–*détente* II cycles. Even in the darkest hours of Cold War II, the European members wished to keep open the trade door to the Soviet Union, not only as a market for their products, but also as a device to promote more stable and cooperative long-term political relations. On this point, they disagreed fundamentally with the Reagan Administration which tried to isolate the Soviet Union in all arenas, including trade (Wallerstein, 1984).

It is only the final trade/conflict relationship that matches the expected correlation, with a value of –0.24. This set of non-NATO countries is mainly composed of neutral states or states well removed from the European frontline. Like the values of the NATO countries, trade steadily increased to the mid-1980s, when the difficulties of hard currency payments struck the Soviet Union. The conflict score ebbed and flowed in no apparent pattern or rhythm; it was seemingly unrelated to the Cold War/*détente* patterns of the superpowers. This apparent anomaly may be due to the diverse political

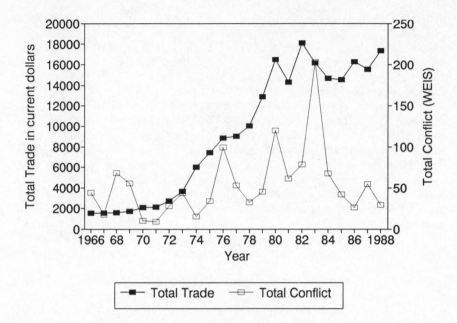

Figure 4.7   Trade and political conflict in the nonNATO OECD-Soviet relationship, 1966-88. Data sources are IMF Direction of trade statistics, Vienna Center data and WEIS databank.

composition of the group; overall, their total conflict score with the Soviet Union remained much lower than the scores for either the US or the NATO members in Europe. Despite the (non-significant) negative correlation between trade and conflict, the level of imports and exports of non-NATO members of OECD with the Soviet Union was motivated in both directions by considerations other than political ones.

The evidence in this section provides very little support for the thesis that the Soviet Union was adversely affected by the nature of its relationships with the Western powers. With the exception of the specific incidences of US grain sales and embargoes, determined by the state of the superpower relationship, trade was little affected by international politics. Instead, it was the nature of Soviet trade, specifically the composition of its exports, that adversely affected the ability of the country to muddle along in a changed global economy. Ironically, the Western industrial states were by-standers to the course of events.

Conclusions and postscript

The Soviet Union's economy collapsed in 1988–91 as a result of political developments. These were not, however, the kind of international effects that might have been expected to bring the country to a time of great change. It was not the usual trauma associated with a defeat on the battlefield that propelled change. Though the Soviet Union could ill afford the Cold War, it competed for a long time with the richer and stronger superpower, the US, backed by a massive array of political alliances. In the process, the Soviet Union damaged its domestic economy as its military nature determined the priorities of Soviet life. Though the Soviet Union had fallen on hard times in earlier years, domestic discipline, a clear agenda for policy and the fortuitous windfall from rising oil rents kept the country afloat. None of these conditions were available in the late 1980s.

Fundamentally, the reasons for the Soviet collapse point to Gorbachev. In not too dissimilar circumstances in the early 1980s, Yuri Andropov returned to traditional Soviet practices to turn the economy around. Gorbachev, as has been noted by many authors (Draper, 1992; Ellman and Kontorovich, 1992) allowed the political and economic worlds to drift, undermined the authority and role of the Communist Party without offering a replacement and as part of a global perestroika, waved goodbye to Eastern Europe. Once Eastern Europe had left the fold and the other socialist allies in the Third World had been left to their own devices, the Soviet Union lost its captive markets and reliable trading partners. The country had avoided coming to terms with the global restructuring of the Kondratieff IVB phase and remained a resources exporter with an antiquated Fordist industrial structure geared, in the first place, to military needs.

Returning to our basic conception of the USSR as a semi-peripheral actor in world affairs, its relations with Third World states and with the West suggest that it played the classic intermediate role of a semi-peripheral state (Chase-Dunn, 1990). Leavening its trade relations with its ideological principles, the Soviet Union attempted to support, through negative terms of trade, its poorer and weaker ideological allies in CMEA, tried to win export and import market shares in LDCs and at the same time, gain technology and necessary foodstuffs from ideological opponents in the West. The Soviet Union was a special kind of semi-peripheral state. Though we can easily recognize a core or peripheral state, the semi-peripheral states of the world system come in all manner of composition (Martin, 1990). The Soviet Union was the core of an ancillary Socialist world-system and at the same time, was a semi-peripheral in the larger world arena. In the current era of economic restructuring, it has been the flexible economies of East Asia that have profited most while the traditional industrial model has suffered most, in Eastern Europe, in parts of Western Europe and in the 'Rustbelt' of the United States. The particular timing of the collapse of the Soviet economy was a function of the political decisions of its leader and the radically-altered nature of its closest allies. But the overall structural determinants of the collapse were set a long time ago in the Stalinist period and in the specific route that the country pursued in the world economy. When the time for change arrived, the Soviet Union was unable to respond.

References

Becker, A.S., 1986, 'The Soviet Union and the Third World: the economic dimension', *Soviet Economy* **2** (3): 233–260.

Blank, S., 1991, 'Paying for Lenin's illusions: the economic dimensions of Soviet foreign policy', *Comparative Strategy* **10** (4):365–92.

Boswell, T. (ed.), 1989, *Revolution in the world-system*, Greenwood Press, Westport, CT.

Boswell, T. and Peters, R., 1990, 'State socialism and the industrial divide in the world-economy: a comparative essay on the rebellions in Poland and China', *Critical Sociology* **17** (1): 3–34.

Brada, J., 1988, 'Interpreting the Soviet subsidization of Eastern Europe', *International Organization* **42** (4): 639–58.

Bunce, V., 1983, 'The political economy of the Brezhnev era', *British Journal of Political Science* **13** (2): 129–58.

Bunce, V., 1985, 'The empire strikes back: the evolution of the Eastern bloc from a Soviet asset to a Soviet liability', *International Organization* **39** (1): 1–46.

Bunce, V., 1989 'The Polish crisis of 1980–81 and theories of revolution', in T. Boswell (ed.) *Revolution in the world-system*, Greenwood Press, Westport CT, pp.167–88.

Chadwick, M., Long, D. and Nissanke, M., 1987, *Soviet oil exports: trade adjustments, refining constraints and market behavior*, Oxford University Press, New York.

Chase-Dunn, C., (ed.), 1982, *Socialist States in the World-System*, Sage, Beverly Hills, CA.

Chase-Dunn, C., 1989, *Global Formation: Structures of the World-Economy*, Basil Blackwell, Oxford.

Chase-Dunn, C., 1990, 'Resistance to imperialism: semi-peripheral actors', *Review* **13** (1): 1–32.

Dipalma, G., 1991, 'Legitimation from the top to civil society: politics and cultural change in eastern Europe', *World Politics*, **44**, (1): 49–80.

Draper, T., 1992, 'Who killed Soviet Communism?', *New York Review of Books*, June 11, 7–14

Economist, 1990, 'Perestroika: and now for the hard part – a survey', April 28, 22 pages.

Ellman, M. and Kontorovich, V., 1992, 'Overview', in Ellman, M. and Kontorovich, V., (eds), *The disintegration of the Soviet economic system*, Routledge, London, pp. 1–42.

Firebaugh, G. and Bullock, B.P., 1986, 'Levels of processing of exports: new exports for 73 less-developed countries in 1970 and 1980', *International Studies Quarterly* **30** (3): 333–350.

Frank, A.G., 1980, 'Long live transideological enterprise! the socialist economies in the capitalist international division of labor and the West–East–South political economic relations', in A.G. Frank, *Crisis in the world-economy*, Holmes and Meier, New York, pp. 178–262.

Franklin, D., 1988, 'Soviet trade with the industrialized West', *SAIS Review* **8** (1): 75–88.

Fritsche, K., 1989, 'Dritte-Welt-Politik unter Gorbatschow: wachsende Rolle der ökonomie', *Ost-Europa* **39** (4): 332–342.

Gardner, J., 1988, 'Restructuring the Soviet foreign trade system', *Columbia Journal of World Business* **23** (Summer): 7–11.

Gasiorowski, M., 1986, 'Economic interdependence and international conflict: some cross-national evidence', *International Studies Quarterly* **30** (1): 23–38.

Gasiorowski, M. and Polachek, S., 1982, 'Conflict and interdependence: East–West trade and linkages in the era of detente', *Journal of Conflict Resolution* **26** (4) 709–729.

Goldman M.I., 1967, *Soviet foreign aid*, Praeger, New York.

Grote, G. and Kühn, H., 1988 'Comparative advantage and its use in the foreign trade of the socialist countries', *Soviet and Eastern European Foreign Trade* **24** (3): 31–53.

Hardt, J.P. and Boone, J.F., 1988, 'The Soviet Union's trade policy' *Current History* **87** (October): 329–332

Hewitt, E.A., 1984, *Energy, economics and foreign policy of the Soviet Union*, Brookings Institute, Washington DC.

Ivanov, I.D., 1987, 'Restructuring the mechanism of foreign economic relations in the USSR', *Soviet Economy* **3** (2): 192–218.

Jackson, M.R., 1985, 'The economics and the policies of East–South relations in the 1980s: an overview and review of the literature' *Soviet and Eastern Europe Foreign Trade* **21** (1): 3–26

Kanet, R., 1986, 'Economic aspects of Soviet policy in the Third World', *Soviet Economy* **2** (3): 261–268.

Kennedy, P.M., 1987, *The rise and fall of the great powers: economic change and military conflict from 1500 to 2000*, Random House, New York.

Khanin, G., 1992, 'Economic growth in the 1980s', in M. Ellman and V. Kontorovich (eds) *The disintegration of the Soviet economy*, Routledge, New York, pp.73–85.

Kuran, T., 1991, 'Now out of never: the element of surprise in the east European revolution of 1989', *World Politics* **44** (1): 1–7.

Levinson, C., 1978, *Vodka Cola*, Gordon and Cremonesi, New York.

Liebowitz, R., 1983, 'Finlandization: an analysis of the Soviet Union's "domination" of Finland', *Political Geography Quarterly* **2** (4): 275–88

Liefert, W., 1990, 'The Soviet gain from trade with the West in fuel, grain and machinery', *Wirtschaftliches Archiv* **126** (1): 78–96.

Martens, J.A., 1984, 'Quantification of Western exports of high-technology products to the USSR and Eastern Europe', in G.B. Smith (ed.), *The politics of East–West trade*, Westview Press, Boulder, CO., pp. 33–59.

Martin, W.G., (ed.), 1990, *Semi-peripheral states in the world-economy*, Greenwood Press, westport, CT.

McAuley, A., 1991, 'The economic consequences of Soviet disintegration', *Soviet Economy* **7** (3): 189–214.

McMillan, C.H., 1973, 'Factor proportions and the structure of Soviet trade', *ACES Bulletin* **15** (1): 57–81

Moe, A., 1991, 'The future of Soviet oil supplies to the West', *Soviet Geography* **32**, (3), 137–67.

Nove, A., 1982, *An economic history of the USSR*, Penguin, New York.

O'Lear, S., 1992, 'Perestroika in perspective: the international trade and political relations and civil disorders of the Soviet Union; 1985–88', Unpublished Masters thesis, University of Colorado, Boulder.

O'Loughlin, J., 1989, 'World-power competition and local conflicts in the Third World', in R.J.Johnston and P.J. Taylor (eds), *A world in crisis: geographical perspectives*, Basil Blackwell, Oxford, pp. 289–332.

Pitzer, J.S. and Baukel, A.P., 1991, 'Recent Soviet oil and productivity trends', *Soviet Economy* **7** (1): 46–82.

Polachek, S., 1980, 'Conflict and trade', *Journal of Conflict Resolution* **24** (1): 55–78.

Pollins, B.P., 1989a, 'Conflict, cooperation and commerce: the effect of international political interaction on bilateral trade flows', *American Journal of Political Science* **33** (3): 737–761.

Pollins, B.P., 1989b, 'Does trade still follow the flag?', *American Political Science Review* **83** (2): 465–480

Roeder, P.G., 1985, 'The ties that bind: aid, trade and political compliance in Soviet Third World relations', *International Studies Quarterly* **29** (2): 191–216.

Sagers, M.J., 1991, 'Review of Soviet energy industries in 1990', *Soviet Geography* **32** (4): 251–90.

Schroeder, G.E., 1985, 'The slowdown in Soviet industry, 1976–1982', *Soviet Economy* **1** (1): 42–74.

Seppain, H., 1990, 'The divided West: contrasting German and US attitudes to Soviet trade', *Political Quarterly* **61** (1): 51–66.

Smith G.B., (ed.), 1984, *The Politics of East–West Trade*, Westview Press, Boulder, CO.

Smith, D., and White, D., 1987, 'An empirical analysis of commodity exchange in the international economy', *International Studies Quarterly* **32** (2): 227–46.

Syzmanski, A., 1982, 'The socialist world-system', in C. Chase-Dunn (ed.) *Socialist states in the world-system*, Sage Publications, Beverly Hills, CA., pp. 57–84.

Sweezy, P., 1991, 'Class societies: the Soviet Union and the United States', *Monthly Review* December, 1–17.

Taylor, P.J., 1991, 'The crisis of the movements: the enabling state as Quisling', *Antipode* **23** (2): 214–28.

Tilly, C., 1990, *Coercion, capital and European states, AD 990–1990*, Basil Blackwell, Cambridge, MA.

Valkenier, E.K., 1979, 'The Soviet Union, the Third World and the global economy', *Problems of Communism* **28** (4): 17–33.

Vanous, J., 1984, 'Comparative advantage in Soviet grain and energy trade', in G.B. Smith (ed.) *The Politics of East–West Trade*, Westview Press, Boulder, CO., pp. 95–108.

Wallerstein, I., 1979, *The capitalist world-economy*, Cambridge University Press, New York.

Wallerstein, I., 1984, *The politics of the world-economy*, Cambridge University Press, New York.

Wallerstein, I., 1991, *Geopolitics and Geoculture*, Cambridge University Press, New York.

Wolf, T.A., 1985, 'An empirical analysis of Soviet economic relations with developing countries', *Soviet Economy* **1** (3): 232–260.

Zhukov, S.I., 1990, 'The geography of the USSR's foreign trade with bordering socialist countries', *Soviet Geography* **31** (1): 46–53.

5 Geopolitical transitions in agriculture: the changing role of American food policy in Eastern Europe, 1955–91

Janet E. Kodras

The Cold War woke in me a passion for geography.
Bruce Chatwin

Even in the ebullient, cathartic days of 1989, as Mstislav Rostropovich sat in the rubble of the Berlin Wall playing Bach on his cello, nascent political regimes were beginning to address problems inherent in Eastern Europe's transition to market economy. One immediate question concerned the lifting of state controls on food prices and the hardship and social instability that might ensue. The longer-term prospects for the food situation in Eastern Europe involve decisions on how best to proceed with the privatization of agriculture. Given differences among the countries in the agricultural systems originally in place, with the most privatized forms in Yugoslavia and Poland, and given disagreements as to the extent and pace of change needed, each country faces a distinct set of issues. Due to the tight integration of the global agricultural economy, the developing food situation in Eastern Europe will be affected by external forces, as well as domestic decisions. Understanding what lies ahead for Eastern Europe requires consideration of the world political economy of agriculture.

The purpose of this study is to examine the changing role of US foreign food policy in Eastern Europe over the past four decades, to illustrate the dynamic interplay of these external forces in the region. The study focuses upon American policy because the US exhibited disproportionate control over the global agricultural economy during the post-war period and remains the dominant power, governing more than half of international agricultural trade and providing two-thirds of the world's food aid (Wood, 1986).

It is the thesis of this chapter that alterations in US policy reflect larger shifts in the geopolitical position of Eastern Europe since World War II. During the early years of the Cold War, when Eastern Europe served as an ideological battleground between the US and the Soviet Union, the US sent food assistance to the region in a strategic attempt to entice Eastern European satellites out of the Soviet orbit. Currently, the region is emerging as a primary terrain of competition between the US and the European Community, as each seeks to enter its developing markets. The types and purposes of American food policy in Eastern Europe have been altered to conform with these new realities.

The Soviet Union was eventually replaced by the European Community (EC) as the major American competitor for Eastern Europe, as the Cold War gave way to a period of intensified intercapitalist rivalry. This shift was due in part to Soviet withdrawal from the region and subsequent disintegration into a Commonwealth of

Independent States (CIS), but also reflects the decline of the US as the hegemonic power of the capitalist world. I argue below that during the early years of the Cold War, the US was sufficiently in control of the capitalist political economy that it was able to support the agricultural expansion of other advanced capitalist nations. By the early 1970s, however, American power was faltering to the point that the US ceased such sacrifices to stabilize the system and began to use its still considerable power in an attempt to bolster its own position. The US, as a hegemonic power-in-decline in the Gramscian sense, was forced to compete against the EC for agricultural markets, one of the remaining sectors over which it retained some control. Eastern Europe has arisen as an important setting for that competition, as it provides new markets with relatively great potential for penetration and growth.

The chapter consists of five sections. The first provides a brief review of US foreign food aid policy, as a background for understanding its multiple uses in Eastern Europe. The second section describes the distribution of food assistance to the region during the early Cold War era, when the US used agricultural commodities in an attempt to wedge fissures in the Soviet bloc. The third section reviews how the declining status of the US during the later years of the Cold War forced a change in the world political economy of agriculture. The result was a decline in US food aid, accompanied by intensified trade competition. The fourth section reports on recent shifts in American foreign food policy in Eastern Europe, as the US simultaneously attempts to help rebuild economies along capitalist lines and to position itself to compete with the EC for the markets thus developed. The final section of the chapter comments on the current instability of the global agricultural economy, as reflected for example in the US–EC deadlock over GATT agricultural trade regulations, and implications for the future food situation in Eastern Europe.

Outline of US foreign food assistance

Approximately one-quarter of all US official development assistance since World War II has been food aid (Wood, 1986). Food assistance is one of the most flexible components of American foreign policy at the disposal of the president, because it consists of surplus agricultural commodities purchased and stored by the government. It is therefore not a visible component of the national budget and is rarely subject to the scrutiny of Congress in the annual funding process. Should circumstances warrant a change in US foreign policy, the administration can call upon food reserves much more readily than capital forms of assistance, without seeking legislative approval (Wallerstein, 1980).

As a result, food assistance has been used to address the international priorities of each of the succeeding presidential administrations, and the policy has come to serve a complex, often contradictory, set of purposes (Shapouri and Missiaen, 1990; Singer, Wood and Jennings, 1987; Tarrant, 1980). This is schematically presented in Figure 5.1. First, US food aid addresses both the domestic and foreign policy realms, with a constantly shifting tension between obligations to the domestic agricultural sector and the imperatives of foreign policy.

Two prime policy objectives in the domestic sphere are the disposal of agricultural surpluses, which plagued the sector during most of the post-war era, and the development of markets for US commodities, so as to increase export sales. The clear

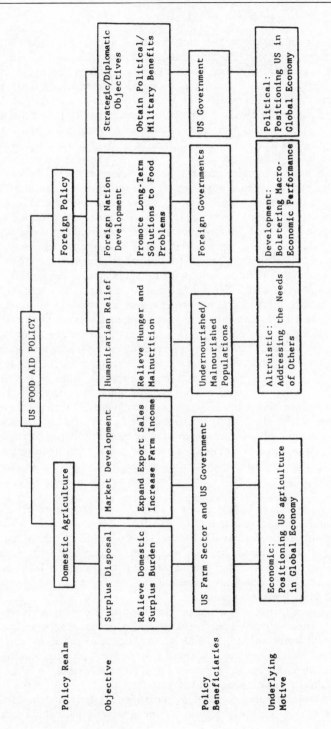

Figure 5.1 Objectives of US foreign food aid

beneficiaries of a food policy serving these domestic concerns are the US farm sector, particularly export-oriented agribusiness, and the US government itself, which curries the favour of an agriculturally-based constituency through such a policy.

There are three main policy objectives associated with the foreign policy realm: to provide humanitarian relief to the world's hungry, commonly assumed to be the primary beneficiary of food policy; to promote economic development through long-term solutions to global food problems; and to serve diplomatic and military interests on the foreign front, where the acknowledged beneficiary is the US government in obtaining political and strategic rewards.

The process is more complex than this heuristic diagram reveals. As shown below, internal dynamics between actors involved in the process – such as sporadic competition between the executive and legislative branches, bureaucratic politics, pressure from the agricultural constituency or agribusiness, and policy-capturing by particular groups with a stake in the outcome – can dramatically affect which motives prevail, thus influencing the geographic distribution of food aid to different nations at any given time and shifting the agenda for the programme over time. The diagram nevertheless provides a useful starting point for studying the allocation of US food assistance, as it makes visually explicit the general conclusion of the empirical literature that donor interests are at least as important as recipient needs in US foreign policy decisions. (See Poe, 1991, for a current review and interpretation of this literature.)

Examples of the many motives for US foreign food aid include its use to hold a favoured regime in power (bolstering India's Congress I party against Communist forces during the 1950s and 1960s); to institute political sanctions (cutting food aid to Chile when the Allende regime expropriated copper holdings of the Anaconda Corporation and other American multi-national companies in the early 1970s); to gain access to military base rights (shipping multi-million dollar food aid allotments to wealthy Iceland during the 1960s); to establish production sites and markets for US corporations (using food aid proceeds to open poultry raising operations in South Korea for the Ralston-Purina Company in the mid-1970s); and to create leverage in diplomatic negotiations (bringing India and Pakistan to the bargaining table over the Kashmir border dispute in 1965). (See Wallerstein, 1980, for accounts of these and other uses of US foreign food aid.)

The post-war outline of US foreign food aid policy was established in 1954 under the Agricultural Trade Development and Assistance Act, Public Law 83-480. The policy, commonly referred to as PL-480, provides for several types of aid, two of overriding significance. Title I is the most important, accounting for more than 70 per cent of all food aid administered by the US government since 1955. Title I authorizes the *sale* of agricultural commodities to 'friendly countries' on concessional terms, to be repaid in long-term, low-interest loans.

The advantage accruing to the foreign government is that by purchasing food for below-market prices, currency is freed to address other financial concerns. In addition, the foreign government may sell PL-480 commodities to its own population, which generates capital for the government to invest in other areas. Although dealing in food commodities, this arrangement is actually a type of cash transfer, and the 'aid' is a loan, with all the dependency strings that implies.

The advantage accruing to the US government is a decline in agricultural surpluses, particularly in wheat, feedcorn, and the non-food commodities tobacco and cotton. As loans are repaid, capital is generated from the disposal of those surpluses, which were permitted under domestic agricultural programmes in the first place. As a result, it has been estimated that the real cost of the US food assistance programme has been virtually nil during the post-war period, as the price supports and storage costs that would have been required in the absence of such a programme approximate the costs of running the programme (Wood, 1986, p. 14).

The second important element of PL-480 is Title II, under which the US government gives food commodities as outright grants to foreign nations. Although this is often the image projected of all US foreign food aid, it has in reality been a comparatively minor component of the programme. It is clear from the relative importance of selling food under Title I versus granting food under Title II that the benefits of the US food assistance system accrue to the donor as well as to the recipient, demonstrating the larger significance of food aid as the US pursues its global objectives.

In the years since its inception in 1954, PL-480 has been altered many times and implemented in diverse economic, political, and cultural contexts, rendering overall assessments of programme efficacy difficult (see Tullis, 1986, for a recent review of the literature examining the positive and negative effects of PL-480).

US food aid, 1955–1970

At the end of World War II, the US held fully 70 per cent of global financial assets (Cafruny, 1989, p. 115). By means of investment, political intervention, and trade and aid policies, the US used these considerable resources to solidify its hegemonic status within the global capitalist system and to challenge the position of the Soviet Union for control of its bloc (Wallerstein, 1991). During the early years of the Cold War, the essential US position in Eastern Europe was aimed to find a middle path between passive acceptance of the Soviet-dominated status quo and 'unrealizable liberation' against Soviet expansion (Gordon, 1987). The failure of the West to take a stand during the 1956 Hungarian uprising was the telling event signalling that the US would not use military force to counter Soviet influence in the area.

As an alternative, the US sought to further its position in Eastern Europe through its food policy, among other intermediate measures. Although the true purpose underlying the decision to give food aid is often complicated by intervening circumstances and camouflaged by the humanitarian rhetoric of the donor, the reason for US food assistance to Eastern Europe during the early Cold War was clear and widely acknowledged: food resources were deployed as strategic leverage to wedge fissures in the Soviet bloc (Wallerstein, 1980). Those countries demonstrating the greatest potential to show weakness in Soviet control of the region received the largest allocations. In this way, the use of US foreign food aid in Eastern Europe was consistent with the larger American policy of 'differentiation', i.e.,

that East European countries are not regarded as members of a monolithic Soviet bloc, like component republics of the Soviet Union itself, and that they are to be treated differently from one another. The grounds for more favorable treatment have consistently been two: East European foreign policies at variance with those of the USSR and favorable to Western (or US) interests, and measures of domestic economic, political and cultural liberalization (Gordon, 1987, p. 74).

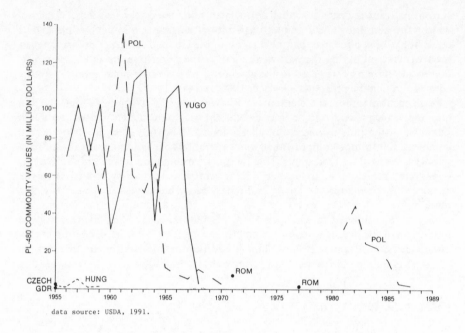

Figure 5.2   US foreign food aid to Eastern Europe, 1955-1989

An examination of the selective geographic allocation of PL-480 to Eastern Europe illustrates how this larger policy of differentiation was implemented through US foreign food aid. There was substantial intraregional variation in the receipt of PL-480 commodities within Eastern Europe during the Cold War (Figure 5.2).[1] Albania and Bulgaria obtained no food allocations under the programme; Czechoslovakia, Hungary, Romania, and the German Democratic Republic received very little, and this only sporadically; while Yugoslavia and Poland drew the overwhelming amount of PL-480 commodities. Yugoslavia received 58 per cent of the regional total ($US 1 billion) and Poland 41 per cent ($US 700 million), leaving one per cent for the other six countries combined.

The geographic pattern of PL-480 allocations does not accord well with the regional distribution of needs for food assistance. A comprehensive set of national nutrition studies on Eastern Europe during the period described the Albanians as the most dependent on low-nutrient foods, as a result of the country's physical geography and its isolation in the struggle against both the USSR and the US (May, 1963, 1966). Yet Albania received nothing, while Yugoslavia and Poland, with lesser needs for food assistance but greater potential to destabilize Soviet control, obtained the large majority of US agricultural surpluses sent to the region.

In Yugoslavia, moreover, the levels of assistance fluctuated in accordance with President Tito's ricocheting relations with Moscow.[2] In 1955, Yugoslavia and the US signed a food aid agreement for $US 43 million in wheat and cotton (the latter not a particularly succulent commodity, but one in substantial oversupply within the US agricultural sector). This allocation was 'an attempt to coax the Tito regime further away from the Soviet sphere of influence by nurturing independent political inclinations which already seemed to exist' (Wallerstein, 1980, p. 122). Barely five months later, however, when Khrushchev visited Belgrade, the flow of aid was decreased, and in the coming months, when Tito's stance turned pro-Soviet during a visit to Moscow, it was cut altogether (Markovich, 1968). After the Hungarian uprising the following year, Yugoslavian relations with the USSR worsened and the flow of aid was reinstituted. The Administration considered that the nation was a 'showcase of the suffering experienced by Communist satellites and afforded the best leverage for encouraging independence among the other satellite nations' (Kaufman, 1982, p. 70).

Further ricocheting occurred in 1961, following the Belgrade Conference of Non-Aligned Countries. Tito's pro-Soviet stance at the conference was of direct concern to the US Administration, as he was seen to play a pivotal role in the non-aligned movement (*Congressional Record*, July 9, 1962; Hoffman and Neal, 1962). President Kennedy reacted sharply to Tito's statements and warned, 'in the administration of [foreign aid] funds, we should give great attention and consideration to those nations who have our view of the world crisis' (*New Republic* October 16, 1962, p. 3). Negotiations on a Yugoslavian aid package were then postponed.

By the following year, however, when the US Congress took up the issue of aid to communist-dominated countries, the Administration strongly favoured preserving the food-aid relationship. US Secretary of State Dean Rusk argued:

> US economic assistance has been one of the principal factors in enabling Yugoslavia to resist the effects of Soviet economic pressures and to complete its successful schism from the bloc . . . Tito's assertion of independence set in train a series of developments bringing into question the basis on which the world Communist movement had previously functioned (Rusk, 1962, pp. 4, 6).

Those seeking to end the flow of assistance to countries such as Yugoslavia argued that PL-480 and other programmes furthered the cause of communism, rather than resisting it. Senator Dodd of Connecticut represented the argument, as follows:

> Our experience should make it abundantly clear the Communist regimes in Poland and Yugoslavia regard American assistance as a powerful weapon in building up their own prestige and strengthening their dictatorial control over the people. To suggest, therefore, that it is possible to help the people of Poland and Yugoslavia without strengthening the Communist regimes which control them is to defy a long record of evidence to the contrary (*Congressional Record*, July 9, 1962, 12112).

One of the outcomes of this vigorous five-year debate was a 1966 amendment prohibiting Title I agreements with any country trading with or aiding Cuba or North Vietnam. This spelled the end of Cold War food aid to Yugoslavia, which was engaged in trade with Cuba and sending medical supplies to North Vietnam (Wallerstein, 1980, p. 274).

The Administration's argument that food aid enticed Eastern European countries from the Soviet realm was more difficult to justify in the case of Poland. While admitting these differences, US Secretary of State Dean Rusk issued such a justification in 1961:

Poland, unlike Yugoslavia, is clearly a member of the Soviet bloc. It is bound to the USSR not only through such formal instrumentalities as the Warsaw Pact, but also because of its exposed geographic position and its heavy economic dependence upon the Soviet Union. Even more important is the fact that Soviet troops are still present in Poland . . . In developing US policies toward Poland, it would be erroneous and dangerous to base such policies on the illusion that Poland is not tied to the Soviets within the bloc, or is likely to be detached from the bloc in the immediate future. On the other hand, it is apparent that Poland enjoys a significant measure of autonomy and thus affords an opportunity for US initiatives that is not now available in any such degree in the rest of the bloc (*The Winds of Freedom*, 1963).

An intersecting reason for Poland's success in obtaining PL-480 aid has been the political force of Polish American citizens, who have influenced relations between the two countries (Drachkovitch, 1963). Relative to other Eastern European groups, the Poles were successful in influencing American foreign policy because the magnitude and geographic concentration of the community was sufficient to translate into political power, expressed through the Polish American Congress and personified in Clement Zablocki, US House Representative from Milwaukee, 1949–1983, and chair of the influential Foreign Affairs Committee (Bukowczyk, 1987). Following a study mission to Poland to analyse whether US aid helped the Polish people or contributed to their domination, Rep. Zablocki cautiously concluded that the net effect was positive:

> . . . the course of United States-Polish economic relations during recent years has served to open new contacts between Poland and the West, and to reduce that country's dependence on her Communist neighbours. This has been heartening to many of the Poles whose contact with the West was severely curtailed prior to 1957. The tangible evidence of US interest in the people of Poland has tended in our opinion to strengthen the bonds of friendship which have long existed between the peoples of our two countries (quoted in Drachkovitch, 1963, p. 62).

A more emotional argument was presented during the Congressional debates of the early 1960s:

> Through American aid we have helped to keep alive the spark of religious freedom. We have helped to keep alive the privilege of the Polish farmer to have title to his little plot of land. We have helped to keep alive the hope of individual political freedom, personal dignity, and an eventual return to the family of free nations (*Congressional Record*, June 7, 1962, p. 9180).

Influence such as that exerted by the Polish American Congress was instrumental in maintaining the flow of PL-480 commodities to Poland, even after the ban imposed by Congress in 1966. From the late 1960s through the end of the 1980s, Poland obtained primarily Title II commodities, not subject to the ban on trading with Cuba and Vietnam, but in 1981 and 1982 it garnered $US 47 million in Title I commodities during the rise of Solidarity and the Soviet imposition of martial law (USDA, 1991).

In summary, the US followed a policy of differentiation in its food aid to Eastern Europe over the course of the Cold War, reflective of its larger foreign policy stance of favouring those countries most at variance with the Soviet Union.[3] The essential reason why Yugoslavia and Poland received particular attention was their potential to show weakness in Soviet control of the region. Domestic factors, such as Polish American pressures on the US Congress, had an effect in specific cases.

Finally, it should be noted that the very fact that PL-480 commodities were sent to any Eastern European nation, at any time during the period 1955–1989, demonstrates how Cold War priorities outweighed other concerns in the selective allocation of US food aid. As illustration, in 1965 the US sent more than $US 100 million in PL-480 commodities to Yugoslavia but only about a half million dollars worth of commodities to Ethiopia (USDA, 1991). Yugoslavia contained approximately two-thirds the population of Ethiopia at that time, however, and the two nations clearly differed in their respective needs for food assistance. Extensive hunger had been reported in several Ethiopian provinces for more than a year, the start of spiralling events which would lead to the great famine of the early 1970s, but urgent requests for food had provoked little US response (Giorgis, 1989, pp. 257–8). In contrast, a nutritional study of Yugoslavia at the time found that diets had steadily improved from the early 1950s and there was no evidence of individuals going without food (May, 1963). And yet, Belgrade received over 200 times the amount of PL-480 commodities obtained by Addis Ababa. With the US engaged in competition against the USSR for spheres of influence, the support of Tito was evidently more important than the inclinations of Haile Selassie, who was consistently loyal to the US This example underscores the position of the US during the Cold War, specifically, that it would direct food aid to a state on the pivot point between the superpowers rather than to one solidly in its own camp, despite greater need.

Geopolitical transitions

Although the immediate cause for disruption in the flow of US foreign food aid to Eastern Europe was the 1966 change in regulations imposed by the US Congress, the shifting position of the US within the global political economy played an underlying role. For twenty-five years following World War II, the US, as the hegemonic power of the capitalist world, so controlled global agriculture that it was able to bear the costs of stabilizing the world system which best served its overall purposes (Wallerstein, 1991). Specifically, the US limited its own food exports through a set of domestic policies designed to curtail overproduction. This involved reducing acreage in production, guaranteeing price supports to its farmers, and using foreign food aid to distribute remaining surpluses (Cafruny, 1989; Hopkins, 1980; Wallerstein, 1980). In particular, the US protected Western Europe from the American farmers' comparative advantage in agriculture, permitting the governments to establish import quotas and export subsidies, mechanisms designed to encourage agricultural production in the region (Tracy, 1982).

Although these policies were initiated by individual Western European countries, the Common Agricultural Policy (CAP) of the EC coordinated them into a coherent mechanism. Established in 1960, CAP became the 'marriage contract' of the regional organization (European Community Commission, 1985, p. ii), bonding the Western European countries in an alliance which protected them against the potential agricultural power of the US. The impact of CAP was to encourage relatively inefficient agricultural production to the point that EC commodities eventually saturated domestic markets and were pushed onto the world market (Cafruny, 1989, p. 122). Although the US had originally supported the export-oriented agricultural policies of advanced capitalist allies, the emphasis on such policies would set the EC on a 'collision course' with the US by the early 1970s (Cafruny, 1989, p. 123).

It was at that time that the US began to falter visibly as the uncontested power of the capitalist world, as foreign corporations challenged US control of international markets for manufactured goods and cut into its domestic market, as well. These ascendant corporate powers were located in advanced industrial nations, which had completed recovery from the destruction of World War II and were becoming globally competitive (Agnew, 1987; Harvey, 1989). In addition, a number of Third World nations began to assert control over their resources, many of which had been cheaply exploited for US production (Noyelle, 1983). This increased the cost of manufacturing and drove down profits.

A major US response to the resultant balance of payments deficit, which began in 1971, was to exploit its comparative advantage in agriculture (Revel and Riboud, 1986). In the early 1970s, the US government removed many production controls and substantially increased export subsidies, with the effect that agricultural exports increased from $7.7 billion in 1971 to $21 billion in 1975 and $44 billion in 1980 (Cafruny, 1989, p.123). The changing position of the US in the global agricultural economy can be viewed as an example of the Gramscian hegemonic power-in-decline, which loses its ability and willingness to bear the costs of the system that previously worked to its own best advantage. It chooses to use its remaining and considerable power to compete against its ascendant rivals, rather than to promote the stability of the system (Gramsci's treatment of hegemony appears in Hoare and Smith, 1971; for an application to changing Atlantic relations in agriculture, see Cafruny, 1989).

It was in this shifting context that the US began to use its agricultural power as an increasingly important element of its international economic strategy, actively competing against the EC, which was also under considerable pressure to increase food exports. Food aid yielded to food trade as the US began to compete for global markets. As a result, PL-480 was substantially cut in the early 1970s, particularly the grant-based Title II. In 1972, the US sold one-half of its agricultural surpluses, normally used for PL-480, and cuts to Title II forced a 50 per cent reduction in food programmes worldwide (Wallerstein, 1980). To make matters worse, this decline in US foreign food aid occurred during the early 1970s world food crisis, when the need for assistance was particularly high.

Given the declining availability of food aid in the early 1970s and the withdrawal of US assistance to 'Communist-dominated' countries, the countries of Eastern Europe were clearly not in a position to receive American food assistance during the later years of the Cold War. By this time also, the locus of competition between the superpowers had shifted to the Third World and the US government had for the most part come to accept Eastern Europe within the Soviet sphere of influence. (See Nijman and van der Wusten, Chapter 3 of this volume). Thus, the predominant reason for sending food aid to Eastern Europe, destabilization of the Soviet bloc, had diminished by this time. It was not until the late 1980s, when transformations in Eastern Europe began to provide potential markets for US agricultural exports, that the US systematically reasserted its food power in the region.

US food policy since 1989

As the countries of Eastern Europe begin the process of transformation from centralized systems to market economies, their efforts are assisted by governments in the advanced capitalist countries. Because the US is no longer the hegemonic power it was at the end of World War II, however, it does not dominate the process. There will be no American Marshall Plan for the recovery of Eastern Europe in the early 1990s as there was for Western Europe in the late 1940s. Given its own budgetary difficulties and persistent public attitudes against capital-based foreign aid, the US government is substantially constrained in the amounts of direct financial assistance it can provide.[4] The US State Department readily admits that 'ninety-five per cent of the burden of making economic and political reform in Eastern Europe work will have to be done by the East Europeans themselves. We in the West can make a 5 per cent contribution to the process with advice, education, limited assistance, and encouragement' (McCormack, 1989, p. 2).

US food policies are an important component of this 'limited assistance', because the US still retains relatively great control over the global agricultural system. These policies not only assist in regional recovery, but help to position the US to compete in the markets thus developed. In particular, the emerging markets in Eastern Europe provide an important setting for the ongoing, and indeed intensifying, agricultural trade competition between the US and the EC.

The Eastern European market is particularly attractive to both the US and the EC because it provides an altogether new opportunity for capitalist penetration. Relative to agricultural markets in much of the rest of the world, where the debt crisis has dampened food demand, those in Eastern Europe exhibit growth potential. In addition, the major commodities exported by the US and the EC, such as wheat and dairy products, best accord with the dietary preferences of Eastern Europeans, thus providing a ready market. This emergent rivalry with the EC for the future Eastern European market is reflected in the following statement by a US Department of Agriculture administrator, who treats the current regional transformations only in terms of their commercial potential for the US:

> The economic and political changes sweeping through Eastern Europe may hold great market opportunities for US agricultural exporters . . . Competition for the Eastern European market promises to be stiff, and is already gearing up. The European Community (EC) in particular has an advantage in its proximity, and some EC countries are resuming traditional special relationships with certain East European countries, notably West Germany with Czechoslovakia and Hungary, and France with Romania (Lambert, 1990, pp. 5,8).

US concern over the development of market-oriented economies in Eastern Europe, and importantly, the future role of US agricultural exports in those markets, has resulted in two sets of food policies, those which assist in the region's recovery and those which seek to penetrate emergent markets. Each set is reviewed below.

Recovery mechanisms

Traditional food assistance programmes, such as PL-480, have been reintroduced to Eastern Europe since 1989. According to the US State Department, the purpose is humanitarian: 'to relieve deprivation and give a new government some breathing room' (Eagleburger, 1990, p. 2). But need for assistance is not the only criterion used in the selective geographic allocation of PL-480 in the 1990s. As was the case during the Cold War, the US government uses differentiation criteria to favour countries aligned with its interests. Aid is conditional on a country demonstrating:

• progress toward political pluralism, including free and fair elections;
• progress toward economic reform through development of a market economy with a substantial private sector;
• enhanced respect for internationally respected human rights; and
• a willingness to build a friendly relationship with the United States (US Department of State, 1991, p. 1).

US Secretary of State James Baker made the point explicit while outlining a framework for US economic assistance to Eastern Europe in 1990: 'We will proceed on the basis of a new democratic differentiation. Any backsliding in the movement to create legitimate governments will isolate a nation from the support we provide' (Baker, 1990b, p. 2). In other words, assistance is targeted to those countries making an effort to create democratic, market systems, where the potential for global capitalist expansion is greatest. A specific example is provided in Title I of PL-480. In order to qualify countries must now demonstrate support for certain political freedoms within their boundaries. In particular, there can be no restriction on citizen emigration, according to the Jackson-Vanik provisions of the 1974 Trade Act.

Two of the seven Eastern European countries have obtained Title I commodities since transformations began in 1989. Poland received $US 45 million in 1990 (Lambert, 1990, p. 5) and negotiated to continue Title I in 1991.[5] Romania also received Title I in 1990, although it was technically ineligible as it lacked a Jackson-Vanik waiver from the State Department. US government lawyers advised that Rumania be dropped from the programme in 1991. Albania is ineligible due to the emigration restriction and Bulgaria, although it became eligible in 1991, was unable to participate as it lacked hard currency for a down payment. Finally, Czechoslovakia, Hungary, and Yugoslavia are considered more suitable to participate in the market development programmes, discussed below, than to receive traditional forms of food aid, such as Title I.[6]

The most important need-based programme in Eastern Europe is referred to as Section 416. Like the PL-480 Title II programme it has largely replaced in the region, Section 416 provides food donations from US agricultural surpluses. As such, it is an outright grant of food, not a loan demanding repayment, and requests for assistance are judged according to the relative need of applicant countries. Czechoslovakia, Hungary, and Yugoslavia are currently ineligible, due to comparatively high per capita incomes. Poland, Bulgaria and Romania have obtained commodities, particularly feedcorn to prevent widespread livestock slaughter following the summer drought in 1990. Albania has not yet received 416 assistance, although it is considered a prime prospect. Widely regarded as Europe's poorest country, Albania is currently threatened by severe food shortages, particularly in rural areas.[7]

Finally, the US government is involved in agricultural development efforts, specifically the re-establishment of privatized production in the region (US Department of State, 1991). Working through private voluntary organizations or directly through its own agencies, the US government has created programmes to build efficiency and profitability in Eastern European agricultural systems. Current examples include the Farmers-to-Farmers programme, which sends American farmers and agricultural experts to Eastern Europe to help with privatization and the establishment of agribusiness, and the Cochran Middle Income Exchange programme, which draws Eastern European farmers and other professionals to the US to study agricultural and agribusiness practices (US Department of State, 1991). In addition, both the US Department of Agriculture and the US Agency for International Development run research extension projects to help establish private agriculture in the region. Notably, emphasis is placed on large-scale, agribusiness-oriented systems, as the US has introduced elsewhere in the world, with highly controversial results (Lappe and Collins, 1986).

While PL-480 and Section 416 provide immediate food assistance, this last set of initiatives seeks to build long-term agricultural productivity in the region. Rather than creating substitutes for American goods, however, these programmes are expected to increase markets for US agricultural commodities, as the sale of Eastern European commodities to advanced capitalist countries will build hard currency earnings and therefore import capability. Romania, for example, expects to export wheat and wine while importing feedcrops for domestic livestock production (Lambert, 1990). Through such initiatives, the US seeks to strengthen Eastern European markets. In a related set of programmes, it is gearing up to compete in those markets, as described below.

Market penetration programmes

The US government is actively pursuing the market penetration of Eastern Europe through a set of programmes that bolster the competitive position of the US relative to the European Community.[8] Presented here are three examples of US policies used to enter the agricultural markets of Eastern Europe. One strategy is the Export Enhancement Programme (EEP). The aim of EEP is to help private US agricultural exporters meet foreign price competition, under conditions deemed to be unfair trade practices. The US Department of Agriculture first identifies a particular commodity and country where subsidies by a foreign power make competition by US firms difficult. US exporters are then granted bonuses from government agricultural stocks for agreeing to enter that market.

The primary competitor targeted by EEP is the Economic Community, whose Common Agricultural Policy makes use of export subsidies to offer normally high-cost EC agricultural goods at lower prices (Smith and Ballenger, 1989). The effectiveness of EEP in generating price competition between the US and the EC is evidenced by the estimate that at least one-third of the recent increase in EC wheat subsidy costs is attributable to the introduction of EEP (Bailey, 1988).

A second market development policy is the Targeted Export Assistance programme (TEA), which makes funds available for the promotion of US commodities, particularly brand-name products, that are considered disadvantaged by unfair trading practices. These promotions include food exhibitions, advertising high-value, processed foods so as to accustom Eastern Europeans to American brand names. It has long been acknowledged within the Department of Agriculture that: 'free sampling is one of the oldest and most effective types of market development' (Hensman, 1971,

p. 256). In this particular context, one USDA official notes: 'Practical demonstrations for food professionals and point-of-sale contacts with consumers could be particularly effective in the East European countries after their years of isolation' (Lambert, 1990, p. 5).

The third market development strategy is an export credit guarantee programme, known as GSM. Essentially, GSM allows countries to purchase US agricultural commodities at commercial rates, with the US government guaranteeing payment to US lending banks if the foreign country's bank defaults on the loan used to purchase the commodities (USDA, 1990). The advantage accruing to the importing country is greater access to US farm commodities than would normally be possible, due to uncertain credit worthiness. US agricultural exporters benefit by expanding risk-covered markets at taxpayers' expense.

The selective geographic allocation of GSM depends upon analyses to identify those countries which are considered relatively good credit risks (although insufficient to obtain non-guaranteed loans from US banks) and at the same time provide strong potential for US market penetration. Only Yugoslavia and Hungary have made arrangements under GSM in the current time frame. In fiscal 1990, Yugoslavia obtained $US 40 million in guarantees and Hungary received $US 26 million (Lambert, 1990, 5). Czechoslovakia is eligible; indeed the US Department of Agriculture has expressed interest in making an agreement given this state's high credit rating within the region, but Czechoslovakia has shown little interest, as it seeks to minimize its short-term debt and maximize its foreign exchange. Poland is ineligible due to its previous default on $US 400 million in guarantees, while Albania and Romania cannot participate because they do not meet the 1974 Trade Act freedom of emigration stipulation. Finally, Bulgaria is eligible, but the large amount of food aid received under traditional food aid programmes suggests that it may not be in a position to obtain substantial assistance under GSM.

Considering the total package of US food policies implemented in Eastern Europe since the 1989 transformations began, it is evident that the region is developing as an important terrain of competition for the US as it seeks to bolster its position in the changing world political economy of agriculture. Current US food policy continues to assist a more general policy stance, simultaneously attempting to rebuild Eastern European economies along capitalist lines and to position itself to participate in the proceeds of that development. As American geopolitical imperatives during the Cold War have given way to the necessities of competing in the global agricultural system at present, the purpose, structure, and geographic distribution of US foreign food policy have been altered accordingly.

Prospects for the future

The global economic system of agriculture is highly unstable at present, due largely to the declining status of the US as the post-war hegemonic power. In particular, the intensifying competition between the US and the EC for global agricultural markets, currently symbolized in their deadlock over the agricultural component of the General Agreement on Tariffs and Trade (GATT), has important implications for the food prospects of Eastern Europe and indeed all nations, net exporters and importers alike.

GATT was established in 1947 as a regulatory mechanism controlling trade among the advanced capitalist countries. Although agricultural trade has been included as a component of GATT since 1960, both the US and the EC manoeuvred around the vaguely-worded regulations for many years (Cafruny, 1989, p. 124). Since the late 1970s, however, the US has increasingly pushed for a liberalized agricultural trading environment, so as to give American exports an edge over the relatively inefficient, and heavily subsidized, agricultural commodities produced by the EC (Bhagwati, 1991). The EC responds that one of the cornerstones of the Community is its Common Agricultural Policy, whose 'principles and mechanisms shall not be called into question and are, therefore, in no way a matter for negotiation' (US Congress, 1986, p. 16).

In the current round of GATT negotiations, the US seeks to eliminate export subsidies and tariff barriers, while the EC argues that these mechanisms have not caused it to corner more than its fair share of the global agricultural market and that, in any case, the US also violates such provisions. Indeed, the 1985 US Farm Bill substantially increased American export subsidies to increase competition with the EC and force it to reconsider its position (*Congressional Quarterly Almanac*, 1985, p. 527). An agricultural trade war between the US and the EC has ensued, which is proving enormously expensive for the governments involved and disastrous for many Third World countries, whose domestic production cannot rival cheap, heavily subsidized imports (Cafruny, 1989, p. 133).

Substantial international debate has arisen over the implications of GATT for different nations (*World Press Review*, 1992). From the perspective of Eastern Europe, an end to the current agricultural trade war would be clearly advantageous, given its financial inability to compete with the treasuries of the US and the EC, which currently subsidize their exports. The EC's relaxation of import restrictions could help Eastern European countries expand agricultural markets, although only Hungary and Rumania are expected to emerge as substantial grain exporters in the foreseeable future (Lambert, 1990). Clearly, the ability of Eastern European countries to earn hard currency through increased exports is a key to their future economic solvency, and some experts call for the EC to open its markets to the region through preferential trading agreements (Gati, 1990). Over the short term, several Eastern European nations, particularly Poland, Albania and Romania, are expected to face serious food shortages, which require assistance from the traditional food aid programmes of the advanced industrial nations (Lambert, 1990).

This study has focused on US foreign food policy as one component of the external forces influencing the food prospects of Eastern Europe. Given the instability of such external forces, and given the pace of economic and political changes occurring within the region, it is premature to forecast specifically the implications of Eastern Europe's incorporation into the global capitalist system of agriculture. Nevertheless, distinct possibilities can be identified, given what we know about the operation of capitalist economies. A major question regards the extent of hunger and destitution likely to emerge in Eastern Europe as a result of restructuring along capitalist lines. It is entirely reasonable to foresee rising societal inequalities, including hunger and destitution among groups left out of the economic growth in Eastern Europe. The prospect of hunger in Eastern Europe is as likely as the reality of hunger in the United States.

Notes

1. Although the Cold War is popularly characterized as an unrelenting period of hostility between the US and the Soviet Union, substantial fluctuations in superpower rivalry can be identified. Halliday (1986) has divided the post-war period into four phases: the first Cold War, 1946–1953; a period of oscillatory antagonism, 1953–1969; *détente*, 1969–1979; and the second Cold War, 1979–1986. The great majority of US food assistance sent to Eastern Europe during the Cold War was allocated during the period of oscillatory antagonism, defined by Halliday as a phase in superpower relations in which attempts to lessen tensions alternated with new confrontations. US foreign food aid was one of the mechanisms used during this period of active give-and-take between the superpowers.

2. Yugoslavia also received US food assistance prior to the establishment of PL-480. In 1950, the US Congress passed the Yugoslav Emergency Relief Assistance Act (PL 81-897), granting $US 50 million to ward off incipient famine, partly attributable to political problems between Yugoslavia and the Soviet Union. The Soviets eventually demanded that the US suspend food assistance to Yugoslavia, as the two competing powers sought to carve out their respective spheres of influence (Wallerstein, 1980, pp. 32, 122)

3. The Soviet Union practised its own form of differentiation in Eastern Europe during the Cold War, placing greater political restraints on countries of greater strategic importance. This differentiation had a geographic component, such that those on the Soviet front line of defence, East Germany, Czechoslovakia and Hungary, were given the least latitude in political affairs. By implication, these governments would have been much more hesitant than Yugoslavia's, for example, to consider a substantial offer of food assistance, had the US proposed it. Indeed, these three received only minimal amounts and only in the very early years of the programme, as noted on Figure 5.2.

4. In fact, the State Department's 1991 budget request asked for only $US 300 million 'to support the dramatic changes underway in Eastern Europe', which is little more than the $US 270 million requested for a new embassy building in Moscow and far less than the $US 500 million sought for Panama alone (Baker, 1990a, p. 3).

5. The 1991 negotiations ran into trouble due to the restriction that Poland suspend export of a 'like product' in order to receieve a PL-480 commodity. The Polish government expressed concern about offsetting export of its rapeseed meal in order to receive soybean meal.

6. Despite judgement by the US Department of Agriculture that Hungary was overqualified for Title I commodities, a decision was made by the Bush administrtaion, following the Hungarian President's visit to Washington, to offer Title I. Subsequent negotiations broke down over the terms of repayment, however, and by the time these problems had been ironed out, Hungary was no longer in need, having purchased feedgrains on the commercial market.

7. US Secretary of State James Baker, visiting Tirana in June 1991, offered food surpluses left over from US action in the Gulf War as food aid to Albania. Negotiations were initiated to send 6,000 metric tons of Section 416 nonfat dry milk to avert impending famine and establish a food relationship between the two countries.

8. The European Commission estimates that the Group of 24 wealthy industrial nations has pledged 33 billion ecus in aid to Eastern Europe, although only 3.5 billion is in the form of grants. Members of the EC account for 73 per cent of the total and 58 per cent of the grants. The single largest contributor is Germany, promising 20 per cent of all grants and 55 per cent of trade and investment guarantees (*The Economist*, 29 June 1991, p. 43).

References

Agnew, J., 1987, *The United States in the world economy*, Cambridge University Press, Cambridge, MA.

Bailey, K., 1988, 'What explains wheat export rise?' *Agricultural outlook* July: 1–23.

Baker, J., 1990a, 'US foreign policy priorities and FY 1991 budget request', *Current policy*, US Department of State, no. 1245.

Baker, J., 1990b, 'From revolution to democracy: Central and Eastern Europe in the new Europe', *Current policy*, US Department of State, no. 1248.

Bhagwati, J., 1991, 'Jumpstarting GATT', *Foreign Policy*, 83, Summer: 105–18.

Bukowczyk, J., 1987, *And my children did not know me: A history of Polish-Americans*, Indiana University Press, Bloomington, IN.

Cafruny, A., 1989, 'Economic conflicts and the transformation of the Atlantic order: The USA, Europe,and the liberalization of agriculture and services', in *Atlantic relations: Beyond the Reagan era*, ed. Stephen Gill, pp. 111–38, St. Martin's Press, New York

Chatwin, B., 1977, *In Patagonia*, Jonathan Cape Ltd, London.

Congressional quarterly almanac, 1985, 'Farm bill granted a limited win on all sides', 517–39.

Congressional Record, June 7, 1962.

Congressional Record, July 9, 1962.

Drachkovitch, M., 1963, *United States aid to Yugoslavia and Poland: Analysis of a controversy*, American Enterprise Institute, Washington, DC.

Eagleburger, L., 1990, 'America's opportunities in Eastern Europe', *Current policy*, US Department of State, no. 1250.

The Economist, 1991, 'Aid to Eastern Europe: The scorecard', 29 June: 43.

European Community (EC) Commission, 1985, *Perspectives for the common agricultural policy*, EC, Brussels.

Gati, C., 1990, 'East-Central Europe: The morning after', *Foreign Affairs*, **69**: 129–145.

Giorgis, D., 1989, *Red tears: War, famine and revolution in Ethiopia*, Red Sea Press, Trenton, NJ.

Gordon, L., 1987, *Eroding empire: Western relations with Eastern Europe*, Brookings Institute, Washington, DC.

Halliday, F., 1986, *The making of the second cold war*, 2nd. ed. Verso, London.

Harvey, D., 1989, *The condition of post-modernity*, Basil Blackwell, Oxford.

Hensman, C., 1971, *Rich against poor: The reality of aid*, Penguin, London.

Hoare, Q., Smith, G. N., (eds) 1971, *Selections from the prison notebooks*, Lawrence and Wishart,London.

Hoffman, G., Neal, F., 1962, *Yugoslavia and the new communism*, Twentieth Century Fund, New York.

Hopkins, R., 1980, *Global food interdependence: Challenge to American foreign policy*, Columbia University Press, New York.

Kaufman, B., 1982, *Trade and aid: Eisenhower's economic policy, 1953–1961*, Johns Hopkins University Press, Baltimore.

Lambert, M., 1990, 'US government programmes help open doors to Eastern Europe', *AgExporter*, July: 4–8.

Lappe, F.M., Collins, J., 1986, *World hunger: Twelve myths*, Grove Press, New York.

Markovich, S., 1968, The influence of American foreign aid in Yugoslav politics, 1948–1966, PhD dissertation, University of Virginia, Charlottesburg, VA.

May, J., 1963, *The ecology of malnutrition in five countries of Eastern and Central Europe*, Hafner, New York.

May, J., 1966, *The ecology of malnutrition in Central and Southeastern Europe*, Hafner, New York.

McCormack, R., 1989, Challenges to the international economy of the 1990s, Current policy, US Department of State, no. 1223.

New Republic, October 16, 1962: 3.

Noyelle, T. J., 1983, 'The implications of industry restructuring for spatial organization in the United States', in *Regional science and the new international division of labor*, eds F. Moulaert and P. W. Salinas, pp. 113–33, Kluwer Nijhoff, Boston.

Poe, S., 1991, 'US economic aid allocation: The quest for cumulation', *International interactions*, 16: 295–316.

Revel, A., Riboud, C., 1986, *American Green Power*, Johns Hopkins University Press, Baltimore, MD.

Rusk, D., 1962, Secret memorandum for the President, 13 January. Office of the Secretary of Agriculture, 1961, Washington, DC.

Shapouri, S., Missiaen, M., 1990, *Food aid: Motivation and allocation criteria*, USDA Foreign Agricultural Economic Report no. 240.

Singer, H., Wood, J., Jennings, T., 1987, *Food aid: The challenge and the opportunity*, Clarendon Press, Oxford.

Smith, M., Ballenger, N., 1989, 'Agricultural export programmes and food aid', in *Agricultural-food policy review: US agricultural policies in a changing world*, USDA Agricultural Economic Report no. 620: 169–86.

Tarrant, J., 1980, *Food policies*, John Wiley, New York.

Tracy, M., 1982, *Agriculture in Western Europe: Challenge and response 1880–1980*, Granada, London.

Tullis, F. L., 1986, 'Food aid and political instability', in *Food, the state, and international political economy*, eds F. L. Lamond and W. L. Hollist, pp. 215–36, University of Nebraska Press, Lincoln, NE.

US Congress, 1986, *Agriculture in the GATT: Toward the next round of multilateral trade negotiations*, US Government Printing Office, Washington, DC.

US Department of Agriculture, 1990, Credit protection for US agricultural exporters, *Factsheet*, US Government Printing Office, Washington, DC.

US Department of Agriculture, 1991, *PL-480 commodity values by recipient country, annually 1955–1989*, machine readable data base.

US Department of State, 1991, *US assistance to Central and Eastern Europe: An overview*, US Government Printing Office, Washington, DC.

Wallerstein, I., 1991, *Geopolitics and geoculture*, Cambridge University Press, Cambridge.

Wallerstein, M., 1980, *Food for war - Food for peace: United States food aid in global context*, MIT Press, Cambridge, MA.

The winds of freedom: Selections from the speeches and statements of Secretary of State Dean Rusk, January 1961 – August 1962, Beacon Press, Boston.

Wood, R., 1986, *From Marshall Plan to debt crisis: Foreign aid and development choices in the world economy*, University of California Press, Berkeley, CA.

World Press Review, 1992, 'The GATT talks', 39, February: 7.

6 Post–Cold War security in the new Europe*

Simon Dalby

With the end of the Cold War, the demolition of the Berlin wall, and the demise of the Warsaw Pact, most of the dangerous geopolitical 'certainties' that used to define the conventional limits of security discourse in Europe have disappeared. By the end of 1991, with the exception of the area of the former East Germany, the Soviet Union's military presence in Eastern Europe had been nearly completely dismantled and repatriated. A Soviet military threat is no longer a serious concern to Western European military planners, although the ultimate fate of the Red Army's nuclear weapons and the dangers that they may fall into the 'wrong' hands have generated some continuing concern. With the demise of the geopolitical confrontation, ongoing arms control initiatives and the wholesale reduction of the numbers of nuclear weapons poised to wreak destruction, many Europeans can, for the first time in decades, be confident that the prospect of a devastating nuclear war in Europe has receded to the point where it ceases to be an immediate concern.

In the West, the language of the North Atlantic Treaty Organization (NATO) has shifted from preoccupations with the 'Soviet threat' to managing the security 'risks' in the European area and further afield in the Persian Gulf. Many of the Western defence institutions of the Cold War remain, trying to adapt and articulate new and coherent rationales for their existence. They are doing so against the backdrop of a fundamental questioning of the role and structure of military forces in the aftermath of the Cold War. At stake in the current debates about defence and security in Europe are numerous political questions about the future of the continent (Buzan *et al.* 1990).

The most important factor in creating the new security situation in Europe was the drastic change in Soviet security thinking in the late 1980s. The key to understanding much of what transpired in Eastern Europe lies in the reconceptualization of Soviet security policy. Just because the consequences of this rethinking have subsequently spread far beyond the initial calculations of its adherents, the significance of these changes in unleashing change should not be overlooked. In addition, other critical thinking on security in the European peace movements and academic research centres has played its part both in influencing Soviet thinking and inspiring 'dissidents' in Eastern Europe. This chapter reviews these intellectual and political developments which now, in part, contextualize the new meanings of security in the post-Cold War Europe.

While many accounts of the changing security situation in Europe continue to evaluate matters in terms of military power, diplomatic and alliance politics and the

* Research for this chapter was made possible by a Barton Fellowship from the Canadian Institute for International Peace and Security

persistence of great power prerogatives, this chapter takes a different approach. It concentrates on the challenges to conventional Cold War security thinking during the 1980s and the adoption of 'new thinking' in the Soviet Union in the mid and late 1980s. The reasons for focusing on the role of critical and innovative thinking in Europe in the past decade are twofold. First, in parallel with the arguments in critical international relations scholarship (Der Derian and Shapiro, 1989), is to underline the political constitution of security arrangements and how they are understood. Second is to emphasize that within the fluid European geopolitical situation there is considerable room for further imaginative initiatives to enhance security (broadly understood), but also the danger that old narrowly focused military understandings of security will define the future of the European political map.

The new sense of security provided by the end of the Cold War is clouded by the continued presence of military concerns and the political instabilities resulting from the dramatic political changes of 1989. The violent dissolution of the Yugoslavian state is only the most obvious instability. Fears of the long-term possibilities of hostilities within the former Soviet Union persist. In the Eastern half of the continent the new regimes search for a *modus vivendi* with each other, with NATO and with the remains of the Soviet Union. The difficulties in Eastern Europe, in particular, are aggravated by economic and ecological difficulties of major scope. These factors also raise important questions about what it means to be secure in Europe in these turbulent times.

Critical voices in the security debate

'National security' dominated discussions of defence and foreign policy in both superpowers through the course of the Cold War (Buzan, 1991). Priority of place was consistently given to military considerations of 'security'. Security was understood in negative terms as a provision of protection of the political status quo from threat (Paggi and Pinzauti, 1985). It was also understood in terms of the spatial protection of the national territory first, and secondly in terms of geopolitical power projection to areas judged to be of vital importance to maintaining the military balance of power (Dalby, 1990). In at least the early stages of the Cold War in the 1950s the assumption that war was a real if not an immediately imminent threat was widely shared. The result was the build-up of nuclear weapons and their delivery systems, and the construction of semi-permanent military alliances on both sides of the geopolitical divide.

In the 1970s *détente* and arms control suggested the possibilities of political agreements, at least to limit the dangers of confrontation and restrict the development of some classes of weapons systems. 'Realist' thinking accepted the fundamental animosity of the capitalist and socialist systems, the permanence of militarization of international politics, and the priority of military force in international relations. These habits of mind continue even after the events of the last few years in Europe. But while the conventional discussions of the future of European security still focused on the activities of 'high' politics – the activities of statespersons, the conferences and arms control agreements, the movements of troops and weapons and so on – through the 1980s many critical voices were to be heard raising perplexing questions that challenged the dominant discourse on security.

These critical voices influenced the security debate in Europe, and also in the USSR in the second half of the 1980s. In part given vocal political expression in the various peace movements, the innovative ideas simultaneously challenged the Cold War understandings of security and suggested ways that the concept, and the politics justified by the concept, could be reformulated. These ideas have penetrated the halls of academe (Booth, 1991a; Klare and Thomas, 1991), and shifted the priorities of at least some European policy-makers and politicians. At least four interconnected themes are of importance.

First, even as the Second Cold War became intense in the early 1980s, the Independent Commission on Disarmament and Security Issues (1982) (the 'Palme Commission') was meeting to investigate the possibilities for reformulating security in terms of 'common security'. Focusing on the mutual vulnerabilities of contemporary societies in the face of extended technological, and not just nuclear, warfare, the idea of common security challenged states to abandon the assumptions that unilateral military measures offered the possibility of assuring national security. Instead they argued that security can only be assured in a world where mutual vulnerability is recognized and policies of mutual cooperation and disarmament are followed. The ultimate goal is one of a world legal regime where law replaces force as the arbiter of international disputes. Since the work of the Palme Commission in the early 1980s Europeans have used the term 'common security' to emphasize the importance of recognizing the interconnectedness of peoples in a world of nuclear weapons and their missiles (Stockholm International Peace Research Institute, 1985).

Second, other European thinkers were enamoured with ideas of 'nonprovocative' or 'nonoffensive' defence (NOD) (Alternative Defence Commission, 1987; Boserup and Neild, 1990). Inspired by the search for alternatives to the military confrontation on the central front in Europe they developed ideas of alternative defence postures that do not rely so heavily on weapons of mass destruction and on massed conventional forces. Given the propensity for offensive force capabilities by one state to raise fears in another nearby state, which in turn begins a military build-up to counter the first state's weapons systems – the 'arms race' phenomenon – nonoffensive defence offers, so its advocates claim, a way of providing for defence without threatening neighbouring states. Emphasizing the potential for high technology 'smart' weapons and careful defensive preparation, they argued that aggression can be rendered too risky or expensive to be attempted.

Nonoffensive defence and common security clearly complement each other (Moller, 1992; Wiseman, 1989). Good-will and confidence building measures reassure other states of non-hostile intentions more effectively if accompanied by military postures that are nonoffensive. Even if good-will gestures are not understood or accepted, the lack of an offensive military capability reassures potential adversaries that intentions are relatively benign given the fact that serious or dangerous aggression is not militarily feasible. On the other hand they deter aggression by making conquest very difficult. Unilateral adoption of nonprovocative defensive force structures is possible for any state, although a mutual adoption by two rival states would obviously further reduce the possibilities of hostilities by removing the technology needed for offensive military operations from both sides.

Third, through the 1980s the European Nuclear Disarmament movement (END) actively campaigned to denuclearize all Europe. They explicitly refused to operate in terms of the East and West, them and us. Out of this logic grew the political programme of 'dealignment' and the practical policies of constructing '*détente* from below' by initiating a dialogue between activists in both East and West and linking practical campaigning on peace with work for human rights and freedom (Federowicz, 1991; Kaldor, 1991). An important premise explicitly stated in the dealignment writings (Kaldor and Falk, 1987; Smith and Thompson, 1987), is that the Atlantic Alliance was more about alliance cohesion and superpower hegemony over Europe than about the need to provide 'security' against an ostensibly expansionist Soviet Union. Likewise it was argued that the Kremlin was using the threat from NATO to justify its continued presence in Eastern Europe (Kaldor, 1990).

In response to this, a political programme to unravel bloc politics and the inherent militarization of 'security' provision was deemed essential. Dealignment extended to consider matters of the militarization of technological development, the environmental consequences of 'the Atlantic technology culture' and the difficulties of democratic politics in states preoccupied with matters of (military) security. Dealignment was concerned with moving 'beyond the blocs', in the sense of transcending the superpower confrontation, rather than just moving 'out of the blocs'; hence its distinction from a policy of neutrality, or simple non-alignment. The arguments for rethinking politics and security were inherently 'anti-geopolitical' in that they directly challenged the bloc definitions of politics and security (Dalby, 1990–91).

Fourth, recently numerous writers have focused on the links between security and environmental issues (Dalby, 1992; Fairclough, 1991; Homer-Dixon, 1991; Renner, 1989; Rowlands, 1991). Linking conflict and ecological degradation offers a further extension of the concept of security. Not only does environmental damage undermine the economic health of a state by damaging its resources and imposing clean up costs, it also often directly endangers public health and the long term viability of economic activity. At the larger scale of the global environment, concerns with environmental security point to the dangers of disruptions caused by global climate change and the long-term dangers of uncontrolled 'economic growth'.

All these contributions have extended the meaning of security in new ways. They point to the necessity of including more than the operation of military threat and deterrence in any discussion of security (Ullman, 1983). Human rights issues have been linked to security also in terms of individual security within states. Cultural survival for many ethnic groups and aboriginal peoples are also an issue. Feminists have made it clear that the conventional discourses of international politics have written women out of the political script and rendered them particularly insecure (Enloe, 1989; Peterson, 1992). The necessity of democratizing security is thus also recognized (Johansen, 1991). All of these modifications of security distanced it from the traditional 'realist' concern with external military threats and domestic 'order'. They also recognized that security is not a somehow objective situation but a political one; security supposedly provided by states is not necessarily congruent with many populations' needs for protection (Hettne, 1988). What is rendered secure is a political order and a particular political identity (Campbell, 1990).

A common theme in all these critiques is that the political order perpetuated by conventional security thinking premised on blocs and nuclear weapons was a particularly dangerous one. The political identities of East and West, capitalist and communist and their Manichean presumptions were perpetuating confrontation and hence nuclear danger. There was an increased recognition through the 1980s in the West that the dangers of nuclear war outweighed the dangers of the 'Soviet threat'.

Likewise critics in East Europe focused on the dangers of continued military confrontation and its relation to the repression of human rights in Eastern Europe (Konrad, 1984). In combination these critical voices challenged the fundamentals of security thinking in Europe and raised questions of the politics of security in ways that could not be ignored.

Perestroika and Soviet 'new thinking' on security

Much to the amazement and delight of the peace movement activists, with the accession of Gorbachev and a reformist political orientation in the Kremlin, dramatic new foreign policy initiatives emerged, designed to end the arms race and shift the understanding of international security away from the bloc confrontation and the perpetual threat of nuclear war. While at first these initiatives were treated with complete scepticism in Washington, they were more favourably received by Western publics that had been substantially scared by the Reagan administration's bellicose rhetoric and the introduction of a new generation of nuclear missiles into Europe. By the time the Intermediate Nuclear Forces agreement was signed late in 1987 committing Moscow to destroying missiles, not only in the European area but also in Asia, it was clear to any commentator not intellectually crippled by Cold War ideological sclerosis that there had been a sea change in security thinking in the Kremlin (Bluth, 1990).

Given the enormous impact the Soviet rethinking of international politics has had on Europe it is worth summarizing the changing priorities of Soviet political and consequently military thinking, matters that are often shrouded in confusion. In particular most accounts of the changing Soviet situation during the period of glasnost and perestroika focus on domestic and economic rationales for policy changes. But the dramatic foreign policy initiatives came first. The political presumptions in 'new thinking' have usually not been immediately obvious, in part because scholars have not looked at the overall political logic of Soviet security discourse, but by careful historical detective work the overall outlines are now quite clear. From Michael MccGwire's (1987, 1991) detailed analyses it is possible to construct the following summary of the crucial historical developments in Soviet security thinking and see their importance in ending the Cold War.

With the Second World War as ample evidence, in the aftermath of that conflict Marxist–Leninist thinking argued that war between capitalism and socialism was inevitable although not necessarily imminent. Avoiding war was the highest Soviet priority, but the ability to survive a war was essential if socialism was to eventually triumph over capitalism. The Soviet Union faced daunting tasks of reconstruction, and initial fears were that a rebuilt Germany, possibly in league with a reconstructed Japan, would present a threat of attack fifteen or twenty years into the future. Constructing a *cordon sanitaire* in East Europe and imposing crippling reparations on Germany were consequent security priorities. These concerns quickly changed to worries about a more general war with the capitalist world led by the United States. Given the US nuclear arms building programmes in the 1940s and its bellicose rhetoric of 'rollback' in Eastern Europe, the Soviet Union's priority became preparing to survive such a war when it was launched by the 'imperialists'.

After Stalin's death attention focused more on the dangers of an airborne nuclear attack rather than a land-based assault. As a result of subsequent assessments of the implications of nuclear missile technology the Soviets assumed that the war, when it came, would involve intercontinental nuclear exchanges, and delivering the first blow would probably be decisive. This required a build-up of Intercontinental Ballistic Missiles to attack the US and the forward deployment of naval elements to destroy the nuclear potential of the US navy. Conquering West Europe would, if it were not too seriously damaged, they hoped, provide resources to rebuild the Soviet Union.

In the 1960s, the Soviets concluded that a war might not inevitably involve a nuclear exchange. This presented the possibility of a war that did not devastate the Soviet Union but which also maintained the US industrial base intact. This required that the US be denied a beachhead on continental Eurasia so that its forces could not threaten a conquest of the Soviet Union. The resulting changes of strategy, and force composition carried out through the 1970s, called for a blitzkrieg capability in Europe allowing the Soviet Union to evict US forces from Europe by entirely conventional means. The resulting force build-up in Europe helped raise fears of Soviet aggression, an unfortunately counterproductive development for Moscow. This strategic assessment also allowed for serious arms control to limit nuclear forces.

The late 1970s and early 1980s produced the novel possibility of a limited war with American forces in the Middle East and the possibility of going onto the defensive in Europe while containing the conflict to the South West Asian theatre. By this period Brezhnev and subsequently Andropov were clearly stating that a nuclear war could not be fought and won. Similarly new NATO weapons including the 'Euro-missiles' were calling into serious question the practicality of a successful Soviet offensive in Europe. In the early 1980s, while expanding weapons procurements in response to the US build-up under Reagan, the Soviets played down the importance of immediate offensive action in Europe. This shift to a more defensive posture in Europe should, they then argued, alleviate destabilizing fears of the 'Soviet threat' in Europe. This more practically reinforced the primary Soviet objective of avoiding a world war. In line with theorists of nonoffensive defence, the Soviet 'new thinkers' of the 1980s had absorbed the idea that unilateral actions on their part might avert the dangers of war.

But 'new thinking' went much further. It no longer held to the Leninist assumption that world war was generated inevitably by the capitalist system. Neither did they agree with the assumption that the 'war of the worlds' between capitalism and socialism was inevitable (Meiskins, 1987). The 'new thinking' on international relations thus removed the fundamental assumption underlying all earlier Soviet thinking; that of the inevitability of war between the social systems as a result of capitalism's inherent tendency to instability and war. Focusing on the large-scale environmental and nuclear dangers facing humanity as a whole, the Gorbachev administration argued that world war had to be prevented by political means, because its consequences would be too terrible for any social system to survive. Unlike all the regimes before it, the Gorbachev administration calculated that it was possible to avert the dangers of war by political means alone. This was the crucial change from conventional Cold War politics to 'post-Cold War security thinking'.

The political means to reduce the dangers of war included unilateral disarmament moves, summit conferences, the adoption of a quasi-NOD posture in conventional forces and a doctrine of 'reasonable sufficiency' in strategic armaments. This shift of priorities drastically changed the role of the Soviet military and its tasks (Gareyev, 1988). With the military doctrine reoriented towards a strictly defensive posture its *cordon sanitaire* in Eastern Europe was no longer strategically necessary either for the protection of the territorial integrity of the Soviet Union, nor crucially, as the launching pad for a blitzkrieg offensive into Western Europe in the event of war. Large unilateral conventional force cuts were subsequently made in Eastern Europe, removing any remaining capability the Soviet Forces retained to launch such an offensive.

Coupled to the INF agreement and the evolution of the 'Sinatra' doctrine in Eastern Europe, whereby Moscow did not intervene in political changes in the Warsaw Pact states, the transition to a defensive posture as a war avoidance strategy was finally evident to all. What has often been less clear is the political re-evaluation of the probabilities of global warfare and the possibility of politically preventing such a disaster. These crucial changes are often obscured because, amongst other reasons, the end of the Cold War is so frequently written about in triumphalist terms as a simple Western victory (Fukuyama, 1989).

The politics of Eastern European security

The history of the political change in Soviet thinking is complex but at least to some degree it was influenced by the discussions of alternative strategy and security in the West (Holden, 1991). Gyorgy Arbatov, one of Gorbachev's key political advisors had been a member of the Palme Commission which developed the theme of common security. Gorbachev wrote about the importance of the Palme Commission as well as ecological and scientific opinion, the Non-Aligned movement, and various anti-war organizations in influencing the formulation of 'new thinking' (MccGwire, 1991, p. 180). The former head of the Soviet-orchestrated World Peace Council, Tair Tairov, has subsequently emphasized the importance of END in inspiring new thinking and in providing practical suggestions for political change. He argues that even as END was being vilified by the official peace organizations in Moscow, the new leadership was listening attentively to its proposals for depolarization and denuclearization (Tairov, 1991).

Obviously, once the Gorbachev leadership had come to realize that it was essential to democratize to ensure the operation of perestroika, international peace and the end to the Cold War confrontation became even more necessary to the reform movement. The alternative foreign policy came well before the internal democratization and before the power of the Communist Party began to crumble. In part the policies of 'new thinking' may well have accelerated its demise, but they were an innovation in place before the pace of reformist events plunged the Soviet system into confusion. The end results of these changes in international relations have in part been eclipsed by the subsequent implosion of Soviet power. Domestic reforms, once unleashed, developed a dynamic of their own. When Soviet capabilities were then so rapidly constrained the virtues of the new NOD posture became a political and military necessity (Garthoff, 1990).

For all the triumphalism in the West following 1989, it was, as Thompson (1991) takes some pleasure in reminding us, the social movements in Eastern Europe that challenged the status quo in ways that it could no longer resist. Many of the leaders of the 'revolutions' of 1989 were linked to the END network. Jiri Dienstbier (subsequently Czechoslovakia's foreign minister) contributed a chapter to Smith and

Thompson's (1987) book *Prospectus for a Habitable Planet*. Pastor Rainer Eppelmann, a leading East German peace movement activist, became East German defence minister prior to German unification in 1990. Jacek Kuron (subsequently Polish Labour minister) was at the END convention in Lund in 1988. Vaclav Havel wrote for the *END Journal*. Their insistence on '*détente* from below' was designed to bypass the formal state negotiations and develop a movement that would bring human rights and demilitarisation into clear focus (Fedorowicz, 1991). This is not to suggest that END or its related Eastern European dissidents were single handedly responsible for the end of the Cold War, although the 'double zero' of the INF agreement was originally a peace movement demand, before the Reagan administration adopted it. It is only to suggest that critically re-evaluating the political presumptions of conventional security discourse was part of the process.

The political implication of these developments is to make it clear that matters of security and international politics are not the sole preserve of states, as so much realist international relations scholarship would have us believe. Internal transformations and international non-state actors clearly had important parts to play in the drastic changes of international security arrangements in the late 1980s in Europe.

There is a potentially dangerous irony in the politics of the new security arrangements in Europe. The argument in this chapter is that many of the events of the last few years were substantially affected by the changes in Soviet security thinking in the middle of the 1980s. The crucial policy innovation of prioritizing political over military means for guaranteeing security came from a regime in Moscow that is now widely discredited. The opportunity to gain full measure from Moscow's initiative has probably been missed in the collapse of Soviet power and the Western (mis)readings of the 'lessons' of recent events (Emmerson, 1991). If the experience of the Gulf War early in 1991 suggests anything it is the continued enthusiasm in the US for military solutions to international security problems, and in particular to its difficulties in the 'third world' (Luckham, 1990; Luke, 1991).

Ecological security in Eastern Europe

While it is no longer either a Soviet *cordon sanitaire*, or a potential launching point for a Warsaw Pact attack on NATO, the end of the Cold War is far from the end of Eastern Europe's security difficulties. Economic and, in particular ecological questions, may yet raise many dangers and instabilities (Schreider, 1991). Refugees and economic migrants could once again, as they did in 1989, substantially increase political pressure on European borders. The environmental protest movements in both the Soviet Union and in Eastern Europe formed an important dimension in the emergence of glasnost and the subsequent political overthrow of the Communist regimes across the continent (Ely, 1990).

The centralized planning system of Eastern Europe emphasized the massive use of natural resources to boost the production of industrial goods (Kabala, 1991). In the case of East Germany, Poland and Czechoslovakia the widespread burning of 'Brown Coal' with a high sulphur content in power stations led to persisting acid rain and smog problems. Poland faces serious air and river pollution problems, some of them 'imported' from Czechoslovak factories. Bulgaria faces difficulties from the deposition of heavy metals, chlorine pollution in the Danube and some nuclear power reactors of dubious safety. Rumania and Yugoslavia also face significant energy and pollution problems. Through the 1980s the costs of resulting environmental degradation became obvious in terms of polluted water supplies, forest damage and increasing health problems amongst the populations of the industrialized areas (ZumBrunnen, 1990).

The dangers of environmental pollution and the destruction of forest ecosystems in particular threaten the safety, health and well-being of populations directly. If security is understood in its broad sense to encompass substantial human-generated threats then clearly the legacy of the industrialization patterns of Eastern Europe continues to render large numbers of people insecure. Pollution is no respecter of boundaries, political or administrative. Thus problems in one location generate health and environmental difficulties elsewhere. Political tension can often result, although, despite some dire earlier warnings (Heilbroner, 1980), these matters themselves have rarely (so far) led to overt conflict (Homer-Dixon, 1991). In the case of the Gabcikovo-Nagymaros project to dam the Danube, ecological protest in Hungary has forced the complicated renegotiation of the project and compensation for failure to deliver contracted electrical power to Austria and Czechoslovakia. Further international tensions over pollution in international waterways are also likely; the issue of chlorine pollution in the Danube has already caused tension between Bulgaria and Rumania.

The Chernobyl disaster in the Soviet Union reminded policy-makers of the transboundary implications of an environmental disaster and launched a series of largely unsuccessful appeals for restitution from, and compensation by, the Soviet government. Chernobyl focused attention on the dangers of nuclear power in particular, but also on the inadequate environmental safeguards and preparations for dealing with an environmental disaster across Europe. It also drew attention to the need for a new politics that focused on alternative development modes (Mackay and Thompson, 1988). The legacy of 'actually existing socialism' has been one of inefficient industries, rampant industrial pollution and nuclear disaster.

The development problems facing Eastern European states offer some potential for hope, provided that a long-term vision is allowed to shape events. A rapid conversion to Western-style industry might well be a major mistake. In retooling production the potential to innovate by adopting highly efficient ecologically sensitive technology may well pay off in the long run (French, 1990). But the difficulties of this approach are considerable, not least the tardiness with which Western states, for all the rhetoric about international environmental cooperation, are tackling their own industrial structures. Failure to restructure the economies of Eastern Europe and solve at least the worst of the health threatening pollution problems may lead to the appearance of 'environmental refugees' across Europe (Jacobson, 1988). This destabilizing phenomenon could aggravate the existing political tensions generated by migration into and within Western Europe (Heisbourg, 1991; Widgren, 1990).

The new geopolitical context

In the aftermath of the Cold War, all geopolitical bets are off. The USSR has left the field of geopolitical rivalry, initially at its own volition as a result of the far-reaching analyses of new thinking, more recently as a result of its internal disintegration. The future role of the US in Europe remains unclear, but it will obviously be a much reduced military presence. Just how reduced depends on how isolationist US policy becomes in the absence of a clear military and ideological threat. Europe will be 'dealigned' to a much greater extent than any period since the 1930s.

Within Europe the most difficult issues are clearly the instabilities of Eastern Europe, although there will no doubt remain concerns over how Germany uses its increasing power. Once the glacier of the Cold War melted, political disputes of ancient lineage once again appeared. Numerous nationalist movements have rapidly surfaced leading to ethnic tension, political refugee difficulties and in Yugoslavia, civil war (Gow, 1991). The new regimes of Eastern Europe also fear the long-term dangers of either a civil war in the remains of the Soviet Union or renewed threats to their territorial integrity from an expansionist Russia. At least initially NATO was not keen to extend formal security guarantees to these new regimes for fear of raising fears of Western expansionism and involving NATO in all manner of disputes in an unstable region. Thus Poland and Czechoslovakia in particular may have to remain satisfied with associate membership of the EEC and some friendly communications on military matters with NATO members.

In the absence of the immediate formal extension of NATO, the Western European Union and the EEC, East European states are looking to temporary regional cooperative agreements to improve some cross-border issues. But they face dramatic difficulties in constructing institutions that can deal with their security situations (Gasteyger, 1991). There will undoubtedly be serious social costs and political difficulties in demilitarizing and converting the economies of Eastern Europe (Nelson, 1991). In terms of military power there will in all probability remain a 'vacuum' in Eastern Europe after the final withdrawal of Soviet troops from Germany is accomplished. While this may trouble some 'realist' theorists of international politics (Mearsheimer, 1990), the potential instabilities are unlikely to lead to a confrontation between the remains of the Soviet Union and a reconstituted NATO. Far more likely are efforts of political cooperation by the major European powers to limit the spread of violence in a war situation (Ullman, 1991). The recognition of the importance of political solutions to security problems offers considerable hope in this regard as does the possible institutionalization of collective security ideas.

The most obvious conventional security threat in the new Europe is the rise of chauvinist nationalisms. These problems are present not only in Yugoslavia and the remains of the Soviet Union. Minority ethnic populations, either understanding themselves as victims or with clearly irredentist aspirations, remain a potential source of tension. The Hungarian population in Rumania, the Turkish population in Bulgaria and the Slovaks in Czechoslovakia are obvious sources of further potentially serious tensions. In Western Europe xenophobic politics is clearly a political factor in France and Germany as visible immigrant minorities attract the attention of right-wing populist politicians and less than savoury political organizations.

The potential of populist nationalisms to cause trouble will no doubt be related to the economic performance of Eastern European economies. In the absence of substantial economic aid from the West, and their difficulties adapting to their new positions in the global economy, these polities may be increasingly vulnerable to populist enthusiasms. If a 'golden curtain' of wealth replaces the military 'iron' division of the continent, frustrated economic aspirations could play into the hands of politicians of a less than peaceful disposition. These dangers challenge the EEC to provide a coherent policy response to facilitate economic restructuring. Given the limitations of existing Western European institutions to absorb new member states or, as graphically illustrated in the case of Yugoslavia, effectively intervene to prevent conflict (Gow, 1991), it can well be argued that the challenge in Europe is now to substantially reform the Western part of the continent (Kaldor, 1990–91).

The institution most often pointed to as the alternative framework for a European-wide security system is the Conference on Security and Cooperation in Europe (CSCE) (Chalmers, 1990–1). This organization has no military forces or permanent command structure. Rather it is a formalized series of political fora and channels of communication that allow the discussion and, hopefully, the resolution of differences in a peaceful manner. CSCE obviously does not (yet?) alone offer the possibility for a security structure for Europe, given the continued presence of military capabilities and unresolved rivalries in various places. But it does obviously point to the necessity for politics in the place of military confrontation, and towards the recognition of the common fate of European peoples on a planet faced with huge problems. More specifically it points in the direction of 'common security' and the possibility of dramatically rethinking security now that the Cold War confrontation is over. But clearly for the foreseeable future the CSCE cannot offer military guarantees nor enforce peaceful relations between European states; it is not a form of defence alliance. But that is precisely why it is interesting.

Ken Booth's argument about the importance of developing the attitude and political habits of mind that emphasize common security and political solutions instead of violent conflict is germane. What is needed, he argues, are shared principles and tacit agreements to act collectively to resolve problems (Booth, 1990). This is probably much more important than the precise formulation of new security institutions, helpful though flexible institutions obviously will be in the future. And while these new tendencies may seem extremely fragile to a 'realist' they are nonetheless present and in need of cultivation rather than dismissal as inadequate to deal with the complexities and dangers of the new situation. But 'new thinking' also refers to the global security predicament, the onrush of technological innovation and the growing impact that humanity has on the ecosphere. Conventional security thinking has yet to substantially incorporate these themes. As with superpower rivalries, thinking in the geopolitical terms of spatial containments and the zero-sum rationales of the 'realist' focus on power politics is clearly counterproductive in the emerging context of global interdependence.

Security for the twenty-first century

There remain very considerable conceptual and political difficulties with 'security'. As noted above, its conventional formulation has for long referred to a stable status quo-oriented political order and preparations to use massive violence to maintain that order. The reinterpretations of security in the 1980s were concerned to challenge the political status quo, as the social movements did so obviously in Eastern Europe. Despite the departures of 'new thinking', peace movement activities and the globalization of culture, politics is still predominantly understood in terms of states; imagining global political subjects is still a very difficult political task in face of a myriad of sectional and local interests (Walker, 1990). Given these limitations and difficulties there are very real concerns that coupling environmental issues in particular to the language of 'security' may be a political and conceptual mistake (Dalby, 1992; Deudney, 1990); unless, of course, new understandings of security become hegemonic.

Faced with the daunting problems of Eastern Europe the question of how one might usefully reconceptualize security to encompass the aspirations of the peoples of its area remains; this chapter can offer no definitive suggestions as to what course the political debates of the future will take. Conventional liberal politics and the reasoning of realpolitik are ill suited to dealing with environmental security problems (Prins, 1990), difficulties that are all too obvious in Eastern Europe. Booth's (1991b) theoretical reformulation of the concept offers useful conceptual clarification. Turning conventional assumptions upside down he calls for security in terms of human liberation. Pointing to the needs to protect people from the arbitrary exercise of political power Booth insists that security involves political liberty and the respect for human rights. But a reformulated concept of security also needs to consider the matter of structural violence and the life-restricting constraints of absolute poverty. To be able to enjoy the benefits of political liberty one also needs the economic wherewithal to make the liberty meaningful. To a substantial extent the populations of Eastern Europe have gained the first of Booth's requirements. The second remains a major challenge. In addition there remains the necessity of reorganizing society to ease the burden of human activities on the natural environment.

It is perhaps overly harsh to suggest that Eastern Europe consists of a series of states whose populations have first-world aspirations but third-world prospects. Its future security prospects are clearly tied to economic change. The challenge is to simultaneously demilitarize, provide jobs and clean up the environment, hence reducing the inducements to large-scale destabilizing migration and potential transboundary disputes. None of these things is easy to do, and the simplistic adoption of monetarist policies or blind faith in 'the market' to solve all problems are not solutions (Galbraith, 1991). Neither have either the EEC or the US been forthcoming with large aid packages that might facilitate rapid modernization of East European economies.

In so far as these societies succeed with policies to alleviate environmental degradation, maintain nonprovocative military force postures, deal with ethnic tension and migration issues and seek political rather than military solutions to disputes, they will point to the possibilities of a less violence-prone, more 'secure' future for all of humanity. Should these efforts be substantial failures they may herald a series of political upheavals and violent episodes which will be ominous portents. The politics of security are about these profound questions, and how they are answered, will determine the European political map into the next century.

References

Alternative Defence Commission, 1987, *The politics of alternative defence*, Paladin, London.
Binnendijk, H., 1991, 'The emerging European security order', *The Washington Quarterly* 14 (4): 67–81.
Bluth, C., 1990, *New thinking in soviet military policy*, Pinter, London.
Booth, K. 1990, 'Steps towards stable peace in Europe: a theory and practice of coexistence', *International Affairs* 66 (1): 17–45.
Booth, K. (ed.), 1991a, *New thinking about strategy and international security*, Harper Collins, London.
Booth, K., 1991b, 'Security and emancipation', *Review of International Studies* 17 (4): 313–26.
Boserup, A. and R. Neild (eds), 1990, *The foundations of defensive defence*, Macmillan, London.
Buzan, B., 1991, *People, states and fear*, Lynne Rienner, Boulder.
Buzan, B., M. Kelstrup, P. Lemaitre, E. Tromer and O. Waever, 1990, *The European security order recast: scenarios for the post Cold War era*, Pinter, London.
Campbell, D., 1990, 'Global inscription: how foreign policy constitutes the United States', *Alternatives* 15 (3): 263–86.
Chalmers, M., 1990–91, 'An unstable triumvirate?: European security structures after the Cold War', *Current Research on Peace and Violence* 13 (3): 155–74.
Dalby, S., 1990, 'American security discourse: the persistence of geopolitics', *Political Geography Quarterly* 9 (2): 171–88.
Dalby, S., 1990–91, 'Dealignment discourse: thinking beyond the blocs', *Current Research in Peace and Violence* 13 (3): 140–155.
Dalby, S., 1992, 'Security, modernity, ecology: the dilemmas of post-Cold War security discourse', *Alternatives* 17 (1): 95–134.
Der Derian, J. and Shapiro, M.J. (eds), 1989, *International/intertextual relations: post-modern readings of world politics*, Lexington Books, Toronto.
Deudney, D., 1990, 'The case against linking environmental degradation and national security', *Millennium* 19 (3): 461–76.
Ely, J., 1990, 'Green politics and the revolution in Eastern Europe', *Capitalism, nature, socialism*, 4: 77–97.
Emmerson, D.K., 1991, 'Diversity, democracy and the "lessons" of Soviet failure: Western hopes, Asian cases', *Pacific review* 4 (4): 423–47.
Enloe, C., 1989, *Bananas, beaches and bases: making feminist sense of international politics*, Pandora, London.
Fairclough, A.J., 1991, 'Global environmental and natural resource problems – their economic, political and security implications', *The Washington Quarterly* 14 (1): 81–98.
Fedorowicz, H.M., 1991, 'Getting beyond the Cold War "from below": East-West dialogue towards democratic peace', *Peace research reviews* 11 (6): 1–80.
French, H.F., 1990, *Green revolutions: environmental reconstruction in Eastern Europe and the Soviet Union*, Worldwatch Institute, Worldwatch Paper No. 99, Washington.
Fukuyama, F., 1989, 'The end of history?' *The National Interest* 16, Summer: 3–18.
Galbraith, J.K., 1991, 'Revolt in our time: the triumph of simplistic ideology' in M. Kaldor (ed.), *Europe from below: an East-West dialogue*, Verso, London, 67–74.
Gareyev, M., 1988, 'The revised Soviet military doctrine', *Bulletin of the Atomic Scientists* 44 (10): 30–4.
Garthoff, R., 1990, *Deterrence and the revolution in Soviet military doctrine*, Brookings, Washington.
Gasteyger, C., 1991, 'The remaking of Eastern Europe's security', *Survival* 33 (2): 111–24.
Gow, J., 1991, 'Deconstructing Yugoslavia', *Survival* 33 (4): 291–311.
Heilbroner, R.L., 1980, *An inquiry into the human prospect*, Norton, New York.
Heisbourg, F., 1991, 'Population movements in post-Cold War Europe', *Survival* 33 (1): 31–43.
Hettne, B., (ed.) 1988, *Europe: dimensions of peace*, Zed, London.

Holden, G., 1991, *Soviet military reform: conventional disarmament and the crisis of militarised socialism*, Pluto, London.

Homer-Dixon, T., 1991, 'On the threshold: environmental changes as causes of acute conflict', *International Security* 16 (2): 76–116.

Independent Commission on Disarmament and Security Issues, 1982, *Common security: a programme for disarmament*, Pan, London.

Jacobson, J.L., 1988, *Environmental refugees: a yardstick of habitability*, Worldwatch Institute, Worldwatch Paper No. 86, Washington.

Johansen, R.C., 1991, 'Real security is democratic security', *Alternatives* 16 (2): 209–42.

Kabala, S.J., 1991, 'The environmental morass in Eastern Europe', *Current History*, November: 384–9.

Kaldor, M. and R. Falk (eds), 1987, *Dealignment: a new foreign policy perspective*, Basil Blackwell, Oxford.

Kaldor, M., 1990, *The imaginary war*, Basil Blackwell, Oxford.

Kaldor, M., 1990–91, 'Avoiding a new division of Europe' *World Policy Journal* 8 (1): 181–93.

Kaldor, M. (ed.), 1991, *Europe from below: an East-West dialogue*, Verso, London.

Klare, M.T. and D.C. Thomas (eds), 1991, *World security: trends and challenges at century's end*, St. Martin's, New York.

Konrad, G., 1984, *Antipolitics*, Harcourt, Brace Jovanovich, New York.

Luckham, R., 1990, *American militarism and the third world: the end of the Cold War*, Australian National University Peace Research Centre, Working Paper No. 94, Canberra.

Luke, T., 1991, 'The discipline of security studies and the codes of containment: learning from Kuwait', *Alternatives* 16 (3): 315–44.

Mackay, L. and M. Thompson (eds), 1988, *Something in the wind: politics after Chernobyl*, Pluto, London.

MccGwire, M., 1987, *Military objectives in Soviet foreign policy*, Brookings Institution, Washington.

MccGwire, M., 1991, *Perestroika and Soviet national security*, Brookings Institution, Washington.

Mearsheimer, J., 1990, 'Back to the future: instability in Europe after the Cold War', *International Security* 15 (1): 5–56.

Meiksins, G., 1987 'War of the worlds', *New Left Review*, no. 162, March/April: 10–11.

Moller, B., 1992, *Common security and nonoffensive defence: a neorealist perspective*, Lynne Rienner, Boulder, CO.

Nelson, D.N., 1991, 'The costs of demilitarization in the USSR and Eastern Europe' *Survival* 33 (4): 312–326.

Paggi, L. and P. Pinzauti, 1985, 'Peace and security', *Telos* 63, 3–40.

Peterson, V.S. (ed.), 1992, *Gendered states: feminist (re)visions of international relations theory*, Lynne Rienner, Boulder.

Prins G., 1990, 'Politics and the environment' *International Affairs* 66 (4): 711–30.

Renner, M., 1989, *National security: the economic and environmental dimensions*, Worldwatch Institute, Worldwatch Paper No. 89, Washington.

Rowlands, I., 1991, 'The security challenges of global environmental change' *The Washington Quarterly* 14 (1): 99–114.

Schreider, H. 1991, 'The threat from environmental destruction in Eastern Europe', *Journal of International Affairs* 44 (2): 359–91.

Smith, D. and E.P. Thompson (eds), 1987, *Prospectus for a habitable planet*, Penguin, Harmondsworth.

Stockholm International Peace Research Institute, 1985, *Policies for common security*, Taylor and Francis, London.

Tairov, T., 1991, 'From new thinking to a civic peace' in M. Kaldor (ed.), *Europe from below: an East-West dialogue*, Verso, London, 43–8.

Thompson, E.P., 1991, 'ENDS and histories' in M. Kaldor (ed.), *Europe from below: an East-West dialogue*, Verso, London, 7–26.

Ullman, R.H., 1983, 'Redefining security', *International Security* **8** (1): 129–53.

Ullman, R.H., 1991, *Securing Europe*, Princeton University Press, New Jersey.

Walker, R.B.J., 1990, 'Security, sovereignty and the challenge of world politics', *Alternatives* **15** (1): 3–27.

Widgren, J. 1990, 'International migration and regional stability' *International affairs* **66** (4): 749–66.

Wiseman, G., 1989, *Common security and nonprovocative defence*, Australian National University Peace Research Centre Research Monograph No. 7, Canberra.

ZumBrunnen, C., 1990, 'The environmental challenges in Eastern Europe', *Millennium* **19** (3): 389–412.

Part III
Social and political transformations

7 Ethno-national aspirations in the Soviet Union and its successor regimes: juggling with options

Petr Dostál

Since the beginning of reformist policies and the paralysis of totalitarian communist power in the erstwhile Soviet Union under Gorbachev, an impressive tide of national self-assertion quickly arose in all ethnic regions of that multi-national state. The famous communist doctrine of self-glorifying 'proletarian internationalism', to be spread among ethnic groups (Connor, 1984), denied latent national grievances and ethnic aspirations. The communist containment of ethno-national aspirations by force instead of democratic accommodation by free majority choice has effectively destroyed the basis for peaceful coexistence of ethnic groups. The Soviet Union has now disappeared but ethnic issues are, on the contrary, far from settled.

The reformist policies initiated by the leadership under Gorbachev were an impressive attempt to achieve both real modernization of the Soviet economy and an effective mobilization of Soviet society. Indeed, effective mobilization is a necessary condition for any effort to improve the economic and administrative performance of the country. Centrifugal tendencies threatening the very existence of the Union soon resulted from the expression of far-reaching aspirations by the national movements of titular groups in the former Soviet republics and other 'autonomous' units. Titular groups were the inhabitants of an administrative unit entitled to some degree of autonomy in that area that they and their namesakes elsewhere considered their homeland. These national movements of titular ethnic groups have frequently been opposed by countermovements of non-titular ethnic groups. To accommodate the disputes democratically and in a peaceful manner, new and effective institutional (notably constitutional) arrangements must be established. Preceding the actual demise of the Soviet Union at the end of 1991, there have been frequent calls and some more elaborate arguments for alternative institutional options that would change the Soviet multi-national state into either a renewed looser federation, a confederation-like entity or a break-up by secession of some of the union republics (Lapidus, 1989; Dostál, 1989; Kux, 1990).

The main aim of this essay is to ponder the options for institutional change, before and after the Soviet system definitely fell apart. Under all circumstances, certain crucial conditions connected with the intermingling of ethno-territorial configurations and the mutual interdependence of regional economies have to be considered. The rest of this essay is organized in four parts. The next section describes conditions set by ethno-territorial intermingling and assimilation. Using some new data from the Soviet census held in January 1989, it is shown that the old option of 'russification' and 'internal colonization' of the non-Russian parts of the Soviet Union by the Russian

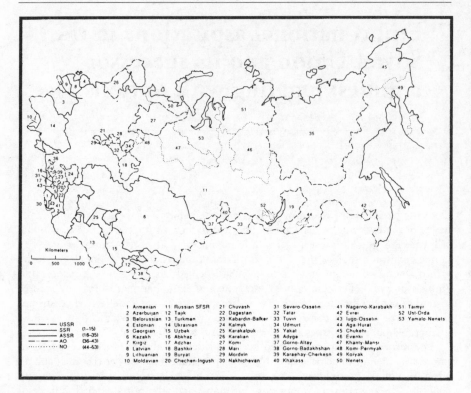

Figure 7.1   Autonomous regions and territories in the former Soviet Union

majority had to be abandoned, even if only for quantitative reasons. It is also shown that the lack of inter-ethnic assimilation has seemingly contributed to the recent rise of ethno-nationalism. The third section outlines some major characteristics of the ethno-national movements that emerged and their countermovements. Movement mobilization in various parts of the former Soviet Union is characterized by a number of stages of ethno-national assertiveness. Finally, in the last section, I speculate how, after the August 1991 coup and the final demise of the Soviet Union, the host of ethnic issues and the inevitable economic interdependence will haunt the successor regimes and condition future life on the territory of the former largest state on earth.

Ethno-territorial intermingling and assimilation

Part of the communist heritage was the hierarchical government structure of the Soviet federation comprising fifty-three more or less autonomous units (see Figure 7.1). Within some of the fifteen union republics (UR), in particular in the Russian Soviet Federal Socialist Republic (RSFSR), autonomous territories were defined as the official homelands of some of the Soviet ethnic groups. Consequently, they were the titular groups in that particular area. In the Soviet Union, twenty (autonomous) republics

(AR), eight (autonomous) provinces (AP) and ten (autonomous) districts (AD) formally provided varying degrees of autonomy (Feldbrugge, 1990) for less than half of its more than one hundred ethnic groups. These lower status autonomous homelands also contributed to the mosaic of the multi-national state, in which tensions between the numerous national movements and countermovements emerged.

The spiralling process of mobilization by national movements and countermovements in a number of areas is to some extent conditioned by the numerical strength of the various population segments. Three proportional figures are particularly relevant: the size of titular ethnic groups *vis-à-vis* non-titular groups in the fifteen union republics; the proportion of Russians within the regions of the Soviet Union and the assimilation of non-Russians with the Russian populations, expressing the intertwined processes of russianization and russification; the proportion of the non-titular population adapting to the culture (language) of fifty-three titular groups.

Ethno-territorial configuration

It is interesting to establish the relative numerical strength of titular ethnic groups in their respective states of the Commonwealth of Independent States (CIS), that replaced the Soviet Union. This question is important because the most extreme secessionist aspirations of national movements of titular groups and the opposing

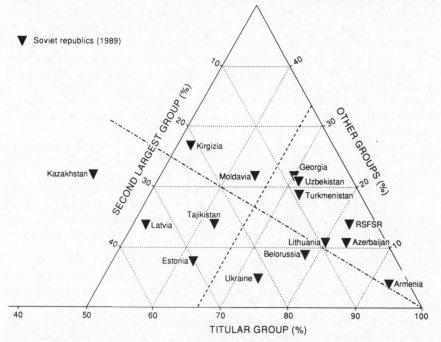

Figure 7.2 Shares of titular and other ethnic groups in the population of the Republics of the former Soviet Union 1989.

Source: Dostál 1991.

demands of countermovements of non-titular groups have at first occurred at the level of the fifteen states of the CIS. Power relations are, if not dominated, at least affected by these proportions. As the political system becomes more democratic, their importance grows. Assuming referenda on constitutional issues, threshold values of, for example, 66.6 per cent might be vital.

In Figure 7.2, a triangular diagram shows the shares of three population groups of the fifteen former union republics. It is necessary to show here only the right part of the triangle because each of the titular groups has at least a relative majority in its republic. On the horizontal axis, the percentages of the titular groups of the former republics are indicated. Next, the left axis shows the shares of the second largest ethnic groups. On the third axis, the shares of other ethnic groups are shown.

The triangular diagram reveals a wide range of variation in shares of the titular groups in the former republics' populations. In Transcaucasia, the Armenian union republic has a highly homogeneous population. The numerical position of the titular group of Armenians (93 per cent) has been strengthened there since the recent exodus of the Azeri group following the violent conflicts associated with the issue of Nagorno-Karabakh Autonomous Province (Dostál and Knippenberg, 1988). Moreover, despite recent earthquakes, there has been considerable immigration of Armenians to Armenia from other parts of the USSR. In Azerbaijan, partly as a consequence of the Armenian exodus and immigration of the Azeri from Armenia, the share of the Azeri increased in their republic to 83 per cent. Due to the Armenian exodus, the second largest ethnic group in Azerbaijan became the Russians (6 per cent). In the third Transcaucasian republic, Georgia, the share of the titular group is much smaller but it is still over two-thirds of the total population (70 per cent). The second group in Georgia are the Armenians but the share of other ethnic groups is also considerable, reflecting the heterogeneity of the non-titular population of this republic. It is interesting to note that the share of the Russian population has always been very low in Transcaucasia. Russians as well as other non-Caucasian ethnic groups now emigrate from the region. This is due to the violent conflicts over Nagorno-Karabakh AP in Azerbaijan but also due to the ethnic strife in Georgia where inter-ethnic conflicts in the Abchazian ASSR and South Ossetian AP were accompanied by much violence.

In the Baltic region also, the differences between the three former republics are considerable. Only in Lithuania does the titular group have a share of over two-thirds of the population (80 per cent). The Russians are the second largest group with 9 per cent and the Poles dominate in the share of other ethnic groups. In Latvia and Estonia, the Russians account for about one-third of the population. During the 1980s, moreover, the shares of non-titular ethnic groups were increasing in Latvia and Estonia to the detriment of the two indigenous nationalities, now less than two-thirds of the population.

In the southern republic of Moldavia, the titular group has a relatively small share of 64 per cent. The Moldavian non-titular population is relatively heterogeneous. Here, the Ukrainians are the second group, but other ethnic groups account for 22 per cent of the total population. In the Slavic states of Ukraine and Byelorussia, the titular groups have a clear majority of about three-quarters of the total population. The Russians are the second largest group in these two former republics. The Russian share is considerable in the Ukraine (22 per cent) where they live in the eastern and southern parts of the republic. Moreover, the triangle diagram also shows that the Russians dominate the non-titular population of the Ukraine. Their numerical position in Byelorussia is weaker (13 per cent) due to a significant share there of the non-titular population with the Polish ethnic group.

In Central Asia and Kazakhstan, there are considerable differences between the ethnic composition of the five states. Only in Uzbekistan and Turkmenistan do the titular groups account for over two-thirds of the population. The numerical positions of the second ethnic groups are weak. In Uzbekistan, the Russians and the Tadjiks both account for 8 per cent and in Turkmenistan, the Uzbeks have a share of 9 per cent. The Uzbeks are also the second largest group in Tadjikistan where, however, they account for 24 per cent of the total population. Given the Tadjik share of 62 per cent, the numerical position of the Uzbeks is strong there. By contrast, the ethnic composition in Kirgizia is quite heterogeneous. During the 1980s, the share of the titular group was increasing steadily and the Kirgiz now account for over half of the population. The second largest group are the Russians (22 per cent), but the share of the Uzbeks is important too. According to the 1989 census, there were over half a million Uzbeks living in the eastern part of the Fergana Valley on the Kirgiz side of the border, a scene of recent violent ethnic clashes over land, water and housing between Kirgiz and Uzbeks. In comparison with the other union republics, the numerical position of the titular group of Kazakhstan is extremely weak. The Kazakhs account for only 40 per cent of Kazakhstan's population. During the 1980s, they became the largest group with the Russians still having an impressive share of 38 per cent. Moreover, the Russians, Ukrainians and other European ethnic groups not only live in the largest cities and industrial centres of the republic but in numerous northern and eastern provinces of Kazakhstan, their shares are over 50 or even 75 per cent. In the past decade, the Kazakhs experienced an increase of 24 per cent while the Russian population grew by only 4 per cent. These numerical changes suggest, that in spite of their strong political and economic positions, many Russians are leaving Kazakhstan.

From Kazakhstan and the other four republics in Central Asia, the Russians and other European ethnic groups are now tending to move to the large Russian SFSR. The share of Russians in the RSFSR is 83 per cent and the position of the second largest group there (Tatars) is quite weak, accounting for only 4 per cent of the total population. In terms of the number of autochthonous and allochthonous ethnic groups, the RSFSR is obviously a highly heterogeneous entity. However, in the past, all of the autonomous units as well as the Russian administrative provinces have experienced a process of russianization in the sense of increasing shares of the Russians in regional populations (Dostál, 1989A). Nowadays, the Russians and the other two large Slavic groups, the Ukrainians and Belorussians, very often form majorities in the numerous autonomous territories of the RSFSR. The Slavic groups now have strong numerical positions in the European as well as in the Asiatic parts of the Russian federation.

Looking at the enormous differences in ethno-territorial mosaics indicated in Figure 7.2, a general conclusion can nonetheless be drawn. Only in a few of the states of the CIS concerned do the titular groups occupy overwhelmingly strong numerical positions *vis-à-vis* the non-titular ones. As titular groups are currently radicalizing their national aspirations, demanding secession, they have to cope with many other numerically strong ethnic groups living within their respective states.

Old option of russification and internal colonization

Since the end of the 1950s, many foreign observers have doubted whether the old option of 'russification' was still available for the central government in order to reconcile the interethnic tensions and conflicts and keep the nationality problems effectively under control. The 'russification' strategy implies 'internal colonization' by the Russians (Dostál, 1989). The Russian elite in non-Russian regions would have to become stronger with respect to both economic and political control. It is obvious that this option would also require an intensified strengthening and spread of the Russian language and culture. The assimilation of the non-Russian ethnic groups with the Russian nation would be intensified. There is little doubt that under Stalin and his successors, Khrushchev and Brezhnev, the option of russification as a concomitant of economic centralization was chosen as a long-term 'solution' of the intertwined issues of national and economic development. The rationale of this choice was voiced openly by Khrushchev at the Twenty-Second Party Congress (XXII Syezd, 1962). It was based on the idea of 'sblizhenie' among nationalities (i.e. on rapprochement and mutual knowledge of each other's culture and language). Yet, the ultimate aim was 'sliyanie' (i.e. merging or assimilation and adaptation of each others' culture). The Russian language had to become the lingua franca of the multinational state (Kirkwood, 1991). In contrast, 'sliyanie' refers to a process of assimilation which has a dramatic socio-psychological consequence: the identification of individuals and groups with other cultures and languages. On account of the dominant position of the Russian

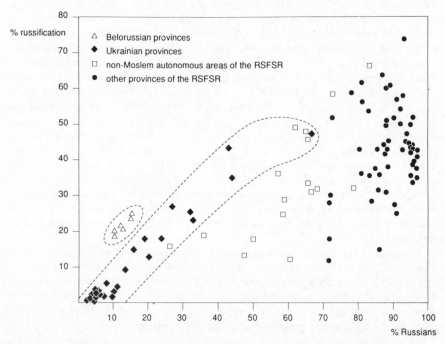

Figure 7.3   Russification and Russianization of selected territories in the former Soviet Union 1989.

Source: Soviet Census January 1989.

language and culture, such a process in this case implies the assimilation of the non-Russian ethnic groups with the Russian one.

Two components of the catch-all notion of 'russification' (Aspaturian, 1968) can now be distinguished. On the one hand, there is the capacity to have (instrumental) contact with Russians, their language and culture (russianization). On the other hand, there is the identification of non-Russians with the Russian language and culture, i.e. the actual assimilation (Dostál and Knippenberg, 1979). In spite of the unmistakable tendencies of the non-Russian ethnic groups towards russianization, and even to some extent russification, the traditional option of accelerated russification as real assimilation has for some time proved unattainable. This can be seen from the 1989 census results.

In Figures 7.3 and 7.4, two statistical indicators referring to regional populations of 169 Soviet territories, are correlated. The two indicators roughly correspond to the two components of 'russification' distinguished above. On the horizontal axis, the share of Russians in regional populations are shown, indicating regionalized chances of the non-Russians to have direct frequent contact with the Russian population. In brief, in the non-Russian parts of the Soviet Union, this variable describes the intensity of 'internal colonization' of the country by the Russian majority of 50.8 per cent and very probably indicates the degree of 'russianization'. The share of thoroughly-russified non-Russians is shown on the vertical axis. This latter indicator refers to those persons who declared at the moment of the census that the Russian language was their first, that is, their native language (*rodnoy yazyk*, mother tongue), although their nationality is non-Russian.

The scatter diagram in Figure 7.3 shows the relationship between these two indicators for the regional populations in the Byelorussian and Ukrainian union republics and also for the regional populations of all provinces and autonomous territories of the Russian SFSR, except those of the Moslem and Buddhist autonomous areas. With a few exceptions, the scatter diagram reveals a clear correlation between the two indicators. In the six Byelorussian and twenty-five Ukrainian provinces, the shares of Russians in the population correlate, very clearly and in the same direction, with the intensities of russification of the non-Russian population group. Within these two Slavic former republics, the presence of one member of the Russian nation in the regional population tends to correspond to the russification of one member of the non-Russian population group. However, it must also be noted that in all Galician provinces of the western part of Ukraine, the russianization as well as the russification are zero as a result of the ethnic homogeneity of this region. In contrast, in the russianized eastern part of the Ukraine in Donbass and Lugansk regions, and particularly in Crimea, the russification of the non-Russians is more than one-third.

A similar trend can be established among the populations of the seventeen non-Moslim and non-Buddhist autonomous areas of the Russian SFSR. The population of the Jewish autonomous province shows the most extreme scores on the two indicators. However, the lowest degree of russification is in the Mordva republic in spite of a 61 per cent Russian population. Within the set of Russian provinces, relations differ. In one group of ten provinces, russification affects less than one-third of the non-Russians. These Russian administrative provinces are the traditional homelands of the Tatar, Baskir, Kazach and Mordva ethnic groups. It is also interesting to note that Gorbachev's home base, Stavropol region, belongs to this group in which a high level of russianization has not led to a corresponding high intensity of russification.

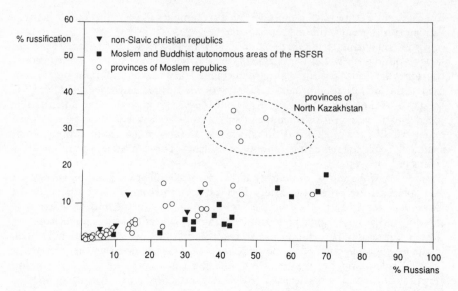

Figure 7.4   Russification and Russianization of other territories in the former Soviet Union 1989.

Source: Soviet Census January 1989

In conclusion, immigration of Russians into the administrative areas of the former Slavic republics, Byelorussia and Ukraine, has facilitated russification. Obviously, this trend is due to the relatively short cultural 'distance' between the Slavic indigenous populations and the Russians (Dostál and Knippenberg, 1979; 1981). Moreover, also in the autonomous areas in the Far North and East of the Russian RSFSR, the presence of the Russians also seems to stimulate the russification of the non-Russian population. The Russians are immigrating into these areas in order to exploit coal, gold, oil and other natural resources and are occupying the influential positions within the regional population (Argumov, 1988). In spite of the clear tendencies in these parts of the CIS towards russification, however, the effect of the presence of the Russians in the regional population must not be exaggerated. Only relatively high shares of Russians in the regional population lead to corresponding high degrees of russification.

By contrast, Figure 7.4 reveals a quite different but again systematic correlation between the two indicators. This scatter diagram shows the relative positions on the two components of 'russification' for regional populations in the non-Slavic Christian states of the CIS, the provinces of the Moslem union republics and the southern Moslem autonomous republics and autonomous territories in the Russian SFSR. The elasticity of the increase of russification corresponding to an increasing share of Russians in the regional population is evidently less steep in comparison with the area we considered earlier. In general, the regional share of Russians must be five times higher in order to accomplish similar levels of russification of the non-Russian population group. Only the provinces of North Kazakhstan diverge from this very systematic trend. These territories cover the so-called 'virgin lands' colonized under

Khrushchev's leadership, particularly by the Ukrainians, Byelorussians and Russians. It is interesting to note that the populations of the Christian non-Slavic states, Estonia, Latvia, Lithuania, Georgia and Armenia, exactly fit this pattern formed mainly by the Moslem-dominated regional populations. The only significant deviation from this trend is the position of the population of Moldavia where the russification level corresponds to the trend established for the populations of the neighbouring Ukrainian provinces.

Looking in particular at the very consistent statistical pattern in Figure 7.4, the general conclusion must be drawn that the traditional option of the Russian 'internal colonization' – inducing high levels of russification as a means to control inter-ethnic tensions – leads nowhere, particularly in the non-Slavic part of the Union. In Byelorussia and Ukraine, the indigenous Slavic populations are not sufficiently sensitive to the presence of the Russian population group to show the required level of russification within their own autonomous areas. Even in those parts of the former Soviet Union, where the Russians had a clear absolute majority and where the russification of the non-Russian groups had reached impressive levels of 40 or 50 per cent, further increases in russification do not seem a realistic option. A main reason is the very unfavourable demographic trend towards low birth rates, high death rates and, importantly, even absolute decreases in some traditionally Russian areas (Kozlov, 1975). The share of the Russians in the total population of the former Soviet Union in the year 2000 will be less than 50 per cent and that of the Moslem population nearly a third (Feshbach, 1983).

Adaptation to titular languages

A third numerical indicator conditioning inter-ethnic strife is derived from the notion that it is not so much russification but the assimilation of non-titular groups to the culture of the titular group in the region that counts. In Figure 7.5, two statistical indicators concerning the populations of the fifty-three autonomous units are correlated. On the horizontal axis the shares of the titular population in total populations of the fifteen former Union Republics, twenty Autonomous Republics, eight Autonomous Provinces and ten Autonomous Districts are shown. The shares of the members of non-titular populations who claim the titular language as their native tongue plus those who claim its fluency are shown on the vertical axis. In short, this latter indicator refers to those members of non-titular populations who tend to adapt to the titular culture (language) of the autonomous units concerned.

At the level of the former union republics, the scatter diagram shows a clear correlation between the two indicators, implying that stronger numerical positions of the titular groups within their republics tend to stimulate the non-titular populations to adapt to the local language. On the whole, the level of adaptation to the titular group's culture is low. The position of the RSFSR is exceptional indeed. The relatively small share of the non-Russians of 18 per cent is associated in the Russian federation with a high share of knowledge of the Russian language of 88 per cent. This outcome is not surprising given the long-term goal of Soviet language policy to promote Russian as a compulsory 'second mother tongue' in the RSFSR as well as in all other autonomous units of the Soviet Union (Kirkwood, 1991).

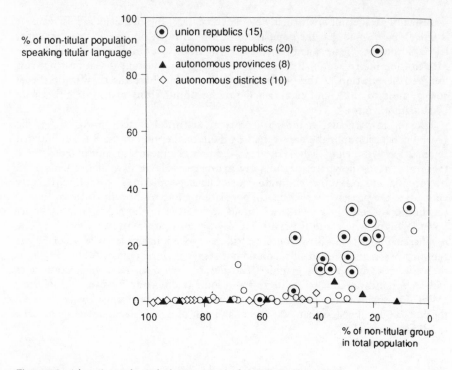

Figure 7.5   Adaptation to the titular languages in the former Soviet Union 1989.

Source: Dostál 1991.

For ARs, APs and ADs, there is no inclination of the non-titular population groups to adapt to the titular languages of these lower status autonomous territories. Moreover, Figure 7.5 also reveals that in most of these territories the non-titular population is numerically dominating. Consequently, the titular ethnic groups of most union republics, but in particular of the autonomous republics, provinces and districts are confronted with other population groups hardly inclined to assimilate. It is therefore no surprise that the strengthening of the role of titular languages and cultural institutions have played an important role in the recent rise of the ethno-national assertiveness at all levels of the fifty-three official homelands, leading to far-reaching aspirations in cultural and educational affairs.

Ethno-territorial movements and their countermovements: stages of assertiveness

Many attempts have been and are still being made under the constitutional successors of the Soviet Union, by both titular and non-titular ethnic groups, to change the formal status of the official homelands or (re-)establish new ones. Two major types of movement act as the vehicles for this ethnic assertiveness. There are national movements of ethnic groups with autonomy over their republic and countermovements that oppose these movements of titular groups (Dostál, 1991).

The term ethno-national movement (Connor, 1973) is used here as an overarching concept for organized ethnic assertiveness of titular ethnic groups. In an ethno-national movement, one titular ethnic group is dominant. Having initially promoted national consciousness and national dignity (nation-building), several ethno-national movements have gradually evolved towards the advocacy of more political autonomy in cultural, socio-economic, environmental issues and then towards full independence (state-formation). Ethno-national movements have united large numbers of associations with a cultural, socio-economic, environmental and party political interest that had originated within the titular ethnic group. The nature of some of these interests occasionally enabled the mobilization of interest groups from the non-titular ethnic groups. Soviet ethno-national movements also included factions of republican communist parties of so-called 'sovereign communists', inclined to emphasize territorial autonomy against the pressure of the centre. Yet, the most important aspirations were institutional demands based on the titular group's predominance in its republic, on its effective sovereignty over its homeland.

Countermovements emerge in response to the surge of ethnic assertiveness of titular ethnic groups (Goubuglo et al, 1990; 1990b). They are usually multi-ethnic and usually also unite a wide range of interest groups (workers' trade unions, consumer associations or cultural societies). Parts of the countermovements have allied with so-called 'old structures', the mainstays of the communist political and economic regime. These conservative interest groups thus sought to defend their privileged political and socio-economic positions appropriated in earlier phases of the communist regime. Countermovements also embrace interest groups of so-called 'imperial communists' emphasizing 'internationalist values'. Some of their members belonged to the titular ethnic group, e.g. as members of the federal Communist Party. Countermovements particularly articulated the demands of immigrant populations, non-titular ethnic minorities having historical homelands within the autonomous homelands of the titular groups, parts of the titular groups of union republics that happened to inhabit so-called autonomous subunits where the local titular group had started a movement for increased autonomy.

When examining the dynamic nature of the national movements, it is necessary to pay some attention to the nature of the elites engaged in the mobilization of titular groups. It appears that the national movements have been guided in a cumulative way by a number of elites belonging to the titular groups (Drobidzheva, 1989; Goubuglo et al., 1990; 1990). Considering the participation of different elites and their clienteles enables us to sketch the evolution towards the mass nature of national movements in clearer terms. Broadly, four stages can be distinguished (Dostál, 1991):

(i) The preservation and strengthening of the national language is usually the principal demand. The cultural and scientific elites of the titular group are particularly active demanding the independence of cultural and educational institutions from the federal institutions;

(ii) Autonomy in economic and social affairs is demanded. There is a close connection between the extra-regional control of the economy by the federal government and a growing focus on environmental issues and demands within the homelands. During this stage, the cultural and scientific elites are joined by representatives of the mass media and the managerial and technical elite of the titular group. The national demands gain massive support among the members of the titular group;

(iii) Demands for political autonomy are articulated. After new and more or less free elections, this radical stage of aspirations of the titular groups gains momentum. The national movement establishes its legislative powers. New politicians gain control over the administrative apparatus of the homeland. However, their legislative and administrative powers are constrained both by the existing federal legislation and the apparatus of the federal institutions; and

(iv) The most radical aspirations of the titular group, full sovereignty and secession from the federal state are brought forward. Will this stage really be the final one? After gaining full independence and sovereignty, some of the titular groups have been willing to re-associate their state entities with the other republics of the former Soviet Union in a much looser confederation of uncertain future.

It is quite obvious that the countermovements have tended to reflect these four stages of radicalization of the titular group's aspirations (Prikhozhaev, 1989). As national aspirations of the titular groups expand, the opposition radicalizes. However, in those republics where the Communist Party has long been able to retain many of the key political positions, there have emerged only weak or unimportant counter-movements. The main reason for this is that the republican 'sovereign communists' have been willing and able to adopt a number of the less radical demands of the national movements. Such reformed communist parties have for a time been able to dampen national aspirations by preventing the secessionist demands characterizing the final fourth stage of national assertiveness. After the coup of August 1991, however, they have also taken the road to full sovereignty and have remarkably adapted to the new rules of the political game. The question arises *where* in the Soviet Union *what stages* of ethno-national assertiveness have emerged at what time. We expect that pattern to be connected with the numerical relations of population groups encountered in the preceding section. This will hopefully help us better understand the next acts of the dramatic demise of the Soviet Union.

The Baltic region

Broad national movements initially emerged in the Soviet Union in 1988. They took the organizational form of Popular Fronts that were associated with many very different and numerous interest groups. They started in the three Baltic republics, only in 1940 forcibly incorporated into the USSR. Especially after winning the free republican elections in the spring of 1990, the national movements in all three Baltic republics extended their demands from second and third stage reforms to the far-reaching radical demands of the fourth stage. The newly elected parliaments in Estonia and Latvia proclaimed regaining full independence after a transition period. The new Lithuanian parliament adopted a declaration (March 11, 1990) demanding restoration of full sovereignty in the short term by way of secession from the Soviet Union. Opinion polls at the time suggested that about one-quarter of the non-titular population in the three Baltic republics supported independence from the Soviet federation. These non-titular supporters of independence seemed to be attracted by prospects of a post-communist democracy and an expected increase of the level of living by a rapid integration into the European economy (Kionka, 1991).

This rapid process of increasing national aspirations was reflected in the countermovements of non-titular minorities in the three republics. They initially opposed new legislation strengthening the position of the titular language. The mobilization of non-Baltic ethnic groups increased when the autonomy in economic and environmental questions turned out to imply the curbing of immigration into the Baltic region (Prikhozhaev, 1989). A number of conservative Russian-dominated interest groups emerged known under the broad heading of 'intermovements', in order to oppose the demands of the titular groups. The republican communist parties split losing liberal communists and the conservative communist factions took part in the counter movements. These worked closely with members of the Soviet armed forces and other organizations dominated by non-titular conservative groups such as the so-called 'councils of labour collectives', 'committees defending the USSR constitution', 'Russian-Slavic cultural societies' or 'public salvation committees'. Membership of these interest groups partly overlapped (Gouboglo et al., 1989). These countermovements and their composite interest groups and organizations emphasized the support coming from the federal government and the all-union communist party in Moscow. The federal leadership considered the supremacy of republican legislation over all-union laws and decrees as unconstitutional. It provided far-reaching support to the Baltic countermovements through an economic blockade and by even permitting violent actions by parts of the Soviet military forces in the Baltic region.

Transcaucasia

The aspirations of the titular groups in this area also led very quickly to the third and fourth stage of national assertiveness. The conflict over Nagorno-Karabakh has had a catalyzing impact on the mobilization of the titular groups in the Transcaucasian region. In spite of their majority of 76 per cent in this autonomous province of Azerbaijan, the Armenians have, in effect, lacked the status of a titular group there. In consequence, they have sought support from the Armenian republic where the national movement mobilized the overwhelming majority of the titular group. The non-communist candidates of the Armenian Pan-National Movement dominated the new parliament. Parliament passed a declaration of independence intended to spark off a process towards full sovereignty of the republic. In the three former Transcaucasian republics (Georgia, Azerbaijan, Armenia), the ethno-linguistic demands have played a relatively minor role. The core of national assertiveness has been more closely connected with ethno-territorial issues. The presence of Russian and other non-Caucasian ethnic groups has always been much weaker in this region than in other parts of the Union (Suny, 1988).

After the violent repression of Georgian assertiveness in April 1990 by the military forces of the Soviet federal government, violent conflicts escalated between the titular Georgian population and the titular groups of the Abchazian ASSR and the autonomous province of South Ossetia. In these two formally autonomous areas within the Georgian republic, the titular groups have demanded the transfer of their homelands from Georgia to the Russian federation. In Abchazia, the national demands for effective autonomy have been stimulated by socio-economic circumstances (Dostál, 1989). This small region has a very attractive natural environment. For decades, it experience an one-sided expansion of recreational activities. Only few members of the agrarian titular group could participate in that expansion. Ethnic groups from other republics and in particular the Georgians have benefited.

The Georgian national movement has emphasized demands, which are both anti-Russian (anti-Centre) and against the ethno-territorial aspirations of the Abchazian and the Ossetian ethnic groups. Free elections were a triumph for the Georgian non-communists who put forward radical demands for the precedence of republican legislation over all-union legislation and for full secession of the republic from the Soviet Union. Besides the Abchazians and the Ossetians, there are no strong countermovements in Armenia and Georgia. Only conservative factions of the communist parties represent significant countervailing power groups.

In Azerbaijan, the conflicts between the titular and non-titular groups were much more violent. The question of Nagorno-Karabakh provided a radical wing of the Azerbaijani Popular Front a sufficient excuse to start a wave of anti-Armenian pogroms. The violence was contained in January 1990 by violent intervention of the Soviet armed forces and through the declaration of the state of emergency on the pretext of preventing the seizing of power by nationalist forces demanding secession from the Soviet Union. Strongly emphasizing the republic's territorial integrity (Nagorno-Karabakh), the Azerbaijani Communist Party was able to win the elections and adopted a cautious line on economic autonomy and the possibility of secession from the USSR (Fuller, 1991). In this way, the national demands were shifted back to the less radical third stage. Here, the local Communist Party has fulfilled the role of an effective countermovement.

Moldavia, the Ukraine and Byelorussia

In the former Moldavian republic, national aspirations have in a very short time reached the fourth stage of demands for secession. Especially after the republican elections, power passed from the Communist Party and non-titular ethnic groups to the Moldavian Popular Front and associated organizations. New legislation again demanded precedence of republican laws over all-Union legislation and institutions, economic autonomy, indigenous self-controlled police force, demilitarization, the right to have international representation, etc. The countermovement of Moldavian non-titular ethnic groups gained momentum when the Russian and the Ukrainian population launched a secession campaign on the eastern bank of the Dniester declaring a so-called 'Dniester republic'. They were accompanied by the Gagauz ethnic group demanding autonomy for their small historic homeland in the southern part of Moldavia (Socor, 1990). These irredentist and countervailing demands of the non-titular groups have been supported indirectly both by the central leadership in Moscow and the local communists. The countermovement forced the Moldavian government to stall the demands for full sovereignty and independence. However, the Moldavian Front re-emphasized its secessionist demands.

In Ukraine and Byelorussia, the national movements until August 1991 put forward more limited demands. The Ukrainian Front 'Rukh' did not win the republican election where the majority of seats was taken by the communist candidates. However, the Front was able to push the new parliament into accepting demands characterizing the third stage of national aspirations. A Ukrainian declaration of sovereignty was accepted by the new republican parliament. The declaration proclaimed a wide range of radical demands (Radyanska Ukraina, July 16, 1990) like priority of republican laws over all-Union legislation, Ukraine's ownership of land, natural resources, primary means of production, inviolability of territory and borders, own banking system, direct economic relations and trade with foreign countries, etc. (Mihalisko, 1990). A far-reaching provision of the declaration stipulated the right to have armed forces and the intention to become a permanently neutral state without nuclear weapons. Here, the shadow of the Chernobyl nuclear disaster of 1986 can be felt. These demands have been supported especially in the western provinces of the Ukraine where the national movement has been particularly strong.

In the eastern and southern heavily industrialized parts of the former republic, the Rukh's assertiveness has been restrained by the presence of an active multi-ethnic workers movement dominated by the Russian ethnic group, for example in the coal mining region of Donbass. This independent trade union movement put forward radical socio-economic demands opposing both the federal and the republican governments. The countermovement in the Ukraine has been led by the republican Communist Party apparatus in which numerous important positions are still occupied by the Russians (Solchanyk, 1991). Clearly, the countermovement dominated by 'old structures' was for a time able to dampen the Ukrainian national aspirations and to prevent radicalization to the stage of secessionist demands. After the miners' strike in 1991 a breakthrough came which demonstrated that national aspirations were merged with a general process of democratization. A faction of so-called sovereign communists has cracked the monolith of the communist majority defending an emphasis on the republic's demands for far-reaching autonomy from the centre in Moscow (*Moscow News*, no. 27, 1991).

In Byelorussia, the national movement has been able to mobilize the titular group to a limited extent. The demands for strengthening the position of the Byelorussian language and cultural institutions and the criticism concerning environmental and health consequences of the Chernobyl disaster have brought the national demands to the second stage of the titular group's aspirations (Mihalisko, 1991). The first multi-candidate elections were won by candidates from the ruling Communist Party. A reform-resistant and orthodox organization, the Communist Party was able to hamper the registration of the Byelorussian Popular Front and instead to give support to cultural organizations dominated by conservative Russian groups. The Communist Party also supported claims of the Byelorussian authorities to territories given to Lithuania after its inclusion in the Soviet Union in the 1940s. Yet, the cultural intelligentsia, the Writers' Union and the small non-communist fraction of the Byelorussian parliament were able to mobilize sufficient support for a declaration of state sovereignty. In comparison with the Ukrainian declaration, however, the Byelorussian one stipulates more moderate demands.

In summary, formal demands of the Byelorussian titular group have been moving slowly from the second towards the third stage of national assertiveness. After strikes in the spring of 1991, there emerged a more articulated package of demands from an All Byelorussia Strike Committee concerning democratization and more independence from the All-Union decisionmakers and institutions (*Moscow News*, no. 16, 1991).

Central Asia and Kazakhstan

Within this Islamic region, radicalization of national aspirations of the titular groups has taken place in all five former union republics. Moreover, there is convergence of demands among the authorities as well as among the Popular Fronts of the five former republics (Globe, 1990). In Uzbekistan, the Popular Front 'Birlik' has mobilized the titular group on issues concerning the environment, socio-economic development and the status of the Uzbek language and cultural institutions. The dissatisfaction with the results of social, economic and cultural development and environmental affairs exceeds the boundaries of the Uzbek republic. The issues are interconnected and closely associated with several regional-economic decisions taken by the all-union government and ministries in Moscow in the past. For decades, the population of the Soviet Central Asia has been confronted with these issues, partly due to the fast population expansion, which contributed considerably to structural overpopulation (Rumer, 1989). There is a serious structural shortage of jobs in Uzbekistan, Turkmenistan, Tadjikistan and Kirgizia and parts of Kazakhstan.

In Uzbekistan, investments in the agricultural sector have in the past been allocated one-sidedly to cotton production. This has had far-reaching negative effects on both the economy and the environment of the region. (See also Chapter 12 by Vladimir Kolossov in this book.) The cotton monoculture has required substantial water resources which are obviously scarce in this arid part of the Soviet Union. Moreover, it has caused considerable water pollution due to intensive use of synthetic fertilizers and pesticides over a long period of time. Ninety per cent of the Soviet cotton comes from this region but only about 10 per cent of the labour-intensive cotton processing and textile industries are located there. It is therefore hardly surprising that these similar and overlapping problems have caused a convergence in the national demands of the Islamic titular ethnic groups concerned. This happened in spite of a recent wave of violent conflicts between themselves in the troubled Fergana Valley and elsewhere (Cristchlow, 1991).

The power of the Communist Party was paralysed, but in all five former republics, 'sovereign' communists were able to win the majority of seats in the new republican parliaments. They adopted several of the demands of the Popular Fronts, yet they were able to dampen the most radical ones. The conservative authorities in Turkmenistan were the last in the region to declare their titular language as the state language of the republic in May 1990 and members of the unregistered Front 'Agzybirlik' succeeded only in part in pressing Turkmen demands from the second to the third stage of national assertiveness (Carlson, 1991).

In the other former republics of the Central Asian region, demands had already reached the third stage. Obviously, the demands are connected with the heart of the above-mentioned issues. Ever since Soviet power was instituted many administrative, managerial and skilled industrial jobs have been occupied by Europeans while the overwhelming majority of enterprises were subordinated to the all-union ministries in Moscow. It is therefore important to note that in late June 1990, the government leaders and top officials of communist parties of all five republics reached agreements on mutual cooperation in order to strengthen their position within the Soviet Union (Globe, 1990).

In this region, the countermovements have been relatively weak, yet some oppositional reactions of the non-titular groups in Kazakhstan were significant

(Brown, 1991). Many Russians have opposed what they and other Slavic ethnic groups considered excessive concessions by the republican authorities to Kazakh demands. The Russian-speaking population have opposed the passage of a law declaring Kazakh the state language of the republic and requiring its widespread use in public life. The Russians and other Europeans have been frightened by the charges of internal colonialism which have been levelled at them by radical Kazakh groups. Part of the Russian-speaking population organized in a Kazakhstan 'internationalist' movement has demanded annexation of several northern and eastern provinces of Kazakhstan by the Russian republic.

Such irredentist counter-demands have been opposed by the Kazakhs who have been pointing to the fact that the territories are part of their historical homeland (Carlson, 1990). The Kazakh president and Communist Party leader tried to dampen the issue, emphasizing that contemporary Kazakhstan was a result of the labour of the entire population giving all ethnic groups the right to share in its riches. These attempts to moderate the aspirations of the titular groups did not ease inter-ethnic tensions in the region. Considerable emigration of the Russian and other European populations from the five republics to the Russian and other European republics occurred. Naturally, this narrowed the base for forming effective countermovements in this region. Despite the declarations of sovereignty adopted by the new parliaments of the five republics and the agreements on regional cooperation, the communist leaders have emphasized the limitation of sovereignty and clung to the idea of a new looser Soviet federalism, i.e. to demands characterizing the third stage of national aspirations.

The Russian federation

Since the beginning of Soviet power, the largest of the fifteen former union republics has been a complex federation of a number of autonomous territorial formations. Within the territory of the Russian Soviet Federative Socialist Republic (RSFSR) there are sixteen autonomous republics (ASSR), five provinces (AP) and ten districts (AD). Under the RSFSR constitution, however, these were not designated as sovereign entities (Konstitutsiya RSFSR, 1989, articles 71 to 84). In spite of constitutional limitations, in all of these partly-autonomous territories, the titular ethnic groups have pressed the local parliaments (ASSR) or soviets (AR and AD) to adopt various declarations on sovereignty (Sheehy, 1990). The declarations have involved raising the status of the autonomous unit concerned. The declarations on sovereignty have emphasized the following claims in particular.

First, various demands for strengthening cultural autonomy, the role of titular languages and indigenous educational institutions have been articulated. According to the results shown in Figure 7.5, the non-titular groups do not speak the titular languages. This illustrates the weak position of the local cultures. Second, some autonomous entities have proclaimed exclusive rights on the natural resources in their territories. Effective decentralization of economic and financial decision-making towards the regional level of the autonomous entities has also been demanded. Third, the declarations until August 1991 did not demand secession from the RSFSR and accepted the primacy of several basic Russian laws over the local legislation, such as the right to change the status of the autonomous territories concerned (*Sovetskaya Rossiya*, October 2, 1990). A clear exception is the Tatar republic. In Tataristan, the 'sovereign' communists followed the national movement boycotting the attempts of the RSFSR authorities to restructure the intra-republican arrangements. The Tataristan authorities have tried to deal directly with the all-Union authorities (*Moscow News*, no. 8, August 1991). Yet, the constitutional changes which are necessary to give the numerous declarations the force of law have still to be made. It seems that the demands of the numerous titular ethnic groups possessing a degree of autonomy within the RSFSR are characterizing the first or the second stage of national assertiveness.

In the meantime, the authorities of the RSFSR demanded a considerable increase in their own sovereign rights *vis-à-vis* the competencies of the all-Union government and institutions. The Russian government pushed ahead with legislative projects that spelled out the powers of the RSFSR and its constituent parts. Such legislation might make the numerous declarations on sovereignty redundant. In the first proposals on the legislative project concerning a new Russian federal treaty, a far-reaching decentralization of legislative, economic and socio-cultural competencies was envisaged (Proekt Federativnyy Dogovor RSFSR, February 2, 1991). It is interesting to note that the proposals intended to give far-reaching competencies to the numerous autonomous units as well as to Russian administrative provinces or their regional associations. Such regional subjects of a renewed Russian federation would be political units having as their titular groups in some cases the existing autonomous minorities and in others the Russian population groups.

These interesting proposals were designed to remedy the dissatisfaction of the Russian population with their formal status. The national demands of the Russians have opposed any separatist tendencies of the autonomous units. The emergence of the RSFSR as a political force in its own right has basically been a reaction to the increased demands of titular groups of other union republics as well as to the national assertiveness of the titular groups within the Russian federation. The increased assertiveness of the Russian authorities has prevented the emergence of significant counter-movements of Russian and other non-titular ethnic groups within the numerous autonomous units of the Russian federation.

Looking at the developments in the fifteen former republics up to mid-1991 the following conclusions can be drawn. First, all of the republics are multi-ethnic states in which any fulfilment of radical aspirations of the titular group has to take into account the ethno-territorial mosaic as a complicating factor. The presence and political strength of the Russians is obviously the most important complicating factor to be accommodated in mutual reconciliations among the titular and non-titular ethnic groups. The territorial intermingling of ethnic groups with the numerically-dominant group of Russians has resulted in considerable russianization (i.e. 'internal colonialization') of non-Russian areas as well as in some 'russification' (i.e. assimilation) of the non-Russian groups. However, the intensity of russification did not weaken significantly the cultural and other aspirations of the titular ethnic groups. The strengthening of the role of titular languages and cultural institutions was an important initial ingredient of the rise of national assertiveness of titular groups at all levels of the fifty-three official homelands.

Second, in mid-1991, the demands of the titular groups of the fifteen former union republics reached the third or the fourth (secessional) stage of ethno-national assertiveness. It appeared that radical and basically reactive demands put forward by the countermovements of non-titular groups were not able to oppose effectively the demands of the titular groups. The countermovements and their composite interests groups were supported by the federal government and the all-union communist party in Moscow. The federal leadership considered the supremacy of republican legislation over all-union laws and decrees as unconstitutional. Yet, even far-reaching support provided by the all-union leadership such as economic blockade or violent actions by parts of the Soviet military forces proved to be ineffective in preventing radical (secessionist) demands of the titular groups.

Finally, a dramatic outcome of the tensions came in August 1991. After sixty hours of an unsuccessful *coup d'état* attempted by so-called 'imperial communists', the option of re-imposing a totalitarian 'order' on the collapsing Soviet Union was closed. In a few days, the Soviet system and the Communist Party fell and a new stage of juggling with options for accommodation of the ethnic issues and the inevitable economic interdependence started.

Juggling with options: federation, confederation and secession

The issue of the character of successor regimes of the Soviet state has become crucial. The Soviet Union was a totalitarian communist state in which the *de jure* federal system was *de facto* functioning like those of unitary state systems. The distinction between the *de jure* federal structure of competencies and the *de facto* unitary system of power is nowadays essential for understanding the option of a renewed federation of the multi-ethnic states concerned.

In a *unitary system*, the central authority has the political capacity to centralize or decentralize more or less power to territorial subunits. Any delegation of powers is revocable and amendable in its scope (Duchacek, 1986). The communist political elites tended to find that a highly centralized *de facto* unitary system of power served their main goal of maintenance of the one-party control in all parts and hierarchical levels of the federation better. Their ideological commitment to 'unified proletarian class-building' played an important role here. The communist elites believed that a unitary power system of one party is more manageable and effective in the era of modern warfare, technology and long-term planning aiming at uniform development of all parts of the federal state. In brief, the unitary system of power of the communist federal states was based upon the largely *extra*-constitutional political culture of a single totalitarian party. The fear of the newly-elected authorities in the republics for the maintenance of this unitary extra-constitutional political culture in the centre of a new federal structure of the multi-national state was a major source of dissatisfaction with numerous reform proposals put forward by Gorbachev's leadership in 1990 and 1991. It prevented any real acceptance of a new treaty on a renewed Soviet Union.

In a genuine federal state, the key constitutional principle is the *irrevocability* of the power division between the centre and constituent parts. A permanent division of competencies and political powers between a central authority and constituting territorial components is freely agreed among the authorities of respective territorial domains. The powers of the distinct levels are neither derived from nor dependent on each other and elimination of territorial autonomy is ruled out (Duchacek, 1986). Federalism seems to be appropriate for territorial communities which desire self-government but wish to achieve a number of additional aims by combining their resources and domains in a large composite entity which is distinct from and interacts with other states. The additional aims are usually economic advantages to be derived from a common large market, common protection against external economic or military pressures. An awareness of cultural affinity and common destiny can also contribute to federal assertion of constituent units *vis-à-vis* other states. It is important to note that the *irrevocability of power division freely agreed* between the centre and constituent republics must prevent the emergence of a 'war of laws' between the federal and the republican legislations. The Soviet Union was a federal system in which the principle of sovereignty of *nationalities* (i.e. constituent states in the federation) had to be combined with democratic principles of parliamentary rights of *individuals* (i.e. the right of forming majorities by the voting population of the whole federation). In brief, there was a tension between, on the one hand, the possibility of 'tyranny' of a majority of constituent republics and, on the other hand, the possibility of 'tyranny' of a popular majority of the whole Soviet population.

Formally, the bicameral system of the all-union Supreme Soviet with its Soviet of the Union and the Soviet of Nationalities had to try to accommodate this tension (Feldbrugge, 1990; Kux, 1990; Kolossov, 1990). The Soviet of Nationalities was indirectly elected in accord with the hierarchical system of the official fifty-three homelands: each UR eleven seats, each AR four seats, each AP two seats and each AD one seat. Yet, also under the leadership of Gorbachev and his associates this latter Soviet proved to play a marginal role because numerous legislative commissions and committees have been dominated by the work of the Soviet of the Union (Kux, 1990). The Federal Council instituted in 1991 did not change the asymmetry in a significant way because this new body of highest representatives of the republics and other autonomous areas was given only consultative functions.

This federal institutional system could not accommodate demands from the Ukraine, Russia and Byelorussia and the Central Asian republics or Kazakhstan to build up a new federation 'from below'. A wave of horizontal treaties among these republics showed in 1991 the determination of their authorities to by-pass the attempts of the Gorbachev leadership in Moscow to institute a new Treaty on Union of Soviet Sovereign Republics 'from above'. This in spite of the fact that Gorbachev's provisional Treaty on Soviet Union of Socialist Republics was formally accepted by just over 50 per cent of the voters of the Soviet population in March 1991, a referendum in which the population of the six break-away republics did not participate. The RSFSR signed treaties with the Ukraine, Byelorussia and Kazahkstan in which the republics agreed to recognize each other as virtually independent political and economic entities in order to institute a horizontal framework for economic integration.

An important consideration to keep in mind is that these arrangements among sovereign economic entities no longer gave the federal centre in Moscow the prerogative of deciding on what it wanted to keep first and delegating the remaining powers afterwards to the republics. Instead, according to the instituting of a federation 'from below' the sovereign republics decide by mutual agreement which competencies are to be granted to the federal centre. For example, a treaty between the RSFSR and Kazakhstan stipulated direct co-operation in a wide range of affairs which would limit the role of a future federal centre to a very modest scope of competencies (Dogovor, 1991). In this way, the possibility of the re-emerging of the *de facto* extra-constitutional unitary power in the federal centre would be precluded.

It is this process of delegation of authority from the bottom up and its political and economic ramifications which formed the core of national aspirations demanding genuine sovereignty of republics within a renewed federation with a relatively weak, yet *democratic* (post-communist) centre. This willingness of the *core republics* (i.e Russia, Kazakhstan, Central Asian republics and the Ukraine) to accept a weaker, but democratic centre of coordination had an important background. The former republics depend heavily upon each other for trade of goods and services as well as for use of natural resources (see Table 7.1).

Table 7.1   Inter-republican trade in the former Soviet Union 1988

	Trade as % of GNP	Total (bn roubles)
Turkmenistan	76	7.9
Belorussia	49	32.4
Tadjikistan	47	5.0
Kirgizia	45	5.5
Azerbaijan	43	11.7
Uzbekistan	41	20.6
Kazakhstan	32	22.0
Ukraine	32	83.1
Russia	15	138.2
Republics with secessionist aspirations before the coup:		
Armenia	57	7.7
Estonia	52	5.7
Moldavia	52	9.8
Latvia	50	9.1
Lithuania	49	11.7
Georgia	46	10.7

Source: PlanEcon 1990.

In order to maintain a necessary degree of stability of their relations, they cannot avoid a renewed coordination of regional-economic cooperation in which distributive and egalitarian measures are kept in balance. Distributive principles of economic policy must be based on actual economic achievements and correspond to the shares which individual republics deserve proportionally.

The effect of such market-driven distributive principles would be that comparatively more efficiently functioning republics would be able to improve their position within the inter-regional pattern of efficiency and welfare, while weaker ones such as those in Central Asia would be further restricted to positions in which their economic performance is likely to decrease further. Therefore, any economic mechanism of cooperation in a federation must provide for measures which will dampen the effects of too harsh distributive principles (Dostál, 1984). In adopting elementary egalitarian principles of inter-regional redistribution, the fundamental equality of composite republics would be emphasized. Such elementary egalitarian principles would necessarily include a package of measures supporting basic regional infrastructure and, importantly, a certain equality of economic opportunities that too often are absent in the less-developed republics. This general regional-economic argument will also play an important role in a future, looser post-communist cooperation based on the market-driven economies of its composite republics.

It is obvious now that the option of a renewed, looser and post-communist federal system could not accommodate the radical secessionist demands of the republics. In contrast to federal arrangements, a *confederal* system is not committed to institute a supra-sovereign entity of an overarching state. The sovereign states associated in a confederal arrangement do not accept subordination to a numerical majority of other participants, except in a few marginal matters. The confederal parties combine some of their efforts into a cooperative association, yet they retain veto rights in collective decision-making on all important issues (Dostál, 1989). The cooperation is for the purpose of executing several specific common tasks such as economic matters or defense. Common confederal institutions are therefore bodies which are not entitled by the associated states to enact rules or make decisions which directly affect citizens of the participating states (Duchacek, 1986). A confederal citizenship is absent, yet free movement of persons or organizations across boundaries is generally accepted. Accordingly, legislation of associated states cannot be overshadowed by confederal measures and their political and economic sovereign powers are maintained. In short, confederal arrangements based on democratic association usually declare the assertion of sovereign self-rule against interferences in domestic affairs by common confederal institutions as well as guaranteeing the territorial sovereignty of participating states allowing them secession or disassociation from the confederal compact.

Yet, the failure of the coup served merely to accelerate the disintegration of the post-communist Soviet Union whereby even the option of a confederative structure became unpopular. Western countries recognized the independence of the Baltic republics setting a precedent for other secessions. The demise of the all-union Communist Party greatly weakened Gorbachev's presidency, the only union-wide institution that really survived the coup. Furthermore, resulting from its size and economic power, the problem of the dominant position of the Russian federation arose. Following the coup, power was essentially transferred to the republics. The 'hiatus institutionnel' was partly filled up by a new State Council of heads of state of the republics. Issues of international positions of the republics forced them to consider new confederation-like options. The four republics with strategic nuclear weapons on their territory (Russia, Belarus, Kazakhstan and the Ukraine) were involved in international discussion on nuclear disarmament. At the same time, the ever-worsening economic situation and the need to present some semblance of order if the country was to receive international assistance made it more urgent to reach agreement on economic and political cooperation. Ten of the twelve remaining republics signed a treaty on an economic community. Gorbachev's leadership insisted that a new compact would be a 'confederative state' rather than a confederation. This option met serious opposition from both the republican leaders and the parliaments. It was rendered obsolete after the Ukrainian referendum on independence on 1 December 1991.

The implications of the overwhelming vote in favour of independence of the Ukrainian republic were far-reaching. Without the Ukraine, the Russian federation would find itself in a compact with Belarus and the largely impoverished Moslem republics of Central Asia and Kazakhstan. Moreover, if Ukraine would not be part of a new compact with Russia, there was also the threat of Russian claims on southern and eastern parts of the republic. Without the participation of Gorbachev's leadership, the Slavic republics (Russia, Belarus and Ukraine) signed an agreement on 8 December 1991 to create a Commonwealth of Independent States (CIS). Also a declaration on the coordination of economic policies was signed (Sheehy, 1992). The declaration of the three Slavic republics declared that the Soviet Union ceased to exist 'as a subject of international law and a geopolitical reality'. The creation of the CIS is an attempt (i) to preserve a minimum of economic cooperation, (ii) to coordinate policies on nuclear weapons and division of the former Soviet armed forces, and (iii) to prevent the separation of the Ukraine declaring recognition of each other's borders. Importantly, Article 3 of the agreement declares that it will promote distinctiveness of the national minorities and take them under protection.

The CIS has been open to other republics. On 21 December 1991, a protocol was adopted to the agreement under which Kazakhstan, the four Central Asian republics, Moldavia, Armenia and Azerbaijan became also founding members of the CIS. This implied that twelve former Soviet republics became members and only Georgia did not take part in this new very loose compact. A Council of Heads of State and a Council of Heads of Government were set up to coordinate the activity of the former republics. Ministerial committees were instituted in such areas as defense and foreign policy, economy, transportation, and social security affairs. *(Izvestiya*, 23 December 1991). It was made clear that there would be no commonwealth citizenship since the CIS was not a state.

The most interesting question now is what kind of compact this CIS actually seems to be in the initial stage of its establishment. The CIS can be described as an inter-governmental association rather than a confederation. It is an association of disunited nations and certainly not an entity separate from or above its national components. It seems to evolve towards an international regime based on sets of arrangements that are meant to affect relationships among the republics through inter-sovereign cooperative frameworks. The CIS regime seems to represent sets of rules, norms and procedures that are based on a perceived convergence of national interests in spite of secessions of the republics from their former union. It can evolve towards a *confederal inter-sovereign association* provided that its character will be regional (i.e. integral) and not only functional (i.e. focused on solving specific issues). Its aim would be to coordinate actions and policies of sovereign states within the territory of a majority of the former Soviet republics. Two characteristic features of the CIS would be: (i) need for cross-boundary cooperation and regulation and (ii) common opposition to a federal agreement that would result in a delegation of significant competencies to a common supra-national authority.

Conclusion

It seems that inter-sovereign association between a majority of the former Soviet republics with a renewed post-communist and democratic Russian federation would provide for *necessary internal stability of the parties involved.* On the one hand, the secessionist aspirations of the national movements would be satisfied and complex negotiations on economic division of the communist economic heritage and its adverse consequences would be less difficult. On the other hand, economic, military-strategic and other interests of the renewed Russian federation would be satisfied, yet counterbalanced by the independence of the other states participating in the association. In all of the sovereign republics, the demands of the titular groups have realized the aspirations characterizing the fourth stage of national assertiveness. When reconstituting themselves as *democratic* multi-national states, they apparently have to search for flexible and also diversified forms of their re-association. Especially the southern less-developed Soviet republics would prefer to participate in the new association of the CIS in order to maintain some responsibilities of the more developed republics for financial support and expertise for long-term development of their less-advanced economies.

It is obvious that the process of re-association would have to proceed 'from below', allowing only for limited coordinative agencies and inter-sovereign balances of power. It would be necessary to institute a flexible (i.e. diversified) structure of cooperation. A new structure in which relations between the republics as well as relations between their autonomous areas and the republican centre would be varied allowing for their specific demands for sovereignty. Within the sovereign republics, the autonomous areas would be granted well-defined irrevocable veto-rights in economic, social and cultural affairs in order to delineate more clearly their sovereignty from the republican centre in these matters, which are obviously important for the maintenance of the political and cultural identity of the titular ethnic groups concerned. Given the military and economic interests of the core (largest) republics of the confederal inter-sovereign association as well as the interests of their often numerically strong minorities, it would be necessary to search for well-balanced agreements on the issue of citizenship of non-titular minorities and their rights. This search would be necessary because the radical irredentist aspirations of ethnic minorities by-passing the option of a possible loose confederal re-association would increase both the internal instability of non-cooperative republics as well as the instability of the participating republics in the CIS.

Behind the ethno-national demands of minorities loom economic interests and democratic interests. The failure of the former communist governments to satisfy economic and social needs, the inability of the communist centre to provide efficient economic and effective political leadership necessitated radical abolition of the rigid federal arrangements of the Soviet multi-national state. The ability of the republics to assert their sovereignty is crucial here because the *coup d'état* has shown that the centres of long-term effective sovereignty are now located below the supra-republican level. In other words, what remains is the survival of republican governments legitimized in the new elections and their willingness and also ability to mobilize both the titular and the non-titular ethnic groups to reconcile their different aspirations and demands on a new base. Radical democratic reform seems to be the source of future stability of the Soviet multi-national continent.

References

Argumov, I.A., 1988, *Sotsialnaya sfera obraza zhisni v Yakutskoy ASSR*, Yakutsk.

Aspaturian, V., 1968, 'The non-Russian nationalities', In A. Kassof (ed.), *Prospects for Soviet society*, Praeger Publishers, New York, pp. 143–198.

Brown, B., 1991, 'Interethnic tensions, unsolved economic problems'. *Report on the USSR*, January 4, pp. 29–30.

Brzezinski, Z., 1989, 'Post-communist nationalism', *Foreign Affairs* 68 (5): 1–25.

Bungs, D., 1990, 'Migration to and from Latvia', *Report on the USSR*, September 14, pp. 27–33.

Carlson, C., 1990, 'Kazakhs refute Russian territorial claims', *Report on the USSR*, August 19, pp. 18–20.

Carlson, C., 1991, 'Inching towards democratization', *Report on the USSR*, January 4, pp. 35–36.

Connor, W., 1973, 'The politics of ethnonationalism', *Journal of International Affairs* 27 (1), 1–21.

Connor, W., 1984, *The national question in Marxist-Leninist theory and strategy*, Princeton University Press, Princeton.

Cristchlow, J., 1991, 'The crisis deepens', *Report on the USSR*, January 4, pp. 36–40.

Dogovor, 1991, Dogovor mezhdu RSFSR i Kazakhskoy SSR. Postanivlenie RSFSR, February 7, no. 583–I. Moscow.

Dostál, P., 1984, 'Regional policy and corporate organizational forms: some questions of interregional social justice', in M. de Smidt and E. Wever (eds), *A profile of Dutch economic geography*, Van Gorcum, Assen, pp. 12–38.

Dostál, P., 1989a, 'Regional interests and the national question under Gorbachev', in A. Bon and R. van Voren (eds), *Nationalism in the USSR: problems of nationalities*, Second World Center, Amsterdam, pp. 28–43.

Dostál, P., 1989b, 'Nationale kwesties and Gorbatsjovs opties: de Georgische les', *Internationale Spectator* 43 (7): 422–426.

Dostál, P., 1991, 'Nationale aspiraties en autonomie in Sovjet-Europa: nieuwe opties onder Gorbatjov?', in T. Zwaan et al. (ed.), *Het Europese labyrint: nationalisme en natievorming in Europa*. Boom, Meppel, pp. 31–48.

Dostál, P., Knippenberg, H., 1979, 'The russification of ethnic minorities in the USSR', *Soviet Geography* 20 (4), 197–219.

Dostál, P., Knippenberg,H., 1988, 'De kwestie Nagorno-Karabach', *Internationale Spectator* 42 (10): 602–610.

Drobizheva, L.M., 1989, *Rol intelligentii v razvitii natsionalnogo camosoznaniya narodov SSSR v uslovijakh perestroyki*, Academy of Sciences of the USSR, Moscow.

Duchacek, I.D., 1986, *The territorial dimension of politics: within, among, and across nations*, Westview Press, Boulder, CO..

Feldbrugge, F.J.M.,1990, 'The constitution of the USSR', *Review of Socialist Law* 16 (2): 163–224.

Feshbach, M., 1983, 'Population and labour force', in A. Bergson and H.S. Levine, (eds), *The Soviet economy: towards the year 2000*, Allen and Unwin, London, pp. 79–111.

Fuller, E., 1991, 'Democratization threatened by interethnic violence', *Report on the USSR*, January 4, pp. 41–44.

Globe, P., 1990, 'Central Asians form political bloc', *Report on the USSR*, July 13, pp. 18–20.

Gouboglo, M. et al., 1990a, *Grazhdanskie dvizheniya v Latvii 1989*, Moscow.

Gouboglo, M. et al., 1990b, *Grazhdanskie dvizheniya v Tadzhikistane*, Moscow.

Kionka, R., 1990, 'Migration to and from Estonia', *Report on the USSR*, September 14, pp.20–24.

Kionka, R., 1991, 'Economic woes and political disputes', *Report on the USSR*, January 4, pp. 45–47.

Kirkwood, M., 1991, 'Glasnost, "the national question" and Soviet language policy', *Soviet Studies* 43 (1): 61–81.

Kolossov, W.A., N.W. Petrov and L.V. Smirnyagin, (eds), 1990, *BECHA 89. Gografiya i anatomiya parlamenskikh vyborov*, Progress, Moscow.

Konstitutsiya RSFSR, 1989, Osnovnoy zakon, Moscow.

Kozlov, B.I., 1975, *Natsionalnosti SSSR: Etnodemografichekiy obzor*, Moscow.

Kux, S., 1990, *Soviet Federalism: a Comparative Perspective*. Institute for East-West Security Studies. Occasional Paper Series, no. 18.

Lapidus, G.W., 1989, 'Gorbachev and the 'national question': restructuring the Soviet federation', *Soviet Economy* **5** (3):201–249.

Mihalisko, K., 1990, 'Ukraine's declaration of sovereignty', *Report on the USSR*, July 27, pp. 17–19.

Mihalisko, K., 1991, 'Tug-of-war between the ruling party and its challengers', *Report on the USSR*, January 4, pp. 20–22.

Niklus, M., 1989, 'Account of some events in the National Movement of Estonia', in A. Bon and R. van Voren (eds), *Nationalism in the USSR. Problems of Nationalities*, Second World Center, Amsterdam, pp. 96–106.

Prikhozhaev, Y.G., 1989, 'Latviya 1989: fronty, soyuzy, assotsiatsii (analiticheskiy obzor)', in M. Goubuglo et al. (eds), *Grazhdanskie dvizheniya v Latvii 1989*, Moscow, pp. 22–58.

Proekt Federativnyy Dogovor RSFSR (1991). Moscow.

Rumer, B.Z., 1989, *Soviet Central Asia: 'A Tragic Experiment'*. Unwin and Hyman, Boston.

Sheehy, A., 1990, 'Fact sheet on declarations of sovereignty', *Report on the USSR*, November 9, pp. 23–25.

Sheehy, A., 1992, 'Commonwealth of Independent States: an uneasy compromise', *RFE/RL Research Report*, January 10, pp. 1–5. .

Smith, G., 1989, 'Gorbachev's greatest challenge: perestroika and the national question', *Political Geography Quarterly* **8** (1): 7–20.

Socor, V., 1990, 'Moldavian lands between Romania and Ukraine: the historical and political geography', *Report on the USSR*, November 16, pp. 16–18.

Solchanyk, R., 1991, 'The uncertain road to independence', *Report on the USSR*, January 4, pp. 22–24.

Suny, R.G., 1988, *The Making of the Georgian Nation*, Indiana University Press, Bloomington,IN.

XXII Syezd, 1962, Syezd Kommunisticheskoy Partii SSSR. Moscow.

8 Pluralist mobilization as a catalyst for the dismemberment of Yugoslavia

Snjezana Mrdjen

The political changes in East-Central Europe and in Yugoslavia that occurred in the wake of the pluralist elections of 1989 and 1990 have a number of similarities. They demonstrate democratic, nationalist and, particularly, anti-communist orientations. Yugoslavia was a bit different or, perhaps we should say, somewhat more radical. Because of the multi-national nature of the country, the ethnically-mixed character of many parts of the territory and the latent conflicts between these groups since World War II, pluralism has readily degenerated into inter-ethnic violent conflict. 'Large' and 'small' peoples and ethnic groups with different languages and cultures have opposed each other with greater or lesser chances of realizing their goals. They have all been searching for their national identity and have grasped the occasion that did not arise before.

The national questions have resurfaced as centrifugal forces that have destroyed the cohesion of the Yugoslav state and its territorial integrity. The problem of the eventual future borders of so-called 'ethnically pure' states is foremost in all minds. Such issues dominate the Yugoslav crisis and have led to war. Will Yugoslavia, after breaking into Slovenia, Croatia, Bosnia-Hercegovina and the Yugoslav Federation (Serbia), then be reconstituted as a confederal community? Will there eventually be four independent states (Slovenia, Croatia, Bosnia and Macedonia) and a Greater Serbia (Montenegro, Serbia, the Serb Republic of Krajina and the Serb Republic of Bosnia-Hercegovina) or will still another configuration of political units appear in the end? I will tackle these questions by analysing the dynamics of the current stage of the conflict at the beginning of 1992 and by mentioning some of the conditions that have marked the situation ever since Yugoslavia was established. The events of World War II get less attention, however important they have been. It seems that the war aggravated patterns that are much older, pushed in the background after 1945 but once again at the centre stage in full force.

The well-worn Yugoslav crisis

The League of Yugoslav Communists has been divided for a long time at the level of republics and autonomous provinces between a reformist and a dogmatic wing. These two wings clashed irrevocably at the Party Congress in early 1990, symbolizing the disappearance of the post-war Yugoslav model. The ensuing elections in 1990 cast the communists, as the losers, into the role of parliamentary opposition in Slovenia and Croatia. Elections in the other republics followed in November and December 1990. The results divided Yugoslav politics into a non-communist and confederal Northwest and a communist, federal East.

Looking back to the very beginning of the South Slav state, the situation after the elections of 1990 turns out to have a clear precedent in the circumstances of the earlier time. The elections of 1920 for the Constituent Assembly were complex, the situation delicate. The different parties had opposing views on the organization of the state. Mr Korochetz, the priest that led the clerical Slovene party at the time, stated the fundamental political question that still divides the Yugoslavs in these terms: 'Should one apply the system of centralization to the new state or better the federal system, that was the problem that we had to solve as regards the future organization of our state' (Rivet, 1919, p. 40). The Serbs on their part have always supported the centralist model and the unity of Yugoslavia, whereas Croats and Slovenes have always tended towards autonomy and federalism. For them, the national aspiration was always stronger than the wish for the unity of Yugoslavia. Almost nothing has changed. The restructuring of political life is in the direction of traditional patterns. National ideologies come to the forefront, carried by new parties that spell out these ideas as if communist rule has been nothing more than an insignificant interruption.

Why, in fact, was Yugoslavia created at all, if from the start such divergent and hardly compatible opinions, ideologies and political viewpoints were promoted? After the demise of Austria-Hungary and the Ottoman Empires, a state was created on the territory of the South Slav peoples not only because of political events that led to 'a new equilibrium among European powers' (Ivsic, 1926, p. 9) but also because of a policy based on the national tendencies of the South Slav peoples themselves. The unit created on December 1, 1918 presented the idea of 'three peoples' or 'tribes of one nation'. Consequently, the name of the country was Kingdom of Serbs, Croats and Slovenes. These were, at the time, the only nationalities recognized within that country. In 1931, the Kingdom was renamed Yugoslavia. All three peoples at the time wanted to collaborate in the construction of the new state while respecting each others' positions and perspectives. The Kingdom, in fact, brought together the inhabitants of a number of earlier states: the Kingdom of Serbia, the Kingdom of Montenegro, Croatia and Slovenia that had been part of the Austro-Hungarian Empire until October 29, 1918 and Bosnia-Hercegovina, Ottoman territory until 1878 and subsequently occupied militarily by Austria-Hungary.

Some people in Croatia had earlier supported the idea of an autonomous community within Austria-Hungary. But this became impossible as the empire dissolved. The only possible solution became the creation of a community of the South Slav peoples. Although the Croats and Slovenes never had such strong national sentiments as the Serbs, they understood that they could in the context of post-World War I politics only acquire maximal freedom on condition that they reunified with that nation (Pribitchevich, 1933, p. 53). Therefore, the Croats and Slovenes did not at the time emphasize their national individuality, for they belonged to one of the defeated powers. They ran the risk of being proclaimed defeated countries and thus becoming bereft of their national sovereignty. Serbia existed already as a national state and it played the same role as Piedmont did for Italian unification, the liberator of the other South Slavs. Its aim was to unify all Serbs and to create a new state with the Slav brothers.

Slovenes and Croats - autonomist oppositions

The main representative of Slovene aspirations in 1920 was the Popular Party (SLS, *slovenska ljudska stranka*); it had a clerical dominance. In Slovenia, it had a strong majority although the social democratic opposition made significant inroads. The Slovene clergy played a decisive role in support of the federalism of the Serb, Croat and Slovene nationalities, that is, to form a common cultural and economic autonomy which implied sovereignty (*samosvojnost*). At the same time, this clergy accepted the Yugoslav framework because they wanted to protect their territory against Italian aspirations. These aspirations were predominantly economic and political (Rivet, 1919, p. 28). One has to keep in mind that the Italians already occupied the west of Slovenia after the Rapallo Treaty of 1920. This was another inducement for Slovenia to become allied to Serbia. Rivet (1919, p. 11) concludes: '(Slovenia) accepts centralization, at least as a temporary solution to oppose the Italian and Austro-Hungarian danger'.

In Tito's Yugoslavia (1945–80), the separatist aims of the Slovenes were touched off as the aspiration of economic freedom and the anxieties about the 'Yugoslav yoke' became more and more articulate. All political agitation, and the initiative to organize a referendum about the separation of Slovenia, came from a coalition of seven parties called DEMOS that eventually won the elections in April 1990 (Figure 8.1a). In their desire to govern, they wilfully or incidentally created a coalition between opposing forces where ex-communists and liberals met. The collective presidency constituted by five persons originating from different political parties underlined pluralism as a factor of political equilibrium. This was reinforced by the acting president of the republic, who is a member of the reformist party (ex-communist).

After a year, Slovenia nonetheless proclaimed its independence without making much progress in resolving long-standing differences in domestic politics or in the international arena. This has led to chaos within the Slovene government. The differences of opinion concerning church–state relations have been accentuated while the economy has deteriorated further. This has led to quarrels between the parties constituting DEMOS, particularly between Christian Democrats and Democrats.

In Croatia in 1920, federalist and republican tendencies opposing the newly instituted unitary monarchy were much stronger. Stjepan Radich's Farmers Party won an immense electoral success with 75–100 per cent of the votes in continental Croatia (excluding the islands), with particular strength around Zagreb. One contemporary observer called the Croats living in the region between Zagreb and the old borders of Styria and Hungary, 'the real Croat, the Croat in the true meaning of the word' (Mousset, 1921, p. 81). Radich held very radical opinions: 'We are all federalists in Croatia. Our history, our geographical situation, our orientation towards Hungary - a European state - make us federalists in order not to become dependent on the Balkans' (Pezet and Simondet, 1933, p. 39). He then painted his ideal of a Croatian Farmers republic within the borders of Yugoslavia as the international treaties had prescribed and, if need be, in the framework of a federal monarchy.

Now as then, the Croats discovered that a fundamental ideal separates them from Belgrade, the Serbian capital. 'Given our historic experience, we do not see any other solution than an alliance of sovereign states united within the framework of the European Community; the Croats and the Slovenes on the one hand and the Serbs on the

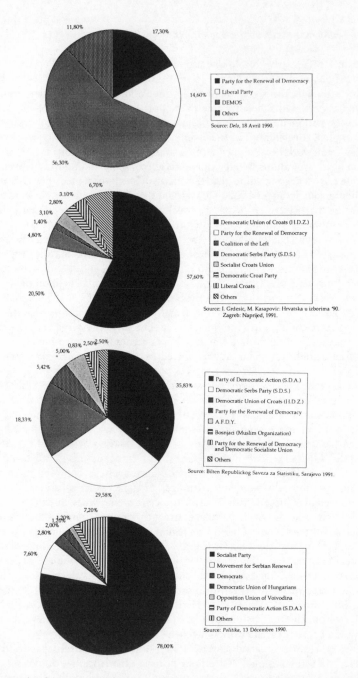

Figure 8.1   Results of the 1990 elections in the individual republics a) Slovenia b) Croatia c) Bosnia-Hercegovina and d) Serbia

other belong to two completely different civilizations' (Franjo Tujdman quoted in *Le Monde*, October 2 1990). Tudjman is the president of the Croatian Democratic Community (HDZ), the most powerful party in Croatia that won a resounding victory at the polls in April 1990 particularly in the Northwest (Figures 8.1b and 8.2). He apparently spoke the language of the majority of Croatians. The HDZ presented themselves as the national movement. 'We have realized the unity of the Croat fatherland and the emigrant Croats and of all the classes of the Croat people. We want to live on our own territory and we want to decide our own fate' said Tudjman on the day of national celebration, May 30, 1990 in Zagreb *(Vjesnik* May 31, 1990). Since late 1991, HDZ often considered itself as a Christian Democratic party after it swallowed a small local Christian Democrat party (*Danas* November 19, 1991).

The elections of 1990 were a real plebiscite of the Croat people and turned out to be a victory for national frustration that had deepened ever since the creation of the Yugoslav state. HDZ dominates Parliament and holds all reins of power. There is hardly any real opposition. The two-block parliament consists of one strong block with HDZ as the core power and a weak communist opposition (Figure 8.1b). Though unlikely, it is true that after all declarations of democracy, a one-party system has replaced another. Contrary to the elections in Slovenia, Serbia and Montenegro, the citizens of Croatia have not elected a president nor a presidential college (or a collective presidency). Since the deputies picked the president, the citizenry has not directly participated in the selection of the most important political office-holder.

Real pluralism in Bosnia-Hercegovina

Bosnia-Hercegovina is situated in the very centre of Yugoslavia. It is a crossroads of peoples, cultures and religions, now also caught up in the maelstrom of ethnic violence. The idyllic Bolshevist image of this republic has now been spoilt and all efforts to disguise the differences between the ethnic groups have been abandoned. Bosnia is re-emerging with a new image, multi-national, multi-cultural, multi-religious. The Serbs (31.3 per cent in 1991) are Orthodox, the Croats (17.3 per cent) Catholic. The Slavs who follow Islam (43.7 per cent) are the largest group. Tito's Yugoslavia allowed them the status of 'Muslim' nation since the national sentiment of these Slavs had at the time become clear when they stubbornly refused to be called Serb or Croat. The communists could not accept a large number of people without nationality and therefore decided to create a new nationality (Gace, 1988). This Bosnian national configuration is different from all the others because there is no majority, as is also the case for the whole of the former Yugoslavian state. Bosnia demonstrates an authentic pluralism in terms of numbers that exists in few other places.

Bosnia has specific arrangements for the ethnic composition of parliament, not deviating more than 15 per cent from the distribution of population in order to safeguard the equilibrium of nationalities. Thanks to this system of quotas, a situation as in Croatia, where a single party has been replaced by another, has not occurred. The presidential election is also subordinated to the composition of the population. According to the new constitution in Bosnia, the president is elected for one year by a secret vote of the seven members of the collective presidency. The current president is Alija Izetbegovic, a Muslim, but he agrees, and the constitution prescribes, that he will be succeeded by a Croat and then by a Serb.

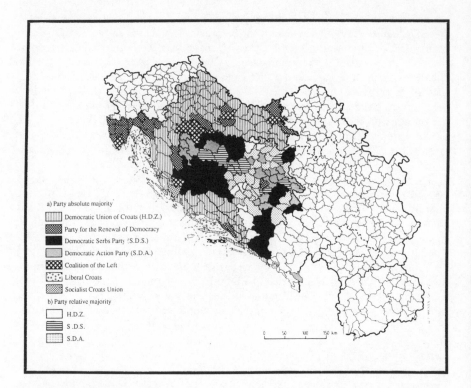

a) Party absolute majority
- Democratic Union of Croats (H.D.Z.)
- Party for the Renewal of Democracy
- Democratic Serbs Party (S.D.S.)
- Democratic Action Party (S.D.A.)
- Coalition of the Left
- Liberal Croats
- Socialist Croats Union

b) Party relative majority
- H.D.Z.
- S.D.S.
- S.D.A.

Figure 8.2 Geographic distribution of the electoral support for the parties in Croatia and Bosnia-Herce-govina in the 1990 elections

During the election campaign, a poll showed that the nationalist parties did not mobilize the strong majority of voters that they expected. The poll indicated the communists and reformists as the popular favourites (*Danas*, 13 November 1990). The actual election had a different outcome: apparent brotherhood and unity protected during nearly fifty years by a communist regime was threatened at the last moment by a multi-party situation. The authorities in Bosnia-Hercegovina tried unsuccessfully to block the lawful entry of the nationalist parties into the electoral arena in order to avoid inter-ethnic conflict. The three parties that represented the three nationalities have won (Figures 8.1c and 8.2). The Muslims have organized a powerful Party of Democratic Action (SDA). The Serbs, united around the Democratic Serb Party (SDS) orient themselves openly towards Belgrade while the same applies to the Croats with respect to Zagreb. They have regrouped as the Democratic Croat Community (HDZ). At the same time that they maintain their links with Croatia, they are trying to establish a coalition with the Muslim leadership. The opposition to this internally-divided nationalist bloc is constituted by the bloc of parties of the left: the Party of Democratic Renewal (PRD, ex-Communist Party) and the Alliance of Reformist Forces within Yugoslavia (AFRJ), better known as the party of the former prime minister of Yugoslavia, the Croat, Ante Markovic.

The Bosnian Parliament is bicameral (Chamber of Citizens and the Chamber of Municipalities) with 240 deputies in parliament in total. The analysis of the distribution of seats in parliament shows that seats are proportional to the shares of nationalities. While the nationalist parties drew their deputies from a single nationality group, Markovic's party (AFRJ) and the Communist Party do not have a majority of any nationality. Their deputies belong to all the different nationalities. The three national parties have different preferences as to the role of a newly created state of Bosnia-Hercegovina in the 'new' Yugoslavia. The Croats, quantitatively the third largest population in Bosnia, accept HDZ policy, that is to say a sovereign republic that could eventually engage in a confederal community with the states of Slovenia and Croatia. The Serbs do not oppose the creation of a sovereign republic, on the condition that it remains within the framework of Yugoslavia. For the Muslims, the largest people, the territorial integrity of Bosnia is very important. Their attachment to Bosnia is very strong mostly because they have no other republic to which they can go.

Back in 1920 during the elections for the Constituent Assembly, there appeared a Yugoslav Muslim Organization (JMO), that called itself a class party (Mousset, 1921, p. 62) despite its confessional name tag. It represented at the time nearly all Muslims in Bosnia. It opposed agrarian reform as nearly all large landowners in Bosnia at the time were Muslims. Banac (1988) gives a figure of 91 per cent of all land in their hands. The party also declared itself strongly in favour of the monarchy in order to protect itself against the division of territory, as indicated by the constitution of Vidovdan (1921). For administrative purposes, the kingdom was divided in regions (*oblasti*), subregions (*srezovi*) and municipalities (*opstine*) aimed at limiting the emergence of alternative powers based on regional, ethnic solidarities and interests. Bosnia-Hercegovina was divided but thanks to the JMO party, the administrative regions in the end were larger and the division as a whole respected the traditional borders of Bosnia.

Macedonia - southern instability

In Macedonia, situated between Serbia, Greece, Bulgaria, Albania and Kosovo, many groups (Macedonians, Muslims, Albanese, Turks, Romanies, Wallachs, Greeks and also 'Egyptians') live together (Mrdjen, 1991). The Serbs (2.3 per cent in 1981) do not exist according to the new Macedonian constitution even if they are larger in number than some other peoples (Muslims 2.07 per cent, Gypsies 2.3 per cent, Wallachs 0.3 per cent). This is one of the paradoxes in this heterogeneous republic.

The nationalist party VMRO (Revolutionary Nationalist Macedonian Organization) and the Albanian party PDP (Party for Democratic Prosperity) have won clear victories in the recent elections, like their equivalents in the other republics (Bosnia and Croatia) where two or three competing nationalities live together. All seventeen Macedonian parties, including the social democrats (ex-communists), without exception refer to the dangers that threaten the young Macedonian nation. In particular, they fear the Serbs. 'For the Serbs, the Macedonian population consists of Serbs, the Bulgars call them Bulgars, the Greeks Slavonic Greeks. Only the communist movement of the interwar years and the Yugoslav regime after 1945 have recognized their separate identity. Thus the Macedonian republic within Yugoslavia came into existence' (Panayote, 1991, p. 180). In the municipalities populated by the Albanian minority, situated in the west of Macedonia, there exists the fear that VRMO will come to power. VRMO has, more than other parties, promised the Macedonian people that they will expel the Albanians towards Kosovo and liberate the whole territory that the communists had offered (*Nin*, 27 October 1991). This Albanian minority totals 20 per cent of the population of Macedonia. It is concentrated in seven municipalities where their fears have been expressed by a massive support for the PDP. This is for example the case in Skopje, where 150,000–200,000 Albanians live, making it one of the largest Albanian cities in the world. Skopje is increasingly a Muslim city, with Islam growing at the expense of the formerly predominant Orthodox character.

As a result of the referendum held in September 1991, Macedonia was proclaimed a sovereign and independent state. This has satisfied Bulgaria but it has unnerved Greece. Bulgaria has recognized the Macedonian state but not the nation. For Bulgaria, there is no Macedonian nation. Greece has recognized neither the state nor the nation, indicating that it does not want to take chances that the 'pseudo question of Macedonia' gets another lease of life. One-third of the population has not agreed to the question in the referendum, with Albanians and Serbs only weakly participating. The conclusion is that the Macedonians can only have their sovereign and independent state if they know how to solve the problem of the municipalities with Serb majorities. Will an eventual demarcation provoke a Serb-Macedonian conflict? How will Bulgaria react in those circumstances?

Serbia and Montenegro – communist fidelity

The elections in the different republics of Yugoslavia have resulted in two victories for (ex-)communist parties and they have therefore remained in power. The Socialist Party won 77.6 per cent of the parliamentary seats in Serbia and 66.4 per cent in Montenegro (Figures 8.1d and 8.2). In Serbia, Slobodan Milosevic won the presidency with 65.3 per cent of the votes. This Serb adherence to communism is striking. The Albanians boycotted the elections while a large number of people belonging to other minorities have preferred their own nationalist parties, for instance the Hungarians and Croats in Voivodina and the Muslims in Sandzak.

The elections in Serbia have placed younger age groups and some of the intellectuals in opposition to the Socialist Party and to old age pensioners and civil servants. Opposition to socialism was also significant among workers and farmers. Everyone made a self-serving argument but fear and uncertainty about the future were decisive. The opposition groups stressed that the demise of communism was imminent and that the future was paved with uncertainties while the political insiders understood that inevitable change could only degrade their established rights.

The existing monolithic single-party system has not disappeared overnight but it was seriously undermined in March 1991 as a result of student demostrations organized by the opposition parties. They aimed at the enlargement of the freedom of the press and an end to the monopoly of the Socialist Party (*Nin*, 27 September 1991). Concessions at this point had to be granted and political structures would certainly have changed if the war in the north of Yugoslavia had not started. It is important to stress that the Serbian government has had to defeat opposition in the minds of many citizens since that day (Kerorguen, 1992, 130–135).

This student movement was first of all a cultural, ethical phenomenon beyond ethnocentric nationalism, opposing militarized leadership in politics as well as populist democracy. This was the last chance for Yugoslavia and its peoples but the Slovenes and Croats failed to grasp the chance of building bridges to the Serbian opposition. The same conjuncture passed in 1968. Then, the students and intellectuals of Belgrade organized street demonstrations to spur a process of democratization. But in Slovenia, the best solution was seen as economic liberalization, decentralization and less commitment to a poor and inefficient 'South' (Gace, 1988).

The consequences of the events of March 1990 have become slowly evident. First of all, Yugoslav central government collapsed in December 1991, not so much because of an opposition that was still weakly organized, but as a result of its own weakness and lack of strength to execute its programme and to deliver on its promises (*Vjesnik*, 26 December 1991). The fidelity to the Socialist Party has therefore changed. According to opinion polls conducted at the end of December 1991, the voting intentions were 29.8 per cent for the Socialist Party, 15 per cent for the Radicals, 12 per cent for the Democrats and only 6.8 per cent for the Movement for Serb Renewal (*Nin*, 20 December 1991). Is this increasing variety the prelude to real pluralism and parliamentary democracy?

Territorial sovereignty and/or sovereignty of nationalities

The current problems of Yugoslavia are perceived in terms of a novel ethno-politico-territorial structure that will have to define all future relations between the little states now being born. To establish a new territorial division, there are two principles that one could or should apply. At the political level, a continuation of either territorial sovereignty or of a sovereignty of nationalities should be created by way of referendum. No republic apart from Slovenia is homogeneous. They all have more than one nationality on their territory and most nationalities do not live in one republic only. In this context, the issue of territorial rights is very complex. Will the referendum apply to the Yugoslav citizens or to the Yugoslav peoples independently from the republic where they live? Will the referendum invoke the notion of territory? If yes, at what level, republics or municipalities?

Yugoslavia represents the worst case of ethno-territorial mixing that one could imagine. Everyone has chosen their own bailiwick where they feel stronger than others. Thus, the Serbs insist on the right of self-determination for nationalities and not for republics because 3 million Serbs live outside Serbia. The Croat policy naturally defends the self-determination of republics because in this way, Croatia might retain dissident Krajina. The first conception is not acceptable for a nationality that wants to have its own state in the current borders. Therefore, the Croats decided on the basis of republican territory in a referendum on 25 July 1991. But such a preference is anathema to nationality groups living as a minority in a republic, like the Croats in Voivodina and Bosnia, the Serbs in Bosnia or in Macedonia.

Does the right to self-determination apply to Yugoslav peoples only (Serbs, Croats, Slovenes, Muslims, Montenegrins, Macedonians)? Or does it also apply to national minorities (Hungarians, Albanians, Italians, etc.)? Fifty years of communism have demonstrated that the categories of nationality are unstable. Some have disappeared while others have been created. Self-determination can then easily be withdrawn or have conditions attached to it. A good example is the constitution of the 'new Croat democracy' of October 1990. The Serbs (12.2 per cent in 1991) lost their statutory position of nationality in Croatia, which they had held in all the preceding constitutions of the post-war period. Croatia had so far been defined as the state of the 'Croat people and the Serb people'. The new status of the Serbs as a national minority reduces the rights of that people. At the same time the government of Croatia considers the Croats of Bosnia (17.3 per cent in 1991) as a constituent nationality of that republic, as under the former communist constitution and also under the present one. Consequently, these Croats preserve the right of self-determination and the right of territory. The same applies to the Albanian minority in Macedonia, which is claiming the status of 'people' and wants to be considered as one of the constituent elements of the Macedonian state (*Le Monde*, 16 November 1991). Serbia could well become a prisoner of its own minority populations and would be encircled by the Albanians in the South and by the more than twenty-eight different populations in Voivodina in the North if it granted the right to independence or self-determination to its 'national minorities'. These national minorities have traditionally benefited from rights that extend beyond various international documents and conventions. These rights have not only been granted to Albanians and Hungarians, who are the most numerous groups, but also to Bulgars, Italians, etc. (Komatina, 1981, p. 51).

The second principle that has become threatened, as the Yugoslav state breaks up, is the inviolability of internal and external borders. Paradoxically, the republics that have proclaimed their independence (Slovenia and Croatia on June 25 1991, Macedonia on September 8 1991 and Bosnia-Hercegovina on October 15 1991) have appropriated the external borders of Yugoslavia guaranteed by international treaty, while they received, at the same time, the borders determined by a communist regime whose legitimacy they disputed. Individuals will once again not be able to agree on border problems if they base their claims on historical borders as Tudjman, the Croat leader, has done or on ethnic and administrative borders as Milosevic, the Serb leader, has done. For the Serbs, the borders between republics are of an administrative nature, formed in accordance with the communist spirit. They are therefore not historical, geographical, cultural or economic.

In conclusion, the actors in the Yugoslav drama play with definitions fed by different logics. These are all implied by the Yugoslav Constitution of 1974 where Yugoslavia is described as 'a statal community of peoples and republics' (Constitution of the Socialist Federal Republic of Yugoslavia, article 1; Constitution 1974, p. 87). In other words, the right of self-determination is granted to the Yugoslav peoples (Serbs, Croats, Slovenes, Montenegrins, Macedonians, Muslims) and at the same time to republics (Serbia, Croatia, Slovenia, Montenegro, Macedonia, Bosnia-Hercegovina). In the current phase of Yugoslav reconstruction, a bipolar conflict is taking shape. Everybody is trying to become the inheritor of Yugoslav sovereignty. Some have ambitions to modify the borders of the republics (the case of Serbia and Montenegro, who claim that Yugoslav sovereignty is transferred to peoples), while the peoples do not always identify with a single territory (republic). Others wish to deny the republic as an entity that serves as homeland to different peoples at the same time as was proclaimed by Tito's Yugoslavia (this is the case of Croatia). Nation-states are called for on all sides. The only ethnically homogeneous republic is Slovenia, where secessionism does not pose any additional problem with the rest of Yugoslavia.

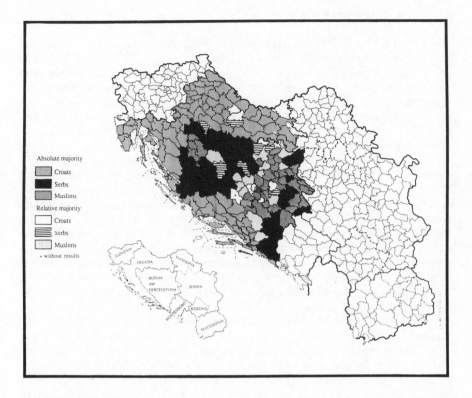

Figure 8.3   Absolute and relative population majorities in the communes of Croatia and Bosnia-Hercegovina (1990 Census)

Will the republics experience the same fate as Yugoslavia?

After the pluralist elections in 1990, the interest in a society based on the democratic ideal has replaced the ideal of national sovereignty based on the model of a 'Bolshevik' society. Inevitably all these nations wanted to construct their own state. However, the ethnographic map of Yugoslavia, the product of a cohabitation of peoples and of more than twenty nationalities, convincingly shows a distribution best qualified as a 'tiger coat pattern'.

How can we territorially rearrange Yugoslavia if every region proclaims itself as an independent republic? Today this applies perhaps to Krajina, Slovenia, Sandjak, Kosovo, tomorrow maybe to Istria and West Macedonia. Will the republics disappear as units? Between the ethnic regions, there are not always clearly distinctive borders indicated by language, cultural heritage differences, religion or nationality. Not all these attributes go together at the personal level. The largest difficulties of demarcation are to be found in Bosnia-Hercegovina and Croatia (Figure 8.3).

Switzerland as an example of cantonization

The mosaic of Bosnia-Hercegovina presents an image of Yugoslavia at a reduced scale where different peoples are in complete mutual interaction. This is where Yugoslavia will pass a national test or will fail. A Bosnian paradox is the incapacity of the three nationalist parties to govern together as they had set out to do. Due to permanent disagreement, government does not work but no party has switched into opposition (*Nin*, 25 October 1991). All decisions are taken by majority vote and are never unanimous. This means that a Croat–Muslim coalition can always ignore the position of the Serbs. This was evident during the vote on the memorandum concerning sovereignty. Bosnia-Hercegovina has asked for recognition of its independence by the European Community. 'There is no choice: there will be an equal status to that of the other republics or it (Bosnia) will be incorporated in greater Serbia' said president Alija Izetbegovic (*Vjesnik*, 24–26 December 1991). This act disturbed the tripartite equilibrium. Izetbegovic, president of the republic and at the same time president of the SDA party, has aligned himself with one people (the Croats) against another (the Serbs) voting for a sovereign Bosnia-Hercegovina in October 1991. The Serbs have rejected this decision of the presidency and the government of Bosnia and they organized a referendum in the municipalities with Serb majorities. They proclaimed their attachment to Serbia and propose a partition of territory within Bosnia-Hercegovina following the ethnic line of division.

A few months later (in February 1992), the erstwhile coalition of Muslims and Croats split over a proposal for a referendum where the electorate of Bosnia will in effect have to choose for or against a sovereign and independent republic. The Serbs and the Croats boycotted the referendum scheduled for 29 February and 1 March, 1992. The Serbs continued their stand of November 1991. The Croats fear becoming national minorities in independent Bosnia where the Muslims will dominate with their 43.7 per cent of the population in the 1991 census. It is well known that the regions of Bosnia populated by the Serbs do not wish to leave Yugoslavia for one important reason; the Serbs of Bosnia want to live with the other Serbs and with other nationalities but in one state. They dispute any project that associates Bosnia with the secessionist republics of Slovenia, Croatia and Macedonia.

If Bosnia wants to preserve its unity and territorial integrity and if it wants to leave behind this chaotic situation, the only possible solution is 'cantonization', with all three peoples taking part. This would be the only situation in which a Bosnia-Hercegovina of Muslims, Serbs and Croats would be viable. Such division or cantonization should be based on the territorial distribution of the nationalities characterized by the ethnic concentration that at the same time reflects the results of the elections of 1990.

The Muslims in Bosnia are the most numerous group, though not a majority (43 per cent in 1991) and they are situated in two separate regions (Figures 8.3 and 8.4). They inhabit an enclave in the West (the Krajina of Bihac and Cazin) where the SDA party has gained an important electoral success. There are four municipalities where the Muslims form over 90 per cent, surrounded by one Croat and some Serb municipalities. This region is not contiguous with the other Muslim region in Bosnia situated in the middle of the republic, 'the old pachalik of Sarajevo'. (A *pachalik* was an administrative division under the Ottoman empire). This unit is populated by 50 per cent of the Muslims in Bosnia plus 400,000 Serbs and a Croat minority. Although the Muslims do not occupy a homogeneously Muslim territory, their role as a people is unprecedented because their geographical situation results in a political disequilibrium that helps to prevent a 'Greater Croatia' as well as a 'Greater Serbia'. In Hercegovina, the demarcation is less complicated than in the remainder of the republic. The Neretva river separates two communities. The right-hand side is populated by Croats, the left-hand side by Serbs. The Croat majorities are solid, over 85 per cent, forming the natural continuation of the Croatian coast of Dalmatia. On the other side of the river, six Serb municipalities bordering Montenegro primarily contain Serbs with some scattered Muslim enclaves.

The first region (one could use the term 'canton') created in Bosnia was the 'Krajina of Bosnia' (the Serb Republic of Bosnia and Hercegovina) (*Le Monde*, 28 December 1991). The fifteen municipalities in the West of Bosnia around Banja Luka have signed an agreement to create an autonomous region (*Nin*, 19 April 1991) that has been widened by the signature of seven other municipalities after the proclamation of a sovereign Bosnia-Hercegovina. The Serbs are the absolute or relative majority in these twenty-two municipalities and the Serb party SDS predominates (Figure 8.4). The creation of this region has certainly not been accepted by SDA and HDZ nor by a large number of parties concentrated in the 'left bloc' (SDP, reformist communist and liberal parties). As they see it, the creation of territorial autonomy is the consequence of an ethnic problem aimed at undermining the territorial integrity of Bosnia. SDS on the other hand derives the logic of this association of communes from an economic, geographical and historical unit. During the Ottoman Empire, Banja Luka constituted the pachalik. Almost the same territory was Vrbaska banovina, also an administrative unit with some territorial autonomy under the Austrian-Hungarian occupation and during the Yugoslav kingdom. After the war Banja Luka became the centre of an administrative division (as *okrug, srez*) that contained twenty-one municipalities nearly identical to the present situation.

Bosnia's Krajina extends into Krajina in Croatia. The Serbs here have proclaimed an autonomous territorial unit called the Serb Republic (SAO) of Krajina (19 December 1991). It covers a territory of 20,000 square kilometres, larger than either Slovenia, Montenegro or Kosovo. This region has proclaimed its attachment to Serbia without taking into account the serious disadvantage of its territorial separation of the 'mother' republic (Figure 8.4).

What regionalism in Croatia?

Election results as well as the distribution of nationalities allow us to divide Croatia into various regions since the republic, like others in former Yugoslavia, was never homogenous. Northwest Croatia (former Civil Croatia) and Dalmatia are the heartlands of Tudjman's HDZ (Figure 8.2). Istria has largely voted communist and the communes that constitute the SAO Krajina, populated by Serbs, have split their votes between SDS and communists. The Serb–Croat conflict came to the surface after the elections and became grim after the proclamation of the new Constitution (25 October 1990) in which the Serbs were downgraded from a constituent nationality to a national minority without any right to cultural autonomy.

In 1920, the Serbs, particularly in Krajina, were opposed to any Croat independence, as proposed by the Democratic Party of S. Pribitchevitch. They always believed that Yugoslav unitary government was the best political solution. Now the Serb

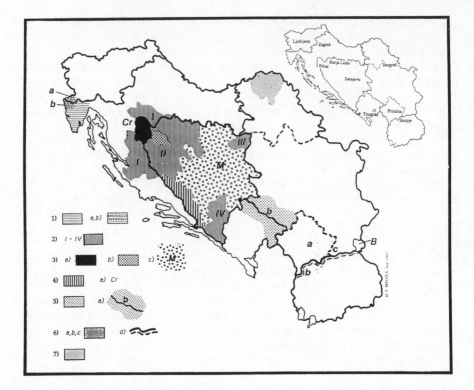

Figure 8.4 Major political problems related to population distribution in Yugoslavia. Numbers refer to those on the map.

1. Istrian peninsula divided between Slovenia and Croatia. The Italian minority a) in Slovenia 2,200 in 1981 and b) 19.000 in 1991 in Croatia.
2. The Serb regions I) 11 municipalities in Croatia, where the Serbs have an absolute majority (more than 57.4 per cent in 1991) have proclaimed the Serb Republic of Krajina on 19 December 1991. This represents 11.8 per cent of Croatian territory and 3 per cent of the population of this republic (580,761 people). Krajina, as a novel entity, has only partially resolved the problem of the Serbs because only 25 per cent of the Serbs in Croatia (144,340) live there. The others are concentrated elsewhere, either in Slavonia, or in the big cities where they are a more or less important minority, Zagreb (between 60,000 and 100,000), Rijeka, Split, Zadar. II) Serb municipalities in Bosnia-Hercegovina that proclaimed the Serb Republic of Bosnia-Hercegovina on 12 December 1991. III) Municipalities in Northwest Bosnia adjoining Serbia. IV) Municipalities in East Hercegovina with the option to join Montenegro.
3. The Muslims a) Enclave in Northwest Bosnia (Binacka Krajina) encircled by Serbian municipalities and one Croat municipality. The Muslims represent 66.6-97.6 per cent of the 1991 population. b) One municipality where the Muslims have a relative majority (47 per cent in 1991). c) The Muslims (M) in central Bosnia who inhabit this region together with sizable populations of Croats and Serbs.
4. The Croats in Bosnia-Hercegovina are concentrated in 10 communes (more than 90 per cent Croatian) that are a territorial extension of Dalmatian Croatia a) The Croat municipality that interrupts the territorial continuity of Krajina.
5. Sandjak – region populated by Muslims. A referendum on territorial and political autonomy was held on 25 October 1991. a) It belongs to two republics (Serbia and Montenegro) since the Balkan wars of 1912-1913. It acts as a barrier of communication between these two republics.
6. The Albanians, a) majority population in Kosovo where they were 77.4 per cent of the population in 1981 and about 80 per cent in 1991; b) in West Macedonia and c) in two municipalities in Serbia;

d) 'The wall of the Albanians' - communication between Serbia and Macedonia can be broken by these Albanian municipalities and one municipality populated by Bulgarians (B), 66.4 per cent in 1981.
7. In Voivodina, Hungarian minority (16.9 per cent or 340,960 people in 1991) is concerned about its prospects.

Democratic Party (SDS) has taken the role of protector of the Serb population and has refused to remain in an independent Croatia. This party has confronted the Croat power embodied by the HDZ party by establishing a National Serb Council, representing eleven communes. The Council organized a referendum on cultural autonomy in August 1990 and it has finally formed the autonomous government of SAO Krajina. This new politico-administrative unit has not accepted the rules imposed by the HDZ government on its ethnic territory, basing its disapproval instead on historical precedent. Krajina in Croatia forms an old military border zone (Vojna Krajina) that existed from 1522 to 1878. Its ethnic character still justifies its separate existence. In the eleven communes, the Serbs are in the majority, as in the adjoining Krajina of Bosnia, and they form the most western frontier region of Orthodoxy.

In October 1991, the Croat parliament accepted a new text on the problem of national minorities, that is, compatible with Council of Europe norms concerning minority rights. This law is applicable to the municipalities where the Serbs and other national minorities are the majority population according to the 1981 census (*Vjesnik*, 5 October 1991). However, the results of the recent census of 1991 have already been published and the rights of the Serb population in two municipalities (Pakrac and Patrinja) are ignored since the Serbs became the majority in these municipalities between 1981 and 1991.

The Istrian peninsula (Figure 8.4) has supported leftist parties in the elections. Consequently this part of Croatia expressed its adherence to a democratic federalism where the regions have an important say in their own destiny (*Delegatski vjesnik*, 12 April 1990). This regional attachment was clearly indicated in the results of the 1991 census where between 11 and 35 per cent of the inhabitants of Istria's municipalities declared their regional attachment (the census form allowed for such expressions). The chances for regional autonomy granted by the Croatian parliament are minute. The Italian Union of Istria and the Democratic Union of Istria have come out against the secessionism of Slovenia and Croatia and this feeling divides the peninsula and its populations (Croats, Slovenes and Italians). At the same time, Italian nationalists (MSI) have become concerned about the Italian community in Istria and have asked for a revision and change of borders. A revision of borders is necessary following an agreement signed between Belgrade and Rome but not between Rome and Ljubljana, the Slovenian capital (*Le Monde*, 5 October 1991).

The future of Istria is uncertain but one thing seems sure. For the first time in history, the peninsula will be divided between two countries, Slovenia and Croatia. Since the proclamation of the Slovene state, official border and customs checks have been instituted (*Courrier internationale* 55, November 1991).

Conclusion

The Yugoslav problem again threatens peace in Europe. It demonstrates the difficulty of solving a fundamental political question, regarding the constitutional issues that divide republics becoming increasingly independent and also dividing nations that, in intricate ways, compose the Republic populations. In 1918, seven different administrative territories and systems of law met in what was Yugoslavia: Austrian, Croat, Hungarian, Bosnian, Montenegrin, Serb and Turk. These areas had never in their history been parts of the same state; they became Yugoslavia. Unfortunately, the desire to be one people has not been realized because national interests have prevailed over the Yugoslav ideal (Pribitchevitch 1933, p. 12). Croat nationalism has not accepted the Yugoslav idea because it represented the negation of its self-identity with the danger of unitary government at the same time. Serb nationalism has tried to merge the idea of its own state with the Yugoslav idea.

At this point in time (early 1992), a Croat national conscience and a Serb national conscience are clearly incompatible and in mutual conflict. Consequently, there has always been tension between these two peoples and the Serb–Croat conflict has continuously poisoned political life since the creation of Yugoslavia (*Tribune de la Presse* 1992, pp. 12–13). In the second version of Yugoslavia installed after 1945, the communist leaders played the card of integral nationalism looking for some sort of balance and vainly hoping for a model multi-national community. After the elections of 1990, this model has been revealed as an infinitely complex entity, being at the same time highly artificial and therefore explosive. Political liberalization has permitted the constitution of new parties that have aroused the traditional political ideology, based on old tensions and ethnic conflicts. This clash has led to the current crisis and the civil war. The climate of mutual fear encouraged by nationalist discourse has provoked a rallying around the idea of the different nationalities and has encouraged each of the nationalist parties to create its own statelet.

Yugoslavia has lost its sovereignty. It has fallen into as many pieces as there are republics. As a result, antagonism is no longer only between nations (Serbs against Croats) but also between nationality and state (Serb against the Croat state). In particular, the issue of the recognition of cultural autonomy for minority nations has destroyed the sovereignty of republics. Territorial claims are necessarily based on the problem of ethnic borders or electoral frontiers. These do not always coincide with the borders of republics. The necessary and only possible way out seems to be arbitration under international supervision.

Apart from Slovenia, a model of ethnic and linguistic homogeneity, Yugoslavia shows a mosaic of peoples demonstrating a mixture of languages, religions and heritages. How is Yugoslavia to be divided if one can visualize as many national states as peoples? We know that territorial continuity will not be assured because the frontiers of the republics do not correspond with those of the peoples. Should one regroup municipalities into new regions or devise new territorial units (like cantons) based on the principle of majority nationality? Whatever territorial division is chosen, at least nearly 1,600,000 persons (*Vreme Belgrade*, 9 September 1991) will be affected by such territorial and political redefinition. They will be held hostage as minorities, repressed or forced to emigrate. (Currently, there are over 1.2 million refugees from the fighting.) What should one do, for example, with the enclaved regions within Bosnia like 'Bihacka Krajina' where a Muslim minority is encircled by Serbs and Croats? Will new massive waves of people hit the roads as has already happened in Baranja and Slavonia? The future of the multi-national state is bleak indeed.

References

Banac, I., 1988, *Nacionalno pitanje u Jugoslaviji*, Naprijed, Zagreb.

Banitch, M., 1933, *La Yougoslavie vu par un Croate*, Pierre Bossuet, Paris.

Castellan, G., 1960, 'Aspect de la politique des nationalités dans la Fédération Socialiste Yougoslave', *Revue Française de Science Politique* 1, 83–107.

Ceratini, R., 1987, *La force des faibles. Encyclopédie mondiale des minorités*, Larousse, Paris.

Djuric, I., 1991, 'Les racines historiques du conflit serbo-croate', *Etudes* 1, 293–303.

France, Vreg., 1991, 'Perspektive politickog pluralizma u Jugoslaviji ili "sjaj i bijeda" novih demokracija', *Politicka misao*, no. 1, 95–110.

Gace, N., 1988, *Jugoslavija, Suocavanje sudbinom*, NIGP Glas, Beograd.

Ivsic, M., 1926, *Les problèmes agraires en Yougoslavie*, Rousseau, Paris.

Janjic, D., 1987, *Drzava i nacija*, Informator, Zagreb.

Komac, M., 1991, 'Nationalités et minorités en Yugoslavie', *L'événement européen* Octobre no. 16, 156–75.

Krulic, J., 1991a, 'Deux sociétés civiles, plusieurs nations', *Le Débat*, Mars–Avril, no. 59, 31–49.

Krulic, J.,1991b, 'Les populismes d'Europe de l'Est', *Le Débat*, 67, Novembre-Décembre, no. 67, 84–91.

Mousset, A. 1921, *Le royaume des Serbes, Croates et Slovènes*, Paris n.p.

Mrdjen, S., 1991, 'Tragédie: le dernier recensement de la Yougoslavie', *Populations et Sociétés*, no. 263 INED, Paris

Nestorovic, C., 1991, 'Question nationale ou question constitutionelle?', *Cosmopolitiques*, Février, 65–69.

Nouzille, J.,1991, *Histoire de frontiéres, l'Autriche et l'Empire ottoman*, Berg Internationale, Paris.

Panayote, E.D. (1991) Minorités: une ou moins pour la Gréce. *L'événement européen*, no. 16, Octobre, Paris.

Perovic, B., 1988, *Jugoslavenstvo i nacionalizam*, Gardos Beograd.

Pezet, E., Simondet, H., 1933, *La Yougoslavie en péril*, Blond et Gay, Paris.

Pribitchevitch, S., 1933, *La dictature du roi Alexandre*, Pierre Bousset, Paris.

Rivet, C., 1919, *En Yougoslavie*, Parrin, Paris.

Sisic, F.,1937, Jugoslavenska misao, Rad, Beograd.

Yovanovitch, N., 1924, *Etude sur la Constitution du Royaume des Serbes, Croates et Slovènes du 28 juin 1921*, Pierre Bousset, Paris.

9 Gypsies in Czechoslovakia: demographic development and policy perspectives

Kveta Kalibova, Tomas Haisman and Jitka Gjuricova.

The Romany peoples (in popular terms, those called Gypsies) add an extra piece to the mosaic of population groups that inhabit Eastern Europe. They deviate considerably from the other population groups in their social, economic and cultural life and in their demographic behaviour. These differences are due not only to their quite separate historical evolution in ancient times outside Europe but also to their isolation during long periods after their immigration to the region. There have been traditionally very few marriages between Gypsies and other inhabitants.

The country of origin of the Gypsies is India. They have been leaving India over a long period but the most significant outmigration occurred in the tenth century, with the majority of the Gypsies coming to Europe. The first traces of Gypsies in the central part of Europe date from the fifteenth century (Caratini, 1986). Gypsies live in almost all European countries, most of them in the Balkan and in the Danubian region. Nowhere are they the majority population in territories larger than a few villages. Even their largest concentrations with more than a thousand people form only enclaves in regions dominated by others. Most Gypsies live dispersed in small groups, usually of relatives or just in separate families.

Anthropologically, socially and even ethnically, Gypsies are far from homogeneous. Only their common origin enables us to consider them as a separate nationality (Chaliand and Rageau, 1991). The original differentiation of Gypsies occurred in India, where a social structure was found; the structure of monoprofessional castes, implying the territorial movement of people. Gypsies in India belonged to the castes of blacksmiths, musicians and middlemen. Members of these castes lead a nomadic life in India, even today. The secondary differentiation of Gypsies was the result of varying national, cultural and socio-economic conditions in the different European regions, where they came to live. In some countries in East-Central Europe–for example, in Hungary and Slovakia – Gypsies had more reasons to abandon their nomadic style of life. Most of them settled permanently during the last two centuries. To the east, they continued their nomadic life as was the case with a significant portion of the Gypsies in Rumania and Bulgaria. The intra-group differences among permanently settled Gypsies are less significant than among those Gypsies who still practise a nomadic life style.

Estimates of the number of Gypsies in the world and in various countries vary tremendously. A comparison of published data demonstrates methodological helplessness more than anything else. In some places, all people without permanent address or all inhabitants with the lowest social rank are classed as Gypsies. Therefore, it is not easy to say how many Gypsies live in the world and even who can be and should be considered as a Romany. According to the different sources, there are about 8–15 million Gypsies in the world and approximately 5–6 millions Gypsies in Europe. The Romany Congress in 1978 put their number between 6 and 15 million in the world and about 4 million in Eastern Europe (see Table 9.1). Indira Gandhi estimated the number of Gypsies in the world at 15 million at the International Festival of Gypsies in Chandigar in India in 1983.

Table 9.1   Estimates of the number of Gypsies in the former socialist countries

Country	Number of Romanies	Percentage of Population
Hungary	400,000–800,0000	5.6
Bulgaria	300,000–500,000	4.5
Rumania	500,000–1,500,000	4.4
Yugoslavia	700,000–1,000,000	3.5
Czechoslovakia	300,000–500,000	2.6
Poland	30,000–80,000	0.2

In this chapter, we concentrate on the position of the Gypsies in Czechoslovakia, emphasizing the specifics of their position in the Western part of Eastern Europe. In the Czech and Slovak Federal Republic, the Gypsies constitute, *de facto* as well as *de jure*, an ethnic minority (Puxon, 1975). Sometimes they are described as a historical minority, but in any case they certainly represent one of the largest and most identifiable minority groups in Czechoslovakia. After a short historical overview, we first concentrate on the demography of the Gypsy population in recent times as an indication of the social profile of this group. We then move on to the difficult questions of policy toward the Gypsies under communism and in the post-communist period.

Historical overview

The separate and different development of the Czech Lands and Slovakia between the fifteenth and nineteenth centuries was also reflected in different emphases in the history of the Gypsy population in the two parts of the present state. Their itinerant style of life was not at all accepted in the Czech Lands (as was also the case in Western Europe) and their failure to adapt resulted in even more pronounced nomadism and separation from the settled population. On the other hand, a specific kind of sedentarization typical in the Balkan region and some form of mutual adaptation resulting in more symbiotic coexistence characterized the social status of the Gypsy population not only in Slovakia but more broadly in the Eastern parts of Europe and, especially, the Balkans.

Because their style of life was considered as sponging off others, the Gypsies were severely persecuted during parts of the sixteenth and seventeenth centuries. Their situation improved slightly under the reign of Maria Theresia and Joseph II in the middle of the eighteenth century. This was the first time the problem of Gypsies was considered more as a social than as an ethnic problem. Efforts were made to make them settle on a permanent basis and to provide education and regular jobs. Their situation was further improved in the nineteenth century, particularly after 1848. Even so, the Gypsies were only slightly incorporated in the economy and the majority population shunned contact.

In the late nineteenth- and early twentieth-century, population censuses of the Gypsy population were held separately in the Czech Lands and in Slovakia. In the Czech Lands, some 5,000-7,000 people were labelled as 'gypsies'. They formed a social stratum rather than a specific ethnic group: 'vagabonds', including Gypsies, mostly engaged in marginal trades occupying the lowest rung on the social ladder. According to the 1893 census, Slovakia was the home of about 36,000 people described as 'gypsies'. These figures suggest that the number of Gypsies living on the territory of the present-day federation has increased about tenfold.

The Gypsy population was apparently concentrated in Slovakia, mostly in the eastern poorest parts, in the late nineteenth century. The 1893 census recorded a substantial portion of the Gypsies in Slovakia, depending on agriculture for their livelihood by various forms of cooperation with the local (i.e. ethnically different) population, while a high proportion had left the countryside, their traditional habitat, altogether. During the First Czechoslovak Republic (1919–1938), divergences between the lifestyles of the Gypsies and the other population groups in Slovakia were underlined. The approach of the civil service in the Czech Lands in preventing the circulation of 'vagabond gypsies' was also introduced in Slovakia to prevent a territorial redistribution of Gypsies (mostly men) seeking work. This brought about a deepening pauperization of the Gypsies and a cumulation of the problems already signalled in the preceding period. Until World War II, the Gypsy population probably hardly increased at all.

The years of World War II spelled disaster for the Gypsies. The Czech Lands lost 6,500–7,000 Gypsies in the war-time 'gypsy camps' and the gas chambers of the Auschwitz concentration camp, while Slovakia was deprived of the last remnants of mutual tolerance and economic and social symbiosis between the majority and this ethnic minority.

The demography of the Gypsy population in Czechoslovakia

A marked growth of the number of Gypsies in Czechoslovakia started after World War II. The data presented in Table 9.2 demonstrate the increase of the number of Gypsies since 1921. Data for individual years were collected through different methods and they are not strictly comparable. The situation is also complicated by the fact that Gypsies were not considered as a separate nationality between 1945 and 1990 and neither their maternal language nor their ethnic group were recorded in population censuses. In the last population census of 1991, Gypsies had the opportunity of declaring their nationality as 'Gypsy' but the results of this census are rather surprising. Only a small number of Gypsies took advantage of this chance of ethnic identification.

Table 9.2   Estimates of the number of Gypsies in Czechoslovakia, by different sources (1921–1991)

Year	Number of Gypsies	Per cent of pop.	Source
1921	8,284	0.06	census
1930	31,415	0.22	census
1947	101,190	0.83	police
1966	221,525	1.55	local authorities
1970	219,554	1.53	census
1980	288,440	1.89	census
1980	310,598	2.03	local authorities
1991	114,116	0.73	census

Local authorities are National committees, Bureau of Social Care for Problematic Families and Persons

The demographic characteristics of the Romany population in Czechoslovakia have been elaborated on the basis of the analysis of the census results in 1970 and 1980, when a special form of identification of Gypsies was carried out using similar methods. In fact, the census enumerator decided whether the person belonged to the Gypsy ethnic group. As a basis the census enumerator took records of local authorities plus his/her own judgment of characteristic features of the respondent (character of family, style of living, cultural level, knowledge of languages, anthropological features). This practice has often been criticized from the point of view of human rights because alleged Gypsies did not know about it. It was not used in the 1991 census.

In the early post-war years, the increase in the numbers of Gypsies was partly caused by their immigration from Rumania, Yugoslavia and Hungary. The results of the population census in 1991 are not comparable because of the different method of investigation. The total number of Gypsies in Czechoslovakia increased by one-third between 1970 and 1980. Due to a large immigration to the most heavily industrial and urbanized regions of the Czech republic (around Prague), their population growth was here noticeably higher than in the Slovak republic (see Table 9.3). The yearly average

Table 9.3   Gypsies in Czechoslovakia in 1970 and 1980

Area	1970 Gypsy pop.	1980 Gypsy pop.	Increase 1970–80	Per cent 1970	Per cent 1980	Per cent of country 1970	Per cent of country 1980
Czechoslovakia	219,554	288,440	31.4	1.53	1.89	100.0	100.0
Czech Republic	60,279	88,587	47.0	0.61	0.86	27.5	30.7
Slovak Republic	159,275	199,853	25.5	3.51	4.00	72.5	69.3

Source: Czechoslovak population census 1970, 1980

rate of growth was eight times higher among Gypsies in the Czech republic than among other inhabitants and over 1.5 times higher than among Gypsies in the Slovak republic. The overall population growth of around 3 per cent puts the Gypsy growth rate with the populations of developing countries. It can be stated, however, that in no country has such a growth lasted for more than one generation. Due to the fact that Gypsies are not classified separately in the vital statistics, no crude rate of natural increase can be calculated. It can only be estimated on the basis of population census data supposing that the size of external migration is negligible. That is a reasonable assumption for this period (see Table 9.4).

Table 9.4   Average yearly rate of population growth (percentage) in Czechoslovakia, 1970–1980.

Area	Gypsies	Other inhabitants
Czechoslovakia	2.71	0.62
Czech republic	3.80	0.49
Slovak republic	2.26	0.91

Source: Czechoslovak population census 1970, 1980

The territorial distribution of Gypsies is very uneven in Czechoslovakia with their rate of migration much higher than that of the rest of the population. This has led to their dispersion over the whole territory but it also gives rise to new concentrations and consequently new social problems. In the Czech republic, Gypsies live mainly in urban areas (80.8 per cent), a fact that strongly affects their demographic behaviour. In the Slovak republic, the ratio in urban areas is only 40 per cent. At a more regional level Gypsies have traditionally concentrated in East Slovakian districts (see Figure 9.1). Here their share was 7.7 per cent of the population in 1980, while the figure was 2.9 per cent in the Central Slovakian region, 2.6 per cent in the West Slovakian region and 2.07 in North Bohemia, the only Czech region where their share is sizable.

As mentioned above, Gypsies in Czechoslovakia were not considered a separate nationality and they had to declare one of the other nationalities during the population censuses in 1970 and 1980. About three-quarters declared a Slovak nationality, 15 per cent a Hungarian one and 10 per cent adopted the Czech nationality in that year. The number of Gypsies of other nationalities was negligible. In comparison with 1970, the highest increase was enumerated among Gypsies with a Czech nationality (121.3 per cent), both in the Czech and Slovak republics. The increase of Gypsies of Slovak nationality was only 29.9 per cent and those of Hungarian nationality 20.2 per cent. In most cases, the Gypsies declared their nationality according to place of tempo-rary residence. They apparently do not take the majority nationality where they live in all cases.

The differences in demographic behaviour between Gypsies and other inhabitants of Czechoslovakia are evident from the age structure (see Table 9.5), a result of previ-ous conditions and consequently of previous levels of mortality, fertility and migra-tion. Gypsies have an obviously progressive type of age structure with a high share of children and low share of the aged due to a high level of fertility and also a relatively

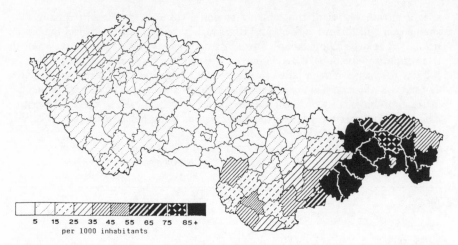

per 1000 inhabitants

Figure 9.1   Percentage of the Gypsy population by district in Czechslovakia 1980

higher rate of mortality (see Figure 9.2). Any reduction in mortality rates in this type of age structure leads to even higher population growth. The population of the Czech republic had this pyramidal type of age structure in the nineteenth century; it has long maintained a stationary type and has acquired a regressive type of age structure after 1970, with slow population decline. By contrast, the Slovak republic has had slight population growth up to the present.

Table 9.5   Age structure of Gypsies and whole population in Czechoslovakia (per cent)

Age Group	Gypies 1970	Gypsies 1980	Czechoslovakia 1980
0–14	48.7	43.1	24.3
15–59	46.2	52.4	60.0
60 +	4.5	3.6	15.7
unknown	0.6	0.9	–

Source: Czechoslovak population census 1970, 1980

The specific age structure of Gypsies also affects their distribution according to marital status. There are many more single men among Gypsies (65.5 per cent) in comparison with the Czechoslovak population (43.7 per cent). The corresponding percentages for women were just 60.5 and 35.4 in 1980. The share of Gypsies living in marriages is significantly lower (31.7 per cent among men in comparison with 51.0 per cent in Czechoslovakia and 33.2 per cent among women in comparison with 48.6 per cent in Czechoslovakia). Gypsies enter into marriages at a younger age than other population groups but they also remain more frequently single. The relative share of widowed persons is higher in all age groups, certainly due to a higher mortality level. In examining these data, it has to be mentioned that some Gypsies consider a marriage as an unnecessary formal legal act and live in *de facto* marriages as common-law husband and wife. In 1980, about 5.5 per cent of common-law marriages in the country were Gypsy marriages. That is significantly more than the share of Gypsies over 15 years of age (1.4 per cent).

Besides a progressive age structure, high fertility and families with many children, a low education level is a noticeable characteristic of the Gypsy population. There are several reasons for this fact, including insufficient knowledge of either the Czech, Slovak or Hungarian languages, bad conditions for education in large families and little interest in the value of education and vocational qualification. In 1980, more than three-quarters of all Gypsies had only completed elementary education, and about 7 per cent (30 per cent in 1970) had not even completed elementary school. Only 1 per cent of Gypsies completed a high school of any kind in or before 1980 and 0.2 per cent of them completed university or technical school. The education level of Gypsy women has been especially low.

A certain improvement can be found between 1970 and 1980. There were more trained Gypsies in 1980 and fewer without a primary school education. In spite of this progress, the educational level of the Gypsy population remains very far below the level of the other inhabitants of Czechoslovakia. The low educational level of Gypsies has negative consequences in the kind of jobs they acquire and in the education of their children. The continuation of this pattern certainly seems to hinder their social integration. Society at large did not provide sufficient inducement for education because there were sufficient numbers of jobs that did not require any kind of qualification and were relatively very well paid. The specific age structure of the Gypsy population also affects their economic activity. The level of economic activity of Gypsies increased between 1970 and 1980 but it is still considerably below the level of the general population. The activity level of Gypsies is only higher compared to the majority population until the age of 24.

The sex structure of the Gypsy population is also peculiar, with men outnumbering women (see Figure 9.2). There was even a small decrease of the share of women between 1970 and 1980. This may partly be the consequence of the under-registration of women but again it also reflects population characteristics comparable to those of a developing country. In 1970, the female proportion in percentage terms was 49.3, dropping to 49.2 in 1980 while the sex ratio (males per 100 females) went from 102.6 to 103.4.

The demographic reproduction of the Gypsy population has to be estimated on the basis of Czechoslovak population censuses, because of the lack of information from the vital statistics. Gypsy women have a high level of fertility during the whole childbearing period; procreation ends usually at the age of 30 among other women in Czechoslovakia. The average number of live-born children for every Gypsy woman was 6.0 in the age group 45-49, but only 2.3 for the whole population (including Gypsies). Significant changes in the demographic behaviour related to the process of the demographic transition have continued during the 1970s and later. The number of live-born children from present marriage had decreased by 20.5 per cent in 1980 from 1970 (0.5 per cent for the total population). The fertility-level decrease was evident in all age groups but especially in the younger groups. The total fertility rate (average number of live-born children per woman during the whole reproductive period) was estimated at 5.78 between 1970 and 1980 and about 4.00 children in 1990. This estimate is based on population projections of the Gypsy population up to 2003.

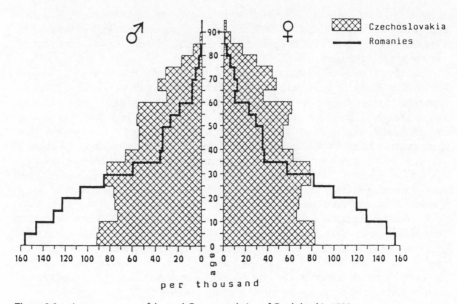

Figure 9.2   Age-sex structure of the total Gypsy population of Czechslovakia 1980

In spite of the fact that a decrease in fertility level among Gypsies during the last two decades is evident, Gypsy women still have a much higher level of fertility in comparison with other women in Czechoslovakia. The high fertility level of Gypsies creates a specific structure of families with many children and it affects their standard and style of living. It is considered by many to be a factor slowing down the integration of Gypsies into society at large.

The analysis of mortality suffers from the same paucity of hard information as the analysis of fertility (Kalibova, 1989a). It must be based mainly on comparison of the age structure provided by the 1970 and 1980 censuses. There is no doubt that mortality figures have improved during the last decades but still only a small share of Gypsies are over the age of 60 (3.6 per cent in comparison with 15.7 per cent for the whole of Czechoslovakia). The lower level of economic activity of Gypsy men in the age groups over 50 indicates a high level of work disability. There were only 79.4 per cent of economically-active Gypsy men in the age group 50-54 and 71.8 per cent in the age group 54-59. The corresponding percentages for all Czechoslovak men were 92.7 and 84.2 per cent.

The registration data from health institutions provide only partial data on infant mortality. In 1985, the infant mortality of the Gypsy population oscillated at about 24 per 1,000 in the Czech republic and reached the value of about 35 per 1,000 in the Slovak republic. However, in isolated East Slovakian areas, this rate is certainly much higher than that. A poor diet of mothers during pregnancy and inadequate care of infants have been cited as reasons for such figures. It should be mentioned that the perinatal mortality of Gypsy children born in hospitals is practically the same as that of the other children.

An effort has been made to estimate the life expectancy of the Gypsy population on the basis of 1970 and 1980 population censuses. Various simplifications and assumptions had to be made. The mortality table has to be constructed for the whole country in spite of the fact that the mortality level of Gypsies is different in Czech regions and Slovak regions. We assumed that external migration of Gypsies into and out of Czechoslovakia has been negligible but internal migration between Czech and Slovak regions has been rather high (Kalibova, 1990). The second assumption was that the same persons were recorded in both population censuses in 1970 and 1980. The probability of survival between 1970 and 1980 was the first function that was calculated and the probability of death, the introductory function to mortality tables, was derived from it. Life expectancy at birth of Gypsy men calculated in this way was 55.3 years and for Gypsy women it was 59.5 years in the period 1971–1980. Levels such as these are frequently found in developing countries.

Gypsies have retained certain specific features of demographic reproduction that are characteristic of other groups in the past. Changes in the demographic behaviour are occurring very slowly as a consequence of changing social and economic conditions. The example of the Czech and Slovak populations can be mentioned: they have lived during three generations (since independence in 1918) under comparable conditions but they still maintain slightly different demographic behaviour due to a different historical evolution. At the same time, the differences between the two largest Czechoslovak population groups in the past were considerably smaller than between Gypsies and the other inhabitants of Czechoslovakia. Without doubt, there has been social and economic progress of Gypsies in Czechoslovakia since World War II. Efforts to assimilate Gypsies into the society at large, affecting their culture, language and traditions, can be seen as an infringement on their human rights. On the other hand, their material situation was improving as can be seen from demographic indicators, such as a slight decrease in fertility levels. The question that then arises is why demographic progress is so slow? It is a well-known fact that a certain time lag always exists between social and economic change and the demographic response. Such a time lag cannot be measured in calendar years but is rather a function of the passing of successive female cohorts with different life experience. Consequently we can expect further demographic changes among Gypsies in the future.

Policy toward Gypsies

During the early post-war years, a sizeable part of the Gypsy population migrated from Slovakia to the mines and heavy industries in the Czech borderlands. Some years later, the collectivization of agriculture forced a further migration flow to the Czech and Slovak industrial centres. The pauperization of the Gypsies continued. Now it was the consequence of massive displacement from the economic and social environment where they had won a precarious existence. The major state policy of the post-war years towards the Gypsies, interrupted for a short time around 1968, was pressure to assimilate. The methods to solve the so-called gypsy question during the first five years after the war were especially heavy-handed. From the beginning of the 1950s, the 'people's democracy' operated on the principle that nothing but harsh government measures could be successful in 'doing away with the gypsies' backwardness'. Although the subsequent period of the 'beginnings of building up socialism' brought a *de jure* liquidation of discriminatory legislation, the leading ideology of communism was unable to grasp the real sources of the Gypsies' social misery or to value the distinctive character of their civilization and culture. One elaboration of this experiment in social engineering was the adoption in 1958 of the Anti-Itineracy Act No. 74, which, centrally and by way of persecution, asserted the principle of the Gypsies 'reeducation'. According to this Act, Gypsies were forced to settle in one place. The Act and its follow-up measures were not successful. In 1965 even more drastic measures were taken. The Gypsies' social and cultural assimilation was to be achieved by means of their centrally-organized dispersion on government orders. In this process, their traditional as well as newly-formed communities would be ruined.

In 1968, at the time of the 'Prague Spring', these programmes were dropped. Two independent organizations emerged in the next year to protect and advocate the interests of the Gypsies. In 1970, they both participated in drafting a new concept of a government policy to solve the so-called Gypsy question. It was based on an idea of social integration that clearly departed from the assimilation approach of the past decades in favour of respect for the distinctive character of this population group. But the hopes for a new approach on the part of the government did not outlive the ban on the Gypsy organizations.

After 1973, a retreat from the integration approach back to assimilation was increasingly evident both on the Czech and on the Slovak side. During the 1970s, centrally controlled programmes for the Czech lands and Slovakia were formulated to transform the way of life of the Gypsy population. Where clear 'successes' were not reached quickly, both the Czech and the Slovak programmes introduced ever more drastic means to try to achieve their aims. A typical example is the attempt to lower the birth rate among Gypsy women, which resulted around 1980 in a gradually elaborated programme of female sterilization.

The post-war time of communist rule, marked off by the turning point of 1989, can be described as one of paternalistic manipulation. The Gypsies became an object of policy and a victim of solutions imposed by the authorities. Little consultation of the Gypsies was undertaken. The government based its philosophy on the premise that improvement of the Gypsies' material conditions alone would change their manner of thought and their spiritual world. In executing this policy, the government exceeded the limits laid down by basic human rights and aimed at latent as well as unconcealed ethnocide, as the Gypsies were forced to abandon their cultural background and change their style of life through forced assimilation. The regime rejected the existing ethnic character of the Gypsies and was not interested in the development of Gypsy culture and language. By suppressing Gypsy representation in the early 1970s, it quelled the forces of internal activism and the development of a political movement in the Gypsy minority. In fact, the socialist regime only provided chances to the Gypsies well-adapted to the host society. All the rest became isolated at the margins of society.

November 1989, the time of the 'velvet revolution' and the end of the communist period, was followed by a brief period of bilateral euphoria, a time when society at large, but above all the Gypsies themselves, succumbed to the illusion of an easy solution to the social problems of Gypsies in Czechoslovakia. November 17 1989 became an important landmark for the Gypsies in the process of becoming aware of their national identity and their search for emancipation. For a brief moment, relations with the public at large became unencumbered. Addressed only on isolated occasions and often   haphazardly in the past, the Gypsies suddenly found   themselves a focus of interest of many people and political groupings. The Czechoslovak public, but mainly the Gypsies themselves, increasingly yielded to the illusion that the Gypsies were able to solve the problems derived from their marginal position by themselves.

The third period is a time of disillusionment. It has not yet ended and it is hard to guess when it will. For many reasons, the system of social care for the socially-weak Gypsy population is currently collapsing without being replaced by effective development programmes. Social care systems were designed to respond to the social conditions of the entire population of particular regions regardless of people's ethnic background. Disintegration of social care is now erroneously regarded as an expression of liberalism, democracy and social justice. The problems of the Gypsies' life in Czechoslovakia represent a latent danger of destabilization in whole regions with high concentrations of Gypsies as in the industrial centres of North Bohemia and North Moravia. More than anything else, fear characterizes the present day-to-day relations between the Gypsies and the rest of society. Fear is present on both sides. Fear generates a need for defence and repression, on the part not only of the government but of individuals as well.

The traditionally-low educational level of the Gypsy population and consequently the low level of their vocational qualifications condition their concentration at the lowest levels of the socio-professional structure of society. Gypsy children fail at school at a 14-times higher rate than other children and 30 times as often they leave school before completing the final elementary grade. With a 28-times higher frequency, they are transferred to special schools. A mere 2.5 per cent of Gypsy children attend secondary school, compared with 38 per cent of non-Gypsy children. Among the principal educational problems is an inappropriate school system which does not provide conditions for educating children who are poorly adapted for attending school for social and language ability reasons.

Another, equally important, cause of low educational achievement is the Gypsies' inherent attitude to education, which does not occupy a major place in their value orientation. The Gypsies are rather materialist. They aim at a level of material well-being that equals that of the population at large, to be reached in the shortest possible time. Most Gypsies are unskilled workers; women do menial jobs as auxiliary labour. This determines their contacts with the rest of the population. Other marginal groups often are the sole representatives of the majority society with whom the Gypsies come into touch. This type of role model does not help to inculcate positive attitudes towards education.

A new fact is coming to the forefront at the present moment: large-scale Gypsy unemployment. All the known causes such as low vocational qualifications, problematic working morale and frequent changing of jobs, combine with the important factor of the Gypsies' attitude to their own employment. In the recent past under the communist regime, the right to work was a repressively-enforced duty and this duty to be employed corresponded with the employers' duty to employ. The Gypsies have become accustomed to treating their employment recklessly by making unrealistic demands. Today it is becoming increasingly normal that Gypsies made redundant cannot find new employment and often they do not even qualify for unemployment benefits. The problem of large-scale unemployment of the Gypsies springs *inter alia* from the traditional distrust by employers of Gypsy workers and their reluctance to employ them, much of it based on racial intolerance.

A pronounced threat to the social position of the Gypsies is contained in the privatization of housing since 1989. The bad experiences of home-owners with Gypsy tenants handicap a large part of the Gypsy population, particularly in urban areas. A growing number of Gypsies are becoming homeless. While stopping a further influx of Gypsies to towns and cities, local authorities are beginning to deal with conflicts arising from the coexistence of the non-Gypsy and Gypsy population by isolating the latter in poor ghettos. Urban Gypsy enclaves have been known during the whole postwar period. They were formed in the process of urbanization of the Gypsy population. The experience with building satellite housing estates especially for Gypsies is clearly negative. Forcibly bringing together a larger number of Gypsy families resulted in destruction of the original social ties entailing group control. This created the conditions for a general social regression. Social, health and hygiene problems on the estates deepened the isolation of these artificial communities from the rest of the population. The new social conditions led to further deterioration. The decreasing living standard of the inhabitants of the satellite housing estates has caused the Gypsies' heavy frustration that reflects in their increased aggressiveness as can be seen from the high incidence of violent crime.

In the mid-1980s near the end of the communist era, a 'mere' quarter but possibly one-third of all Gypsies in Czechoslovakia lived well below the poverty line but also – and perhaps more importantly – without any perspective of improvement. In 1989, the new government faced the task of practically having to deal with the problem all over again. On 9 January 1991, the Federal Assembly of the Czech and Slovak Federal Republic adopted the Charter of Basic Rights and Freedoms, a document which reflects the humanistic concerns of current democratic systems and their attitudes to ethnic minorities. The Charter of Basic Rights and Freedoms has provided the legislative frame from which the policy of CSFR in relation to the Gypsy ethnic minority should derive from now on. Let us hope that this charter will result in some significant improvements in the social situation of the Romany population in Czechoslovakia.

References

Caratini, R., 1986, *La force des faibles: encyclopédie mondiale des minorités*, Larousse, Paris.

Chaliand, G. and J.-P. Rageau, 1991, *Atlas des diasporas*, Odile Jacob, Paris.

Kalibova K., 1989a, 'Charakteristika umrtnostnich pomeru romske populace v Ceskoslovensku' (Mortality characteristics of Gypsy population in Czechoslovakia), *Demografie* **3**, (3): 239–250.

Kalibova K., 1989b, 'Gypsies in Czechoslovakia and the process of the demographic revolution in this population', *Acta Universitatis Carolinae* **1**, (1): 23–32.

Kalibova K., 1990, 'Prognoza romske populace v CSFR do roku 2005', (Prognosis of Gypsy population in Czechoslovakia till 2005), *Demografie* **3**, (3): 219–224.

Puxon, G., 1975, *Les Romanis: ces gitans d'Europe*. Minority Right Group. Rapport no. 14, London 1975, 24 pp.

10 The stolen revolution: minorities in Romania after Ceauşescu

Leo Paul

On Christmas Day 1989, an execution squad put an end to the lives of Nicolae and Elena Ceauşescu, the uncrowned King and Queen of the Dacian Empire. It seemed that the death of the dictator would bring an end to the suffering of the population of Romania, and would improve the situation of the minority groups. But now, more than two years after the 'revolution', many people are disappointed, although the real terror is over. The 'nationality question' is one of the time-bombs still ticking away in Romania. In fact, the revolution started on account of the minority issue. In December 1989, about 1,000 people demonstrated in Timişoara for the release of Reverend Laslo Tökés, the symbolic leader of the Hungarian minority groups. He was once a hero for many Romanians, but he is now being discredited in the country in an aggressive campaign against all minorities.

This chapter describes the position of several minority groups in Romania since the revolution. To explain why the status and problems of these groups diverge so widely, it is necessary to review their different historical and geographical contexts. Three groups will get special attention: the Hungarians, the Germans and the Gypsies. These groups differ in size and origin, and were treated differently during the Ceauşescu regime. Now they share a common fate in that they all suffer from a rising tide of Romanian nationalism. Violent clashes occur from time to time; should these be seen as isolated incidents or taken as warnings that the time bomb might explode?

Romania, country of many nations

Romania is a country consisting of many nations. According to estimates, about 13 per cent of the total population of 23 million belong to an ethnic minority group. In the communist period to 1989, official figures on ethnic minorities were not always reliable; most experts consider the last accurate census to be the one taken in 1966. Table 10.1 presents the official figures from the last census, held in 1977. According to these figures the Hungarians, the Germans and the Gypsies are the main minority groups. Of these three, the Hungarians are officially the largest group, with about 1.7 million according to this census. We must be careful with numbers, especially with regard to the size of the group of Gypsies. (In this chapter, the term Gypsy will be used because it is the common expression for this group, though the legalistic term Romany is more properly applied.) The census gives a figure of 230,000, while unoffical estimates put their number over 760,000, and some even maintain that the true figure is

Table 10.1   Population estimates for ethnic groups in Romania

Ethnic group	Census 1977	Percentage 1977	Estimates Dec. 1991
Rumanians	19,001,721	88.2	
Hungarians	1,706,874	7.9	2-2.5 million
Gypsies	229,986	1.1	760,000-2.5 million
Germans	358,732	1.7	80,000
Jews	25,686	0.1	15,000
Ukrainians, Ruthenians, Hurzulen	55,417	0.3	
Serbs, Croats, Slovenes	42,358	0.2	
Russians	32,147	0.2	
Slovaks	22,037	0.1	
Tatars	23,107	0.1	
Turks	23,303	0.1	
Others (Bulgarians, Czechs, Greeks, Poles, Armenians)	36,219	0.2	
TOTAL Population	21,559,416	100	23 million

Sources: Mihok, 1990, pp. 205-207; Schöpflin and Poulton, 1990, pp. 5-6; Ghermani 1991b,

two million or above (Helsinki Watch, 1991b). The real number of Hungarians is perhaps over two million (Schöpflin and Poulton, 1990, p. 5). As for the Germans, the official number for 1977 could be correct. But the recent mass emigration of this group to Germany over the past fifteen years makes it difficult to estimate how many of them still live in Romania.

Figure 10.1 is an unofficial map of the geographical distribution of the minorities in Romania, compiled from several sources. This map presents only a general overview and might be slightly incorrect in its details. Ethnographic mapping was not allowed during the last decades of communism. Most of the minorities live in Transylvania, the western part of Romania, covering about one-third of the country. Historic Transylvania was much smaller than the present area, now including the Banat, Crisana and Maramures areas, which the Romanian state took over from the Kingdom of

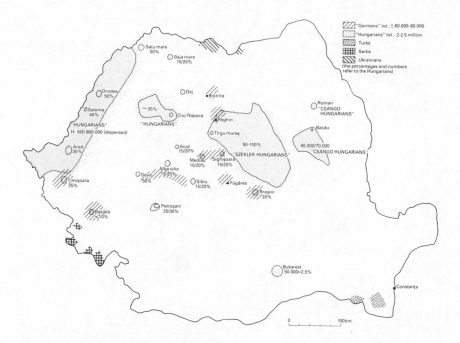

Figure 10.1   Distribution of ethnic groups in Romania

Hungary after 1918. The population pattern of present Transylvania is extremely complex, and the distribution of the nationalities is uneven. The total population of the region is about seven million, of which around three-fifths are Romanian.

Many of the population concentrations in Transylvania are ethnically mixed, but a compact Hungarian area can be found in the heart of Transylvania. This area is populated by so-called 'Szekler Hungarians'. (The area is called Székelyföld in the Hungarian language.) These Szeklers have some typical cultural traditions that deviate from those of the Hungarians in Hungary, but in view of their language and cultural heritage, we can call them Hungarians (or better Magyars). In the 1977 census, the Romanian authorities gave them the opportunity to report their nationality as 'Szekler' instead of 'Hungarian', but only a few did so. This indicates that the Szeklers are conscious of their Hungarian nationhood. On the other hand, the Hungarians in Hungary make a distinction between themselves and the Szeklers and regard the Szeklers as the best of the Hungarian nation. This unusual expression will be discussed below.

Székelyföld comprises the counties of Harghita (Hargita, 80 per cent Hungarian), Covasna (Kovászna, 70 per cent Hungarian) and Mures (Maros, 50 per cent Hungarian). Outside this Szekler area, we find a high proportion (about 50 per cent) of Hungarians in some major cities: in Cluj (Koloszvár), Oradea (Nagyvárad), Tîrgu Mures (Marosvársárhely) and Satu Mare (Szatmár). In Brasov (Brassó), Timişoara (Temesvár) and Arad, about 20 per cent of the population is Hungarian. According to some estimates, between 500,000 and 800,000 Hungarians live scattered along the border with Hungary (Schöpflin, 1978). The third concentration of Hungarians (the so-called

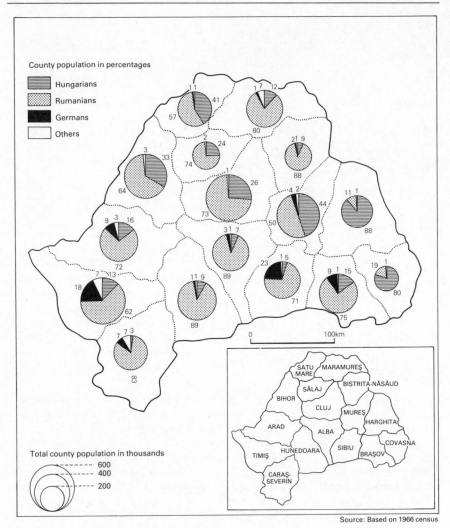

Figure 10.2   Distribution of ethnic groups in Transylvania, 1966 census

Csángo Hungarians), estimated between 40,000 and 70,000, is found east of the Carpathians near Roman and Bacau. It is almost certain that they originate in a group of Szekler Hungarians who crossed the Carpathians in the eighteenth century to escape from the Habsburg army. Because of their isolated location, their language and attitudes differ from those of the Szekler Hungarians.

From the heart of Szekler country to the west, there is hardly any natural barrier: the road leads through wide valleys and the hills gradually slope down to the Great Hungarian Plain. But the territory in between is for the most part populated by Romanians: only near the Hungarian border on the Romanian side do we find a Hungarian-speaking population. This distribution is the heart of the matter: a large group of Hungarians (1.5–2 million) concentrated quite a distance (about 350 km) from Hungary, with a territory in between that is populated mainly by Romanians. Figure 10.2 is a map of the distribution of minorities in Transylvania, based on the more reliable census of 1966. It shows that the German minority is mainly concentrated in the counties of Sibiu and Timiş. In the middle ages, the Germans founded a number of towns that have retained their importance ever since. The German name for Transylvania (Siebenbürgen=Seven Towns) refers to the urban origin of this minority group. They can be subdivided in two groups: the Saxons, living around Braşov (Kronstadt), Sibiu (Hermannstadt) and Cluj (Klausenburg); and the Swabians near Timişoara (Temeschwar), Arad and Oradea (Grosswardein).

The Gypsies are the most deprived minority in Romania. Only since the overthrow of Ceauşescu have they been recognized as an official nationality. They are among the diverse and numerous Gypsy groups who now may number over 6 million throughout Eastern and Western Europe, Turkey and the former Soviet Union. It is difficult to sketch the geographical distribution of this group at any one time-period because of its mobility; about 10 per cent of the Gypsies are moving around in any period. One can state that the group is scattered around the country, and partly concentrated in pseudo-Gypsy areas (Schöpflin and Poulton, 1990, p. 5). The group that is considered 'Gypsy' is in fact composed of at least forty different groups, with differences in tribal loyalty, language and profession. The divisions within the Gypsy population still play an important role. An estimated 60 per cent of them speak Romani (Romanesc or the Gypsy language), but most also speak Romanian or Hungarian. Most Gypsies are no longer truly nomadic, due to policies of forced sedentarization (Helsinki Watch, 1991b).

The small Ukrainian and Ruthenian minorities live mainly in the Maramures and Suceava areas, in closed, homogeneous small areas. The Serbs live mainly near the Yugoslav border. And the Turks have their highest concentration in the area of Constanta in south-east Romania. The reasons behind this unusual scattering of ethnic groups in Transylvania will be discussed later in this chapter.

After the fall

At first, many improvements

After the fall and execution of Ceauşescu, and the violent revolution in December 1989, major changes occurred in Romania, with great positive impact on daily life. Freedom of the press, the right to assemble and to form political parties and other societal interest groups, and the opportunity to travel came into effect for the whole Romanian population, including the minority groups. With respect to the minorities' policy, a radical change seemed to have taken place. The new regime promised to create a special Ministry for Minority Issues, and to pass legislation protecting the rights of minorities. Special efforts would be made to stop discrimination and to preserve and enhance cultural identity. The restrictions on university enrolment by members of minority groups would be lifted. New organizations were founded by the minority groups to promote their interests. Minority groups were allowed to start their own schools again. Gabanyi (1991b) reports that minority schools may have classes with less than the minimum number of pupils (fifteen).

Gyula Horn, the Hungarian Minister of Foreign Affairs, was the first official foreign guest after the 'revolution' of 1989. He reached an agreement with the new Romanian government on improving the situation of the Hungarian minority. The Romanian authorities announced the reopening of the Hungarian consulate in Cluj, although its activities were restricted to consular matters. A Hungarian-Romanian cultural accord was signed in February 1990, which entailed the renewal of Romanian-Hungarian Friendship Societies (Schöpflin and Poulton, 1990). The admission of Hungarian students to the Romanian university in Cluj shows that things had certainly improved. In the autumn of 1990, a Hungarian student told me that the proportion of Hungarian students studying mathematics had grown from a few per cent in 1989 to about 35 per cent.

Streets and villages could be renamed using non-Romanian names if a majority of the people wanted this. In everyday life, the increased tolerance of the Hungarian language was evident. For instance, Hungarian street signs (some streets were renamed after Hungarian heroes like Lajos Kosuth), bilingual names for official buildings, and bilingual signposts at the entrance to every village with a Hungarian community, whether large or small, appeared. The special programmes on radio and television in Hungarian and in German were reinstated. Newspapers and books in all languages could be printed and sold again; in some cases, as for the German press, their publication was even subsidized by the state.

One week after the revolution, the Democratic Forum of Germans in Romania was set up. The German Foreign Minister Hans-Dietrich Genscher spoke with this new organization during his visit to Romania in January 1990. He declared that his government accepted responsibility for the situation of the German community in Romania, as it had before December 1989. But as for the question 'stay or leave', the situation had changed. Before the Romanian revolution, it was hardly possible for the government of West Germany to improve the living conditions of the ethnic Germans in Romania by creating jobs and supporting German schools and cultural activities. Genscher expected this to change after the fall of Ceauşescu and hoped that German investments would prevent the mass emigration of Romanian Germans to the Federal Republic of Germany. But if they wanted to come, 'the door would always be open' (Gabanyi, 1991b, p. 512).

In many respects, the Germans could profit from the general liberalization. Soon it was possible to study the German language as a major subject at several universities again. However, in spite of these improvements, a mass emigration of Germans did take place. Between the revolution and the end of August 1991, about 132,000 Romanian Germans migrated to Germany. That is about two-thirds of the original 200,000 (Gabanyi, 1991b, p. 493). The reasons for this phenomenon and other setbacks to reducing the minority tensions were found in the worsening political and economic situation.

Violent clashes and the outcome of the elections

Gradually in 1990, the general situation in Romania worsened and it was becoming obvious that the former second echelon of the Communist Party was now in charge. In March 1990, a serious riot broke out in Tîrgu Mures because of the decision to reopen Hungarian schools and to allow bilingual signs. The strong Romanian opposition to these plans resulted in riots; officially three people were killed and about 269 injured. (Beyer, 1991, p. 484). There are indications that the Securitate (the Romanian Secret Service, set up by Ceauşescu) helped instigate the tumult, with the help of the 'Iron Guard' (a fascist terrorist organization that was well-known in the 1930s and during World War II), and the new semi-fascist nationalist movement, Vatra Româneasca. Romania accused Hungary of starting the riots. Hungary was said to have misused the permission to aid the Hungarian minority by starting separatist actions – for instance, by sending maps and text books in which Transylvania was presented as Hungarian territory. According to the report of the official inquiry, the riot in Tîrgu Mures 'was started by local extremists, who wanted to destabilize the new government. They received help from "foreign agents", although the latter were not identified' (NRC, 18 January 1991).

In May 1990, the first free parliamentary and presidential elections were held in Romania. During the weeks leading up to these elections, an increasing number of violent incidents took place. They were directed at political parties and independent groups opposing the National Salvation Front. In one case, a breach of the Electoral Law was reported; a Romanian woman, who supported the right of Hungarians to have separate language schools, was prevented from running for office. The court of the Mures county based its judgement on an article of the Election Law that was meant to prevent members of the old nomenklatura from returing to power (Helsinki Watch, 1991a, p. 31).

The elections brought a tremendous victory for the National Salvation Front. Ion Iliescu was elected as president, winning 85 per cent of all votes, and in parliament, the Front took 66 per cent. However, the second-largest party was the Hungarian Democratic Union of Romania, with 7 per cent (about one million) of the votes. According to the electral law, every minority group must have at least one seat in parliament, even if the minimum number of votes is not reached. In parliament, as a result, twelve minorities are represented. After the elections, the 'minority issue' was out of sight, out of mind, as far as the new majority government of the National Front was concerned. In official goverment statements, the problem of the minorities was not even mentioned.

In June 1990, the 'miners' revolt' took place in Bucharest: a student protest against the government was violently suppressed in a 'spontaneous' action by miners. The miners responded to an appeal by President Iliescu to 'restore order' in the Romanian capital. Five people were killed and 462 injured. Again, there are strong indications that the Securitate took part in this operation as well. This event confirmed the suspicions of many who were now convinced that communism was still in power, although with a milder face (Beyer, 1991).

Rising Romanian nationalism

An alarming phenomenon is the rise of right-extremist Romanian nationalism. One of the most fanatic movements is Vatra Româneasca (Romanian Hearth), which provokes a primitive hatred against all minorities, including Jews. One article of their programme illustrates their standpoint on the Hungarian minority:

Unfortunately, the sacred Romanian soil is still being defiled by the feet of Asiatic Huns, Gypsies and other scum. Let us unite to expel them from our country. Away with the Huns, those tramps, who should never have obtained a foothold in our country, away with the Gypsies who disgrace our country! We want a pure and great Romania! We demand all territories back that were robbed from us! Now or never! Do not fear the fight and do not hesitate to shed the unclean blood of the strangers! Those hairy apes have no business in our beloved country (VK, 19 May 1990).

The Party for National Unity (AUR), which shares many of the ideas of Vatra Româneasca, published a 'Declaration for the Solution of the National Issue' in March 1991. In this document, it opposed special schools for minorities and rejected bilingual names for villages and streets. This party only got 2 per cent of the votes during the elections, but its influence is growing.

Central to the national movement is the weekly România Mare (Great Romania), that has a circulation of about 500,000 (Gabanyi, 1991b). In the best fascist tradition, this weekly expresses anti-Semitism and hatred of minorities and all opposition parties. It wrote that 'the Romanian revolution of 1989 was an international intrigue led by the Hungarians'. In 1991, every edition included two pages of anti-Hungarian rhetoric, under the headline '1991: the International Year of the fight against Hungarian terrorism'. In an interview with a Dutch newspaper, the two editors of the magazine (who were ghost writers for Ceausescu) expressed their opinion of Hungarians:

Every right-thinking person knows that Hungarians are animals. They still practise ritual murders. . . Hungarians are worse than Russians. . . . The world is too stupid to see through the great Hungarian plot against Romania. They let important people in Europe marry Hungarian wives. They infiltrate the whole nobility in Europe (VK 27 May, 1991).

The editors cite a lot of examples of Hungarian aggression against and even murder of Romanians. 'The intention of these actions is clear: first autonomy and than unification with Hungary' (VK, 27 May 1991).

The Romanian government has not vigorously condemned these Romanian nationalist organizations. Perhaps it does not wish to do so. It may be afraid to abandon this nationalism, which has been growing among the Romanians, because the popularity of the Front is decreasing. In April 1991, the Romanian parliament paid tribute to Marshall Ion Antonescu, who was executed in 1946 as a war criminal. Antonescu, the fascist leader of Romania during the war, started the pogroms and the deportation of Jews to the concentration camps; he was honoured with one minute of silence in parliament. President Iliescu has condemned Antonescu's behavior during the war but the publications that normally support the government praised Antonescu as a great patriot. According to foreign diplomats, Iliescu shows personal courage in his efforts to run counter to the stream of nationalism (VK, 20 June 1991).

In the course of 1991, ultra-nationalist articles of the kind illlustrated here appeared in an increasing number of Romanian newspapers. It seemed that 'anti-Hungarianism' had become a semi-official state ideology. Laslo Tökés, once the national hero of the revolution, is now the target of the anti-minorities campaign. He is the victim of anonymous letters and phone calls claiming that he will be murdered. Even his son's teacher has been threatened. According to Tökés, 'they use the same methods as before the revolution. In former days the situation was clear, now it is complex. You cannot discover easily where your enemies are, and who they are . . . Nicolae Ceauşescu is dead, but his spirit is alive' (VK, 21 December 1991).

The way back: the stolen revolution

Since the 1990 elections, the situation of the minorities has deteriorated in several respects. Many of the initial promises have not been fullfilled and many measures actually taken have been reversed. The reopening of independent Hungarian schools in Transylvania proceeded very slowly and encountered many difficulties. In Spring 1990, Prime Minister Petre Roman stated that 'it would be a pity if the re-introduction of education in the Hungarian language went too fast' (NRC, 1 March 1990). But in spite of local opposition, many special schools for Hungarians and Germans were created, either separately or as part of other schools. In general, the new education policy is a significant improvement compared to the restrictions on education in minority languages. However, local resistance is severe, and the Romanian government has been slow to enforce these laws on local officials. In some counties, local authorities refused to allow ethnic Hungarian students to take their entrance exams for high school in Hungarian, as is required by law. The head of the Hungarian language school in Bucharest reported to Helsinki Watch (1991a) that his school was vandalized and that school property was damaged.

At the beginning of the school year 1991-92, even the central government was trying to reverse the positive developments. The efforts of Hungarian and German schools to enlarge their influence on the curriculum had to be stopped. It was even announced that Romanian History and Geography had to be taught in the Romanian language again (Gabanyi, 1991b, p. 507). The Hungarian University in Cluj is still not open. Lack of money is not a problem because its financing is guaranteed by the rich community of Hungarians in the United States.

After the 1989 revolution, there was an explosion in publishing (from approximately thirty publications in 1990 to over 900). But the independent press faces great constraints in practice. It is difficult to purchase paper, since all independent publications depend on one single paper mill, where output has dropped sharply due to strikes and the government's apparent failure to guarantee wood for pulping. Many view this as an indirect way of subverting the independent press. Also problems related to the distribution of publications have been reported (Helsinki Watch, 1991a). In February 1991, access of minority groups to the television media was reduced. Half of the programmes broadcast in Hungarian and German were moved from Channel 1, which broadcasts nationwide seventeen hours a day, to Channel 2, which can only be received by about 13 per cent of the population and broadcasts only ten hours a day. The International Helsinki Federation for Human Rights (IHF, 1991) who reported this, has no information on the broadcasts in Serbo-Croatian.

The fact that the Romanian government initially did not keep its promise to guarantee minority rights in new laws and institutions was also criticized by the chairman of the DFDR (Democratic Forum of Germans in Romania): 'we do not want privileges like in the Middle Ages; the only thing we want is a constitutional state, in which we can live and maintain our German culture' (Gabanyi, 1991b, p. 508). The fall of Ceauşescu did not stop the exodus of German emigrants; it even stimulated it. In 1991 each month about 2,600 Germans made the decision to leave Romania. If this continues the German population (about 80,000 at the end of 1991) will disappear almost completely; perhaps only a few old people will stay to die in Romania. The reasons for the on-going migration are simple: a distrust in the new Romanian government, the bad economic situation in this period of transition to a market economy, rising aggression and criminality, and the growth of Romanian nationalism. Vatra

Româneasca and România Mare express a hatred not only of Hungarians, Gypsies and Jews, but also of Germans. Furthermore, the discussions in Germany to limit the ability of Germans abroad to migrate to Germany is an extra stimulus for Romanian Germans not to put off the decision. Now they still can get a German passport and will be financially supported after arrival in Germany. This privilege makes the Germans a very special minority group in Romania.

The Gypsies have been the target of increasingly violent attacks since the revolution. Their homes have been burned down and vandalized; they have been beaten in police custody; and they have been chased out of one village after another. At least five Gypsies have been killed. Gypsies have also lost their property, their security, and any hope they may have had after the revolution for a better life. The observers of Helsinki Watch (1991b) quote the words of a Gypsy woman:

> It was better under Ceausescu. We were left alone. No one bothered us. No one tried to attack us. No one called us 'Gypsy'. Now people insult us. They say all kinds of insulting things. They try to force us out of our homes and villages, out of Romania.

Gypsies have been portrayed in a particularly negative way in the Romanian mass media. State-controlled television has manipulated the stereotype of Gypsies as thieves and black-market dealers for political purposes. The increasing unemployment in the country due to economic reforms has a disproportionately greater impact on Gypsies.

New constitution and local elections

After months of discussion, the Romanian parliament approved a new constitution in November 1991. One month later, about three-quarters of the Romanian population voted in a referendum for this constitution. It guarantees a multiparty system, the protection of human rights, and the introduction of a market economy. But the representatives of the minority groups opposed this constitution, although it recognizes the right of the minorities to 'maintain, develop and express their identity'. The minorities criticize the formulation that 'Romania is a unitary state, with the Romanian language as the single official language'.

The first local elections in fifty years were held in February 1992. The Front of National Salvation, which had split into several groups, was reduced to about 40 per cent of the vote. The opposition parties got about 32 per cent and the extreme-right nationalist parties got less votes than expected (5 per cent) but won in Cluj (NRC, 19 February 1992). For many observers the outcome of this election is important, since it makes it possible to break the power of the local elites consisting of old communists. It could be the beginning of real democracy in Romania.

History as a treasure hunt and history as a burden

Who came first? - the dispute between Hungarians and Romanians

Transylvania plays a central role in the national history and legends of Hungary as well as Romania. For both countries Transylvania is the cradle of culture and civilization. Therefore, the main dispute centres on one question: who was there first?

In the Hungarian version, the Magyars in Transylvania belonged to the stream of

Magyars who came from the region between the middle reaches of the River Volga and the Ural Mountains in the tenth century. They occupied the Pannonian lowlands and Transylvania, regions which they found largely unpopulated. According to this version, the Romanians came later: only in the thirteenth century did Romanian nomads and shepherds cross the Carpathian mountains, and the Hungarians were so kind as to give them the right to settle.

The Romanian version of the settlement of Transylvania is quite different. They claim that the Szeklers were originally Romanians who were forced to become Hungarian. According to official Romanian history, Transylvania was the core of the Dacian Empire, an area that became part of the Roman Empire in the second century. The Romanian national culture was the result of the mixing of Dacian and Roman culture. The Romans left the province of Dacia in 271, but Transylvania remained the crossroads of migrating people for the next seven centuries. The Romanized Dacians did not leave but hid in the woods and mountains, keeping the Romanian culture alive. This theory of 2,000 years of Dacian-Roman continuity justifies Romanian possession of the territory of Transylvania and confirms their primacy as the indigenous inhabitants (see e.g. Kovrig, 1986). According to Georgescu (1991, cited in Deák, 1992) the Romanian princes, keen on resisting pressure from Catholic Hungary, preferred Eastern to Western Christianity, in part because of their running dispute with Hungary.

In the fifteenth century, Hungary was one of the great powers of Europe. But in 1526 the Hungarians were defeated by the Turks at Mohacs, and large parts of Hungary fell under Turkish occupation until about 1700. But unlike the rest of Hungary, Transylvania was spared heavy destruction and remained relatively independent. This is one of the main reasons why Transylvania is so important for present-day Hungarians: only here do they find the remains of the old Hungarian Empire. In 1690, Transylvania was conquered by the Habsburg Emperor, and it remained under Habsburg rule until 1867. In this period, many Romanians came to Transylvania, and soon they outnumbered the Szeklers.

In the twelfth and thirteenth centuries, groups of Germans, now called Saxons (although they came mainly from the Rhineland), were asked by the Hungarian king to help to defend the borders of the Hungarian Empire in the east. In the eighteenth century, another group of Germans, the Swabians, came to the region and settled in the Banat area around Arad, Timişoara and Resita. This part of the Great Hungarian Plain (which now belongs to Transylvania, but was outside the historical province of Transylvania) had suffered under the Turks and had to be repopulated and recolonized. These Roman Catholic Swabians should be distinguished from the Protestant Saxons (Illyés, 1981).

Minorities and social stratification

After the establishment of the Habsburg Dual Monarchy in 1867, some liberal principles were included in the Hungarian constitution. The Romanians in Transylvania gained recognition as a 'nation', but gaining equal rights and true representation in the Habsburg parliament was a more difficult matter. With regards to culture and language, between 1867 and World War I, a true 'magyarization' of the ethnic minorities in Transylvania took place. The Hungarians believed that this transfomation, although compulsory, would be in the interest of the minorities. This magyarization harmed not only the Romanians but also the German population (Mihok, 1990).

The organization of social and economic life in Transylvania was simple. In general, the Hungarians were the land-owners, and the Romanians formed the dependent group of labourers on the estates. A Hungarian bishop put it at the time, 'the position of the Romanians in society could be compared with that of moths in a coat'. This remark illustrates the existence of a class society in which Romanians were not treated well by the Hungarians. According to Verdery (1983, p. 175), the serfs in Transylvania were exploited by an unusually reactionary nobility. It is difficult to judge whether or not her quotation from Prodan (p. 126) is an exaggeration or not: 'It can be asserted without hesitation that Transylvanian serfdom was among the most repressive ever known'. There was an increasing discrepancy between the Westernized and increasingly prosperous urban middle classes on the one hand and the backward rural population, suffering from extreme poverty and malnutrition, on the other. Both the Hungarians and the Germans claimed racial, social and cultural superiority. And this has contributed enormously to the unending trouble between these groups and the Romanian people. Many Romanians feel like second-class citizens in their own country (Deák, 1992).

Who's in charge of what?

In 1878, the Kingdom of Romania was founded (not including Transylvania), and a king was found in one of the German principalities (Verdery, 1983). As an outcome of the First World War, Romania gained Transylvania, the Banat, Crisana and Maramures. During that war, Romania had changed sides several times. But just in time, one day before the capitulation of the Central Powers, Romania joined the Allied Forces and on that basis, it could claim territorial extension during the peace negotiations. Austria-Hungary had to be split up, and according to Woodrow Wilson, the US President, the principle of national self-determination should operate to draw the lines. In this version, each 'nation' should have its own state. But the ethnic mosaic of Transylvania did not allow simple application of such principles. There was no choice but rule by one or the other unitary state, and the victors of the war favoured joining Romania. Establishing a new border between Hungary and Romania was a problem: the strict separation of Romanians and Hungarians would suggest a border with many curves that would cross the important railway Satu Mare-Oradea-Arad several times. A more or less straight borderline was drawn, with the entire railway on Romanian territory, as well as a large Hungarian minority. (see Figure 10.3).

The Peace Settlement of Trianon (1920) still is a trauma for the Hungarians. They felt that a great injustice had been done. In the book *Justice for Hungary* the former minister Count Albert Apponyi (1928) writes:

> The Trianon mutilation has detached from the West territories it had already conquered, and thrown them back into semi-oriental conditions . . . (pp. 19-20).

His message was clear: the conflict over Transylvania was a conflict between West and East, between progress and culture on one side, and backwardness and 'semi-oriental conditions' on the other. Soon after Transylvania had come under Romanian rule, the

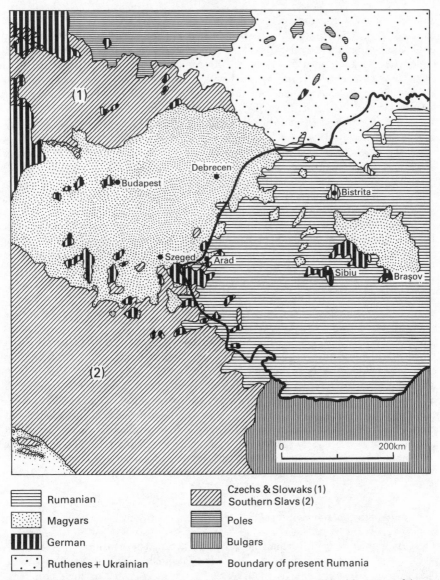

	Rumanian		Czechs & Slowaks (1) Southern Slavs (2)
	Magyars		Poles
	German		Bulgars
	Ruthenes + Ukrainian	——	Boundary of present Rumania

Figure 10.3   Distribution of ethnic groups in South-East Europe 1920 and the delimitation of the new border between Hungary and Romania

number of Hungarians was reduced. At the beginning of the 1920s, about 197,000 of them left Transylvania voluntarily or otherwise, while at the same time a large number of Romanians came to Transylvania from the old Romanian territory (Illyés, 1981, p. 28).

Territorial interests and historical sentiments determined the positions of both Hungary and Romania during World War II. Hungary chose the side of the Germans, with initial success: by Italo-German arbitration in the Treaty of Vienna, Hungary re-annexed the northern and southeastern part of Transylvania in 1940. In these re-annexed lands, the Hungarian authorities often mistreated the Romanian minority population. After the German defeat in Romania in August 1944, Romania abandoned the Axis and joined the Allies. The Romanians then took revenge for the violations committed by the Hungarians a few years earlier. Transylvania was put under Soviet military rule. After the war, the Paris Peace Treaty of 1947 reaffirmed the Trianon territorial settlement (Kovrig, 1986, pp. 475-77).

The war had a great effect on the number of Germans, Gypsies, Jews and Hungarians in Romania. In 1941, Antonescu made a speech calling for the 'elimination' of national minorities. By his orders, more than 26,000 Gypsies were deported to camps located in the Romanian occupied areas of the Soviet Union. A total of 36,000 Romanian Gypsies died during the war period, making the number of Gypsy deaths the highest in any country of Europe (Helsinki Watch, 1991b, p. 12-13).

In 1939 about 800,000 Germans lived in Romania. During the first years of the war, about 300,000 Germans were resettled in Germany or had to join the army. After 1944, a further 100,000 Germans fled or were evacuated. In January 1945, about 75,000 men and women who were able to work were deported to labour camps in the Soviet Union; about 15 per cent of them did not survive these camps.

Romania had a rather large Jewish population before the war (about 800,000 in 1939). The treatment of the Jews took on a strangely dualistic character over the years. Until 1923, Romania was the only European country where native-born Jews were systematically denied citizenship, yet they had a strong economic position with a great influence on trade and finance. During the first years of the war, Romania played an active role in deporting between 200,000 and 300,000 Jews to the concentration camps. The Romanian fascist organization, 'the Iron Guard', played an active role in 'purifying Romania' of Jews. In Hungarian-occupied northern Transylvania, nearly all Jews, perhaps 150,000 in all, were sent to the Auschwitz concentration and extermination camp in summer 1944. The active role of the Hungarians in the initiation of this process was very cynical, as the Hungarian Jews in Transylvania were great Hungarian patriots who were proud to speak Hungarian under Romanian rule. The dual nature of the policy toward Jews can be seen after Romania's change in position in 1943, when it successfully protected the country's remaining 300,000 Jews (Deák, 1992).

The terrible weight of communist politics

The Communist Party of Romania, founded in 1921, had at that time a high per centage of non-Romanian members, largely Jewish intellectuals. At first, they were opposed to a Greater Romania, though later they were corrected by the Comintern. Romanians remembered those facts well and remember too that, after World War II also, the ethnic minorities continued to make up a large part of the Communist Party leadership. Later on, non-Romanian intellectuals were eliminated from the Party and replaced by the sons of Romanian peasants (Deák, 1992, p. 48).

During the first years of communist rule, the Hungarians enjoyed extensive political and cultural privileges. The constitution of 1952 provided the creation of an 'Autonomous Hungarian Province' in the compact region inhabited by the Szekler Hungarians. In 1960, the character of the Autonomous Hungarian Province was changed in two ways: symbolically, by a change of name to 'Mures Autonomous Hungarian Region', and ethnically, by a change of boundaries that reduced the percentage of Hungarians. In the new Mures Autonomous Hungarian Region, Hungarians were reduced from 77.3 per cent to 62.2 per cent, while the Romanian proportion increased from 20.1 per cent to 35.1 per cent (Mihok, 1990, pp. 209, 215). By the end of 1962, Romanian had effectively replaced Hungarian as the official language in the area.

In 1951, a forced deportation of about 40,000 Germans from the Banat took place. These people were resettled in the Baragan Steppe in 'old Romania' to do forced labor under severe conditions (Illyés, 1981, p. 29). But this resettlement was an exception: in contrast to other East European countries, a mass deportation of the German population did not take place. Until 1948, the Germans were discriminated against more than other minorities: they could not vote, and during the land reform, many German farmlands were expropriated. Owing to this fact, the percentage of Germans working in agriculture was reduced from 77 per cent in 1945 to 22 per cent in 1956. They were chased away from their farms and houses, which put an end to their economic independence, but also meant an expulsion from their traditional cultural environment in the countryside. They were 'expelled, but retained in the land of expulsion' ('vertrieben, jedoch im Vertreibungsland zurückgehalten').

In 1948, the period of exclusive discrimination of the German minority came to an end. The official policy of equal rights for citizens of all nationalities now came into effect and also applied to the Germans. In 1950, this minority was given the right to vote. The death of Josef Stalin in 1953 started a general liberalization campaign in eastern Europe that also included Romania. The labour camps at the Danube-Black Sea Canal were closed, and the deported people of the Baragan Steppe could return home. Between 1954 and 1956, a part of the expropriated German possessions was returned. But many events of the past were irreparable: the separation of families, the destruction of economic life and the loss of cultural identity. In general, a deep distrust in the communist rulers festered (Gabanyi, 1991b).

Nicolae Ceaușecsu came to power in 1965. In the new Romanian constitution of that year, the expression 'national minority' was replaced by 'coinhabiting nationalities'. Within three years, the autonomous region was abolished. By territorial reform, thirty-nine new counties were created out of the former sixteen. Only two predominantly Hungarian counties were formed (Covasna and Harghita), in which only one-fifth of Transylvania's Hungarian population were living. In spite of these measures, the first years of Ceaușescu seemed to bring a favorable change in the policy concerning nationalities. In the spring of 1968 several spontaneous demonstrations occurred in Transylvania as an expression of the growing discontent among the Szeklers. In response to this, the Council of Working People of Hungarian Nationality was created that same year, and the Hungarian language was reintroduced in publications, broadcasting and education. There are indications that Ceaușescu made these concessions, after the revolt in Czechoslovakia, for fear that the Soviet Union might seize upon ethnic troubles to punish Romania for its increasingly independent foreign policy (Kovrig, 1986, p. 477).

By the mid-seventies, the liberal policy changed. A true 'romanianization campaign' started, and the development of the 'national (= Romanian) way to socialism' was announced. Even Russian names disappeared from public life and the Russian language was no longer an obligatory subject in primary schools. Ceaușescu, the 'Conductor' (leader) of the people, saw himself as the successor of former rulers of the Dacian Empire. Parallel to the glorification of the Romanian culture and history, cultural activities of other ethnic groups were gradually forbidden (Mihok, 1990). Ceaușescu wanted to eliminate the hold of the traditional Romanian social elite on political power and the influence of German, Hungarian and Jewish minorities on Romania's economy, cities and culture.

Large industrial projects were set up in Transylvania, especially in the less densely populated 'Szekler' counties of Harghita and Covasna, and in the German territories. Romanians from outside Transylvania were forced to settle in this Hungarian territory. Hungarians were kept out of leading positions and speaking Hungarian at work was forbidden. At the same time, Hungarian professionals and skilled workers were forced to accept employment in predominantly Romanian districts. In the development of the urban centers in the 1970s and 1980s, notably of Cluj, Oradea and Brașov, Romanians were given some advantages as regards housing. As a result the per centage of Hungarians in those towns decreased (Kovrig, 1986, p. 481).

The example of Sibiu (Hermannstadt) illustrates the remarkable ethnic and class transformation over time. An ancient Saxon-German city, Hermannstadt was 98 per cent German and two per cent Romanian in 1720. Between 1867 (the reunification with Hungary) and 1910, the German population had declined to 56 per cent (Romanians 21 per cent, Hungarians 19 per cent). Today, the city is almost exclusively Romanian, with its immigrant population consisting mainly of poor rural folk, recruited in Moldavia and Wallachia (Deák, 1992, p. 48).

The gradual Romanianization of education started with the requirement that Hungarian schools (or Hungarian sections of Romanian schools) give part of their lessons in Romanian. Schöpflin and Poulton (1990, p. 13) estimate that in the 1980s, about 40 to 50 per cent of the school-age children of Hungarian nationality were taught in Romanian. History books were rewritten in order to correspond with the Romanian theory of Dacian-Roman continuity. Hungarian historical atlases were strictly forbidden. Outside Transylvania the situation was even worse. In 1958 the Csángós of Moldavia had seventy-two Hungarian-language schools, and they were all closed. At the University of Cluj, the Hungarian teaching staff was gradually diminished and those who remained had to teach in Romanian-language departments (Kovrig, 1986, p. 482).

There were some special radio and television broadcasts in the Hungarian and German languages, but these were strictly rationed (two hours of TV a week) and controlled. Some books in Hungarian could be published, but they were worthless. Like the broadcasts, they contained nothing of interest to the Hungarian community; they reflected official Romanian policy, translated into Hungarian. During the last years of the Ceaușescu regime, even the official newspaper of the Hungarian Communist Party was forbidden in Romania. Hungarian historical monuments, buildings and graves were neglected or destroyed. All elements of bilingualism disappeared from daily life, even in the almost-homogeneous Hungarian towns. By the end of the 1980s, the tensions between Hungary and Romania had reached a critical point. More and more Hungarian Romanians fled to Hungary. In view of the gradual political change in Hungary, the government could now officially accuse Romania for its maltreatment of the Hungarian minority. There was even talk of the threat of a civil war in Romania.

The emigration of Germans started at the end of the seventies, when the German Chancellor, Helmut Schmidt, and Nicolae Ceaușescu made an agreement that allowed 12,000 Germans to migrate to Germany each year. A secret clause of that treaty required West Germany to pay 5,000 Deutche Marks (DM) for each migrant. Five years later, the price went up to 7,800 DM, which allowed a higher number of migrants, about 15,000 each year. The decision to leave the country was made by the Germans at an early stage, right after the war; they had to wait for an opportunity. Even before the fall of Ceauşescu, about half of the German population in Romania had applied for emigration to Germany. This was stimulated by poor living conditions in the eighties (for all people in Romania) and the 'romanianization' campaign of Ceauşescu, which also affected the Germans. The special broadcasting in the languages of the minorities was stopped in 1985, officially to save energy. Starting in 1988, the German press had to use Romanian names for villages and cities. The continuing emigration of teachers and pupils made it difficult to maintain education in the German language (Gabanyi, 1991b, p. 494).

Though life for the Germans was difficult, it was much worse for the Gypsies. The Gypsies, not recognized as an official minority, were frequently placed in the worst housing without basic services, in the worst areas. They were not treated equally in the workplace and have long been directed into the dirtiest and lowest-paid jobs (Helsinki Watch, 1991b). Ceausescu's perverse plan to reduce the total number of villages in Romania from 13,000 to 5,000 or less, by means of the bulldozer (*Sistematizare*), and to house the farmers in blocks of flats without running water, was an assault on all farmers in Romania. It affected the entire farming population of Romania but it was seen by Hungary as a programme especially designed to hit the minorities. Turnock (1991b, p. 259) criticizes this idea. In his opinion the *Sistematizare* was national in scope and also affected the Romanian population. No cases of the bulldozing of Hungarian villages have come to light. The continuation of the programme strongly affected the Gypsy population, with their outlying hut settlements and encampments. But the Gypsy problem did not attract much international attention.

Evaluation and perspective

During the first post-communist years, nationalism is growing in almost every country of the former Eastern Bloc. This phenomenon is observed by many in Western Europe with great disapproval. How is it possible that protectionism and nationalism are dominant in Eastern Europe, while 'modern developments' in Western Europe are focused on cooperation within the European Community? Apart from the fact that the process of Europeanization is accompanied by a lot of national animosity, in my opinion, this attitude is an arrogant 'West European-centrism', that does not respect the right of nations to catch up with 'natural' historical developments. The establishment of nation-states in Western Europe was the outcome of a long process of violent clashes and a struggle for civil and cultural rights. In Eastern Europe nationalism was suppressed by the great empires that dominated the region, in most cases until World War I. Within the Habsburg Empire, the Hungarians were oppressed. When the Hungarians got more influence, after the 'Ausgleich' in 1867, they started a 'magyarization' of the minorities within the Hungarian part of the Dual Monarchy. The right to catch up with history does not imply a kind of modernization theory, whereby the East European countries first have to follow the road of civil wars before they can reach the so-called West European optimum. But the road to better understanding among the several nationalities will be long, and we must take into account the special context in which nationalism is emerging.

History plays a pervasive role in Romania, as it does in the whole of Eastern

Europe. All nationalities have their own 'collective memory', based on (sometimes imaginary) grievances from the past. Historic differences in socio-economic status, in culture and in power have led to frustrations and even to the urge for revenge. From a West European vantage point, the dispute over which nationality lived in Transylvania in the second century seems ridiculous. But we must be aware that the passions raised in this debate originate in the 'magyarization' just mentioned, and the 'romanianization' under the Ceauşescu regime. The two world wars had a great impact on the region. First of all, the territorial disputes determined the borders of Hungary, Romania and the Soviet Union. And these borders had major implications for the various nationalities in Romania. The Hungarians and the Romanians could fight out their old disputes, while the Jews and the Germans were seen as respectively the scapegoats and the aggressors during and after the wars.

The cultural differences between the nationalities in Romania play a great role: the Romanians, whose language is similar to Latin and French, feel surrounded by Slavic and Hungarian speakers. The German group lived in relative isolation, maintaining their German language and culture over the centuries. The Gypsies, with their varied culture and traditions that evolved from ancient origins in India, are considered by all others as outsiders. Cultural differences have led to feelings of cultural superiority, and this has caused irritation. The words spoken by the Hungarian Foreign Minister after the Treaty of Trianon are characteristic: 'the Hungarians are the outpost to defend the moral values of the West against semi-barbaric conditions from the East'. On the other hand, the Romanians created the national myth of being the last bastion of Christianity against the infidel and that Romanian bravery has been ignored by the West (Deák, 1992).

During the communist rule in Romania, the minorities enjoyed short periods of relative tolerance. But most of the time, and certainly since the early 1970s, it was difficult for the minorities to maintain their ethnic and cultural identity. Nationalism was the privilege of the state, manifested most clearly in the ideology of Romanian superiority under Ceauşescu. This state-led nationalism, sailing under a counterfeit flag of communism, became more and more violent and oppressive. This had an enormous impact on the whole population, making Romania the darkest place in Europe at the end of the 1980s. The minorities probably suffered even more than the rest. They were also subjected to policies of resettlement. And they were sometimes sent to labour camps, for example, to carry out the absurd project of building a canal from the Danube to the Black Sea.

Now that the belljar of repression has been lifted, individual feelings can be expressed in Romania. They may lead to xenophobia; this is a negative side effect of an otherwise positive development: that after the fall of Ceauşescu, freedom of speech has been reinstated. Suspicion is raised when local and state authorities do not respond to discrimination and even violence against minorities with conviction; the Romanian government failed to respond after the revolution. One gets the impression that the government is making malicious use of the emotions of rising Romanian nationalism because of its unstable power position. Soon after the enormous electoral victory of Iliescu and the National Salvation Front, the support for the new regime deteriorated. There were justified feelings that the second echelon of the former Communist Party was then in charge. The transition to a market economy, initiated by this government, was accompanied by a serious decline in the standard of living. This fact alone was sufficient to create a fertile matrix for rising Romanian nationalism and xenophobia.

The several minority groups in Romania have been treated in different ways, and each group has its own peculiar way to draw attention to its plight. The Szekler Hungarians are large in number, and their sense of ethnic unity is strong; they are proud of their cultural heritage. Yet another factor is even more important: because the Turks had no great impact on Transylvania, it is the 'homeland' for all Hungarians. Because of their early occupancy of Transylvania, and their strong roots in this region, it is not likely that they will migrate to Hungary on a large scale. Perhaps this would be more likely for the Hungarians who live along the border with Hungary. Their orientation toward Hungary is stronger, and the proximity would make migration easier. Up to now, that migration flow has not occured, but that could change if tensions between Romanians and Hungarians increase. The group of Csángo Hungarians is much smaller, and has deviated more from their original cultural mainstream. No detailed information about their quality of life is available. In general, the Hungarians have good access to the Western media, and they are thus able to express their grievances, which irritates the Romanians. This strengthens the Romanians' opinion that the West is not taking them seriously, imposing on Romanian culture the stigma of 'oriental backwardness'.

The Gypsies are ignored by everybody and, of all minority groups, they suffer the most. Their situation now is even worse than under the Ceauşescu regime, with rising hatred, expulsion, and destruction of their possessions. They are the scapegoats for all the social ills and the government is not actively protecting them. The scapegoats of the past, the Jews, now form such a small group and are so widely dispersed around the country, that we can hardly say they are part of the minority problem. Nevertheless, anti-semitism is clearly manifest in the streets and in the media.

The Germans, the Saxons and the Swabians, who once were invited to immigrate for colonization purposes, have played an important role in urban social and cultural life. World War II had an enormous impact on these groups: many fled to Germany or were deported. The majority of those who were left after the war decided to emigrate to Germany but this became only possible in the seventies and was restricted to a limited number each year. The character of the post-Ceauşescu regime and the deteriorating living conditions explain their urge to leave Romania. In the near future, only 20,000 elderly Romanian Germans are likely to remain of the 800,000 who lived there in 1939. Because of the importance of Germany as a trading partner, every regime in Romania has been interested in a special settlement for this minority group.

Verdery (1991, quoted in Deák, 1992, p. 48) argues that under Ceauşescu, nationalism was becoming the main vehicle by which the party and the intellectuals were able to discredit Marxism and to set out an independent course for Romania, independent from Moscow. In an attempt to gain a monopoly over the formulation of national ideology, academics, historians, philosophers and literary critics battled for a greater share of official patronage. It was their intention to prove the superiority of Romanians over both the Slavs and the Hungarians. According to Verdery, the revolution of 1989 started with the protest of older party leaders again Ceauşescu's attempt to detach Romania from the West. And these old Bolsheviks were still emotionally attached to their Western antecedents, as Silviu Brucan and other former Stalinist ideologues explained in their March 1989 letter of protest to Ceauşescu: 'Romania is and remains a European country. . . .You have begun to change the geography of the rural areas but you cannot move Romania into Africa.'

After the revolution the Iliescu regime repeatedly stated that Romania belongs to Europe. When Romania was accepted as a member of the European Council, this was celebrated as a major victory. Until now, the government has not done its utmost to protect the fundamental human rights of the minorities. The treatment of the minorities could be the European barometer to forecast real democratic reform in the future.

References

Apponyi, A., 1928, *Justice for Hungary*, Longman, London.
Beyer, B., 1991, 'Chronologie der Ereignisse in Rumänien im Zeitraum September 1989 bis zu den ersten freien Wahlen und der Bildung der Regierung unter Petre Roman Ende Juni 1990, *Südosteuropa* **39** (9): 477–492.
Bodea, L. and V. Cândea, 1982, *Transylvania in the History of the Romanians*, Praeger, New York.
Deák, I., 1992, 'Survivors', *The New York Review of Books*, March 5, 43–51.
Engbersen, D., 1983, 'Magyaren en Dako-Romeinen: nationalisme op de Balkan', *Oost Europa Verkenningen* (119): 32–39.
Gabanyi, A.U., 1991a, 'Präsident Iliescu gegen Premier Roman: Frontenbildung in der 'Front der Nationalen Rettung', *Südosteuropa* **40** (9): 423–440.
Gabanyi, A.U., 1991b, 'Bleiben, gehen, wiederkehren? Zur Lage der deutschen Minderheit in Rumänien', *Südosteuropa* **40** (10): 493–517.
Georgescu, V., 1991, *The Romanians: A History*, Ohio State University Press, Columbus, OH.
Ghermani, D., 1983, 'Zur Lage der ungarischen Minderheit in Rumänien', *Südosteuropa* **32** (1): 30–36.
Ghermani, D., 1986, 'Rumäniens Ungarn-Syndrom', *Südosteuropa* **35** (10): 589–600.
Helsinki Watch Report, 1991a, *Since the Revolution: Human Rights in Romania*, March, New York.
Helsinki Watch Report, 1991b, *Destroying Ethnic Identity: The persecution of Gypsies in Romania*, September, New York.
IHF evaluation of the current human rights situation in Romania, June 1991. International Helsinki Federation for Human Rights (unpublished).
Illyés, E., 1981, *Nationale Minderheiten in Rumänien. Siebenbürgen im Wandel*, Wilhelm Braumüller, Wien.
Illyés, E., 1982, *National Minorities in Romania*, Colombia University Press, New York.
Kovrig, B., 1986, 'The Magyars in Romania: Problems of a 'coinhabiting' nationality', *Südosteuropa* **35** (9): 475–490.
Mihok, B., 1990, *Ethnostratifikation im Sozialismus, aufgezeigt an den Beispielländern Ungarn und Rumänien*, Peter Lang, Frankfurt am Main.
Nemzetör (publ), 1965, *Die Siebenbürgische Frage*, Verein Ungarische Bücherfreunde in der Schweiz, Wien.
NRC Handelsblad (NRC), various editions.
Osterhaven, M.E., 1973, *Transsylvanië.: de Hongaren in Roemenië*, Internationale Raad van Christelijke Kerken, Amsterdam.
Paul, L.J., 1991, 'The Hungarians in Romania: portrait of an explosive minority issue', in: Amersfoort, H. van, and H. Knippenberg (eds), *States and nations: the rebirth of the 'nationalities question'* in Europe, pp. 59–78. Nederlandse Geografische Studies, no. 137, Amsterdam.
The Plight of the Hungarian Minority in Romania Since 1918. A Historical Analysis, Institute for Hungarian Studies, 1989, Transylvanian World Federation, Budapest.
Schöpflin, G., 1978, *The Hungarians of Romania*, Minority Rights Group, London.
Schöpflin, G. and H. Poulton, 1990, *Romania's Ethnic Hungarians*, Minority Rights Group, London.
Seton-Watson, R.W., 1943, *Transylvania: a Key Problem*, Leplay Society, Somerville College, Oxford.

Turnock, D., 1991a, 'The changing Romanian countryside: the Ceauşescu epoch and prospects for change following the revolution', *Environment and Planning C; Government and Policy* 9 (9): 319–340.

Turnock, D., 1991b, 'The planning of rural settlement in Romania', *The Geographical Journal* 157 (3): 251–264.

Verdery, K., 1983, *Transylvanian villages: three centuries of political, economic and ethnic change*, University of California Press, Berkeley, CA.

Verdery, K., 1991, *National ideology under socialism: identity and cultural politics in Ceauşescu's Romania*, University of California Press, Berkeley, CA.

Volkskrant (VK), various editions.

11 Environmental politics, democracy and economic restructuring in Bulgaria*

John Pickles and the Bourgas Group

Humanity's historical responsibility is an interpretive task, 'naming' both the potential of the new nature (now synonymous with nature's 'redemption') and the failure of history to realize it. (Walter Benjamin quoted in Buck-Morss, 1990, p. 240).

Introduction

In an essay published at the time of the coup in the Soviet Union, E.P. Thompson (1991, p. 3) suggested that

> one of the great lessons of communism under challenge in the past 10 years - from Polish Solidarity onwards, and above all the East European lesson of autumn 1989 - has been that awe of the state has been falling away: think of Gdansk, Wenceslas Square, and Leningrad this week. Ideological doping no longer works, the instruments of repression are less effective, the rulers have lost confidence in themselves, the people have been re-learning their power when aroused in great numbers.

However, Thompson ends his essay with 'A note of warning'. At the European Disarmament Convention, which ended as the coup in the Soviet Union was proclaimed, Soviet participants were obsessed with national autonomy with human rights and minority rights poor second and third concerns:

> So rejection of the coup may not be an outright victory for 'democracy'; it may also be a victory for populist Russian nationalism against bureaucrats and ideologues. That is not altogether bad, but populist nationalism is by no means an unqualified good either.

With these words, Thompson evokes the dilemma of democratic movements in Central and Eastern Europe in which issues of demonopolization, anti-bureaucraticactions, local

*This chapter draws upon intensive fieldwork carried out by the author and the Bourgas Research Group: Robert Begg, James Friedberg, Boian Koulov, Krassimira Paskaleva, Didi Mikhova, Phillip Shapira, Stefan Velev, Brent Yarnal. and Branimir Zaimor A preliminary version of the chapter was presented to the International Geographical Union Conference on 'Redrawing the Geopolitical Map: Eastern Europe, Central Europe, Europe' Charles University, Prague, Czechoslovakia, August 1991. The chapter has benefitted from discussion with the Bourgas Group, Martin Bosman, Deszu Kovacs, Lazlo Farago, Wolfgang Netter, Sandor Peter, Judit Peter, Lynn Pickles, Michael Watts and Daniel Weiner. The research is supported by a grant from the John D. and Catherine T. MacArthur Foundation Program on Pearce and International Cooperation. The author is responsible for any errors.

power, and individual and civic rights have arisen along with new and old forms of nationalism, ethnic struggle, local competition, core-periphery dominance, the segmentation of consumer markets, and the substitution of political for economic power.

Table 11.1   Environmental movements in Eastern and Central Europe

---

Bulgaria

Ecoglasnost, which played a major role in the overthrow of President Zhivkov, is active as an environmental movement, a non-government organization, and an organization (not a political party) with its own members in Parliament. It recently posted the highest approval rating of any political 'party'. Several of its members serve in influential environmental positions in the government. The Green Party, has recently split into three groups.

Czechoslovakia

Older environmental groups such as Brontosauras and the Czech and Slovak Unions of Nature Protectors are now independent and are being joined by other smaller groups. The Green Circle is a coordinating group for about 33 environmental groups in the country. There is a national Green Party and a Slovakian Green Party called 'Trend for the Third Millenium'.

East Germany

The environmental group in East Germany was fostered greatly with the help of the Lutheran Church. ARK is one such network, which merged with other groups in 1990 to form the Green League. A Green Party was established in 1989. Following reunification there was a merging of environmental groups and Green parties.

Hungary

Several environmental groups and Green parties have formed around particular issues. In Budapest an environmental movement emerged out of a battle against the building of a dam on the Danube. In southern Hungary an environmental group emerged to protect fauna and flora in a mining region. An environmental research institute (ISTER) has been established, along with an Independent Ecological Center serving as a resource centre for local environmental groups. The Regional Environmental Center has been established in Budapest, funded primarily by the EC and the USA.

Poland

The Polish Ecological Club grew out of Solidarity in the early 1980s, and some of its members now hold environmental positions in the government. Several Green parties exist, as well as over 40 other environmental groups, including the Green Federation, Zoology and Health, and the Franciscan Ecological Movement.

Romania

The Ecological Movement of Romania (MER) operates as both an environmental group and a Green Party, and has taken a leading role in politics. There are many local environmental groups with a large membership.

Source: adapted from French, 1991.

These issues find resonance in the three central themes in this chapter. The first theme concerns the central role played by the environmental movement in challenging the legitimacy of the command economy and its state apparatus as the politics of protest erupted throughout Eastern Europe (and the Soviet Union) in the late 1980s. In each of the countries of Eastern and Central Europe the environmental movement seems to have played a distinct and important role in fostering and enabling a broader coalition of political forces to emerge under difficult and repressive conditions (Table 11.1). Specifically, this chapter traces the emergence and successes of environmental politics in Bulgaria in these years and the role played by environmental politics in forging a shift from the reformist democratization policies of the old regime to the democracy movement that led to the new governments and dismantling of the command economy after 1989.

The second theme concerns the evolving tensions between democratic practices and the emergence of new forces of social division in Eastern Europe following the revolutions of 1989–1990. In this regard, the chapter addresses changes in the regional and local structure of power in Bulgaria, focuses upon the shifting balance between centrist/technocratic and grassroots/populist tendencies within the body politic, and assesses their implications for the environmental movement.

The third theme concerns the form of explanation we give to these changes in the political sphere. While some authors (for example, Musil in this volume) suggest that the revolutions of 1989–1990 are an important step in the evolution of a universal history characterized by the expansion of market economies, liberal democratic practices, and recognition of the incompatibility of political democracy and central planning, and that these revolutions were primarily political revolutions without economic or social causes, I take a different view in this chapter. The chapter situates the political changes in the context of the social and economic conditions from which they emerged, and evaluates the implications of these social and economic conditions for the continued success of a grassroots environmental politics. Thus, the first half of the chapter briefly indicates the importance of the fiscal crisis of the central state for the success of the politics of protest, while the second half of the chapter suggests that the environmental politics of mass mobilization that flourished in 1989–1991 has been weakened by the normalization of political life and by the continued deepening of the economic crisis at all levels.

Central planning and the hubris of giganticism

At the end of World War II 80 per cent of Bulgaria's workforce was employed in subsistence agriculture. By the 1960s the economy had been transformed into an 'industrial–agricultural' economy tied to raw material and market supports from the USSR. By 1984 71.9 per cent of Bulgarian exports went to Comecon countries and 55.7 per cent of the total went to the USSR (Pitassio, 1989, p. 205). National growth seems to have occurred along with income equalization (at least until the early 1980s), and social services and social welfare were rapidly improved in aggregate terms.

In contrast to these apparent and real improvements in the quality of life are the terrible consequences of the mechanisms used to achieve them. Property was expropriated. Productive resources were collectivized in the hands of state managers and bureaucrats. Restrictions on movement were introduced and rigid influx controls into the city were enforced. National economic development was achieved by subsuming all other concerns to a productionist ideology in the cities and the countryside. In what Eric Green refers to as the 'hubris of giganticism' (Green, 1989, p.1), Soviet-style central planning and norms were imposed on every sector of production. Among the most visible consequences were environmental and health problems. As in the Soviet Union, the environmental consequences and resulting health problems were tremendous and, as in the Soviet Union, a particular attitude towards the environment emerged:

> our economy conducts itself towards nature like the conqueror of a weak country. Many people are complicit in this, beginning with the managers of the economy and ending with common workers (Frolov, 1988).

The entire economic structure and system of management operated to induce people to pollute, and often such inducements were not only implicit but were made quite explicit, as in the slogan exhorting workers to work harder: 'we cannot wait for favours from nature; our task is to take them from her' (quoted in Green, 1989, p. 2). Michael Colby (1989, p. 6) refers to this model of exploitation as frontier economics, in which the promise of infinite growth is achieved by the application of high-energy, low-efficiency technologies and mechanized production without regard to or knowledge of the ecological consequences of such actions.

Consequently, environmental issues have always been of secondary concern to industry, and the costs of such practices have been externalized to the surrounding community. For example, in the town of Kameno (near Bourgas in southeast Bulgaria, and downwind from one of the largest petro-chemical complexes in Europe) respiratory diseases are 2.7 per cent higher than the (already high) national average, circulatory diseases are 87 per cent higher, blood cancer levels are 97 per cent higher, and Infant Mortality Rates are 50/1000 compared to a national average of 13–15/1000. These 'hot spots' are replicated in several sites throughout Bulgaria: radioactive materials mined from a uranium mine used to be carried in open carts; toxic wastes (including cyanide) derived from production processes in the electronics industry used to be discarded in open dumping sites; for many years irradiated waste was dumped straight into the Bourgas bay where bathers swim; and a zinc and lead smelter at Plovdiv continued until 1991 to emit heavy metal wastes directly into the air and onto the vegetable fields nearby.

Estimates of ecological and economical problem areas run as high as 75 per cent of the total area of Bulgaria. Currently 60 per cent of the value of the total capital assets of the country is in industry, especially in heavy industrial branches, and one half of this industry is in ecologically unsound production, employing 600,000 people. If these plants were to be closed an estimated 400,000 jobs would be lost, a drastic measure given that unemployment in March 1992 stood at about 600,000.

Oleg Chulev (Vice President of Podkrepa, the new radical trade union confederation) has suggested that the form of economic organization that gave rise to such practices should be called 'anti-economy', and that the transition from 'anti-economy' to economy parallels that of other Central and Eastern European countries. This is a transition from a bureaucratic state capitalist (Cliff, 1988) and bureaucratic authoritarian system (Burawoy, 1985), in which the necessity to meet production norms took priority over the protection of environment and health, the provision of social infrastructure, and the effective use of labour. In this context, the local authorities had very little power or effective jurisdiction over the enterprises and their activities, and even when fines were levied they did not go to those who were affected by pollution, but to the national government and the district council. [1] According to the Mayor of Dolno Ezerovo, a small village near the petrochemical complex outside Bourgas: 'Ecology has always been the last chapter in economic development plans'.

From democratization to the politics of protest

Political delegitimation and the environmental crisis

> Ecological problems do not arise spontaneously, they are the consequence of our technological and ecological incompetence, bad management, and irresponsibility (Morgun, 1988, p. 13).

It used to be said that when the Soviet Union sneezed, Central Europe caught a cold, and Bulgaria came down with the flu. Jokes such as these are numerous in Bulgaria, and are meant to reflect the way in which the Zhivkov regime obediently followed the direction of, and directives from, the Soviet Union. Such obedience arose from the enormous material benefits that the relationship brought to Bulgaria. Throughout the 1950s, the transformation of the Bulgarian economy was supported by the USSR. Bulgaria's economy was propped up by a Soviet supply of raw materials, machinery, technicians, and loans, as well as by the guaranteed market it provided for agricultural and industrial goods. Inefficient production, poor-quality goods, and over-centralization of the economy were protected under this arrangement, as was the continued party monopoly of political life and the rapid expansion of social infrastructure, particularly in the urban areas. Despite claims by the central state that it sought to restructure production, decentralize aspects of decision-making, and open markets beyond Comecon, attempts to increase levels of enterprise autonomy by decentralizing decision-making (known collectively as the New Economic Movement) failed to revitalize production or narrow the technology gap with Bulgaria's competitors in international markets. By the mid-1980s, the costs of refurbishing urban infrastructure had become unbearable and the quality of housing in the cities was deteriorating rapidly. The costs of state-controlled production and reproduction increased, while the ability to generate sufficient capital to cover these costs was constrained by outmoded technology, fixed markets, and rigid systems of decision-making within enterprises. The Zhivkov regime turned increasingly to foreign loans to support inefficient production and to increase urban consumption. By 1989 the state had amassed so large a burden of debt that the government was forced to halt repayments, and subsequently also halted payments of interest on the debt. The political crisis of the state of 1989–1990 thus emerged out of a fiscal crisis of both production and reproduction. It is in this context of debt crisis, unproductive enterprises, and declining social infrastructure that the emergence of an effective politics of protest organized around environmental and health issues must be understood. Moreover, it is through this environmental politics of protest that the movement for human rights, the restoration of human dignity and civil liberties, the control of the state, and the struggle for political and cultural pluralism was articulated.

Environmental politics and the ecological defence

The particular origins of the environmental movement as an opposition, democratic movement lie in the formation of local political groups involved in civil disobedience in an attempt to prevent the continued pollution of local communities. These local environmental movements are all the more remarkable because they arose during a period when the central state had placed strict prohibitions on any such civic actions, and in a society in which information about environmental issues was suppressed.[2]

For example, since Bulgaria's uranium mines were a state secret, public debate about the health hazards to residents in nearby villages and to workers in the mines was virtually impossible (Searle and Power, 1989, p. 25). To this day topographic maps are still classified documents and penalties for their use, possession and copying are severe. Under such constraints, how did the environmental movement succeed in becoming a national social and political movement?

Sharp criticism of ecological problems in Bulgaria emerged publicly in July 1987. At a national ecology conference, organized in Sofia by the National Committee for the Protection of the Environment, several researchers revealed that:

> The most severe sanctions known to have been imposed on polluting enterprises are fines, but in 98 per cent of cases courts refuse to fine offenders in accordance with the law, mainly because managers have repeatedly circumvented environmental legislation in order to fulfil plan targets.[3]

In the same year criticism of government policy and of scholars emerged in the April Literary Discussion in Sofia, where Ivan Golev challenged environmental experts to speak out:

> We have so many experts in various branches of science. Where are they? There are many towns and regions in Bulgaria that are already polluted by contaminated air, water, and soil. What about Rousse, this beautiful city of ours that is systematically being poisoned by the industries of our northern neighbours and friends? Where are these experts? They should be standing up as one body to force our government to confront the problem honestly and solve it.[4]

The Rousse Group was the first public opposition group organized around environmental issues. Rousse is the fourth largest city in Bulgaria, with a population of 180,000. The population of Rousse had been exposed to chlorine and other gas emissions from a chemical factory across the Danube in Rumania (Bell, 1990, p. 419). On 2 June 1988 (Children's Day), a demonstration was organized by mothers in the community demanding that the air pollution be stopped. The event was not reported in the government-controlled media, but a documentary film depicting the event resulted in the formation of the Civil Committee for Ecological Defence of Rousse on 8 March 1988 (the so-called Rousse Committee). The Committee was declared an anti-state organization, its members were harassed, and the Institute of Philosophy at the Bulgarian Academy of Sciences (where some of its members worked) was shut down and fifty-four research associates were dismissed.

By the end of 1988, the Sofia Club for Glasnost and Perestroika had been founded and the first regional group of the club – 'Civil Initiative' – was formed in Rousse.

One year later a national movement – 'Civil Initiative' – was founded in Sofia on the principle that meaningful change would not arise out of the 'July concept' reforms of the Zhivkov regime, but from popular defence.[5]

In April 1989 Ecoglasnost was formed as a grassroots social movement striving for 'a democratic public climate and up-to-date ecological consciousness to challenge the stagnating monopolism and demoralizing command centralism in all spheres of social life having to do with ecological problems' (Ecoglasnost, undated).   The group emerged to counter a reformist group of politicians who argued that change would be best achieved within the old system by the gradual reform of the party and the command economy. This reformist position was the basis for the government's own measures to democratize central planning by devolving limited powers to the local and regional councils and to enterprises (Creed, 1990, pp. 45–65; Pitassio, 1989, 204–216). Ecoglasnost and the trade union federation Podkrepa, by contrast, advocated the abolition of the old system, mass mobilization of opposition to the communists, and the creation of a liberal democratic government and market economy.

The major goals of Ecoglasnost are: (1) free access to environmental information; (2) protection of people's health and safety; and (3) the change of the old system and the building of democracy. The Policy Statement of the Social Movement Ecoglasnost argued:

> we should be aware of the fact that [bureaucratic functionaries] are usually entrapped in an all-embracing network of biased administrations, whose apparatus runs like a steam-roller OVER both environment and public opinion, as well as OVER the merely symbolic punitive sanctions applied by official environmental protection agencies. This calls for DEMOCRATIC PUBLIC CONTROL OVER ECOLOGICAL POLICY. Recognizing the need for ECOLOGICAL SELF-DEFENSE of the citizens, the participants in the movement ECOGLASNOST are resolved to unite their efforts for a deep SOCIAL AND ECOLOGICAL RECONSTRUCTION. They see the major strategic weapon of the struggle as FULL ECOLOGICAL GLASNOST, which is the precondition of the people's control over the existing institutional activities (Ecoglasnost, undated, original emphasis).

This explicit call for the building of a 'radical democracy' based on citizen-rights and citizen-participation gave rise to a series of fourteen major demands by the movement ranging from the right to clean air, water, soil, and foodstuffs; the abolition of classified data; full disclosure of nuclear dump sites; medical information about the population; broader access to and dissemination of information as it is collected; expansion of environmentally protected areas; new laws governing the press reporting of environmental issues; freedom to travel and discuss environmental issues; and changes in school curricula to include ecological education.

In early 1989 several other civic opposition groups arose to challenge the hegemony of the Communist Party and the central power of President Zhivkov in particular. The Labour Confederation Podkrepa, the Committee for Religious Rights and Liberties, and the 272 Committee, among others, arose alongside the environmental groups. Approximately fifty organizations formed during 1989, but by the end of the year the most important groups had joined together to form the Union of Democratic Forces (UDF) (Bell, 1990, p. 420). The UDF was extremely effective in organizing mass demonstrations in Sofia, and these demonstrations resulted in an agreement with the communist government to enter into televised roundtable discussions about the future of the country and agreements to legalize political parties, to move towards multi-party elections in 1990, and for the government to provide resources to the opposition press and time on television to be given for debates between the candidates.

The Bulgarian revolution was certainly aided by the sequence of events throughout Eastern and Central Europe in 1989 and 1990, but the nature of the transition in Bulgaria has been somewhat different to that in other countries. In Bulgaria the revolution has occurred (and continues) more cautiously, in a series of stages. First, the popular protests of Fall 1989 led to the ousting of Todor Zhivkov from the Presidency and head of the Bulgarian Communist Party – a kind of coup internal to the party machinery itself. His position was taken by the Prime Minister, Andrei Lukanov (a member of the Bulgarian Socialist Party (BSP), the reformed Communist Party) who led the BSP to an electoral victory and the formation of a new government. However, by November 1990 he was also forced to resign by growing opposition within the country, and directly by street demonstrations and strikes of thousands of people. Before leaving his position Lukanov organized a caretaker or provisional government – a 'government of peaceful transition'. This provisional government operated at all levels from the national to the local, with participation determined proportionally based on seats won in the previous election. The provisional government operated until October 1991 when a new government of Union of Democratic Forces (UDF) was formed. In January 1992 the UDF candidate was elected President with a plurality of votes. The BSP candidate came in second with 47 per cent of the vote and with strong support in rural areas, among the elderly, and in certain industries.

The level of influence exercised by Ecoglasnost in shaping national environmental policy is unparalleled, and is illustrated by its claim in 1991 to be the only environmental NGO operating in Bulgaria, compared to Hungary which had about 200 environmental NGOs at that time.[6] The political role played by the organization depends on the particular issue and its context. Its platform declares that:

> ECOGLASNOST participants wish to be CONSISTENTLY INDEPENDENT from all state institutions in order to keep their ability to stand up for their pluralistic and democratic values and to offer their own radical democratic alternative on every ecological issue (Ecoglasnost, undated, original emphasis).

However, in 1990 Ecoglasnost did run candidates for the Grand National Assembly because that assembly was to write the new constitution and a number of important laws, such as the new environmental law and the law of privatization. Many Ecoglasnost supporters worked in the Ministry of Environment during the period of the provisional government, and, in coalition with other groups such as the Green Party, Podkrepa, and other UDF groups, the environmental movement generally was able to persuade the BSP to allow the new environmental and land privatization laws to pass despite their opposition to them.

At the local level Ecoglasnost boasted several early important victories in its struggles for ecological defence. There are now local groups acting on issues of local and regional concern and affecting local planning decisions. In the harsh winter of 1990 Ecoglasnost, together with the trade unions and other groups, effectively organized a series of local groups to blockade all Black Sea ports, preventing the export of foodstuffs needed at home. In 1991 they managed, along with the local community, to persuade the Deputy Minister of the Environment to reassess earlier decisions on the Plovdiv lead and zinc smelting plant, and to close down the most polluting lines. As an association of over 100 community-based groups, each with between fifty and 100 members, Ecoglasnost has become the principal environmental organization in the country. It has been able to mobilize public support effectively and citizen action around key issues of pollution, democratic control and economy.

How do we account for the emergence and success of such democratic environmental movements, and what changes have begun to emerge in them as broader restructuring processes begin to affect both the body politic and the economy? While many see the revolutions of 1990 as primarily political revolutions (see Musil in this volume), such an explanation in inadequate for understanding the complex and rapid changes occurring in contemporary Bulgaria. In order to understand these changes and the effect they are having on environmental politics it is necessary to consider the economic conditions that led to and permitted the politics of protest to succeed in 1989 and 1990, and the restructuring of the body politic that is currently occurring as civil society is extended and parliamentary politics is normalized.

The 'normalizing' of politics and its effects on the environmental movement

With the rise of new forms of democratic politics, some of them initiated at the level of the state, others forged through popular struggles and ecological defense, new structures of civil society have emerged (but see Zizek's (1990, pp. 50–62) arguments about the 're-invention of democracy' in Eastern Europe). Grassroots environmental movements and the struggle over environment and health have been a central part of this democratic politics. Popular struggles and ecological defence have challenged crucial elements of bureaucratic management, state-enterprise collusion, the destructive effects of productionist ideologies, and the inefficiencies of large state enterprises which are not accountable to workers, the local community or the law. Through these struggles, emerging strong local democratic practices and institutions have been developed.

In fact, environmental politics has attained a surprising degree of legitimacy. For example, in 1991 the authors of the new environmental law, many of the people in the Ministry of Environment, the Mayor of Sofia, and the administrator of Bourgas were all Ecoglasnost members. Moreover, the Green Party claimed that while its share of the 1990 electoral vote was only 4.5 per cent, 69 per cent of the population supported its policies. Even at the international level, policy recommendations for fiscal reform and privatization now involve environmental issues. Thus, for example, in June 2–22 1991 a World Bank, US Environmental Protection Agency (EPA) and US Agency for International Development (AID) Joint Environmental Mission visited Bulgaria to prepare with the Government of Bulgaria an Environmental Strategy Study as part of negotiations for new loans to the country (World Bank, 1991).

However, not all aspects of the transition process can be seen as opening up the spaces for democratic action and ecological defence. Several issues complicate the democratic potential of the process of restructuring and transition, and challenge some of the gains already made by the democratic movements, especially in the realm of environmental protection.

Restructuring government and the economy

As a consequence of the emerging economic and fiscal crisis of the state, the failure of reform politics to deal effectively with the crises of production and legitimation, and the success of social movements (especially the environmental movement Ecoglasnost), rapid changes in government policy and practices occurred after 1989. The democracy movement, seen previously elsewhere in Eastern and Central Europe, emerged in Bulgaria and resulted in a rapid redirection of state policies from bureaucratic centrism, nominal decentralization and self-management, to market-oriented mechanisms, real decentralization of power from central to local government, demonopolization of state enterprises, and privatization of property (especially in agriculture, services, and industry).

These three policies – decentralization, demonopolization, and privatization – form the basis for the current democratization process, and each has important implications for the shifting balance between central state and local state, enterprises and unions, social movements and individuals, rural and urban areas.

One of the major effects of economic crisis and the delegitimation of central planning is the inability of the central state to maintain effective control over all the functions of planning and government. Moreover, the adoption of market-oriented policies is occurring along monetarist lines in which the state is withdrawing from arenas of social and economic life in which it used to be heavily involved. Consequently, new forms and new powers of local government have been emerging in the past two years. At the same time, the demonopolization of state enterprises and the transfer of power from state bureaucrats to individual managers and entrepreneurs have shifted the fields of power operating between local government and enterprises. In many cases, local governments are gaining increased levels of regulatory power over the new enterprises, a situation encapsulated in the new environmental law, which gives local authorities strong powers to regulate and even close polluting enterprises. In other cases, demonopolization is resulting in decreased levels of control. Thus, for example, under central state planning, all enterprises reported directly to the state all information about employment, wages, purchases, sales, etc. In the new circumstances, enterprises report to no state officials or government bodies, and local authorities have even less access to information about the activities of large-scale industry.

In the interregnum, privatization also functions in similarly ambiguous ways. Since the laws are only now being written, many would-be entrepreneurs and investors are wary of committing to specific projects. Less scrupulous or better connected entrepreneurs show no such reticence. Again, in a 'not-yet-regulated' economy the role of the local state is ambiguous. Now able to develop its own laws and regulations to a greater extent than ever before, the local state is also even more captive to the willingness of private companies and landowners to provide information. And, as economic conditions continue to deteriorate, the local state is further captive to the demands and threats of businesses for the reduction of local regulations.

These circumstances of national and regional economic crisis, increasing enterprise autonomy, and an only partially formulated division of powers between the central and local state, have greatly affected the environmental movement.

International organizations and structural adjustment

The reform years and the lead up to 1989–1990 were characterized by one very important economic fact: when the new provisional government took over in 1990 there was no money in the Treasury. The government was effectively bankrupt. Partly as a result of the expenditures of state finances and foreign loans to deal with the effects of the climatically disastrous years of 1984–5, partly from subsidizing social consumption in the reform years, and partly because of propping up unprofitable industries throughout the 1980s, the government had drained its coffers and rapidly increased its debt burden. The consequences of this fiscal collapse were unprecedented in two ways. First, the Provisional Government declared a moratorium on the repayment of foreign loans, later extended to include interest on loans. Second, because of such absolute economic collapse, when new foreign loans were renegotiated with the IMF, Bulgaria had little leverage over the conditions under which the loans were given. The international lending banks and the IMF had *carte blanche* in making their demands to this unreliable borrower. The influence of these international organizations in the current restructuring has thus taken on something of the character of a shadow government, and the impacts are extensive and deep.

IMF policies of structural readjustment are being applied, albeit in amended form. The government is actually being encouraged to slow down the pace of privatization and demonopolization, in order to restructure state enterprises before they are sold and protect the future industrial and employment base from massive plant closure of unproductive lines and sectors. Furthermore, the unprecedented leverage the lenders experience in Bulgaria, combined with their own need to legitimize their lending activities internationally in the face of criticism from environmental groups worldwide, have made the Bulgaria case an interesting one. Indeed, the transition in Eastern Europe generally represents an interesting paradox at the international level. In the past, agencies such as the IMF and the World Bank have been severely criticized for the ways in which their structural adjustment policies have had impacts upon the environment. Criticism has been most strong in regard to IMF/World Bank projects in Amazonia (see Pickles and Watts, 1992). In Eastern Europe, however, international agencies have adopted a very different approach to economic and political restructuring. While their policies and tools bear close resemblance to structural adjustment programmes elsewhere in the world, they have adopted a very pro-active stance on environmental issues. Thus, for example, the IMF team which visited Bulgaria in 1991 took along with it a US EPA team to develop an environmental report, and policy prescriptions for economic change include within them certain environmental requirements.

In a perverse way environmental conditions are improving as a direct consequence of restructuring. Opening Bulgarian industry to international markets and the removal of state subsidies and protections is resulting in the rapid restructuring of production and the closing of inefficient enterprises. Environmental pollution *will* be reduced by these policies, but it will decline as a result of plant closure and technological replacement – both of which will increase the number of the unemployed and result in enormous social costs.

The government has adopted rigorous structural adjustment programmes recommended by the International Monetary Fund (IMF), and current economic policy is based on IMF policies of privatization, price and financial stabilization, reduction in government expenditure, reduction in social programs, increased efficiency, and unemployment. Financial stabilization policies have focused on the liberalization of prices, drastic increases in interest rates, from 3 to 45 per cent basic interest, the formation of a hard currency market, and allowing the lev to float against the dollar (to as high as 30 leva = \$1 compared to a former official rate of 1 lev = \$1).

Since 1 February 1989, when liberalization of prices was initiated, 90 per cent of prices have been liberalized. Controlled prices remain on only fourteen groups of consumer goods, and the only fixed prices are on energy and electricity. The result has been that between 1989 and 1992, prices have risen by 7 to 10 times. Not surprisingly, there has been a massive drop in the levels of consumption of goods, between 50–55 per cent. Typical figures for income and living costs illustrate the impact on the family level. From an income level of 100 per cent (450–670 leva/month), 60–70 per cent is spent on food, 7 per cent on transport, and 20 per cent on electricity, heating, etc. Where a family has a second income, 40–45 per cent of the second income goes on food. Salaries have increased only about 20 per cent in the same time.

The transfer of political to economic power

One important, yet under-theorized element in the transition period has been the role of red and black capitalists. These are businessmen and women who have moved into the new markets and into the demonopolized industries and privatized retail and service outlets from a prior base of economic or political power in the Communist Party or in the black market (arms dealers, smugglers, and other illegal activities). A combination of three factors has been important.

First, the BCP systematically sought to recruit young members into the party who were intelligent and active. Many saw the party either as socially attractive or as socially necessary. Consequently, a large proportion of new capitalists are now being drawn from the ranks of the former BCP, some of whom are proving to be very effective in their efforts. A positive interpretation of this shift is that party leaders were well trained and educated, and hence it should not be surprising that they do well in the new system. A critical interpretation is that we are seeing what Bulgarians call 'chameleon' capitalism at work. 'Chameleon' capitalists are individuals who change their 'colour' to suit the environment in which they find themselves; they survived well under communism, and they are surviving well as capitalists.

Second, the reform politics in the 1970s and 1980s encouraged a greater diversification of party activities and permitted increased levels of autonomous business activity in agriculture and to a lesser extent in industry. Party members were instrumental in implementing these reforms at the level of the enterprise, the cooperative, or local government. Consequently, as these units of management and production have become increasingly privatized, these same individuals have been well placed to benefit from the reforms.

Third and most recent, there has occurred a massive and rapid transfer of political power among party bureaucrats and nomenklatura into economic power. With the recent phase of demonopolization, individuals have taken advantage of their party privilege and connections and have 'jumped' into the new economy, either as enterprise managers prior to privatization, as founders of new banks prior to deregulation, or as service and retail outlet directors prior to privatization. According to researchers at the Independent Trade Union Federation (ITUF) 'There are almost no examples of real privatization without such elements. Privatization is being carried out by people who have power and money' (Interview, Research Institute for Trade Union and Social Studies, Sofia, 6.17.1991). This form of 'bandit' capitalism is an extension of 'chameleon' capitalism, and involves not only the shift of an individual from one system to another (from 'red' to 'blue'), but also involves the transfer of economic resources, either in the form of a state enterprise, money, or other objects of value.

Red and black capitalists are significant because of their economic (and still strong political) power, the depth and intricacy of their system of connections, and particularly for the brand of market activities adopted by the most daring of them. In Reagan's America they might be called 'cowboy capitalists'or 'fast capitalists' (Agger, 1989). Moreover, these 'transfers' often adopt the language of environmental politics, in the face of their personal records in earlier times. In Czechoslovakia they are called 'green meloni' because they are green on the outside, but red on the inside.[7]

Social movements, NGOs and the loss of political momentum

Initially, the environmental movement permitted a diverse array of political interests to mobilize around Ecoglasnost, and to present a common front to the government of Zhivkov. As political life has normalized in the past two years, these groups have begun to articulate independent agendas, new groups have arisen, new problems in the economy have come to light, and the universal support previously given to the environmental groups has begun to diminish. Consequently, a shift has occurred within the environmental groups themselves.

Not only is the mobilization of mass support more difficult because of the normalization of politics generally and the continued economic difficulties facing the country, but environmental groups have to deal with internal tensions resulting from their dual goal of mobilization and democratic organization on the one hand, and the need to organize resources to carry out research on environmental 'hot spots' on the other hand. The 1991 split within Ecoglasnost occurred along these lines, between the 'hippies' and the 'yuppies'. The former supported continued mass mobilization and political action, the latter supported a withdrawal from politics and a concentration on building an effective non-governmental organization (NGO), organized for ecological defence. While the former group sought to extend networks of Ecoglasnost at the grassroots level, the latter group sought to concentrate efforts on distancing itself from political parties in order to maintain and extend links with the emerging international agencies concerned with environmental problems.[8]

A parallel shift has taken place in the Green Party (GP). In distinction to green parties elsewhere in Europe, the Bulgarian Green Party now argues that it is not a social movement, but is engaged in parliamentary politics. Ecoglasnost is seen by the GP as the social movement for the environment, whereas the domain of responsible action for the GP is in government. This is also partly a response to the size of the task facing the new parties (from writing a constitution to writing laws governing every aspects of social and economic regulation) and the limited resources available for such work. But the decision not to concentrate on mass mobilization and environmental and political education through engaged practice becomes more significant when we see this delimitation of the Green Party's activities to parliamentary politics in the light of Ecoglasnost's decision to reduce its own emphasis on popular action and grassroots organization. The consequence is a loss of momentum in mobilizing the grassroots democratic movement around environmental issues.

One consequence of the normalization of politics – the adoption of a Western multi-party and electoral system, the apparent shift from mass mobilization to the creation of a technocratic NGO, and the weakening of the environmental movement nationally – has been a loss of political momentum in the country generally. The turn away from grassroots organization to the formation of research cadres in the environmental movement raises the question as to whether popular struggles for ecological defence will be much less central to the democratic process in future than they have been in the past two years. The failure in the 1991 elections of the Green Party to gain the necessary 4 per cent of the vote to remain in Parliament is indicative of the emerging importance of economic over environmental issues.

Technocracy and democracy

The depth of the economic crisis facing the country seems to have produced a form of politics in which ideological differences are put to one side in the interest of managing the crisis. In the structure of Provisional Government, local and regional councils were represented according to the proportion of seats won by each party in the 1990 election. For example, the Bourgas District Council was run by a provisional executive from the BSP. The Executive Council was composed of eleven people: four from the BSP, four from the Opposition/UDF (including the Deputy Chairman), two from BANU (the agricultural party), and one Independent. At the national level, whole Ministries were divided between political affiliations and responsibilities apportioned accordingly, with environmentalists being given responsibility for dealing with issues such as the writing of the new environmental law. Some argue that this situation was possible because all parties agreed on what had to be done. In interviews, local government leaders indicated that it is rare that a problem is not solved for political reasons: that politics was always secondary to bread and butter issues in provisional council decisions (Interview with Nedelcho Pandev, Chairman of the Provisional Executive Committee of the District Council of Bourgas, 24 June 1991).

In an effort to further foster this tradition of consensual politics, the government created in 1990–1991 a parallel form of management system/provisional government. Throughout the country at local, regional, and national levels – trilateral commissions – comprising political leaders, enterprise managers, and union officials were established. This 'shadow' government emerged rapidly as the forum in which a great deal of coordination occurred and many decisions were made. The purpose and impacts of the trilateral commissions are little discussed, and little is known about them.

Interpreting these emerging traditions of cooperative politics is not easy. Certainly there has emerged an unusual degree of tolerance to those who managed the past, and this is reflected in the still high level of electoral support received by the BSP. There remains a high level of cooperation between groups with ostensibly different interests. Whether this has arisen as a result of past party affiliations, or is emerging out of the need to deal with crisis conditions, is difficult to say. Regardless, there is a strong technocratic and scientistic nature to much of the emerging discourse. As in other parts of Central and Eastern Europe, the intelligentsia and the technically skilled were negatively affected under the old system unless they worked with and within it. They were also the group that gained increasing positional power throughout the 1980s as economic and structural change occurred. These skilled professionals were major actors in the revolutions of 1989 and 1990 throughout Eastern Europe (Ascherson, 1991, 127-128). This was no less true in Bulgaria, and can be seen, for example, in the make-up of the leadership of Ecoglasnost, the Green Party, and the UDF.

Despite their initial support for the mass mobilization of the population, there remains (or is emerging) a deep distrust of popular movements and mass mobilization. In spite of the evidence of its effectiveness in 1989 and 1990, organizers and activists remain sceptical about the 'Bulgarian character'. There is talk of its totalitarian nature, its desire to be led and to be told what to do. Others speak of the absence of democratic traditions in the Balkan lands, particularly among the rural peasantry, and of the need for 'rational' planning and 'skilled' leadership. These views have emerged more strongly with the deepening economic crisis.

The role of the state is particularly problematic in this regard. The rejection of central planning and command systems of management is also a rejection of a strong state, a policy encouraged by Western organizations like the IMF. In keeping with this anti-state perspective, Slavoj Zizek has recently argued:

> Paradoxically, we could say that what Eastern Europe needs most now is *more alienation*: the establishment of an 'alienated' state that would maintain its distance from civil society, that would be 'formal', 'empty', embodying no particular ethnic community's dream (and thus keeping the space open for them all) (Zizek, 1990, p. 62).

However, the question of community in this newly emerging world is a crucial one, with important implications for the success of grassroots social organizations, such as the environmental movement.

In this context, community has two conflicting meanings. One refers to the democratic action of a group of people striving to protect their lives and livelihoods. The other involves a reactionary understanding of community as a defensive closure of one group against another group which constitutes a real or perceived threat. In Bulgaria at the present time, this 'otherness' is not just being asserted, but is being actively constituted, and in such a way as to fragment broadly based social movements along ethnic, regional, and class lines. Ethnically 'otherness' is constituted around the fear of gypsies (*csyginy*) and the Turkish minority. Under increasing economic pressure, such ethnic differences have become increasingly real factors in political action, and they have been reflected recently in the monolithic voting bloc formed by the Turkish minority in voting for Human Rights Party. Socially, 'otherness' is being constituted by the state and the public as both cause of and explanation for economic and social destabilization in terms of criminality. Crime statistics used to be extremely low in Bulgaria. In recent years, crime statistics have begun to rise and the public expresses a great deal of concern and fear about theft and violence. Without challenging the accuracy of these fears, it is important to recognize the functionality of 'crime paranoia' in a society undergoing rapid changes, where the police force was formerly aligned entirely with the old regime and is now seeking to rehabilitate itself, and where the state needs to be able to explain in the short run the frictions in everyday life which emerge out of structural adjustment. Criminality and a growing climate of civil disobedience and petty crime are, in a perverse way, functional to all of these goals.

These tendencies to define 'otherness' have an interesting effect in the economic sphere. The rise of red and black capitalists is a well-known phenomenon in Bulgaria, but there is also a sense in discussions and interviews that red and black capitalism serves as an explanation for the emerging differences in economic power in the society. Thus, it is argued, since only BSP members and arms dealers had money under the previous regime, those who are successful now or who now have money to purchase enterprises must have been communists or black marketeers. The effect of this view is that a broadly held suspicion exists of the economically successful. Thus, while in Bulgaria under Zhivkov possession of a Western car meant privilege within the party, in modern day Bulgaria the white Mercedes is a 'sure sign' of dirty money. The indirect consequence is a redirection of attention away from the general polarizing effects of the modernization process and towards laying the blame on the legacies of party power and influence. In such a situation, theories of conspiracy and corruption can be readily substituted to explain the impacts of broader forces of restructuring.

These processes of social differentiation have a strong spatial component. Locality competition is increasing as demonopolization, decentralization and privatization occur, and will continue especially if the economic crisis persists. The nature of the resultant forms of locality competition will be interesting, creating new forms of state–business coalitions. Given the prior association of local government, community enterprises and party officials, it seems likely that some localities will attempt to recreate these associations as a local state–business alliance for local development. One example of this new alliance for local development is the case of the community enterprise ECOPAN and the town of Malko Turnovo in the southern part of Bourgas, which is attempting to establish a new regional enclave based on regionally specific attributes (natural and historical), geographical location (Malko Turnovo is a market town close to the southern border of Bulgaria and on the road to Turkey), and the power and influence of the community enterprise ECOPAN.

New forms of regional competition combined with ethnic and social conflict, severe economic crisis, and high (and increasing) rates of unemployment pose serious challenges to an effective environmental and grassroots democratic politics. While in some regions and some sectors of industry new forms of private enterprise or state–business coalition have been created to deal with environmental problems (particularly as the monopoly of power of the central state is removed and new powers devolve to the local state and the private sector), in general the relationship between economic and environmental concerns is seen to be one of conflict. The two major trade union federations increasingly find their ability to support environmental positions undermined by the very real threat of plant closure. Workers experiencing rapidly increasing prices, decreasing incomes and uncertain futures, continue to defend long-established practices whereby they are paid higher wages for working in dangerous environments. The economy–environment debate is creating increasing divisions within the newly emerging civil society, undermining the ability to maintain or extend mass support for the environmental movement, and forcing groups like Ecoglasnost to work in different ways to foster increased environmental awareness. Heated debates continue within the environmental and mass democratic movement about the role and form of environmental politics under these conditions.

Conclusion

Environmental problems and local concerns about health have provided the focus for the mobilization of the mass democratic movement *and* have become universally accepted parts of political rhetoric. Thus, the tools or policies of renewal and the problems of the environment constitute important aspects of the struggle for political power.

There has been an extended period of transition from the political dominance of the Bulgarian Communist Party to a system of political pluralism (see Crampton, 1987; McIntyre, 1988). In the emerging situation of political pluralism, the degree of political power and electoral support retained by the communist party (now the Bulgarian Socialist Party) remains quite high. The BSP was the majority party until the October 1991 elections, where they gained 33 per cent of the votes. In this context and in complex ways, perestroika, glasnost, democratization, and decentralization have become both policy adjustments aimed at retaining power for an aging and increasingly delegitimized party bureaucracy, as well as the rallying demands of the democratic movements.[9]

The deepening economic crisis since 1989, exacerbated by the absence of clear national policy and the rapid adoption of market-oriented mechanisms, has created problems for the environmental and the democratic movements. New forms of economic power have arisen in the interregnum, with important implications for both the democratic movement generally and environmental issues in particular. Moreover, bread and butter economic issues have become so pressing that they have reduced the support for environmental issues, and now threaten the emerging civil structures which are so central to effective democratic and environmental politics.

The deepening economic crisis has had a weakening impact on the emergence of an independent policy arena within Bulgaria, and has favoured a (re)assertion of a culture in which solutions are sought from the outside and from technical experts. In these circumstances, international agencies and foreign governmental bodies have been surprisingly influential in the formulation of public and environmental policy, and correspondingly Bulgarians have been surprisingly eager to accept those policy recommendations.

The conjuncture of new challenges to old powers, the difficulty of putting new regulations in place, the emergence of new political forces, and the problems for the environmental movement arising out of economic crisis must also be situated in a broader theoretical and geographical perspective of international restructuring and the emergence of new forms of production, new regulatory environments, and new challenges to environmental politics.

The modern future that will emerge for the new democracies of Central and Eastern Europe is not yet clear. Will an economy emerge which produces any social surplus at all or will Bulgaria emerge as an economy in perpetual crisis? If economic growth can occur, will it permit the development of a Keynesian social welfare state, in which social markets are protected, regulations are institutionalized to protect health, the working day, and to provide insurance and decent wages? Or will Bulgaria emerge into a post-modern world of deregulated markets and fast capitalism, in which speculation in property, services (such as tourism), and finance capital has higher priority than investment in production?

Three issues, in particular, have been central to understanding these processes in this chapter. In Bulgaria, as elsewhere in the region, 'the environment in the pre-revolution days also served as a rallying point from which broader demands for political change emerged. Opposition to the state found expression in struggles over the environment, and protests against pollution quickly turned into protests against Communist rule. Initially perceived by governments as relatively benign, environmental movements in the region soon acquired unstoppable momentum' (French, 1991, p. 93) (Table 10.1). However, while the popular democratic alliances forged across the country between 1988 and 1990 remain strong, and while Bulgarian society has opened up in many ways, there is some evidence that these gains are already in retreat in the face of deepening economic crisis *and* the difficulties of dealing with it. Finally, the process of economic restructuring, revitalization, and environmental reconstruction in Eastern Europe is occurring in the context of a world economic order itself undergoing a rapid and deep-seated restructuring. These parallel and related restructurings have important implications for the nature of regional development processes and the ability to protect democratic practices and rebuild healthy environments in Bulgaria and throughout Eastern Europe.

Notes

1. According to the Head of the Economic Development Section of the District of Bourgas (Interview, 6/24/1991), fines are now apportioned 50 per cent to the Ministry of Environment (for the environmental fund) and 50 per cent to the District Council for the Ecology Fund. This fund was begun in March 1990. 'These funds are absolutely insufficient to meet the needs of the District. They are basically used for some scientific research, not for infrastructure or technological change.' It is still in the interest of the Regional Inspectorates to send the funds to the Ministry of Environment rather than the District Council.
2. The growth of civic organizations and opposition groups in the late 1980s is documented in Radio Free Europe's *Soviet/East European Report* series and in the *Yearbook on International Communist Affairs* (1988–1990).
3. Reported in *Radio Free Europe Research* 8 July 1987, drawn from *Rabotnichesko Delo*, 12 July 1986 and 'The Environment and Eastern Europe' RAD Background Report/42 (Eastern Europe), *Radio Free Europe*, 20 March 1987, pp. 5–6.
4. *Literaturen Front*, no. 17, 23 April 1987. Reported in *Radio Free Europe Research*, 8 July 1987. It is important to bear in mind that the emerging environmental movement was supported and encouraged by Radio Free Europe's broadcasting. Thus, in a 1987 report of ' Ecological Problems' the report begins with a report from Radio Sofia of a national conference, critical commentary on the Romanian polluters and their effects on the city of Rousse, and the quotation in the text. Here the research community is chastised for not standing up – with patriotic zeal – to challenge the Bulgarian government to deal with the Romanian neighbours' and friends' devastating pollution. It is through the 'other' of the Romanian government that popular forces are mobilized against the laxity of the Bulgarian bureaucrats. To clarify the nature of this popular versus centrist appeal to patriotism, the report immediately continues: 'RFE's Bulgarian Service has, incidentally, received repeated telephone calls complaining about the pollution in Ruse caused by Romanian enterprises in and around Giurgiu'.
5. The 'July concept' reforms were initiated in 1987, calling for administrative and economic reorganization, political democratization, the expansion of press freedom, and experiments in multi-candidate elections. The early experiments were short lived: following the exposure of several cases of official corruption, the press was again subjected to strict controls and some editors and journalists were fired (see Bell, 1990 p. 418).
6. This claim is somewhat misleading. Since Ecoglasnost operates as a loose affiliation of local groups, other smaller NGOs such as SOS operate as part of Ecoglasnost.
7. I am grateful to Petr Dostal (Universiteit van Amsterdam) for this observation in discussion of my paper at the International Geographical Union Conference on 'Re-Drawing the Geo-political Map: Eastern Europe-Central Europe-Europe'. Prague, August 1991.
8. Many of these agencies will only fund NGOs.
9. The precise implications of the October 1991 general elections and the December 1991 and January 1992 Presidential elections have yet to be analysed. Despite the fact that the BSP lost the elections, the relatively high percentage of the vote they obtained suggests that they remain a significant political force.

References

Agger, B., 1989, *Fast capitalism. A critical theory of significance*, University of Illinois Press, Urbana and Chicago.

Ascherson, N., 1991, 'Two winners for each loser in Europe's new promised lands', *Europe from below: An East–West dialogue*, edited by Kaldor, M., Verso, London, 127–8.

Bell, J.D., 1990, 'Post-Communist Bulgaria', *Current History* **89**: 32–38.

Buck-Morss, S., 1990, *The dialectics of seeing. Walter Benjamin and the Arcades Project*, MIT Press, Cambridge, Mass.

Burawoy, M., 1985, *The politics of production: factory regimes under capitalism and socialism*, Verso, London.

Cliff, T., 1988, *State capitalism in Russia*, Bookmarks, London.

Colby, M.E., 1989, *The evolution of paradigms of environmental management in development*, SPR Discussion Paper No.1.

Crampton, R.J., 1987, *A short history of modern Bulgaria*, Cambridge University Press, Cambridge.

Creed, G.W., 1990, 'Between economy and ideology: local level perspectives on political and economic reform in Bulgaria', *Socialism and Democracy* **12**: 45–65.

Ecoglasnost, undated, *Policy statement of the social movement Ecoglasnost*, Sofia, mimeo.

French, H.F., 1991, Restoring the East European and Soviet environments, *State of the world 1991*, Norton, New York: 93–112.

Frolov, I., 1988, *Sotsialistichiskaia Industriia*, December 3.

Green, E., 1989, The political economy of environmental protection in the Soviet Union. Paper prepared by the staff of the American Committee on U.S.-Soviet Relations, No. 8, February.

McIntyre, R.J., 1988, *Bulgaria: Politics, economics and society*, Pinter Publishers, London and New York.

Morgun, F., 1988, Speech to the 19th Party Conference, *Pravda,* July 2. Translated by *Foreign Broadcast Information Service, Daily Report on the Soviet Union* (FBIS), July 6 1988, 13.

Pickles, J., and Watts, M., 1992, 'Paradigms for inquiry? Explanation and criticism in contemporary human geography', in Abler, R., Marcus, M., and Olson, J., *Geography's Inner Worlds*. Rutgers University Press, New Brunswick, New Jersey, 301–26

Pitassio, A., 1989, 'Reform politics in Bulgaria', *Telos*, Spring, **79**: 204–216.

Searle, D., and Power, M., 1989, 'Bulgarian authorities close the party door on green activities', *New Scientist*, September **16**: 25.

Thompson, E.P., 1991 Mixed Soviet blessings, *The Guardian*, August **23**: 3.

World Bank, 1991, Aide-Memoire, Joint Environmental Mission, Washington D.C..

Zizek, S., 1990, Eastern Europe's Republics of Gilead, *New Left Review* **183**: 50–62.

Part IV
New electoral geographies

12 The electoral geography of the former Soviet Union 1989–91: retrospective comparisons and theoretical issues

Vladimir Kolossov

Political reforms in Eastern Europe since 1989 have allowed geographers to re-examine the long-hidden political patterns of this large part of the globe. Recent elections and referenda offer researchers an excellent opportunity not only to uncover the main features of a country's political differentiation but also to follow the rapid evolution of the electoral situation in constituent regions of the states of former Eastern Europe. Other opportunities lie in the identification of general trends in the transition period from totalitarianism to representative democracy and the study of the spatial relationships of voting choices and other political phenomena, in particular, ethnic conflicts and nationalism. Of course, work on the political and electoral geography of the former Soviet Union post-dated the 1989 revolutions. The first stage of studies in these fields, the accumulation of primary data and facts, is not yet finished but luckily, it is possible still to incorporate theoretical comprehension of the electoral patterns.

This chapter compares the macro-level spatial patterns brought to light by the elections to the Congress of People's Deputies of the USSR in 1989, the People's Deputies of the former Union republics in 1990, the all-Union and Republican referenda in March, 1991, and the Presidential election in the Russian Federation in June, 1991. Attention in this analysis will be focused on Russia, which, as the largest republic, exerted the strongest influence on all the other republics (now the countries of the Commonwealth of Independent States, CIS). The multi-national Russian Federation included regions which, in a political sense, were moving at very different speeds to representative democracy; to a certain extent, the problems of Russia were repeated elsewhere in what has recently been the USSR Finally, Russia was the first among the former Union republics to hold a general presidential election, thus allowing the introduction of additional variables, due to sharp political distinctions between candidates in this election.

A second aim of the chapter is to review theoretical aspects of the electoral geography of the former USSR and in particular, the opportunities to use electoral–geographical concepts based on Western studies. The first part of this section deals with political cleavages and constraints for electoral–geographical studies of the former USSR. The second part is devoted essentially to the analysis of voter turnouts in four elections in Russia as a universal index allowing the forecast of a large part of political returns; other electoral variables are also considered. In the third section, some geographical issues of the presidential election in the Russian Federation are described. The fourth section is dedicated to an explanation of electoral patterns in Russia and the last section presents theoretical perspectives of the former USSR electoral geography.

Recent elections and political cleavages

Theoretical approaches developed in electoral geography assume that electoral processes are based upon principles of liberal democracy. Taylor (1990) lists some of these principles: political freedom, pluralist elections, universal suffrage, and the consensus about the necessity of the state's funds redistribution. He stresses one other very important condition *sine qua non*, the stability of the political process and political regime. Obviously, in the Soviet Union of 1989–91, the electoral situation satisfied only two conditions and then, not without reservation. First, despite discussion about regions disadvantaged and advantaged by the state, deep egalitarian traditions determined views on the state's redistributive function. Second, though universal suffrage is proclaimed, the principle of 'one man - one vote' was not realized by the biased apportionment and districting. According to the first democratic electoral law of 1988, which regulated the election of People's Deputies of the former USSR, the uni-nominal system of absolute majority was adopted; all the republics, except Georgia, copied it later. At the time, legislators argued that it was the only system possible in the absence of the true multi-party political structure. Furthermore, there was no legal regulation of apportionment and districting. Unlike the usual practice in the Western democracies, seats were apportioned according to the number of electors (voters) and not the size of the population as a whole. Moreover, the execution of this principle was far from perfect. With the exception of biased anti-Russian districting in Estonia and Latvia, it was done very carelessly. In 60 per cent of the Russian oblasts and autonomies, which included more than three-quarters of the districts in this republic, the difference in population between the biggest and smallest districts was more than 20 per cent; there were a large number of examples when it ranged up to 400 per cent. Unfortunately, in the Russian Federation, the lessons of the first electoral campaign not only were not taken into account, but, worse, the districting which has been adopted since 1990 is even more mal-apportioned.

The first democratic (or, more properly, quasi-democratic) election took place in March 1989, after more than seventy years of totalitarian rule. During these decades, the efforts of the regime were directed to removing all existing and potential opposition and all regional identities that might give rise to protest movements. Previous social and territorial cleavages in the society were erased or, at least, strongly modified. For historical comparison, it is possible to look at the returns of only one election, the election to the Constituent Assembly of 1917, contested by organized and sharply divergent parties, on the basis of universal, equal, direct and secret suffrage. Recent elections happened against a background of the late abolition of serfdom (1861), a secular tradition of the life under highly-centralized authoritarian power and of a monolithic 'unity'. Voters, party activists or candidates had no experience of participation in free ballots.

Dramatic events resulting in the dismantling of the Soviet state are reflected in the electoral results. The political issues changed very fast, often in contradictory ways. In periods of revolutionary shifts, institutional and legal changes cannot keep up with public opinion. For example, almost three-quarters of the Ukrainian population supported participation of Ukraine in the Union of Sovereign Republics in March 1991, incorporating the idea of the preservation of the USSR itself. Only eight and half months later, in another election, the same Ukrainian voters buried any option of creating even a vague confederation. But regardless of the electoral outcomes, spatial analysis of these elections reveals fundamentally stable patterns that allow the ecological identification of the political behaviour of voters in the different areas.

Table 12.1 Elections and referendums in the former Soviet Union, 1989–1991

March 1989: Election of People's Deputies of the USSR. The experience of the first democratic election in the Soviet history; the formation of democratic parliamentary opposition at the all-Union level; the formation of party systems in Baltic republics and Moldavia; the creation of large social movements ('People's Fronts') in most other republics.

March–November 1990: Elections of People's Deputies of the Russian Federation and other former union republics and autonomous regions, of deputies of local councils in most Republics. The victory of nationalist-democratic forces in the Baltic Republics, Georgia, Moldavia and Armenia; the beginning of party systems formation in most republics; the strengthening of opposition democratic forces which won many parliamentary seats in Russia, Ukraine, Byelorussia; the victory of old communist elites in Azerbaijan, Kazakhstan and the republics of Central Asia; the 'war of laws' and the beginning of the deep political and economic crisis and of disintegration of the USSR.

January–March 1991: Referenda. 1) The all-union referendum; 2) republican referendums in the Russian Federation, in 3) Ukraine, in 4) the Baltic republics and in 5) Georgia. The adoption of a proposed formula; the moral victory and further strengthening of Boris Yeltsin supporters in Russia by winning in all the major cities and oblasts, and of supporters of the national idea in Ukraine; the legitimization of the declarations on independence in the Baltic republics.

May–August 1991: The election of the president of the Russian Federation and of Georgia. The overwhelming victory of Boris Yeltsin in the first round, legitimization of his power compared to that of Gorbachev, critical tensions between conservatives and democrats in the 'centre'.

August–December 1991: More elections. Presidential elections in Azerbaijan, Armenia, Kazakhstan, the republics of Central Asia and Ukraine; referendums on independence in Ukraine, Uzbekistan, Armenia, Moldavia; first presidential elections in former autonomous republics of Russia (Chechenia, Kalmykia). The disintegration of the USSR as a result of the August putsch; the victory of nationalist forces and the creation of the bloc between 'national-communists' and 'national-democrats' in Ukraine and in several other republics; the strengthening of State structures in republics; legitimation of old elites in Azerbaijan and the republics of Central Asia aspiring to keep power.

In the former Union Republics of the Soviet Union, voters have been called to ballot-boxes no less than three, or, more often, four times since the spring of 1989 (see Table 12.1). In most republics, except in the Baltic ones, in Georgia in 1990 and to a certain degree, in Moldavia, there were no multi-party elections as in Western liberal demo cracies. But the political alternatives were quite clear to the ordinary voter. On the power front, preservation of traditional communist power structures, cosmetic changes or major renovation of power structures in true reforms were offered. On the state-preservation front, whether to retain the large multi-ethnic state or whether separation, autonomization, sovereignty, or independence of the Republics was on the ballots. In 1989 the voter had to choose between candidates of the power establishment, 'chefs', and candidates suggested 'from the bottom', by the people, most of whom, if elected, constituted a parliamentary opposition. In 1990, opposition candidates could unite in common lists under the banner of the movement 'Democratic Russia' or similar banners. This development did not happen in all regions but essentially only in major cities (Moscow, Leningrad, Novosibirsk, etc.). After the election of 1990, the situation evolved to the formation of a *de facto* two-party system: 'Communists' ('conservatives') against 'Democrats' (reformers). In March 1991, in voting in the all-Union and Republican referendums, most electors said yes to both questions but the relation between the share of those who voted favourably for the election of a Russian President (it was clear that this post was destined for Boris Yeltsin) and who rejected the formula proposed by the all-Union 'centre', and those who were against the election of the president of Russia and supported the 'centre', allowed the identification of 'radical' and 'conservative' regions (Kolossov and Petrov, 1991). The vote on the Russian presidential election of June 1991 was more complicated with six candidates. However, the votes for four minor rivals of the two main candidates, Nikolai Ryzhkov, supported by the Russian Communist Party, and Boris Yeltsin, leader of the Democrats, were relatively small. But, importantly, these minor candidate votes shed light on the degree of dissatisfaction with both Ryzhkov and Yeltsin, and the spatial distribution of right-wing and nationalist movements.

Political opinion in the former USSR, as in other East European countries (Vanlaer, 1991), was divided along two main axes: the first, a political one, separates 'occidentalists', supporters of modernization leading to a civic society and the market economy, from those who believe in the 'third way', which could reconcile the need for reform with specific national values and history. The second main 'axis', an economic one, passes between radicals who defend the more or less comprehensive privatization of the economy and those who think that it is necessary to uphold the decisive role of the state in the economic sphere. The latter 'axis' is relatively close to distinctions between right and left parties in the West. In multi-national countries, like Yugoslavia and the former USSR, there is the third very important political 'axis': between adherents of the 'united and indivisible' Union and defenders of the sovereignty of republics. In the Russian Federation this 'axis' was reflected in discussions about relationships between the Union and Russia, on the one hand, and between Russia and the former autonomies on the other.

It is clear that these 'axes' did not coincide well with the most important political watershed in 1989–91, that between 'communists' and 'democrats'. The use of this dichotomy is fraught with the risk of excessive simplification. First, 'Democratic Russia' is a temporary and relatively unstable bloc of different parties and movements, united first by the idea of counteraction to the common rival. Second, and even more important, 'Democratic Russia' is not a party disposing of the network of regional organizations submitted to a common centre. It is an organization of 'cadres' trying to get influence in different localities. The weakness of the opposition was reflected in the fact that, before the attempted putsch of August 1991, it had a majority or a visible role in only five oblasts and large city councils of Russia. In the winter of 1990, a series of 'local revolutions' against corrupt and compromised regional Communist Party leaders did not result in great changes: first secretaries were simply substituted by their former lieutenants. The largest democratic parties have not attracted more than a few ten thousand members and nobody knows their real electoral strength. A number of well-known democratic leaders conscientiously try to keep their distance from any organized structures. Regional democratic organizations have very limited contacts between themselves and often try to avoid contact with headquarters in Moscow, fearing centralization tendencies.

From the social point of view, democratic organizations suffer from the perennial and traditional alienation of Russian intelligentsia from workers' movements. The charismatic strength of Boris Yeltsin is a result of his position as the only one leader popular among workers as well as among intellectuals. Democratic leaders in Moscow undertook great efforts to unite odd local organizations. In autumn 1990, several all-Russian newspapers were founded; though they became popular, until the autumn of 1991, the majority of them were sold in Moscow and Leningrad.

At the same time, the Communist Party (CPSU), merged with state structures, never was a party in the Western sense of this term. The CPSU was very far from being a monolithic political force which has been proven by the creation, in 1991, of dissident movements on both wings. There were many communists in all parliamentary groupings. Besides that, the existing party administrative structures had been widely used as a cover by growing nationalist forces. Thus, it was impossible to measure, even approximately, the influence of the different wings of both of the main political forces.

In autumn 1991, in Russia proper, a typical adherent of the 'third way' was usually close to 'patriots' and even 'nationalists'; s/he usually actively supported the unity of the country and s/he was against the large-scale privatization of the economy. In the fourteen other national republics, the struggle against the usurpation of all power by the 'centre' (Moscow) easily grew into true nationalism, which often became combined with democratic convictions and the belief in privatization. Therefore, the principal distinction between 'communists' and 'democrats' remains valid for the comparison of the four elections in Russia.

Under these conditions of temporarily black and white polarization of political life, can the four elections, appearing very different, be usefully compared? What approach, what indexes, are convenient for such a comparison, if there were no parties in the normal sense of this word? Elections in the former USSR cannot be analysed without some non-traditional indexes, approaches and methods. The need for such methods is based upon the importance of subjective factors in voting. In the 1990 election, people often got bulletins with two or three dozen names. Even for an experienced and educated voter, it was very difficult not only to separate candidates according to their views, but even to extract the essence of these views from the campaign literature. Under such conditions, the subjective characteristics of candidates played an important role. That is why a number of indexes characterizing the social class of a candidate, his rank in the administrative hierarchy, his membership in the CPSU, education, sex and age could contain important information about the electoral campaign and positions of electors. Electors dissatisfied with candidates and elections as a whole protested by striking out all the names from bulletins or taking them, but not putting them down in the ballot-boxes. The campaign intensity was to a degree reflected in the average number of candidates for one seat and by the number of rounds of voting.

As shown in earlier publications (Berezkin et al., 1989; Kolossov, 1991; Kolossov, Petrov and Smirniagin, 1990), the most significant index is the turnout; as a rule, it is well correlated with other variables. In the USSR, the lesser the participation, the

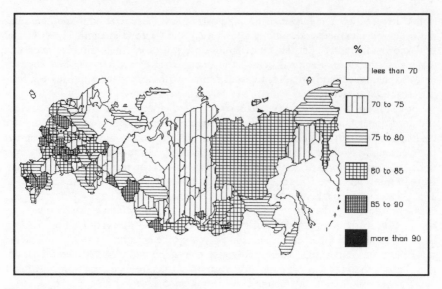

Figure 12.1   Turnout rate in the 1990 election

higher the political activity of the population; this was confirmed by all the elections in Russia. After seventy years, when elections were an obligatory and boring duty, people with more emancipated political consciences felt themselves free to speak their mind. Moreover, turnout is the only index allowing a comparison of all four ballots in Russia. But only detailed 'field' studies can give comprehensive information about the electoral campaign in a district: very often, similar statistical results describe different situations. Only 'field' studies assist in understanding spatial political differentiation at and below the level of electoral districts.

The stability and the predictability of voting

In 1989–91, two types of electoral patterns in the former USSR could be discovered. They are clearly seen on the turnout map for 1990 (see Figure 12.1). First, two linear territorial structures can be distinguished: in the majority of the area to the north-east of a line from Leningrad to Vladivostok, absenteeism was much higher than in the areas to the south-west of this diagonal. Second, absenteeism was much greater in all large cities in Russia as well as in other Union Republics. The turnout patterns remained the same from 1989 to 1991, though the turnout dropped progressively.

The range of spatial variation in participation remained almost the same (see Table 12.2), although in 1990 it would seem that the territorial differences in voting were diminishing. The high correlation coefficients show that the results of the first election in 1989 were not accidental; they occurred as a result of some fundamental cleavages. However, it should be noted that the correlations between turnout levels are lower than in Western countries, where spatial patterns in voting remain stable for a long time. The turnout of the three earlier ballots is correlated highly with the participation of the electorate in the presidential election of 1991 (0.71), a value that is higher than the coefficients of each separate vote. It is easier to predict the activity (and indirectly the results) of parliamentary elections on the basis of previous elections than on the basis of a Presidential ballot or of a referendum. Since turnout is closely related to political activity and the type of political behaviour of the population, the multiple correlation coefficient of turnout on rates of participation in previous ballots reflects the degree of predictability of voting among the constituencies. Mapping of the regressions residuals allows the identification of regions where political orientations have been most dynamic. The multiple regression equation seriously overestimated the turnouts in such remote areas as two Buriat autonomous districts in Irkutsk and Chita oblasts, in Bashkiria, in Dagestan and in Tuva. At the same time, the model could not predict relatively high turnouts in some Caucasian republics, Northern and Ural oblasts, where people came in surprising numbers to support the candidacy of Boris Yeltsin, who was very popular in these areas.

Table 12.2   Correlations of turnout rates in the Russian Federation, 1989–1991

	1989 election	1990 election	1991 referendum	1991 president
1989	1.0			
1990	+0.61	1.0		
1991 ref.	+0.50	+0.66	1.0	
1991 pres.	+0.54	+0.67	+0.55	1.0
Variation %	13.03	8.35	13.72	12.71

Predicting the turnout in the election of June, 1991 using the 1989 data gives the same result: the regression equation underestimates the decrease in the turnout. Stated another way, the degree of radicalization, tiredness, and dissatisfaction of electors with politicians and politics in North-Caucasian and Siberian republics and autonomous districts, and in Kuban, as well as in some areas which were among the most radical from the very beginning of political reforms – the oil-extracting northern parts of Western Siberia, Kemerovo (the main region of miners' strikes), Khabarovsk and Sakhalin regions in the Far East and the big cities of Leningrad and Moscow – all saw sharp falls in turnout. In the regions, where the regression overestimated turnout, Boris Yeltsin was by far the most popular candidate.

The regressions of the turnout on other votes allow an estimation of the influence of the subjective factor. The residuals of these regressions show areas where the process of political radicalization was more developed than in neighbouring republics and oblasts. Among these regions were radical and democratic areas in North-East Russia and the large cities, especially Nijny Novgorod (a heavily industrialized oblast with a poor infrastructure) and Volgograd. In the latter city, such a result undoubtedly echoed events of early 1990, when the first secretary of the local Communist Party committee was dismissed after a series of mass rally protests.

The regression results also reflect the very complicated situation in the Northern Caucasus, where the different attitudes of the native population towards the all-Union and new Russian democrat authorities resulted in varied turnouts and other electoral results, especially in Kabardino-Balkaria, Northern Ossetia and Checheno-Ingushetia.

Northern Ossetia was traditionally considered the main support of Moscow power (the majority of Ossetians are orthodox Christians); the region leans on Moscow's support in conflicts with neighbours. Besides, the South Ossetians saw in the preservation of the Soviet Union the chance to unite or at least to improve the situation of Southern Ossetians who remain in the now-sovereign Georgia. The initiatives of the new Russian authorities, and the personal intervention of Boris Yeltsin on behalf of the Ingushes, while supporting the idea of Georgian independence, were not supported in the Ossetian lands. By contrast, in Checheno-Ingushetia, native discontent with the central authorities was high because of the reaction of the latter to Ingush claims to Northern Ossetia, which had received fertile Ingush lands after the deportation of Ingush people to Central Asia towards the end of World War II.

The hypothesis that turnout on the previous vote is related to choices on quasi-two-party votes, referenda and the presidential election, was examined. Spatial patterns of turnouts conform to the spatial variation of other electoral variables. The average number of candidates for each seat more than doubled in comparison with the March 1989 election. There were a lot of districts where the choice was among more than twenty competitors. As a rule, these very competitive districts are concentrated in socially-active regions, with low turnout most of all in the capitals. This traditional distinction between urban and more rural regions in the number of candidates was becoming less clear by 1990.

The positions of candidates in the administrative hierarchy were evaluated by rank. One rank was given to a candidate who did not occupy any administrative post; the highest, the sixth rank, meant that a candidate was a member of all-Union or all-Russian leadership on the day of election. The average social rank of candidates by oblasts and former autonomies in 1990 was lower than in 1989 (compare Figures 12.2 and 12.3). The averages were 1.87 and 2.20 by territorial districts in 1989 and 1991 and 2.24 and 2.44 by national–territorial ones. These differences reflect democratization of the elections and of the electoral law which eliminated discriminating selection meetings of 'workers' representatives'. The social rank index was usually higher in regions

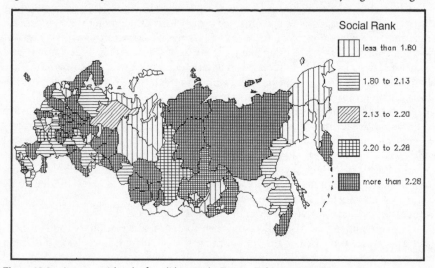

Figure 12.2   Average social rank of candidates in the Russian Federation 1989

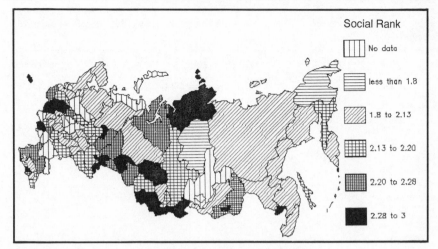

Figure 12.3   Average social rank of candidates in the Russian Federation 1990

with more traditional types of electoral behaviour, in particular, in the southern oblasts and in some oblasts of Central economic region, where almost all the traditional local nomenklatura was balloting (and more often elected). The figures for Moscow and Leningrad are lower than average, though both large cities concentrated on a great number of highly placed leaders. At the same time, in 1990 there were many exceptions; for example, in the Sverdlovsk oblast, one of the democratic strongholds, many local leaders were involved in the electoral campaign. That is why the diagonal 'north-west–south-east', according to this index, was not so clear in 1990 as in 1989 (compare Figures 12.2 and 12.3). The spatial variation of the average social rank also followed the fundamental alignment that regions of high political activity are areas characterized by low turnout, high number of contenders for deputies' seats, and a relatively low social rank of candidates and deputies.

The presidential election in Russia: roots of a multiparty system

The strong influence of Boris Yeltsin's charismatic image, of the widespread belief in a leader proportionate to the Russian national character, resulted in a weaker predictive power of the previous vote turnouts. The results of both election turnouts have higher correlations with the percentage of the votes for Nikolai Ryzhkov than with Boris Yeltsin (see Table 12.3). The high correlations between the results of the referendums and the vote for both main candidates in the Presidential election is more evidence that the quasi-two-party system was formed in 1990–1991, as their territorial spheres of influence are related like a mirror reflection. This conclusion is confirmed by the maps and the statistical indexes describing the vote for all the six candidates to the Russian presidency. As expected, the vote for Ryzhkov is highly negatively correlated with the share of votes gathered by Yeltsin (see Table 12.4). Nikolai Ryzhkov, considered a defender of old Communist Party structures and interests, and more moderate V. Bakatin, former Minister of the Interior, deposed in November 1990 in the period

Table 12.3   Correlations between voter turnout and results of the 1991 Russian presidential election

	'Yes' all-Union referendum	'Yes' on Russian fed. referendum	% Yeltsin	% Ryzhkov
Election 1989	+0.48	+0.32	+0.17	−0.27
Election 1990	+0.72	+0.52	+0.45	−0.46
Referendum	+0.68	+0.82	+0.48	−0.57
'Yes' all-Union referendum	1.0	−0.62	+0.68	−0.73
'Yes' on Russian referendum		1.0	+0.76	−0.78

of the active counter-offensive of the conservatives for his 'too liberal' policy towards the Union Republics, seemed nevertheless to form 'the centre' of the political spectrum in this election.

Choosing between them, voters preferred Ryzhkov who received the official support from the CPSU as well as the Russian Communist Party. Bakatin could obtain no more than a very small percentage of votes in a few regions; his vote shares do not correlate very strongly with the influence of Ryzhkov. The very weak correlations between the percentages of the other three outsiders are most interesting. V. Zhirinovsky, president of the so called liberal-democratic party, and General A. Makashov can be considered as candidates of the extreme right; these candidates attracted people greedy for populist demagoguery and for pseudo-patriotic slogans. By some stretch, the votes for the relatively unknown Amangeldy Tuleyev, the president of Kemerovo oblast council, can be ranked together with support for Zhirinovsky and Makashov because the support of his candidacy meant dissatisfaction with the two principal actors on the Russian political scene; his supporters hoped for a new, fresh and strong face. It is obvious at the same time that two of these candidates, Tuleyev and Zhirinovsky, competed with Boris Yeltsin for the votes of 'protest', the votes against the system: this supposition is confirmed by the significant correlations between the three sets of results and by the maps.

Table 12.4   Correlation of votes for candidates in the 1991 Russian presidential election

Candidates	Yeltsin	Ryzhkov	Bakatin	Tuleyev	Zhirinovsky	Makashov
Yeltsin	1.0	−0.83	−0.17	0.42	0.39	0.14
Ryzhkov		1.0	0.46	0.03	0.19	0.10
Bakatin			1.0	0.05	0.08	0.02
Tuleyev				1.0	0.06	0.03
Zhirinovsky					1.0	0.17
Makashov						1.0

A kind of 'spatial division of labour' between Bakatin, Tuleyev and Makashov can be detected. Each of their support blocs is strongly concentrated in a few areas. Their scores in regions and republics varied very sharply (the rates of spatial variation were respectively 51.72 per cent (Bakatin), 68.71 per cent (Tuleyev) and 50.72 per cent (Makashov). Surprisingly, the votes for Zhirinovsky were distributed over the Russian territory much more evenly (level of variation 33.96 per cent) which testifies to his general populism and the value of propaganda. No less surprising was the considerable territorial concentration of Ryzhkov's best scores (level of variation 45.57 per cent). It is logical that the spatial variation of the votes for the winner, Boris Yeltsin, is the lowest (25.68 per cent).

The geography of the votes for Yeltsin, as noted earlier, is 'larger' than the spatial sphere of influence of the 'democrats': not only personal, but important ethnic factors, intervened. The comparison of his scores in regions and Republics with their 'political temperatures',[1] calculated by Sobianin and Juriev (1990) by the roll-call voting of deputies to the People's Congress, supports the notion of his cross-sectional support: the correlation between these two variables is only +0.24. The average temperature shows, in particular, areas where deputies of different political orientation were elected. The map of Yeltsin's influence (see Figure 12.4) shows his percentages of votes by region divided by the average share for all Russia. Four major strongholds of the Russian president can be identified on this map, *viz.* 1) the industrial core in the centre of the country, with Moscow and Nizhny Novgorod; 2) the industrial oblasts of the Urals and the adjacent areas in Western Siberia, with Yeltsin's native town and political 'capital' Sverdlovsk (now Yekaterinaburg); 3) peripheral regions in the Far East; and 4) three North Caucasian areas - Checheno-Ingushetia, Dagestan and Kabardino-Baklkaria. Two other important, but smaller areas are also identified, the traditionally strongly pro-democratic Leningrad and the more recent democratic 'acquisition'- Volgograd.

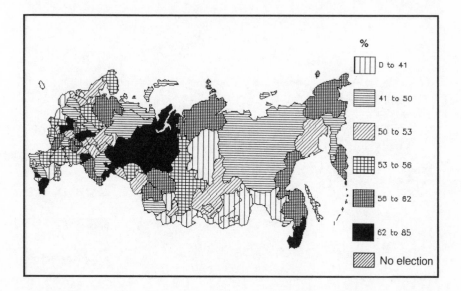

Figure 12.4   Percentage of the vote for Yeltsin in the 1991 Russian Presidential election

The geography of the voting for Ryzhkov (see Figure 12.5) is clearly 'peripheral', with the belt of high support stretched along the western boundary of the Russian Federation, including Pskov and Smolensk oblasts, several oblasts of the Black-soil (Chernozem) region, and along the southern boundary, including the granaries of Siberia and the Far East. In summary, it embraces agricultural, more rural regions. The second category of safe regions for the former prime minister included the rest of the autonomies, especially sparsely-settled national districts. But Ryzhkov clearly lost the autonomous areas as a whole to Yeltsin. He obtained the absolute majority of the votes only in Tuva (his best score all over the Russian Federation) and ran first in two other regions. In contrast, Yeltsin won only by the absolute majority in fifteen areas. Here is an important shift because during the Russian referendum three months earlier, democrats were defeated primarily in autonomous regions, which feared that the traditional centralization policy of Moscow would be inherited by the new Russian authorities. It is impossible to identify exactly to what degree this victory is due to Yeltsin's personal dynamism and attraction.

The vote for V. Bakatin (see Figure 12.6) proves that the well-known 'friends and neighbours' element in voting is valuable also in interpreting the Soviet case. Bakatin was strongly supported especially in the Kirov oblast, where for several years he was the first secretary of the regional Communist Party committee (14.7 per cent of the votes here and only 3.41 per cent nationally). He got unusually strong support also in adjacent regions in the north-east European part of Russia. In other areas where N. Ryzhkov gained support, Bakatin competed with him relatively successfully.

Curiously, Bakatin did not lead in the Kemerovo oblast where he was the first secretary of the CPSU after his stint in Kirov. The winner here was A. Tuleyev, whose main support was in this region, in Eastern Siberia and especially in the Kemerovo area, where he got 44.7 per cent (compared to 6.6 per cent in all of Russia) (see Figure 12.7).

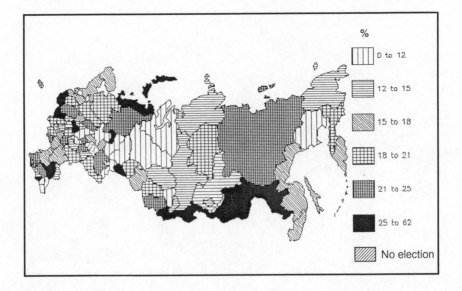

Figure 12.5   Percentage of the vote for Ryzhkov in the Russian Presidential election 1991

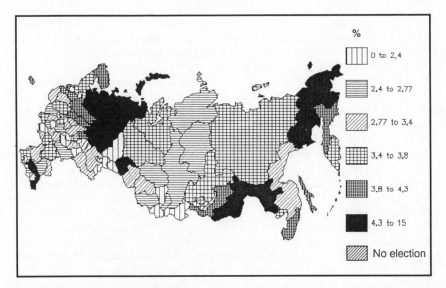

Figure 12.6 Percentage of the vote for Bakatin in the Russian Presidential election 1991

Tuleyev stressed the specific problems of eastern and northern regions of Russia during his electoral campaign. The geography of his influence is the other good illustration of the 'friends and neighbours' principle. But, again, the vote for this candidate also had an ethnic aspect. Probably because of his Kazakh background, Tuleyev got his best support after Kemerovo in the former autonomous regions such as the mountainous

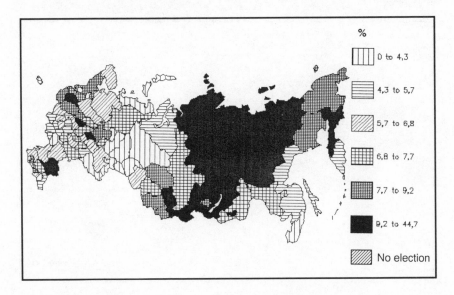

Figure 12.7 Percentage of the vote for Tulyev in the Russian Presidential election 1991

Altaï, Kalmykia, and Mari. Simultaneously, there were several exclusively-Russian oblasts in the European part of the country where Tuleyev was quite successful in gathering 10–15 per cent of the votes due to his image as a new political face.

The Zhirinovsky (ultra-right candidate) area of influence (see Figure 12.8) is strongest in Russian areas adjacent to 'national' Republics, regions of national conflicts and places with out-migration of the Russian population. Zhirinovsky also did well in oblasts and districts of Western Siberia which, since the first election in 1989, have been known as 'regions of protest'. One of the reasons for his support in the northern districts of Western Siberia probably was his demagogic promise to reduce the price of vodka. The Russian part of Northern Caucasus where Zhirinovsky also was quite successful is the area of the revival of the Cossack movement, fighting as they are for autonomy and even special functions and privileges in the Russian state. The relatively rich, fertile and conservative Northern Caucasus became an arena for the usurpation of local authorities, power by posturing Cossack committees, who proclaimed themselves 'defenders of the social order' and opponents of the immigration caused by national conflicts in neighbouring Caucasian regions. The Zhirinovsky appeal found fertile soil here. He was also relatively successful in Russian regions close to the Baltic republics (Pskov, Tver', etc.) for similar reasons as in the Northern Caucasus. Either way, Zhirinovsky received a lot of publicity in the newly-democratic mass media because he was considered very dangerous in his rightist slogans.

General Makashov, a conservative candidate from the position of orthodox dogmatism, had his best scores, first, in regions with high concentration of troops along the Soviet-Chinese boundary, in Kaliningrad oblast (the isolated Russian region on the border with Poland), and in the Kamtchatka peninsula. He ran relatively better in his region in Middle Volga region (he was the commander of Volga-Ural military district) and also received disproportionate support in several former autonomous regions (see Figure 12.9).

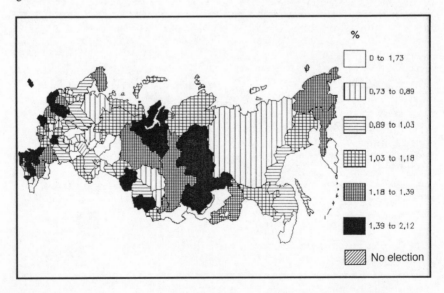

Figure 12.8 Percentage of the vote for Zhirinovsky in the Russian presidential election 1991

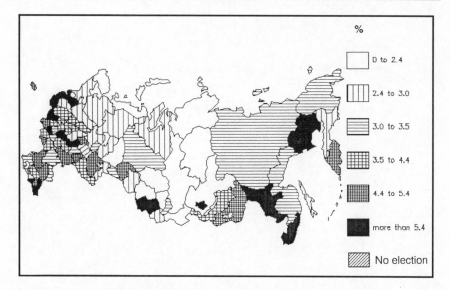

Figure 12.9   Percentage of the vote for Makashov in the Russian presidential election 1991

The triangular diagram (see Figure 12.10) shows the distribution of territorial units according to types of combinations of the votes for all the candidates. They are classified as left (Yeltsin), centre (Ryzhkov and Bakatin), and right (Tuleyev, Zhirinovsky and Makashov). The overwhelming majority of points on this diagram is concentrated around the centre, with a small dispersion to the left. There are relatively few territorial units with a strong deviation from the average. Five types of regions were distinguished on the basis of this diagram (they are mapped on Figure 12.11). In the regions of the first type, Yeltsin won by the overwhelming majority of the votes; Ryzhkov and Bakatin got less than 20 per cent; the influence of the right-wing candidates was insignificant. In Type II regions, Yeltsin obtained the absolute majority with the candidates of the centre gaining 20–35 per cent. In Type III, the proportions obtained by the three 'wings' are similar to Type II but the weight of the protest (right-wing) votes was greater. Type IV was characterized by a higher proportion of votes for the centrist candidates; nonetheless, even here, Boris Yeltsin ran first. Finally, Type V included few units with 'abnormal' combinations caused by small vote proportions for Yeltsin and a relatively strong influence both of the centre and of the right. This figure represents 'the quality' of the Yeltsin victory. He gained the majority of the votes in important centres of Russia, in the regions with the highest economic, scientific and cultural potential and in the major focuses of industrial working-class concentrations.

These cartographic conclusions were confirmed by a more exact method, multi-factor analysis by principal components. The initial matrix included the per centage of absenteeism during the presidential elections and the March referendum and the shares of votes for all the candidates of the former autonomous regions and oblasts. The first four factors accounted for 77.3 per cent of all the variance with the first factor (31.0 per cent) easily interpreted as the main political axis. This component is strongly positively correlated with absenteeism and the votes for Yeltsin and negatively

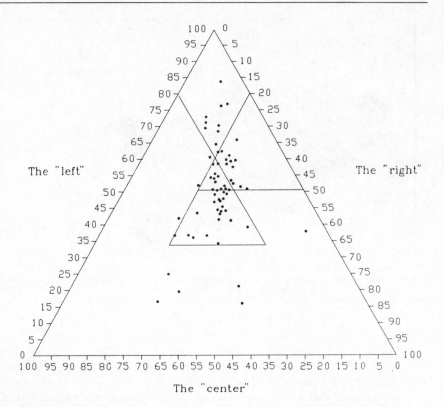

Figure 12.10 Distribution of the types of electoral regions in the Russian Federation, based on the presidential vote 1991

related to the vote for Ryzhkov. The second component (18.6 per cent) describes the vote for Tuleyev and it is also closely correlated with absenteeism. The third factor (14.4 per cent) is essentially connected to the vote for Bakatin, but also a relatively high negative correlation with the vote for Zhirinovsky. Finally, the fourth factor (13.3 per cent) is clearly positively related to the high influence of the right-wing candidates, Zhirinovsky and Makashov. The factor scores are very similar to the patterns in Figure 12.11.

An attempt at explanation

Electoral patterns in the former Soviet Union are still quite dynamic, especially at the local level, where the influence of the subjective factors (personality of candidate, role of local authorities, bias in districting, etc.) is very strong. At the same time, however, four elections in Russia showed a high stability in patterns at the level of oblasts and former autonomies. Surprisingly, similar spatial patterns are revealed in the pre-revolutionary (pre-1917) elections, in particular by the most representative and democratic election in the Constituent Assembly of 1917. It is difficult to compare directly electoral statistics of 1917 and those of recent (post-1989) elections, because of adminis-

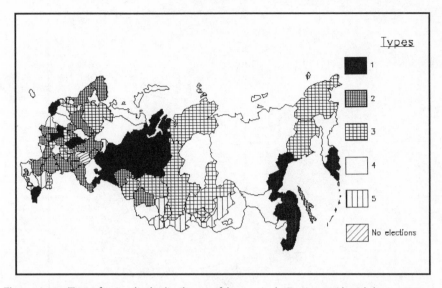

Figure 12.11   Types of regions by the distributons of the votes in the Russian presidential election 1991

trative boundary incompatibilities and lack of detailed data on all the provinces of 1917. Nevertheless, some comparisons can be made, especially for the Central region of Russia where the boundaries between large administrative units have changed little since the time of Catherine II.

The typical 'core-periphery' structure of Russia is clearly seen in the map of the 1917 election (Figure 12.12). The radical, more industrialized and populated core (with two major parts, a larger one around Moscow and a more compact one around Petrograd, now St. Petersburg) was opposed to a more rural and conservative periphery, with a few left-wing urban centres. Even more amazing is that the same historical distinction between a more radical North and a more moderate South is observed. In 1917, the Bolsheviks were supported in the Russian provinces by the industrial workers of Petrograd, Moscow, Ivanovo-Voznesensk (this area was a part of Vladimir province), other industrial centres and by the peasantry in the northern provinces, especially near Moscow and Petrograd, Vladimir, Tula, Tver', Smolensk, Novgorod, and Yaroslavl'. Russian and foreign scholars (e.g., Radkey, 1950) showed that Bolsheviks got more votes in suburban villages and not in towns, except in the above-named industrial centres and capitals. In suburbs, there were many semi-peasants, semi-workers exposed to the propaganda of soldiers of nearby garrisons and from Bolshevik cells in industrial plants. These peasant strata had interests not necessarily connected to agricultural and landlord relations. Analogously, peasants in the Northern provinces, with poor soils which did not allow the population to survive the winter without buying food-stuffs, worked in Moscow and Petrograd; as a consequence, they were socially and spatially more mobile.

In pre-revolutionary Russia, differences in fundamental geographic characteristics, such as the quality of soils, produced a different economic outlook and a different political perspective. These sectional distinctions continue, despite decades of totalitarianism

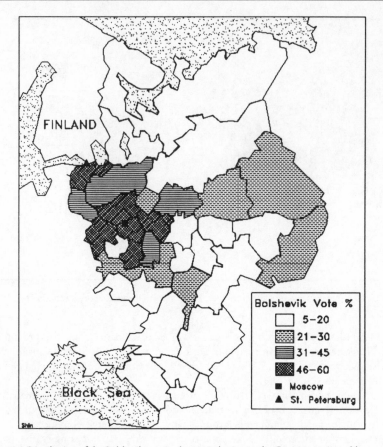

Figure 12.2 Distribution of the Bolshevik vote in the 1917 election to the Constituent Assembly

massive industrialization and urbanization, and the disappearance of the folk culture. North-eastern Russia is more urbanized and more mobile, better connected with regional capitals, not least because of the recreational activity of urban dwellers. Urban-dwellers are more innovative in their political behaviour and more receptive to new political ideas.

However, a lot of differences are observed now in comparison to 1917. The radical core has now shifted more to the north, thereby diffusing to all the North-East of the European part of Russia and a large number of regions beyond the Urals. Some geographically-central provinces (Smolensk, Tver' and Novgorod) are not now among the most radical because of a massive migration of peasants to Moscow, Leningrad and nearby industrial centres, such as Cherepovetz and Murmansk. Most of these places are politically innovative. By contrast, central oblasts became desolate and their populations became elderly. After 1917, Siberia, an exclusively agricultural region far from the influence of large cities and unsympathetic to Bolsheviks, became heavily urbanized and industrialized. With the exception of more rural southern areas, Siberia is now one of the strongholds of the democrats.

Table 12.5   Correlation of socio-economic variables and Russian presidential vote

Variables	Turnout	Yeltsin%	Ryzhkov%	Zhirinovsky%
Sq.Metres	+0.28	+0.24	−0.20	+0.08
Sales	+0.53	+0.19	+0.25	+0.09
Cars	+0.02	+0.01	+0.02	+0.13
CPSU/1,00	+0.32	+0.00	+0.01	+0.01
Services	+0.23	+0.13	−0.23	+0.06
Physicians	+0.34	+0.15	+0.13	+0.16
Kindergartens	+0.22	+0.14	−0.12	+0.04
Higher Educ.	+0.27	+0.34	−0.26	+0.25
Secondary Ed.	+0.22	+0.42	−0.34	+0.24
%Russians	+0.07	+0.20	+0.22	+0.16
Old people	+0.15	+0.12	+0.07	+0.27
% Urban	+0.39	+0.48	−0.41	+0.27
R^2	0.71	0.63	0.61	0.61

Variable definition: *Sq.metres:* per capita living space (in square metres in houses and apartments), in cities,1985; *Sales:* per capita retail sales, in rubles, 1985; *Cars:* number of cars per 10000 inhabitants, 1986; *CPSU/1000:* Number of members of the CPSU per 10000 people, 1989; *Services:* per capita expenditures on personal services in rubles, 1985; *Physicians:* Number of physicians per 10000 people, 1985; *Kindergartens:* Number of places in Kindergartens per 10000 people, 1985; *Higher Educa.:* Percentage of people with University education, 1989; *Secondary Ed.:* Percentage of people with secondary education, 1989; *% Russians:* Percentage of Russians in the total population,1989; *Old People:* Percentage of people older than 60 years in the total population, 1989; *% Urban:* Percentage of urban to total population, 1989; *R^2:* Percentage of total variance in vote accounted for by all the independent variables in a multiple correlation.

Available regional social statistics suitable for explanation of voting patterns are still rather limited and irregular. Nevertheless, it was possible to correlate some representative figures (see Table 12.5). Turnout in the presidential election in Russia is related to the strength of the democratic vote, which in turn, is correlated closely with the variables reflecting the urban/rural/centre/periphery cleavage. Turnover in retail sales, the number of physicians per 10,000 people, living space (size) in urban dwellings, the proportion of people with higher education, as well as the rate of urbanization, are all inter-correlated with turnout and the democratic vote. In the Russian Federation as a whole, the ethnic component *grosso modo* seemed to have no large influence on the electoral patterns; the political behaviour of populations in the former autonomous areas was very different. Comparative analysis in former autonomous regions, on the basis of the national proportions of the population, of the competition for deputies' votes and of the elected deputies (affecting the probability of different national groups being elected), did not reveal obvious biases. This distinguishes the Russian election from the all-Union one a year earlier when such biases were observed in several republics. In summary, the available socio-economic variables explain the variation of the turnout surprisingly well.

The vote for Boris Yeltsin, which was cross-sectional in nature, does not correlate closely with the indexes, except those of education and urbanization. His support was first of all in large cities, where the social infrastructure is often poorer than in the smaller cities. As expected, the independent variables are related to the vote for Nikolai Ryzhkov almost at the same degree but with the opposite sign. The influence of candidate Zhirinovsky was the most spectacular among the 'outsiders'; his vote does not correlate with the socio-economic indexes, at least, at the macro-level. However, Zhirinovsky's vote is slightly correlated with the proportion of poorly-educated voters, urbanization levels and the elderly ratio, groups who respond to slogans about 'the need for order'. We can conclude that the votes for all three candidates are partly explained by socio-economic indicators.

The matrix of correlations at the scale of oblasts and autonomous regions reflects the fundamental socio-spatial cleavages in Russia, that of the deep social distinctions between towns and the countryside, between large metropolises and medium-sized cities, and between the latter and small centres or administrative districts. The strength of democrats is almost directly proportionate to the size of the place. An example from the all-Union referendum is Kuban' (Krasnodar region) where the average regional vote for the democrats was 80.3 per cent but only 68.5 per cent in the regional centre and 87.4 per cent in the countryside. These differences were universal throughout the country, though they sometimes had different manifestations under specific national and local conditions.

Case study: Kzyl-Orda, a politically awakening Kazakh province

Recent elections and referenda played an extremely important role in the population's political awakening in all the republics and the regions of the former Soviet Union. The elections revealed relative solidity and stability of traditional political culture, with its typical organic contradictions. These include the respect for the hierarchical organisation of society and of power; the jealous attitude to real or imaginary privileges of neighbours; total dependence upon the top of the power hierarchy; the widespread belief in the obligation of the 'centre' to solve all local problems; the omnipotence of local elites; the importance of clans and connections and of ethnic divisions; and the decisive role of economic factors, of paternalistic policy which can outweigh clan and tribal affiliations.

These beliefs and processes can be illustrated by the example of the Kzyl-Orda oblast in Kazakhstan, located on the northern and north-eastern coast of the Aral sea. In an analysis of the comparison of the elections to the Congress of People's Deputies of Kazakhstan in March 1990 and the results of the elections of the People's Deputies of the USSR in March 1989, the candidates' electoral programmes clearly show large shifts but in spite of that, stability of electoral behaviour in two regions remained. These two elections were held under similar political conditions and, therefore, such a comparison is possible.

Kzyl-Orda oblast is a huge, sparsely-populated area that is almost a desert. Its population is concentrated in the narrow band of irrigated lands along the Syr-Darya river and along the main railway connecting the European part of the former Soviet union with the republics of Central Asia. The total population of the oblast, according to the

1989 Census, was 625,000, with about 150,000 at the centre. The population comprises 81.6 per cent Kazakhs, 13.8 per cent Russians and 4.6 per cent other groups. In the oblast is the cosmodrome Baykonur, an object of pride for the local population, but since 1990, transformed into a cause of political discussions, jealous comparisons and claims by the all-Union authorities. The formerly 'secret' town of Leninsk, second largest in the region, is populated by servicemen and their families. The third urban centre of the oblast is Aralsk (34,000), the main maritime spot on the Aral sea, which used to be the richest in fish in the world. Now, Aralsk is 120 kilometres from the rapidly-drying up sea. This man-made disaster, affecting all Central Asia, especially influenced the local climate and the economic and social structures of Aralsk.

At first glance, it could seem that the 1990 elections in Kzyl-Orda oblast followed the usual scenario. In 1989, the first secretary of the oblast party committee, E. Auyelbekov, was the only candidate in the Kzyl-Orda territorial district; he was elected a people's deputy of the USSR with 99.3 per cent of the votes in a turnout of 99.94 per cent. The national–territorial districts elections did not produce any surprises either. Far away from Kzyl-Orda, passions became very heated in Moscow, Leningrad and other large cities. Electors in the Kazakh province quietly chose the best candidate of two well-qualified ones, in the opinion of the district party committee.

In 1990, as well, all the candidates to the Kazahk Congress of People's Deputies were carefully analysed by the oblast and districts party committees. For each candidate, a district committee examined his personal characteristics (*kharakeristika*) signed by the so-called triangle (the director, the secretary of the party committee and the president of the trade union committee) of an organization where he worked. In weekly summaries on the electoral campaign sent by district committees to Kzyl-Orda, the social composition of the candidates was usually analysed: the share of the party and the komsomol (the Communist Union of the youth) members was considered the most important but attention was also paid to the proportion of women, persons under thirty, party and Soviets officials, workers and employees. As in the days before the reforms of Mikhail Gorbachev, a district committee was called to balance these percentages, eliminating certain candidates and organizing the nomination of the others.

In 1990 91.5 per cent of the voters in the oblast came to the ballot-boxes. It was a substantially lower figure than in the elections before Gorbachev and smaller than the turnout one year earlier in 1989; it was, nonetheless, an unattainably high turnout according to the standards of Russia and, especially, its large cities. In some districts the turnout was even higher, beyond the limits of accuracy. For instance, in the Kazalinsky district, where the high official, the second secretary of the Communist Party of Kazakhstan (CPK), V. Anufriyev stood against the hardly-known director of a local school, 99.3 per cent of the voters turned out. Anufriyev got 81.8 per cent of the votes here.

Twenty-nine candidates competed for twelve seats, that is, 2.4 for each seat: this was much less than in Russia but enough to qualify the election as democratic. All the leadership of the oblast were elected: the first secretary of the oblast committee of the Communist Party of Kazahkstan (CPK), who was also the president of the oblast council, was successful as was the first secretary of the central committee of the CPK. Leninsk elected three generals to the Supreme Soviet of Kazakhstan, including the commander of Baykonur. At the same time, however, the 'people' were also represented among the deputies from Kzyl-Orda: one textile worker from the oblast capital; two state farm workers, and one army veteran who had been the head of the oblast directorate in the past.

In 1990, therefore, the electorate of Kzyl-Orda as a whole still seemed to be respecting authority and adopting their decisions: local officials did not need to fear a contest here. The people supported more influential candidates consistently because they believed that they really had access to republican and all-Union corridors of power to gain local investment, for construction of a hospital, a school, a road, etc. The official programme of civil construction for 1990 included 64 million rubles of investments though all construction enterprises did not exceed 35 million rubles.

The population of Kvzl-Orda especially appreciated specific promises in a locality or a district, or for the oblast at a minimum. Party and Soviet officials boasted openly of their past successes in bringing investment to the region. 'Ordinary' candidates often stressed local problems, trying to use their local knowledge to win support. V. Dumche, then second secretary of the oblast party committee, included a promise to build a large mechanized bakery in one of the localities of his constituency in his programme; the Kazahkstan Fishing Minister, A. Sarzhanov, promised to provide the fish processing factory in Aralsk (suffering from the shortage of fish after the ecological disaster in the Aral sea), with fish from Sakhalin Island, off the eastern coast of Siberia; the editor-in-chief of the main oblast newspaper, a local party official named E. Khan, promised to construct two new water-pipes.

These local emphases of the candidates made electoral programmes more or less distinguishable from each other. As in other regions, they usually included a mixture of popular slogans and current themes discussed by central mass-media: social justice; attention to deprived social strata; abolition of the privileges of nomenklatura; more economic autonomy to enterprises, regions, republics, etc. Women candidates demanded better social services, more aid to mothers with several children, etc. Veteran candidates worried about pensions and special health services for elderly people. The candidates usually considered themselves not only as the representatives of local interests but also as representatives of the interests of specific social strata.

The influence of general political changes enriched electoral programmes in 1990 with some new elements. Many candidates now appealed to national feelings stressing the necessity to improve the status of the Kazakh language as the state language and to make it mandatory in schools for all who lived in Kazakhstan and suggested that a school be established using the Koran as the basis for instruction. Some candidates supported the idea of the reconstruction of the mosque in Kzyl-Orda.

A lot of candidates touched on the problem of the Aral sea ecological crisis, but in a general form. Only a few of them spoke about more concrete measures such as the change of land-use. The local political elite, who directed this campaign and actively participated in it, found out a politically advantageous way to propagandize the easiest and the most spectacular, but absolutely incorrect way to solve or to soften the problem of this ecological disaster. They realized that the restructuring of the whole Central-Asian economy, a radical solution, is a very complicated and slow matter. Instead of that, they promised to fight for the revival of a project to divert Siberian rivers to Central Asia; they wanted a thirty-year construction project of a channel more than 2,000 kilometres long. The rejection of public opinion in Russia of this project was often interpreted as the 'unwillingness of the Russian people to help the Kazakh people in hard times'. This rejection was further proof for the Kazahks of negative Russian attitudes related to the flight of the Russian-speaking population from the settlements close to the former shore of the sea (for Kazahks, 'it is our homeland and we will never leave it'), to the unfavourable attitude of the all-Union political centre towards Kazakhs, to the wide use of Kazakh lands by central military authorities, especially in Baykonur, to the heavy environmental pollution of the oblast with the remainders of missiles, to the privileges of Baykonur's officers getting an additional 40 per cent over a normal wage as compensation for hard working conditions unlike the 25 per cent given to the people outside the boundaries of the missile range. Under the new political conditions, by explicitly emphasizing the negative role of decisions taken in the centre, local officials got an opportunity to rationalize their own failures.

Arguing for the necessity of constructing the big diversion channel, local authorities started work on a small one, connecting the Syr-Darya and the former Aral sea gulf of Sary-Chaganac. This project had not been approved yet by Moscow experts because the ecological consequences of the creation of a closed, shallow, warm basin, full of chemicals brought by the river from rice and cotton fields, were not clear. But for the local authorities, it was politically very important to prove to the population that they were taking action by starting large-scale construction works and bringing water to the former quays of Aralsk. Most of the electoral programmes of local officials contained oaths of support and support for this project. They totally succeeded in persuading electors that the construction of huge diversion channels is the only way to save the sea and to improve the very poor quality of life in this area.

A typical example of the early electoral changes in a typically traditional area is seen in the events of the electoral campaign in the constituency of Aralsk and its district. According to official statistics, 98.2 per cent of the 37,000 electors in this constituency, of more than 90 per cent Kazakh population, took part in the election. Vitaly Brynkin, a Russian, the president of Kzyl-Orda oblast executive committee of people's deputies, defeated both of his Kazakh rivals, with 53.2 per cent of the votes. Though these figures seem to prove that the electoral behaviour of the population remains traditional, they are the result of very spectacular political events.

Brynkin was, of course, the candidate supported by the whole oblast establishment. The Minister of Fisheries of Kazakhstan, K. Sarzhanov, surprisingly became a formally registered candidate. He organized his nomination among the fishermen of the village where he was born. Then, also unexpectedly, a third candidate, the only one living in the constituency, the president of the district executive committee A. Aymbetov, decided to run for election. Aymbetov was, at this time, the highest official in the district because the first secretary of the CPK committee was away and he suggested nominating somebody living not in Alma-Ata or Kzyl-Orda, but in Aralsk itself. Aymbetov managed to cope with the displeasure of the oblast bosses.

Aymbetov was already sure of his nomination and was waiting for the meeting in the town's cinema, when for the first time in the history of Aralsk, the place became the stage of spontaneous and 'unofficial' political activity. A local youth group promoted the candidacy of the labour force office employee, Kh. Khoatov. Khoatov knew many local young people, including almost all 2,000 unemployed in the town. It was mostly young men who campaigned for him at bus stops, near the shops, etc. Aymbetov had to mobilize all his efforts, blocking the entrance to the cinema under the pretext of overcrowding, organizing the bus transportation of potential supporters from a factory and promising them a free film instead of work; he used procedural tricks for winning the nomination with a score of 450 to 126 votes. Khoatov's supporters protested but the forces were not yet equal. Then, the Khoatov group decided to support the candidacy of Brynkin against Aymbetov and the powerful boss of the oblast accepted the help of an unknown young clerk. Brynkin came to Aralsk specifically to meet the young activists and appointed Khoatov as his adviser for the electoral campaign.

Sarzhanov, actively supported by the members of his clan, by the administration of the fish collective farms (Kolkhoz) and by the workers of the fish factory promised to find jobs for everybody in the constituency, to build new factories processing the local fish, and to restructure the former ship-repairing plant. Aymbetov campaigned in particular on the issue of raising the local wage ratio (coefficient) to the wage level of Leninsk/Baykonur. He also promised to eliminate unemployment and to improve public services. Brynkin underlined his ability to provide Aralsk with better consumer goods and to improve health services. He confirmed his backing of the rivers diversion project and promised to build as quickly as possible the channel from Syr-Darya to Sary-Chaganac and to give water back to Aralsk. Ironically, he was supported by the Khoatov group which carried on its campaign, stressing first of all ecological issues; it organized the first ecological and political demonstration in Aralsk. The people in Aralsk, who are obviously very sensitive to the problem of the Aral sea, found in Brynkin not only a 'chef', a representative of power structures, but also a man who was more able to implement their unrealistic dream of swimming in the Aral sea.

The story of the last election in Aralsk seems very instructive. It combines, on the one hand, the traditional patterns of popular support, belief in the authority of power, the struggle of clans and/or of cadres for power and, on the other hand, the emergence of new forms of political activity produced principally by increasingly severe ecological and economic crisis and the inability of authorities to cope with it. But, of course, the competitiveness of elections plays in it an important role. For traditional local elites grouped formerly in party committees and now in local councils controlled by the interest of the state plants administration, it will be more difficult to cope with new movements recently called 'informal', with the process of relatively rapid politicization and radicalization even in peripheral regions. But will the eventual victory of new forces bring political stability and real democracy or will it contribute to the splintering of society along ethnic lines? Perhaps these changes will produce a serious threat of Muslim fundamentalism, not in Kzyl-Orda, a homogeneous area where it seems unlikely in the near future, but in neighbouring regions like Karakalpakia?

Too many electoral geographies?

Without adequate theoretical guidelines, the emergent electoral geography of the former USSR risks becoming a vague discipline dealing with the collection of case studies and some limited practical problems. The important issue is how useful the theoretical approaches developed in Western electoral geography are in the Russian and former Soviet contexts, considering that they are based on axioms of liberal democracy, a notion that is not yet entrenched in the former USSR.

In his classic works, Stein Rokkan (1970, 1980) named five main social cleavages along which electoral processes were organized: urban/rural, national/local, church/state, labour/capital and between different religious communities. Some researchers have added to this list cleavages such as openness/reticence/different regional orientations in foreign policy, regime support/radical change, liberalism/dirigism, etc. (Johnston, Shelley and Taylor, 1990). The majority of these cleavages can be observed in the former Soviet Union. As has been stressed, the most obvious is the sharp contrast between urban and rural settlements. The difference between urban and rural interests, certainly, exists as was confirmed by the formation of groups of deputies employed in agriculture, in both the all-Union and Russian parliaments. In the future, as private farms develop, urban/rural divergences will become more considerable.

Ascending regionalism and separatism as direct consequences of deep economic crisis are the principal tendencies in current Soviet political life, though they are developing on a new basis due to radical social and territorial changes. Ironically, the cleavage between labour and capital is not yet significant. The most influential churches seem not yet to be playing a significant role in the activity of social movements and of central, republican and local authorities. However, political parties proclaiming themselves defenders of religious values are now being created. Ethnic and religious problems are undoubtedly among the most important issues, but neither in the former Union nor in Russia are nationalist parties yet a universal phenomena. There are republics where such parties are very strong as well as republics where nationalist aspirations are expressed by vague, apparently unstructured movements; as yet, they do not participate in electoral campaigns. Finally, there are republics, especially with large ratios of Russians in the population, where ethnic issues are not yet among the most important on the political agenda. Therefore, the interests of social groups are not yet articulated or translated into activities of parties and electoral campaigns.

The model of 'modernization–nationalization', also based on premises of liberal pluralism, can be useful in retrospective studies. Many questions are still to be answered such as how unification measures and centralization ('nationalization') policy influenced pre-revolutionary cleavages and spatial patterns; how was nationalization combined with radical social changes as a result of collectivization in agriculture, industrialization and urbanization, destruction of traditional peasant conscience and culture, resettlement of peoples, etc.; what structures of the past were more resistant to changes and where were they located?

The 'social welfare' approach can be more efficiently applied in studies at the micro-level; at more aggregate levels, distinctions in political culture rather than economic factors more likely play a greater role. Soviet geographers (Kolossov et al., 1990), studying the 1989 election, believe that political culture and the subjective factors of electoral campaigns are much more important than social welfare variables in understanding voting choices, especially in times of economic stress. Moreover, these variables are more often strongly related to the urban/rural socio-cultural cleavage.

The theoretical perspectives of 'uneven development' and the world-systems framework (Taylor, 1989) could become useful in the near future when the economies of the newly-independent states become more involved in the capitalist world-economy. Until now, the viability of whole branches and regions was artificially sustained by central planning and a controlled prices system. Electoral patterns will be inevitably related to long cycles in regional development which will affect regional structures. It is easy to forecast that old industrial regions will become critical points of national political debates and their evolution will be important for the political evolution of the whole country.

Place–context analysis should be evaluated as a *modus operandi* for (former) Soviet electoral studies, not because it is now 'fashionable' among Anglo-American geographers. It should of course, be considerably modified according to the specific conditions of (former) Soviet realities. The context approach incorporates specific combinations of natural, socio-cultural, historical and economic factors, leading to the formation of particular kinds of regional political climates and to the emergence of different 'subjective' factors. These, in turn, cannot be examined in formal statistical methods and are stably reproduced in time despite the extreme volatility of current politics. In fact, how else could one explain differences between two neighbouring old industrial regions in Central Russia? Ivanovo was until recently relatively 'calm' and more traditional in the political behaviour of its population while Yaroslavl' had important mass movements. Clearly, something beyond different branch structures of manufacturing is at work here.

Problems of explanation also appear at the macro-level where cultural distinctions are usually smoothed over and relatively hidden. The place–context approach corresponds very well to regional disintegration, 'provincialism' and volatility in the current political life in the republics of the former Soviet Union. A similar approach was used by Soviet geographers in 'field' case-studies and this is well connected with the traditional Russian/Soviet regional school in human geography.

The electorate in the former Soviet republics now consists not of segments of a united 'political market', but of many separate arenas of republican or regional size. Each of them has its own, specific electoral geography, even if electoral data are apparently similar. As in many Third World countries, in many areas (especially the East) of the former Soviet Union, representative democratic institutions disguise the quite traditional struggle for power between the elite of local clans created on ethnic, cultural, religious or, more often, purely economic, clientelist bases. Such a struggle is very far from Western ideas about the triumph of liberal democracy as the superior form of political organization. For example, who could imagine, after the bloody events in Baku in January 1990 when Azerbaijan was under the control of the Popular Front, that a few months later, in the Republican parliamentary election of November 1990, candidates of this Front would get less than one-quarter of the votes? The majority of seats were won by local Communist Party leaders, chiefs of the militia and the prosecutor's offices and especially the managers of industrial plants and *kolkozes*. This outcome was due to the existence of a kind of 'cadre party' and a relatively weak coincidence between the 'geography of support' and the 'geography of power', to use Peter Taylor's terms.

When the balance of forces between clans is well regulated and they accept the implicit rules of the game, this system is relatively stable because it corresponds to deep-rooted cultural traditions (collectivism and not individualism, absolute obedience to interests of a clan and to its leaders in exchange their support and personal promotion, etc.) (Berry, 1990). But in the case when there is no such for balance, when new clans appear and their interests are in conflict, as in the former Soviet republics in the period of economic transformations, the implanting of campaigns for representative institutions could potentially lead to destabilization. Signs of this were already seen in the Republican elections of 1990. For example, in Karakalpak republic in Uzbekistan, where voting was very traditional and electors voted for candidates approved by the existing authorities, in some districts of its centre, the city of Nukus, the electorate was split along ethnic lines. Candidates belonging to different ethnic communities seldom dared to vote in the same district. In this region, with an ethnically heterogeneous population, there could be serious consequences. At the same time, in Moscow, Leningrad, and other large cities and highly urbanized regions, representative institutions in terms of liberal democracy have a sufficient socio-cultural basis, due to the existence of a relatively numerous 'middle class'.

It is useful to adopt an eclectic 'compositional' approach to electoral behaviour in the former Soviet Union, taking into account the kind of electoral geography and the scale studied. Approaches useful in studies of Central Russia and at the macro-level could be absolutely unsuitable in studies of the national Republics and/or at lower spatial scales. The recognition of the fact that the contemporary theory of electoral geography is geographically limited because it is based on axioms of liberal democracy and on the conviction that this form of political organization must finally win everywhere is quite accurate (Taylor, 1990). Studies of the electoral geography of the former Soviet republics could help to avoid this bias.

Note

1. Sobianin and Juriev (1990) use the term 'average temperature of a region' for the difference between the percentage of roll-call votes for the most important political issues from positions of 'Democratic Russia' and of the conservative fraction 'Communists of Russia'

References

Berezkin, A.V., Kolossov, V.A., Pavlovskaya, M.E., Petrov, N.V., Smirniagin, L.V., 1989, 'The geography of the 1989 elections of the People's Deputies of the U.S.S.R: the preliminary results', *Soviet Geography* 30 (10): 607–634.
Berry, B.J.L., 1990, 'Comparative geography of the global economy: cultures, corporations, and the nation-state', *Economic Geography* 65 (1): 1–18.
Johnston, R.J., Shelley, F.M., and Taylor, P.J. (eds), 1990, *Developments in electoral geography*, Routledge, London and New York.
Kolossov V.A., 1990, 'The geography of elections of USSR People's Deputies by national-territorial districts and the nationalities issue', *Soviet Geography* 31 (11): 753–766.
Kolossov, V.A., and Petrov, N.V., 1991, 'La géographie du référendum de 1991 dans la Fédération Russe et dans les autres républiques: éléments de stabilité et de dynamisme, *Revue Geographique Belge* 115, No. 1-2-3.
Kolossov, V.A., Petrov, N.V., and Smirniagin, L.V.(eds), 1990, *BECHA 89* (Spring 89: the geography and the anatomy of parliamentary elections), Progress Publishers, Moscow, 1990 (in Russian).
Radkey, O.H., 1950, *The election to the Russian constituent assembly of 1917*, Harvard University Press, Cambridge, MA.
Rokkan, S., 1970, *Citizens, elections, parties*, MacKay, New York.
Rokkan, S., 1980, 'Territories, centres, and peripheries: towards a geoethnic-geoeconomic-geopolitical model of differentiation within Western Europe', in *Centre and Periphery*, J.Gottmann (ed.), Croom Helm, London and New York, pp. 163–205.
Sobianin, A., and Juriev, D., 1990, 'Political temperature of Russia', *Arguments and Facts* No. 37 (in Russian).
Taylor, P.J., 1989, *Political geography: world-system, nation-state and locality*, (2nd edn.), Longman, London.
Taylor, P.J., 1990, 'Extending the world of political geography', in *Developments in electoral geography*, R.J. Johnston, F.M. Shelley and P.J. Taylor (eds.), Routledge, London and New York, pp. 257–271.
Vanlaer, J., 1991, 'Les premières élections libres en Europe de l'Est: systèmes de partis et clivages régionaux', *Revue Géographique Belge* 115, No.1-2-3.

13 Democratic elections and political restructuring in Poland, 1989–91

Joanna Regulska

The fundamental political and structural transformation occurring in Central and Eastern Europe centres on restructuring of central control and the establishment of new political institutions. After forty-five years of totalitarian, centralized and command authority, the goal is to regain previously denied basic democratic freedoms and to secure self-determination. The process of democratization cannot be achieved fully, and will not become an integral part of this transformation except by the passage of new laws by parliament or by the creation of new institutions. If democratic principles are to be central to society, they must not only be absorbed by the central administrative system but more importantly must inform the creation of new institutions at the local level. Furthermore, these institutions need to be empowered in order to be able to fulfil new responsibilities.

The process of democratization and institution-building at the local level was initiated in Poland more than two years ago. Parliament has adopted numerous laws enabling the transfer of power and authority to the local level and citizens have had an opportunity to exercise their newly-acquired liberties by voting in free and democratic elections. The initial faith in democracy allowed Poland to move rapidly. This conviction allowed, even if only temporarily, the legitimization of economic decisions and it provided society with hopes for a better future. Two years later, Poland faces major challenges and barriers to its political and economic transition, and establishment of local self-governance is not excluded from this turmoil. At issue is the political and ideological perspective that defines the role of representative self-government within the context of newly emerging democracy. The historical context of Polish central–local relations under communism is at the heart of the issue. It strongly influenced current state responses regarding the direction of changes in political decision-making, administrative control and fiscal autonomy. Analysis of the changes in post-communist Poland reveals a multidimensional struggle between central and local state, and emerging civil society.

In the sections that follow changing central–local relations in Poland are examined. In the first part, an historical interpretation of intragovernmental relations under communism is given. In the second, efforts to secure autonomy and power, which are essential for re-establishment of local self-government, are documented. This section pays particular attention to the creation of a new legal apparatus and the societal response to newly acquired rights for free local elections. The final section considers the political and social barriers that lie ahead of the emerging local state in Poland.

The path toward decentralization: 1945–1989

The introduction in post-war Poland of the principle of state uniform power meant the fundamental restructuring of political and economic relations. For local government it meant the loss of autonomy, and incorporation into the hierarchical system of power and decision-making. Municipalities became an integral part of the people's council; their property was nationalized and their administration began to serve as an extension of central government, duly fulfilling the centre's directives. Repeated political crises during forty-five years of totalitarian rule almost always resulted in new government legislation pertinent to local government. The state apparatus and political leadership believed that by introducing new legislation, and thus providing the society with a sense of change, they could avoid addressing issues of autonomy, democracy and freedom of self-determination. Thus, the 1945–48 period of the establishment of the communist regime was reflected in the 1950 Territorial Agencies of the Uniform State Authority Act, which declared the end of local autonomy and defined a new status for people's councils (Regulski, 1989).

The 1956 crisis found its reflection first in a 1958 amendment and subsequently in the 1963 amendment. The further expansion of central administrative power and autonomy of individual sectorial departments (horizontally subordinated to particular ministerial offices) was the key element of the 1958 amendment. Although the purpose of this addition was to strengthen central control and hierarchical linkages, the evidence that this goal was achieved was minimal, and the 1963 amendment picked up the issue again. This time the fear was that the local councils were losing political prestige and, therefore, needed to be given a greater role in the decision-making process. By providing councils' committees with special status, the central administration achieved greater control of local affairs and, most importantly, drastically restricted the councils' ability to decide local priorities for themselves.

The tensions of the 1968–70 period laid the foundation for the ill-conceived administrative reform of 1975, which by creating a larger number of units at the local level and eliminating the middle range of the administrative tier was supposed to improve the efficiency of administrative management and to increase public participation. Due to the principle of 'unity of power', however, the effect was to allow the further permeation of society by oppressive branches of the state, military and police. In the end, it facilitated imposition of martial law in 1981.

Legislation passed in 1983 is considered by some as an important step toward the advancement of decentralization through increased authority and independence of people's councils (Zakrzewski, 1987; Zawadzki, 1987). The theory was not, however, translated into practice: it only repeated the well-known paradox, 'we are free to do more, but can do less', and only added to the already serious social dissatisfaction. The retention of administrative barriers, the lack of resources, and the contradictions between new and old legislation were not viewed by local authorities as an expansion of their power and an improvement of their effectiveness. Although the new legislation obliged people's councils to adhere to public consultation, the failure to establish democratic mechanisms for such a process, a priori restrictions on the timing of such consultation, and the lack of free and democratic elections, precluded the development of public participation as a powerful tool.

The final pseudo-attempt to restructure central–local relations took place in 1988, when, as a part of the so-called 'second stage of reform', people's councils were supposed to obtain greater discretionary power in financial and economic   matters, including the ability to raise their own revenues (Chlopecki, 1990). They were also scheduled to undertake a variety of obligations to provide certain services. Communal property again became a subject of debate, with a proposal to restore communal ownership lost in the 1940s. The relevant legislation was to be approved in 1988 and implemented on 1 January, 1989. This did not take place, however. The events of the summer and fall of 1988 moved Poland on a new political trajectory.

In the autumn of 1988, after a series of nationwide strikes, the regime of General Jaruzelski decided that it had no chance to reform the economy without popular support. It opted for what was called the 'historic compromise', the introduction of the opposition into the system. In December 1988, the 'Citizen's Committee of Lech Walesa' was established. The actual terms for the introduction of the opposition into the system were worked out in the 'Roundtable' discussion in February 1989. The debates took place in three large subcommittees: 1) political reforms, 2) social and economic policy, and 3) trade union pluralism. The subgroup on local government negotiated under the first theme. It was led by Professor Jerzy Regulski, future Senator and Undersecretary for Local Government Reform in Prime Minister Tadeusz Mazowiecki's government. The opposition programme concluded from past failures that only fundamental reform could bring back genuine local self-government.

The programme's philosophy reflected unhappiness with the lack of democracy and the political bankruptcy of the regime. The programme stressed that:

1. the centralized political system and overdeveloped state administration, backed by monopolist political power, caused failures of previous reforms;
2. past changes reflected the ideology and objectives of internal governmental policies and not the public interest;
3. the political weakness of local government was, among other things, derived from nondemocratic elections and the absence of public support for local councils;
4. a restricted legal reform would be insufficient to bring about a change.

The programme presented during the 'Roundtable' demanded several fundamental changes. However, the goal of negotiations was not to produce yet another blueprint (in this case for the re-emergence of local self-government). The intent was to change the nature of the state itself. The opposition side made it clear that the purpose of the debate was to remove all barriers and allow subsequently elected and appointed professionals to shape the scope and the content of the local government reform (Regulski, 1989). The outlined programme argued for:

1. the abolition of the constitutional principle of uniform state power: local councils should represent local society and be free from hierarchical dependencies;
2. a new democratic electoral law;
3. communes to be recognized as legal entities with ownership rights;
4. fiscal autonomy of local government with a stable and controllable system of local budgets and financing, free of arbitrary decisions introduced by central administration;
5. a limitation of state interference in local affairs, by abolition of all central administrative regulations;

6. transfer of local state administration to communal control;
7. freedom to establish inter-communal associations, to advocate local interests in the central government; and
8. the right to judicial appeal against decisions made by state (central and regional) administration.

The outcome of the negotiations was far from satisfactory (Porozumienia Okraglego Stolu, 1989, p. 85). Agreement was reached in the areas of electoral law, ownership rights, local financing (partially), limitation of central-state interference, and the right to organize inter-communal associations, although only at the regional (*voivodship*) level. No specific calendar for the implementation of those points was set. Furthermore, no progress was made on key issues, essential to the overall success of the reform: the abolition of uniformity of state power, the transfer of state local administrative responsibilities, the establishment of a clear financial subsidy system for a five-year period, and the freedom of local government to establish national associations (Porozumienia Okraglego Stolu, 1989, p. 87).

This unwillingness of the regime to reform intergovernmental relations should be seen in the larger context of wilful ignorance of the political and administrative decentralization already taking place. The government was too frightened to provide local councils with power to determine their own needs and priorities. The regime did not dare allow the creation of local political lobbies. The Jaruzelski regime resisted yet again the attempt to entrust political power to civil society.

Post-1989 local government reform

The June 1989 parliamentary elections and the establishment of the first non-communist government in the summer of that year initiated widespread political and economic reforms. Local government reform was viewed as an essential element of the overall change. Prime Minister Mazowiecki, in his speech to the Citizen's Parliamentary Caucus, in the spring of 1990, stated, 'no democratic state can exist without real local democracy' (Czechowska, 1990). He proclaimed further that the upcoming local elections will be 'the key political event of this year'.

Building a legislative framework

The Office of the Undersecretary for Local Government Reform began preparations for local elections already in the fall of 1989. Between January and May, seven pertinent pieces of new legislation were introduced. The Sejm's and Senate's Commissions for Local Government debated and redrafted them. Finally, the Sejm enacted them as laws and they were signed by President Jaruzelski. In effect, the entire philosophy and structure of local government were redesigned. Through setting the date for local elections a way was paved for the implementation of reform. Two of the acts are especially significant for the future of local self-governance in Poland, the Local Self-Government Act, cleared by Parliament on 19 March, 1990, and the Local Government Duties and Powers Act, passed on 26 May, 1990. While the first sets the overall structure of the local government, the second establishes the division of responsibilities between local government and state administration.

LOCAL SELF-GOVERNMENT ACT

The eleven chapters of the Local Self-Government Act outline the structure and scope of activities that each municipality (*gmina*), can perform (Dziennik Ustaw, 1990, No. 16). Furthermore, it defines the gminas' authority and ownership rights and establishes their financial independence. The act also contains provisions about freedom to establish gminas, associations and inter-communal (inter-gmina) agreements. Finally, the act discusses the role and status of the second tier of elected officials, the Voivodship Assembly and the overall boundaries of supervision by regional and central authorities. The significance of the Local Self-Government Act is unquestionable. By legally establishing the gmina as a 'self-governing community', the act provides the gmina with powers to govern its own resources and to make independent decisions, in short, to determine its own needs and priorities. Local government no longer represents an extension of state authority. It has become a legal owner of communal property and has obtained rights to govern it in the manner most appropriate for the community. Most importantly, the gmina not only gained new rights, essential to its autonomy, but also secured legal status that permits it to protect its autonomy. Each gmina will govern by its own status, approved by the council.

The act states that 'the scope of activity of gminas shall embrace all public matters of local significance that are not reserved by law for other units . . . and unless otherwise stated, the settlement of all matters rests with gminas' (Dziennik Ustaw, 1990, No. 16, Chapter 2: Art. 6). The act is very specific about the tasks falling under the local jurisdictions and includes virtually all spheres of community needs. The act does not stipulate, however, which of these tasks are obligatory, which are delegated by the central government and which are the responsibility of the regional level. These issues were left to be decided in the Local Government Duties and Powers Act.

The power of Polish municipalities extends beyond pure provision of services, as local authorities are allowed to engage in economic activities by establishing and owning commercial and industrial enterprises. In addition, they will own the assets of such things as water and sewage systems, low-cost housing, and other public utilities. In this manner, the central state abandoned the socialist notion of regional equality and gave legitimacy to uneven development. Consequently, local states emerged.

The Local Self-Government Act also provides the framework for establishment of fiscal autonomy. Municipalities will be responsible for setting local budgets on an annual basis. The revenues will be drawn from a variety of sources, including taxes, government grants, income derived from charges and loans, and earnings from rents, lotteries and special events. The exact proportion in which each source will contribute to local budgets is still a subject of debate. Because the tax reform would not take place until 1992, the proportion of revenues raised through local taxes, as well as the amount that each municipality will be able to withhold for local needs, was left open. This ambiguity later became a major obstacle to the creation of an autonomous revenue system at the local level. Subsequently, it posed a threat to full implementation of local government reform and establishment of fully autonomous local self-government. Newly provided autonomy without fiscal autonomy is *de facto* an old distribution of power under new institutional structures.

THE LOCAL GOVERNMENT DUTIES AND POWERS ACT

The Local Government Duties and Powers Act, often referred to as the Competence Act, defines the areas of responsibilities falling under the jurisdiction of municipalities (Dziennik Ustaw, 1990, No. 34). Additionally, it lays the groundwork for separation of the decision-making power between the municipal level (elected officials) and district level (appointed state administration officials). Within the primary areas of responsibilities of local government are included pre-school and elementary education (on a voluntary basis until 1994, after which it will become obligatory); physical planning, land registry, land use management and property rights, building construction, housing management, public safety, health care, social welfare, public transportation, and highways and roads.

The act also includes provisions allowing for certain functions and powers to be delegated to municipalities by the central government. The most significant are civil defence, foster care, administration of sales and auctions of state property and land, and population statistics. Several other duties will remain as the responsibility of voivodships, the appointed level of state administration. These will include registration of properties, building inspection, environmental protection, determination of citizenship, and car registration and driving licence issuance.

There is no doubt that the approved legislation adheres to the principles of self-government adopted in western democracies and that it moves the Polish local government system towards participatory democracy. Each municipality has received autonomy and a large degree of power. But it is questionable if the new legislative framework did indeed allow for the full transfer of power to the local level. As mentioned earlier, the issue of fiscal autonomy was one of the contested territories. Another was division of responsibility between local self-governing bodies and centrally-controlled regional and district administrations. The power struggle that emerged during the parliamentary debates between the central and local level was to persist.

Exercising new rights: local elections of May 1990

Shortening the four-year term of local government officials elected under the communist regime and setting the date of local elections for 27 May, 1990 did not allow for a long and intensive campaign. The pre-election period was very short and did not permit the citizens to become familiar with the meaning of the decentralization process, with newly-enacted local government legislation, and with the new electoral law. A public opinion poll conducted in April 1990 by the Center for Public Opinion Survey (CBOS) indicated that only 3 per cent of respondents fully understood the new electoral law and only 27.8 per cent were partially familiar with it. The remaining 68.6 per cent were totally ignorant (Centre for Public Opinion Survey, 1990, p. 2). Further questions to validate the claims about the electoral knowledge indicated an even more dismal situation. More than 70 per cent of those who asserted that they understood the electoral law could not point out if their community had a majority or proportional system. Not surprisingly, those who knew more about the upcoming elections were also more inclined to participate: as candidates (7 per cent), in the work of the election committee (12 per cent), in the activities of an electoral commission (13.8 per cent), and as voters (84.7 per cent) (Centre for Public Opinion Survey, 1990, p. 3). Considering the fact that so few people understood the electoral mechanism, one would expect serious conflicts and numerous difficulties surrounding the elections. Indeed, the intensity of the pre-election campaign period increased as the election drew nearer.

PRE-ELECTION DILEMMAS

During the campaign three areas appeared to stir some emotion and controversy, namely 1) the division of Poland into 47,988 districts and the subsequent allocation of the seats, 2) nomination of the local electoral committees, and 3) selection of the candidates (Office of the General Commissioner for Elections, 1990a). The probability for conflicts when defining voting boundaries was high; nonetheless, only twenty-eight complaints were received by the Board of Judges of the General Commissioner for Elections. The electoral rules were rather flexible and some communities felt that gerrymandering took place when the boundaries were set. Other communities did not want to be divided into the smaller units, arguing that they always represented a unified front. Still others were making the opposite argument, stressing that they should not be merged with other communities and should be allowed to preserve their autonomy and to have their own candidates. After review, by the Board of Judges, the majority of complaints were rejected and, actually, only one was sustained.

The second and third areas of controversy reflected the increased politicization process. The complaints filed questioned the nomination process for the local election commission and argued that '(it) was made without taking into consideration all the organizations that are active in the communities' (Office of the General Commissioner for Elections, 1990a, p. 2). Those who ran as independents felt 'that Solidarity-supported Citizens Committees had a monopoly, and candidates who did not run from their lists did not have any chance to succeed' (Office of the General Commissioner for Elections, 1990a, p. 2). Indeed, for Polish society, Solidarity unquestionably meant freedom, strength and hatred of communism. The fact that Solidarity Citizens' Committees had exclusive use of the name and of the logo provided the candidates with almost certain victory. For the same reason many groups tried to use the name 'Solidarity' during the campaign, leading to arguments and conflicts among different political organizations. The closer the day of elections, the more visible were tensions and several of the cases ended in court (Office of the General Commissioner for Elections, 1990b).

Finding a sufficient number of candidates presented an unexpected problem in several communities. Three weeks before the election, 248 districts still did not have candidates (0.5 per cent of total) (Office of the General Commissioner for Elections, 1990a). This number, however, substantially decreased as the elections drew nearer and only forty-five districts remained unfilled the week before the election. In most cases, those lacking candidates were small, rural areas, often isolated from the main stream of political activities. Voivodships most distant from Warsaw, located on the outskirts of Poland, showed a shortage of candidates (Jeleniogorskie in the Southwest, and Przemyskie in the Southeast). In general, the entire eastern and south-eastern part of the country encountered the same problem. The isolation of the region, which has persisted over centuries, surfaced again. The eighteenth- and nineteenth-century partitions of Poland by Russia, Prussia and Austria resulted in Russian occupation of these territories. Because they were located on Russia's periphery, little attention was given to their development. During the communist regime, these areas continued to be

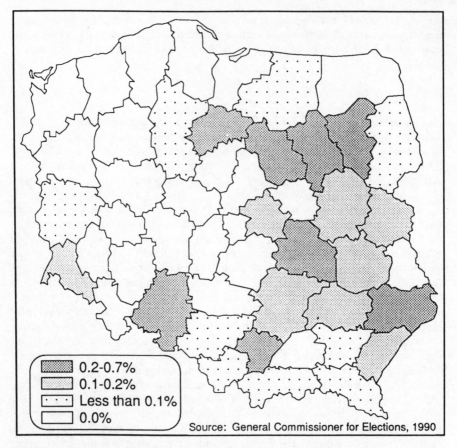

Figure 13.1 Percentages of districts in each region of Poland in which there were no candidates in the local elections, May 1990

referred to as 'Poland B', signifying very clearly the official attitude toward the region. At the time of the local election, in May of 1990, little had changed. The wave of democratic spirit had not yet reached those communities, some of which were distant from large metropolitan centres (Figure 13.1). Besides those districts that had no candidates, many had only one. Of the 47,988 voting districts, in 2,452 (5.1 per cent) candidates were running uncontested. In such cases the fear was that people would not turn out to vote, because they believed that their vote would not influence the final outcome.

Many factors could have contributed to the lower than expected interest in local elections. To a certain extent the lack of candidates stemmed from insufficient time to educate people about the importance of participatory democracy and about the new powers that citizens could exercise at the local level. Under the totalitarian system, where the relationship between state and society was one of dictatorship rather than of partnership, there was no tradition of dialogue. Clearly, the new political forces could not change the old ways of doing things overnight but on the other hand they did not see the importance of creating an environment fruitful for dialogue with society. Furthermore, under pressure of political events, the importance of local government reform diminished, leaving unattended the discussions about the new role that elected officials would perform and about the selection process itself.

Also seen in the electoral campaign were old behavioural patterns developed under communism, the mistrust of official institutions and disregard for governmental structures and law. Society was still uncertain about its future and ambivalent about what to do. On one hand, people did not believe fully that the political changes, originated in 1989, would be sustained and that they were deep enough to force fundamental reorientation of the political system. On the other hand, they believed that local elections were crucial for the further continuation of reforms. The above-mentioned CBOS study reported that almost half of the respondents (47.1 per cent) were convinced that local elections would change people and the ways in which they governed local affairs, 28.7 per cent trusted change in people but not in the system, and 19.2 per cent didn't believe in any change. These results point to caution and hesitance and a persistent lack of trust. They also showed ambivalence about citizens' roles in civil society and about the belief that their participation makes a difference. The same study found that 40.1 per cent of the respondents believed that after the elections their impact on local affairs would not change, but an almost equal number thought that it would increase (36.1 per cent). One fifth remained undecided (21 per cent) (Centre for the Public Opinion Survey, 1990, p. 9).

CANDIDATES AND THEIR POLITICAL AFFILIATION

Only 15 per cent of the candidates were women and they were more likely to run for office in urban areas. The average age of women and men candidates was 41 and 42, respectively (Office of the General Commissioner for Elections, 1990b). One-third of the candidates were farmers (34 per cent), 15 per cent were identified as industrial workers, 14 per cent as technicians and 10 per cent as teachers. Only 4 per cent considered themselves civil servants with administrative experience and only a few represented technical sciences with 3.9 per cent being engineers. The majority of the candidates in urban areas had completed higher education and most frequently represented such professions as teachers, lawyers, economists, engineers, doctors and architects (Office of the General Commissioner for Elections, 1990c).

The candidates for elected office were required to be residents of the voting districts, to have the right to vote themselves, and to present a list of signatures from citizens supporting their candidacy. The electoral system represented a combination of majority and proportional voting. In the voting districts with fewer than 40,000 people, elected officials competed for seats in the single-member districts, with the largest vote-getter becoming the winner. In districts with more than 40,000 citizens, a proportional system was established. In the case of single-seat districts, a minimum of 15 signatures were required while in the multi-seats districts 150 signatures were needed.

Interestingly enough, in smaller communities only 2.6 candidates per seat ran for election. In cities and towns where a proportional system was adopted, there were, on average, 4.6 candidates per seat. This greater competition for seats, in larger urban centres, should be seen as a direct result of emerging pluralism on the Polish political scene. Indeed, by the time of elections more than 1,000 groups, organizations and

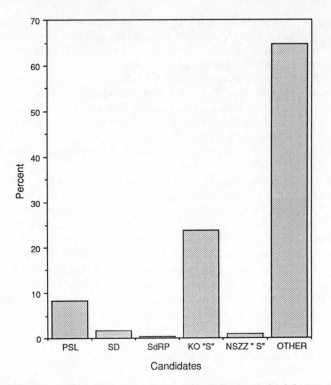

Figure 13.2 Distribution of candidates competing in single-member seats in local elections in Poland, May 1990.

political parties were registered. The final report of the National Election Commission indicated that altogether more than 350 parties participated in the election, including 80 organizations recognized as nationwide political parties and 270 groups representing local parties. Besides political parties, 660 organizations that did not perceive themselves as political entities supported candidates. In order to increase the chances of the candidates put up by smaller and lesser known parties, several groups decided to create coalitions and support candidates on a joint list. By election time, forty such coalitions were recognized, although often they were very fragile and clearly represented a one-time effort. The most frequently occurring alliances were between the Polish Social Democratic Union (PSDU) and the Polish Peasants Party (PPP), and the PPP and the Nationalist Party.

The distribution of support among different political organizations varied between single-seat and multi-seat districts. In the single-seat districts, the Citizens Committees (KOs) represented organizations that supported the largest number of candidates (24.85 per cent). As the old Communist Party as well as its new (SD and SdRP) incarnation were almost non-existent in those districts (2.04 per cent of candidates), the Peasant Party (PSL) (8.3 per cent) and the candidates running as independents or as representatives of small parties (64.75 per cent) gained additional places on the ballots (Office of the General Commissioner for the Elections, 1990d). (See Figure 13.2). The distribution of

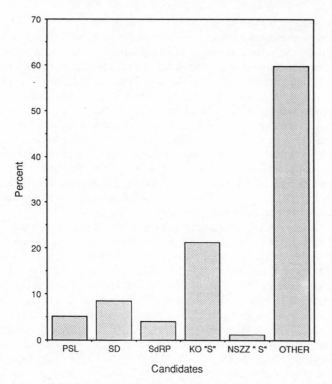

Figure 13.3   Party candidate lists presented in multi-seat districts in local elections in Poland, May 1990

candidates among different parties and groups in multi-seat districts was similar except for the strikingly stronger presence of the communist bloc. The Polish Social Democratic Union (SD) (8.58 per cent) and Social Democracy of the Republic of Poland (SdRP) (4.04 per cent) remained visible under the proportional system. The Polish Peasants Party (5.14 per cent) and the candidates running as independents or who were supported by smaller organizations (54.7 per cent) relinquished their seats (See Figure 13.3).

The emergence of political pluralism was evident. The analysis of political affiliation of candidates in rural and urban areas also revealed differences in the character of parties and groups that supported candidates. In rural areas the majority of the candidates ran as independents (54 per cent). Caution should be used, however, when interpreting this figure in the context of the rural political map. Because single-seat districts represent small communities, often candidates with some political preferences decided not to join any of the parties and thus not to get involved in 'neighbourhood disputes.' Some of them also belonged in the past to the Communist Party but decided at least on the surface to reject this affiliation, in hopes of winning the council seat. In the end, this created a perception of low party affiliation in rural areas, although, again, the Citizens Committees supported the greatest number of candidates in these areas (24 per cent). The peasant movements represented by Polish Peasant Party (8 per cent) and Solidarity-based Peasant Party (SPP) (2.5 per cent) were respectively the second and third largest group supporting candidates in rural areas.

Urban areas represented a completely different political landscape. Only 12 per cent of the candidates ran as independents. An additional 12 per cent represented members of coalition parties. The remaining 58 per cent were distributed among many parties and groups. Among them were the Polish Social Democratic Union (SD) (9 per cent), the Confederation for Independent Poland (KPN) (6 per cent), SdRP (5 per cent), PPP (2 per cent) and several Christian Democratic parties (3 per cent).

Undoubtedly the character of the electoral ordinances contributed significantly to this diversity. These results also reflect different stages at which rural and urban Poland finds themselves on the way to a pluralistic society. The greater visibility of a political scene and greater accessibility to a variety of domestic and international media are but two important factors affecting a more rapid awakening of political consciousness and of particular interests among urban than rural social groups. The more traditional and conservative social dynamic in rural areas also contributes.

In the final period of the campaign, the conflicts between the candidates and groups not only increased but their character changed. Beside the already-known disputes about the use of the Solidarity name, new tensions over the use of TV and radio time emerged. Several incidents were reported in which street posters and other campaign materials were destroyed by competing political organizations. In some cases material contained in those publications was questioned as demeaning and many of those cases did end up in court. Anonymous letters about candidates became an everyday matter in the Office of the General Commissioner for Elections. Some charged candidates with belonging to certain political organizations and others accused them of not being a member of such organizations. The letters questioned the integrity and character of candidates, or accused them of falsifying signatures and withholding information. The conflicts and tensions were spread across Poland and were not specifically confined to one area or another.

ELECTION RESULTS

All citizens of Polish nationality residing in Poland, who were at least eighteen years old, were eligible to vote, but only 42.13 per cent exercised their rights. The elections took place in 2,383 gminas and resulted in the election of 52,028 local officials. More than 147,327 candidates competed, resulting in a ratio of 2.8 candidates per seat. Women won 10.2 per cent of the seats. More than 51 per cent of the candidates were under age forty (Office of the General Commissioner for Elections, 1990d). The turnout on 27 May was considered low in comparison with Western countries but it was higher than the results of similar elections in other Central and East European countries. It was higher in urban, industrial areas (around 50 per cent) than in rural areas (35–40 per cent). The turnout in Warsaw was 43 per cent and in Poznan and Gdansk 50 per cent. In general, southern Poland showed the highest turnout, which was followed by border areas in the east and west (40 per cent). Central Poland had the lowest participation (around 30 per cent) (See Figure 13.4).

Those results voiced the unevenness with which the country moved, during the first year, through the political and economic transition. The areas where local society showed greater ability to mobilize and to organize its resources during the election cam-

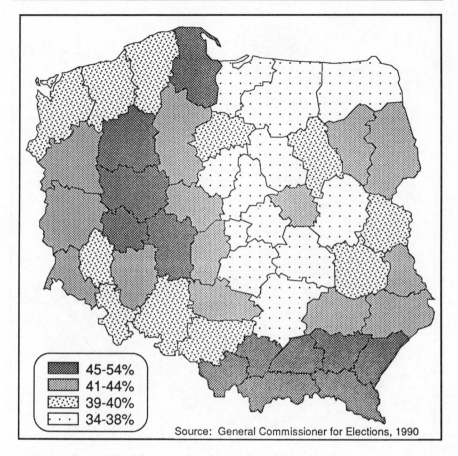

45-54%
41-44%
39-40%
34-38%

Source: General Commissioner for Elections, 1990

Figure 13.4 Turnout in local elections in Poland, May 1990

paign had the higher turnouts. Similarly, areas with a greater number of candidates attracted more voters. Nonetheless, there is cause for caution when those results are interpreted as an early sign of positive change. The striking similarity in spatial distribution can be noticed when the results of local elections are compared with the results of 1989 parliamentary elections. (See Figure 13.5). This uneven regional distribution reflected then not only new transitional trends but also old socio-economic and political patterns, both those pre-World War II and those inherited from communism.

In terms of political results, the candidates supported by Citizens Committees won overwhelmingly (43.02 per cent of the seats). The independent candidates gained 38 per cent of the seats, followed by PSL (5.76 per cent). Other parties fared badly. The old regime structures such as SdRP won only 0.28 per cent of the seats, but even new ones such as the KPN were hurt by winning only 0.1 per cent of the seats (See Figure 13.6). Hundreds of other parties and organizations were simply eliminated.

It is still debatable if the 42.1 per cent should be considered as a low turnout or if

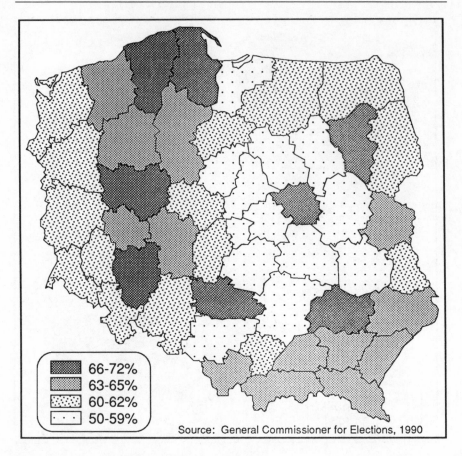

Figure 13.5   Turnout in parliamentary elections, June 1989

instead the expectations for 55–60 per cent were too high. Regardless of the answer, one may still question why people showed such a small interest in the first fully-free elections. Many factors can be blamed. Few, however, were repeated often enough to give the impression that indeed their influence was decisive. The emerging tensions between Lech Walesa and Prime Minister Mazowiecki, and overall rising economic difficulties, especially in rural areas, unquestionably created a climate of uncertainty and disillusionment (Gazeta Wyborcza, 1990). By not voting people, voiced their protest against the economic situation, this time, however, in a peaceful way. As reported by the Office of General Commissioner for Elections, the large number of political parties, organizations and groups presenting candidates created a confusing picture in some areas. The lack of clearly-defined political platforms and political fig-ures, in a country where political culture had no time to rise, left people feeling disori-ented. This, combined with limited understanding of the election process and of appropriate laws, resulted in the last-minute refusal to vote (Office of the General Commissioner for Elections, 1990e). In other regions, voters' numerous choices fostered

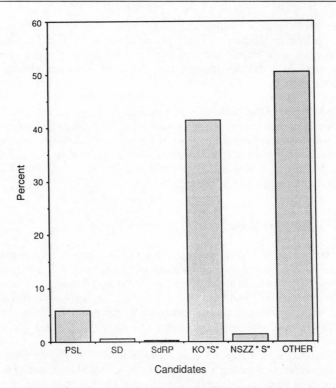

Figure 13.6   Distribution of seats won in single- and multi-seat districts in local elections in Poland, May 1990

a climate of real debate and a feeling that participation in elections would make a difference in the results.

There is no question that after forty-five years of being denied the right to full expression and participation in the governing of their country people wanted immediate and drastic change, but at the same time they did not believe that it was up to them to take the leadership role (Walesa, 1990). They did not grasp the importance of the election, did not realize the extent of power that the newly elected officials would have and the fact that by electing them society will indeed be able to break away fundamentally from the old nomenklatura at the local level (Najder, 1990). This explanation argued that society did not reach for the power that new legislation provided and that people remained sceptical and mistrusting. It implied a continued powerlessnes of the people. An opposite interpretation can be put forward, however. It can be argued that society did exercise its new power by interpreting it as a right to decide, and thus the right not to vote. In this context the absenteeism reflected acceptance of the new democratic rights.

Technical and organizational factors also affected the participation rate. The failure to establish mechanisms for mail ballots, and thus the necessity for students, military and government personnel to travel to their place of permanent residence, deterred many from participation (Regulski, 1990). The large voting districts, especially in the rural areas, also presented a barrier. On one hand, they led to greater isolation of the candidates from the communities, and on the other, with still-limited availability of public and private transportation, many potential voters simply did not bother to get to the polling stations. Finally, one may argue that the majority voting system, adopted in the rural areas, did not generate enough enthusiasm in an already pessimistic environment.

As much as these opinions and interpretations appeared on the surface to be diverse, they point to the difficulties encountered by Polish society and by the new Polish leadership during the period of transition. The conflicts between emerging political pluralism and the old remnants of the old monoparty system inherited from the communist state were acknowledged on the day of local elections. The question for both sides became how to build new political and economic structures, while at the same time attempting to destroy the old one.

Conclusion: the post-election road

The implementation of a newly designed system of local government does not happen without pain. The newly elected officials lack experience in public administration and management. They lack examples of how to implement decentralization and how to move from a centralized, totalitarian way of thinking into a system that requires initiative and independent action on the part of local leadership. They are also presented with the legacy of communist bureaucracy, with its inefficient and apathetic professional staff.

The difficulties are not mounting at the local level only. The government and its central administration is having a difficult time in relinquishing some of the power. A struggle emerged between the public administration sector, composed of the appointed-from-the-top officials, which would like to maintain a semi-centralized system, and the self-governing sector, derived through the elections, which strives to maintain newly acquired power at the local level.

Almost a year and a half after the local elections, the visible tensions and debates can be identified in major areas:

1. In the establishment of the additional tier of central state administration, below the voivodship level, composed of 250 districts. This new layer is charged with the power to oversee and to control many of the activities that were recently passed on to the gmina, the employees of the districts largely represent old voivodship nomenklatura, which was officially dismantled through the establishment of local self-government. Nonetheless, delegitimized political power appeared to have control over the legitimized one.
2. In the division of responsibilities between districts (appointed officials) and gminas (elected officials). Local elected officials feel cheated because of the expansionary tactics of the district administration and the persistent narrowing down of the power recently devolved to gminas. This is interpreted as an attack on decentralization process and a clear unwillingness of the central state to relinquish its power.
3. In the division of property between gmina, central state and private owners. Each gmina is required by law to conduct an inventory of properties on its territory. At stake are the future financial assets of the gmina, possession of which will, without question, have long-lasting financial repercussions for the economic stability of individual units.

4. In fiscal independence of gminas. Legislation introduced by the Ministry of Finance argues for the centralists' solution and a large degree of central control over establishment of tax rates and distribution of centrally collected taxes and fees. The Ministry of Finances will also maintain control over allocation of grants and subsidies offered by the central government. Such an arrangement would, however, mean little financial autonomy for an individual gmina and would question the overall ability of local self-government to maintain its autonomy.

These areas of conflict point to the difficulties with which emerging Polish self-governance is faced. Many of these problems and issues have been dealt with in Western countries, when they went through the process of restructuring their intergovernmental relations. What makes the Polish case, and those of other Central and Eastern European countries, different is a simultaneous attempt to change the law, the institutions and, most importantly, the behavioural patterns of the society.

This often-called 'peaceful revolution', although desired by the people, meets with certain resistance from political elites as well as from the society itself. The resistance is not always conscious or defined as such. While in the past, many political leaders in Poland perceived decentralization as a threat and a step toward the erosion of central monopoly of power and central control, current government leaders often act as if they lack the trust that local societies can handle their own affairs. They disregard the principles of self-determination, which entrust power to people and therefore to local council members as their representatives. In that manner the last two governments (of Prime Minister Mazowiecki and Prime Minister Bielecki) question if elected local officials are the most qualified to make decisions regarding community needs and also the ways in which they should be met. In short, although dreamed of, there seems to be reluctance to accept the ideology of local self-determination.

One year after local elections people were also disillusioned. As the survey conducted by CBOS in April 1991 indicated, people felt alienated and removed from participation in local affairs. When asked if they perceived that they had an impact on the affairs affecting their community, more than 61 per cent responded that nothing had changed in comparison to previous communist local governments. Twelve per cent indicated an actual decrease in their influence. Only 23 per cent believed that a positive change took place.

The new system of self-governance has not managed to break barriers between government and society established under communism. People indicated a certain degree of dissatisfaction and an increased sense that society's interests are the last to be addressed by local councillors. Only 28 per cent believed that newly-elected local council members are concerned with the needs of the gmina residents under their jurisdiction. An equal number (27 per cent) believed that local leadership defend primarily their own interests. The remaining 45 per cent of respondents saw the interests of particular groups as becoming the main focus of local councillors' attention. Among those groups most frequently mentioned were Solidarity (10 per cent), the Church (5 per cent), the old communist nomenklatura (5 per cent), the central government (2 per cent) and other political parties (3 per cent).

The lack of awareness and understanding of what actual powers newly-elected local officials have, while at the same time knowing that many previous attempts to bring change failed, has placed people in a 'wait and see' position. Many still are not sure what the transfer of power means in real terms. As one of the newly-elected officials in a small town told me in the summer of 1991 'they gave us power but they did not tell us what to do'. Polish society has yet to embrace fully what self-governance means and what benefits it can bring to communities. Indeed, many difficulties lie ahead for local democracy in Poland but there can be no doubt that the country is striving to reach it.

References

Centrum Badania Opinii Spolecznej (Centre for Public Opinion Survey), 1990, *Wybory Samorzadowe '90 (Local Elections '90)*, BS/109/40/90, Warsaw.

Chlopecki, J., 1990, *Przestrzen polityczna Polski: konflikt i zmiana (Political space of Poland: conflict and change)*, Instytut Gospodarki Przestrzennej No. 28, Uniwersytet Warszawski, Warsaw.

Czechowska, I., 1990, 'The new system into new hands', *Rzeczpospolita*, March 19.

Dziennik Ustaw, 1990, Ustawa o samorzadzie terytorialnym, (Local self-government act) 19 Marzec, 1990, No. 16, poz. 95.

Dziennik Ustaw, 1990, Ustawa o podziale zadan i kompetencji, (Local government duties and powers act) 26 Maj, 1990, No. 34, poz. 198.

Najder, Z. 1990, Interview, *Rzeczpospolita*, Maj 30.

Najdowski, J., 1991, *Przed wyborami lokalnymi: Komunikat z badan (Before local elections: Survey results)*, Office of the General Commissioner for Elections, Warsaw .

Office of the General Commissioner for Elections, 1990a, 'Sytuacja przedwyborcza na terenie poszczegolnych wojewodztw' (Pre-election situation in individual voivodships), *Bulletin*, May 2.

Office of the General Commissioner for Elections, 1990b, 'Sytuacja przedwyborcza na terenie kraju' (Pre-election situation across the country), *Bulletin*, May 15.

Office of the General Commissioner for Elections 1990c, 'Sytuacja przedwyborcza na terenie kraju' (Pre-election situation across the country), *Bulletin*, May 25.

Office of the General Commissioner for Elections, 1990d, 'Sytuacja powyborcza w poszczegolnych regionach kraju' (Post-election situation in individual regions), *Bulletin*, May 30.

Porozumienia Okraglego Stolu, 1989, (Roundtable agreements), NSZZ 'Solidarnosc' Region Warminsko-Mazurski, Olsztyn.

Regulski, J., 1989, 'Polish local government in transition', *Environment and Planning C: Government and Policy* 7: 423–444.

Regulski, J. 1990, Interview, *Rzeczpospolita*, May 30.

Walesa, L. 1990, Interview, *Rzeczpospolita*, May 30.

Zakrzewski, W., 1987, 'Nouvelle loi sur le systéme de l'autogestion territoriale en Pologne', in *Federalism and decentralization*, Westview Press, Boulder, CO, and Editions Universitaires, Fribourg, Suisse.

Zawadzki, S. 1987, 'Decentralization and optimalisation of the local decision-making process (Poland)', in *Federalism and decentralization*, Westview Press, Boulder, CO, and Editions Universitaires, Fribourg, Suisse.

14 Czechoslovak parliamentary elections 1990: old patterns, new trends and lots of suprises

Petr Jehlička, Tomáš Kostelecký, Luděk Sýkora

The Czechoslovak parliamentary election of June 1990 was one very important event in the post-communist development of state and society after the November 1989 upheaval. On the basis of the results, the federal parliament and both (in the Czech and Slovak republics) national parliaments were formed in a fully democratic way for the first time since 1946. Thus, the 1990 elections allowed further legal steps towards the re-creation of a democratic society of the Western type. Czechoslovakia had already been a democracy before World War II and, with some exceptions, was again a democracy for a short time after the war. The Communist coup in February 1948 transformed the country into a non-democratic 'people's republic'.

In the interwar years, 1919–1939, Czechoslovakia was the only stable democracy in Central Europe, holding regularly-scheduled elections. The electoral law was based on the proportional representation (PR) system and this electoral system has now been restored in a very similar form. In addition, some of the important pre-war political parties survived the communist regime and others were founded again in the wake of its 1989 defeat. These continuities offer the researcher the chance to study the similarities in voting patterns in Czechoslovakia, before and after the communist period.

This chapter begins by providing general information on the Czechoslovak elections. Against this background, some of the most interesting results of the 1990 elections are presented in detail and are interpreted with reference to the historical roots of contemporary voting patterns and in terms of relations between the present voting patterns and the geography of social, economic and cultural phenomena in the country.

The political context

The surprisingly rapid withdrawal of the communists from the Czechoslovak Government started already in December 1989, immediately after the 'Velvet Revolution' of the month before and political events culminated in the elections of June 1990. The 'Government of National Understanding' was set up as the beginning of a transition period in December 1989. The Communist Party occupied only a minority of the ministerial posts in that government. The remaining posts were given to Civic Forum and The Public Against Violence (based on major opposition groups against the Government before November 1989) and to two historical parties, the Czechoslovak Socialist Party and the Czechoslovak People's Party, both of which had survived the forty-two years of one-party rule as satellites of the Communist Party. The formation of this new federal government effectively brought the communist monopoly of political power to an end.

The election by parliamentary deputies of Alexander Dubček (leading figure of the 1968 Prague Spring) as Chairman of the Federal Assembly and of Václav Havel (a founding signatory of Charter 77 and a well-known dissident) as President followed at the end of 1989. In his very first speech in office, President Havel emphasized the need to hold free elections in Czechoslovakia. A further reduction of the role of the Communist Party resulted from co-option of primarily non-party people to the three parliaments in order to replace former Communist deputies. Hence, non-communist majorities were established in both federal and republic parliaments. Czechoslovakia thus became the first country in Eastern Europe in which the organisation of free and competitive parliamentary elections was supervised by the opposition and not by a still-ruling Communist Party (Wightman, 1991).

The structure of contemporary elected bodies was created in October 1968 when the Law of the Federation was approved by the Czechoslovak parliament. In accordance with the federal arrangement of the state, one federal and two parliaments for the republics were founded. The Federal Parliament, called 'Federal Assembly', still has the greatest legislative power. It is composed of two chambers (the Chamber of the People and the Chamber of Nations) with equal rights and responsibilities and each have the same number of members, 150. Members of the Chamber of the People are elected in the whole of Czechoslovakia proportionally to the population of both republics. Consequently, there are approximately twice as many representatives from the Czech Republic as from the Slovak Republic in this chamber. The Chamber of Nations consists of two sections of the same size (seventy-five seats); members of one section are representatives elected in the Czech Republic and members of the other section are elected in the Slovak Republic. In effect, this is similar to the US House of Representatives, based on population, and the US Senate, based on area, with the same number from each place without regard to the size of the place. But to prevent domination by the much larger Czech population, all constitutional laws and other important laws must be approved in both sections separately; Czech representatives simply cannot outvote Slovaks. Besides the Federal Assembly, there are two parliaments for the republics called the Czech National Council and the Slovak National Council. The Czech National Council has 200 members and the Slovak National Council has 150 members. The division of powers between the Federal Assembly and the National Councils is determined by constitutional law.

After the revolution of November 1989, it was generally seen as necessary to change the majority electoral system (only one seat in each electoral district) that was used in the quasi-elections during the communist rule. A new electoral law prescribing a system of proportional representation was approved by the Federal Assembly on 27 February 1990, after several round table meetings of the Communist Party, the Civic Forum, the Public Against Violence and some smaller parties who were the former satellites of the Communist Party. For several reasons, there was a broad consensus concerning the introduction of the PR system. It appealed to the Civic Forum and the Public Against Violence as likely to provide a fairly accurate reflection of the real state of political opinion after forty-two years of communist regime. It was also argued that a majority system would probably produce an undesirable two party structure (Civic Forum together with the Public Against Violence versus the Communist Party). For the Communist Party and its former satellites, a PR system implied more chances to have at least some parliamentary representation. Moreover, a PR system had been used both in pre-war Czechoslovakia and in the 1946 elections.

The electoral law instituted twelve multi-member electoral districts. Names of candidates were listed on official ballot papers in accordance with a party's proposal. Every voter had in fact three votes, two for the two chambers of the Federal Assembly and a third one for his/her National Council. As a change to the pre-war electoral law, a possibility of indicating preferences was introduced; voters could mark from one to four candidates' names on every ballot paper. If any candidate received more than 10 per cent preferences, he/she was shifted to the top of the list. In order to avoid a high degree of party fragmentation, so typical of the Czechoslovak parliament before World War II, a legal threshold was approved. To be represented in the Federal Assembly, a party needed to obtain at least 5 per cent of the votes on the territory of at least one republic. Thus, the hurdle differs from the German case, where a party needs 5 per cent nationally. For representation in the Czech National Council, at least 5 per cent of the votes was necessary; for seats in the Slovak National Council, 3 per cent of the votes was sufficient. It was further determined that parties with more than 2 per cent of the votes in either one of the republics would receive 10 Czechoslovak crowns ($1 = approximately 30 crowns) for every vote from the government. It was simultaneously made possible for the parties to borrow money from the state to finance their electoral campaign.

Historical background

The 1990 elections were the sixth free elections in more than seventy years of Czechoslovak history but the first after forty-two years of communist rule and it was forty-four years since the last free elections in 1946. The first general election took place in 1920 and the next pre-war elections followed in 1925, 1929 and 1935. The electoral system of the first Czechoslovak republic was essentially very similar to the present one; it was also a nearly pure PR system. The most important difference with respect to the present situation was the existence of the single parliament composed of the House of Representatives (300 seats) and the smaller Senate (150 seats). Members of both chambers were elected in the whole of Czechoslovakia proportionally to the population of the respective historical lands (Bohemia, Moravia and Slovakia). Usually about twenty political parties took part in the elections; the most important parties are listed in Table 14.1.

Conditions changed considerably after World War II, when the influence of the Soviet Union and the Communist Party in Czechoslovak politics increased. The participation of political parties in the 1946 elections was restricted in accordance with the Košice Government Programme (1944), based on Communist Party proposals. This was accepted by the Czechoslovak government in exile and served as a basic programme for the first post-war government. Only four parties could participate in the Czech lands or in Slovakia. The Communist Party ran in both parts of Czechoslovakia, but the rest of the party spectrum was different. While in the Czech lands, three historical parties, namely, the Czechoslovak People's Party, the Czechoslovak Socialist Party and the Czechoslovak Social Democracy ran against the communists, in Slovakia, non-communist forces were represented by newly established parties (the Democratic Party, the Freedom Party and the Labour Party).

Table 14.1   A classification of major parties according to the left-right dimension in Czechoslovakia 1920–1992

Time period	Communists	Left	Centre	Centre-Right	Separatist
1920 1925 1929 1935	Communists (#a)-13-10-10)b	Social Democracy (26-9-13-13) socialists (8-9-10-9) German Soc. Dem. (11-6-7-4)	national democracy (6-5-5-6) German agrarians (4-8-5-2)	republican/agrarian (14-14-15-14) People's party (8-10-8-8) Sudeten German party (#-#-#-15)	Hlinka's party (4-7-6-7)
1946 CRc SRc	Communists (40) Communists (31)	Social Democracy (16) Labour Party (3)	socialists (24) Freedom party (3)	People's party (20) Democratic party (62)	
1948-1989	Communists + satellites Socialists and People's Party in the Czech Republic Freedom Party and Slovak Revival Party in Slovak Republic				
1990	Communists (13,13)d	Social Democracy (4,2) socialists (3,0) agrarians (4,2)	Civic Forum (50,-) PAV (-,32) KDH (-,18) Coexistence (-,9) greens (3,3)	KDU (People's) (9,-) Democratic party (-,4)	Slovak national (-,11) Moravians (9,-)
January 1992c- CR	Communists (7)	Social Democracy (13) Liberal Social Union (5)	OH (4)	ODS (21) People's Party (5) ODA (4)	
-SR	Democratic Left (10)	HZDS (27)	KDH (15) Coexistence (4)	ODU-VPN (4) Democratic party (3)	Slovak national (10)

Notes: Electoral results in parentheses are in percentages of total votes.
a) the party did not exist; b) electoral results in (1920-1925-1929-1935); c) CR – Czech Republic, SR - Slovak Republic
d) electoral results in (CR, SR); e) public opinion poll (*source:* Hospodářské noviny, 29.1.1992)

Source: Federal Statistical Office (1920-1946); Svobodné Slovo (11.6.1990), Vol. XLIV, No. 135, p. 1. (1991); Hospodářské noviny, 29.1.1992 (1992)

With one slight exception, all four Czech parties participating in 1946 ran in all pre-war elections as well as in the 1990 elections. (The communists did not participate in the 1920 elections because the party was only founded in 1921). We call these parties 'historical' and their electoral results can therefore be compared very precisely over time. But one should keep in mind that the remainder of the party spectrum changed considerably over time. The analysis of the long-term (from 1920 to 1990) continuity of voting in Slovakia can be focused on the communists only, because no other party was present there also in the pre-war period, in 1946 and in 1990. However, it is possible to recognize two main political streams in the history of Slovak politics. The first one represents forces which have always claimed the autonomy or independence of Slovakia and the other consists of pro-Czechoslovak parties there. A comparison of voting patterns of both camps provides interesting results.

The participation of the Czech historical parties in the six free general elections enables us to establish whether there is a regional continuity of voting in the Czech lands during the entire existence of independent Czechoslovakia. The most intriguing aspect is obviously the more than forty years gap between the elections of 1946 and 1990 and its influence on the voting patterns. Jehlička and Sýkora (1990) attempted to answer whether 'the several decades gap between the 1990 election and the last election that can be considered free (1946) . . . did not obliterate the local cultural and social climate in certain regions, which is the basis for the preservation of the continuity of support for the historical political parties in the Czech lands'. They demonstrated a certain stability of regional voting patterns. The present contribution additionally includes an analysis of the historical roots of Slovak politics and also provides an evaluation of the 1990 election as a whole against a historical background.

General electoral results

The 1990 elections created a solid basis for a pluralist democracy in Czechoslovakia. They took place without serious incidents. An extremely high electoral turnout (more than 96 per cent of those eligible to vote) confirmed the legitimacy of the elected bodies. This very high participation in free elections can partly be explained by a great desire of the people to choose their own future, partly it could be understood as a consequence of a massive campaign in the media, and by most political parties, against non-participation.

Although sixty-six political groupings passed the legal requirements for registration as a political party, only twenty-three of them were registered for the elections. Furthermore, one of those (the Organization of Independent Rumanians) dropped out three weeks before the election day. Eleven parties put up candidates throughout the whole of the country and others formed separate Czech and Slovak organizations within similar sections of the political spectrum. Thirteen of them got more then 2 per cent of the votes in at least one of the republics; these parties are listed in Table 14.2. Eight of them crossed the 5 per cent threshold and as a result entered the Federal Parliament. The Czech National Council was composed of four parties and the Slovak National Council of seven parties, though some of them still preferred to call themselves movements, rather than see themselves as part of the establishment. All parties that gained seats in the Czech parliament did so in the Federal Assembly as well. On the other hand, two Slovak parties (the Greens and the Democratic Party) that managed to get over the 3 per cent limit for the parliament of the republic did not succeed in passing the 5 per cent limit for the Federal Parliament.

It is possible to distinguish some groupings among the political parties and movements running in the elections. A special category are the two movements, Civic Forum and the Public Against Violence, that apparently carried the banner of the November revolution and won the elections. Historical parties such as Social Democracy, the Czechoslovak Socialist Party and the (Slovak) Democratic Party tried to resume their pre-communist traditions and on that basis ran their electoral campaign. Yet, they generally did not get as many votes as expected. Although the Communist Party of Czechoslovakia played a special role in the elections, it is considered as a historical one as well as the Christian and Democratic Union, a coalition with the historical People's Party as the main component. Sizable support for ethnic and separatist parties and movements surprisingly allowed their entrance to the parliaments and drew attention to an increasingly important feature of the multi-ethnic character of the country in the contemporary Czechoslovak political scene. The post-material politics represented by the Green Party also managed to get into a parliament (Slovak

Table 14.2   Results of parliamentary elections in Czechoslovakia 1990

	Federal		Assembly		National councils	
Party	Chamber of People		Chamber of Nations			
	in CR	in SR	in CR	in SR	Czech	Slovak
1.	53.15	–	49.96	–	49.50	–
2.	–	32.54	–	37.28	–	29.34
3.	13.48	13.81	13.80	13.43	13.24	13.34
4.	–	18.98	–	16.66	–	19.20
5.	8.69	–	8.75	–	8.42	–
6.	7.89	–	9.10	–	10.03	–
7.	–	10.96	–	11.44	–	13.94
8.	0.08	8.58	–	8.49	–	8.66
9.	–	4.40	–	3.68	–	4.39
10.	3.10	3.20	3.44	2.58	4.10	3.48
11.	3.77	2.58	3.99	2.10	4.11	2.51
12.	3.84	1.89	4.17	1.51	4.11	1.81
13.	2.75	0.06	2.89	0.06	2.68	0.03
14.	3.25	3.00	3.90	2.77	3.81	3.30
TOTAL	100.0	100.0	100.0	100.0	100.00	100.00

Notes: CR – Czech Republic, SR – Slovak Republic. Party codes: 1. Civic Forum (OF); 2. Public Against Violence (VPN); 3. Communist Party of Czechoslovakia (KSC); 4. Christian Democratic Movement (KDH); 5. Christian and Democratic Union (KDU); 6. Movement for Self-Governing Democracy - Society for Moravia and Silesia (HSD-SMS); 7. Slovak National Party (SNS); 8. Coexistence (coalition of national minorities) & Hungarian Christian Democratic Movement; 9. Democratic Party (DS); 10. Green Party (SZ); 11. Alliance of Agrarians and Countryside (SZV); 12. Social Democracy (SD); 13. Czechoslovak Socialist Party (CSS); 14. Other parties.

Source: Svobodné Slovo (11.6.1990), Vol. XLIV, No. 135, p. 1.

National Council) and their results in some environmentally-damaged regions were also substantial. There were two other parties that got considerable support - the Christian Democratic Movement and the Alliance of Agrarians and Countryside. Among the smallest parties that got less than 2 per cent of the vote, the most interesting were a Friends of Beer Party (a similar party ran in Poland in 1991) and the core of an extreme right-wing party.

Movements

Civic Forum and Public Against Violence were established in November 1989 as loosely-organized movements that united all colours of democratic opinion from reform communists to the right-wing oriented political forces. Their representatives led the revolution, initiated the negotiations with the Communist Party and took crucial steps in pre-election governments and parliaments. The movements were identified in the public mind as guarantors of the return to pluralistic democracy, private ownership and a market economy. They entered the elections with the advantage of their prominent role in the 'Government of National Understanding' in the six months up to the elections and with the presence among their members of some of the best-known artistic and political personalities in Czechoslovakia. Their role was seen as the united opposition to the Communist Party and the elections were viewed as a referendum for or against totalitarianism. The electoral campaign slogan 'Parties are for party-liners, Civic Forum is for everybody!' expressed the general feature of the movements, which was the great variability of ideas under one umbrella with the overthrow of the communist regime as its main task.

Anti-communist feeling found expression in a generally high level of support in the whole country (Figure 14.1). Nevertheless, some interesting differences in the levels of voting support showed a tendency towards increasing the vote percentage for Civic Forum with increasing size of the commune. This occurred in all regions. The spatial pattern of the election returns shows that Civic Forum won its highest support in the cities and suburbs of large cities. The best example of this was Prague and its surroundings. The geographically-different rates of support for Civic Forum in the 1990 election can perhaps be best explained by considering the movement as the diffusion of an innovation touching the different parts of the settlement system sequentially both in a vertical manner (hierarchical diffusion) and in a horizontal direction (neighbourhood diffusion) from the centre. The implication of these processes is that historical parties that had their core strength at the top of the urban hierarchy and its surroundings had most difficulty in competing with these new (only since 1990) movements.

Czech historical parties

The four Czech historical parties usually gained more than 40 per cent of the votes in the Czech lands before the war and they got almost 100 per cent in 1946 because of the restricted electoral participation of parties. Their share of the vote in the Czech Republic in June 1990 was 29 per cent. Only two historical parties gained support comparable to what they received in the past. The Communists received

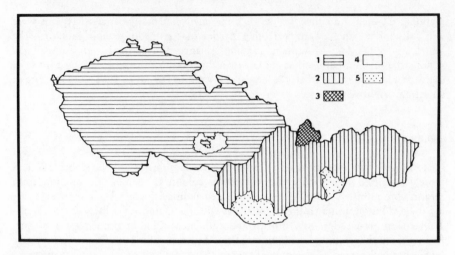

Figure 14.1   Winning parties according to districts: 1) Civic Forum, 2) Public Against Violence, 3) Christian Democratic Movement, 4) Movement for Self-Governing Democracy – Society for Moravia and Silesia and 5) Coexistence and Hungarian Christian Democratic Movement

even more (13 per cent) than they usually did before the war (about 10 per cent) The People's Party, who in 1990 overwhelmingly dominated the coalition of the Christian and Democratic Union (KDU) got 8 per cent in 1990 against approximately 9 per cent before the war. The other two historical parties gained only one third of votes that they did before 1948. The Socialists received about 3 per cent of the vote and the Social Democrats 4 per cent (compare these numbers with those in Table 14.1). Successful or not, the regional continuity of voting survived the communist period as Figure 14.2 shows (Jehlička and Sýkora 1991). This figure portrays on the one hand the regions with continuous high support in the core areas of the respective political parties (dark shading) and, on the other, the areas where parties have traditionally had the lowest support (cross-hatched). Core areas were defined as the areas where the respective parties were most successful in every election. (For a detailed description of the methodology, see Jehlička and Sýkora, 1991.)

In 1990, by far the largest number of votes for the KDU (Christian and Democratic Union) was won in south Moravia. This region always was a traditional stronghold of the Czechoslovak People's Party representing the backbone of the Christian and Democratic Union. The analyses of the 1990 elections showed a negative correlation between the divorce rate and the support for the KDU, confirming the expected positive relationship between religiosity and support for the KDU (Blažek and Kostelecký, 1991). The pro-KDU vote per centage generally increasing with decreasing population size of the municipality. The People's Party retained its traditional core of voters among the Catholics in the south Moravian countryside.

The main feature of the 1990 election results of the communists is their relatively even spatial distribution, both in terms of regional variation and by communities of different sizes. That is contrary to the traditional support pattern of the communists, that used to peak in the industrial regions to the west of Prague (Jehlička and Sýkora, 1991; see Figure 14.2). To some extent, the election results in 1990 were more favourable to the Communist Party than might be expected. One of the possible explanations of the even spatial distribution is the layer of nomenclature cadres formed in the course of the forty years of communist control in all the regions. This resulted more generally in a certain proportion of the population in all regions drawing benefits from the communist regime. The hypothesis that the Communist Party was supported in 1990 by a large part of the former and present-day state apparatus (at least at the lower levels) is verified by the significantly higher vote for the Communists in the capitals of districts, compared to the Communist support in towns without such adminastrative status.

The Czechoslovak Socialist Party was in the past the typical urban, central left-wing party of the middle class in Bohemia. The socialists always emphasized the traditions of the Czech nation and of Protestantism. The dramatic decline of the support for this party in the 1990 elections compared to their pre-war strength resulted from an unattractive campaign which excessively stressed the traditional outlook of the party. This included a narrow class orientation to the 'middle class' which had nearly disappeared

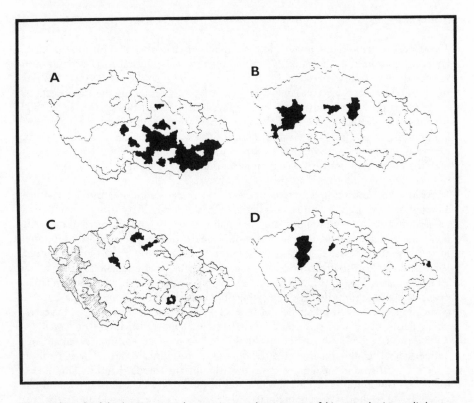

Figure 14.2   Czech lands: core areas, where parties were the most successful in every election studied (shaded), and marginal areas, where parties have not gained at least the average support in any of the elections studied (hatched): A) People's Party, B) Social Democracy, C) Czechoslovak Socialist Party and D) Communist Party

Source: Jehlička and Sýkora 1991

under the Communist regime and could not re-establish itself during the few months since the November 1989 upheaval. The party apparently won only votes from those, presumably the elderly, who remembered its pre-war fame.

Three parties existed during the communist period with the People's Party and the socialists surviving as satellites of the Communist Party. Thus, they had already created a party structure and had a certain amount of party members. On the other hand, the Social Democrats were only re-established in the beginning of 1990. They did not succeed in either creating a serious political programme or in rallying supporters around the party. Moreover, some well-known personalities promoting Social-Democratic ideas were listed on the Civic Forum ballot and this considerably diminished the electoral support of the Social Democrats. However, the party's old western and eastern Bohemian strongholds re-emerged in the voting returns; they gained somewhat greater support than they had before 1948 in the North Bohemian coal basin (north of Prague).

Slovak historical parties

The Slovak situation was much more complicated than the situation in the Czech lands. Apart from the Communist Party, no other Slovak political party with an uninterrupted electoral history exists. Social Democracy did not take part in the 1946 elections. The Democratic Party is only a fairly recent party, contesting the 1946 elections.

As far as the Communist Party in Slovakia is concerned, two main areas of high support were revealed by the 1990 elections. These were identical with the old pre-war Communist cores (Jehlička, Kostelecký and Sýkora, 1991). One of them in southeastern Slovakia is an ore-mining area. It is not without significance that this region, near the Hungarian border, lies just opposite the strongholds of the Hungarian Communists (see the following chapter by Zoltan Kovacs)

Besides the communists, some traces of historical continuity can be revealed, although less precisely. The pre-war Hlinka's Slovak Peoples Party strongly emphasized religion (Catholic), autonomist and nationalist elements and its main programme point was the struggle for the separation of Slovakia; this party was mostly supported in north-western Slovakia. It is in this same territory that both the Slovak National Party and the Christian Democratic Movement gained considerable support in the 1990 elections (Figure 14.3). The former overtly demands the immediate independence of Slovakia from the federal republic; the latter is oriented towards the Catholic population, stressing its preference for independence in less extreme terms. However, a strong nationalistic wing exists inside the Christian Democratic Movement as well.

The pro-Czechoslovak parties in Slovakia before the war, wishing to remain in a united federal republic, represented the opposition to Hlinka's Party. The Republican Party of Agrarian and Smallholders was most important among them. Its Slovak electorate was concentrated in East Slovakia and in the Protestant regions of Central Slovakia. These territories are approximately the same ones, where the Democratic Party (DS) in 1946 and the Public Against Violence (VPN) in 1990 gained most of their votes. The DS won the post-war elections in Slovakia (60 per cent), defeating the Communists there though the Communists were winners in the Czech lands with 40 per cent. In 1990, however, the DS attracted the votes of only 4 per cent of the Slovak electorate, barely sufficient to enter the Slovak National Council.

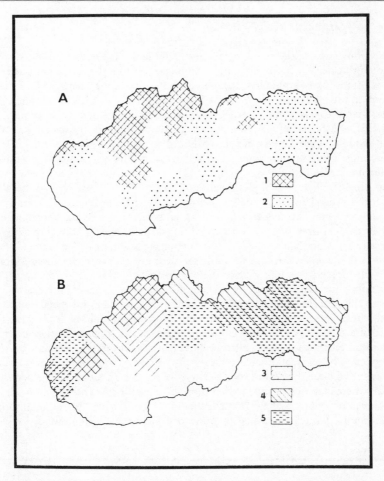

Figure 14.3   Slovakia: Regions with the highest support for selected parties: A) parliamentary elections
1925-1935, B) parliamentary elections 1990; 1) Hlinka's Slovak Peoples Party, 2) Agrarian Party, 3) Slovak
National Party, 4) Christian Democratic Movement and 5) Public Against Violence

From the historical point of view, it is possible to distinguish very roughly three general political orientations of the Slovak voters in three geographical zones:

a) North-western Slovakia represents both the historical and present strongholds of
the separatist forces (the Hlinka's Party before the war and the Slovak National
Party and the Christian Democratic Movement in 1990);
b) Eastern Slovakia always was and is again the most 'pro-Czechoslovak' part of
Slovakia (the Agrarian party at the time of the first Republic to 1939 and the
stronghold of the VPN in 1990); and
c) Southern regions settled by the Hungarian minority, who always expressed their
own interests in elections.

Ethnic and separatist parties and movements

The elections revealed the strength of a seemingly new issue in Czechoslovak politics that could threaten the future of political democracy or even the survival of Czechoslovakia as a state. Three ethnic-based and ethnic-appealing parties managed to get representation in the parliaments. The Slovak National Party (which wants an independent Slovak state), the Movement for Self-Governing Democracy – Society for Moravia and Silesia HSD–SMS (asking for autonomy of the Moravian lands, the eastern half of the Czech Republic), and Coexistence (a coalition of national minorities but in reality drawing most of its support from the Hungarians in southern Slovakia) got into the parliaments (Figure 14.4).

The strength of the Slovak National Party, which won 11 per cent of the Slovak vote for the Federal Assembly and 14 per cent for the Slovak National Council, was totally unexpected. The concentration of its supporters close to the border with the Czech Republic corresponds well with traditional preferences. The voting pattern of the Society for Moravia and Silesia is very interesting as the party wants the territorial lines to be re-drawn on the basis of ethnic self-definition. There were North-Moravian and South-Moravian regions within the administrative structure of the (pre-1990) Czechoslovak Socialist Republic, but their administrative borders did not exactly coincide with the historical Moravian–Silesian lands. The regional (provincial) authorities were abolished in 1990 and the restoration of Moravian autonomy became the main political aim of the Society for Moravia and Silesia party. Support for the Society for Moravia and Silesia party represented well over 20 per cent of the electorate in Moravian regions. The regional differences in the proportion of votes of the HSD–SMS are large; the party came in first in two of twenty-five districts in Moravia. The percentage of votes, where it contested seats, varied from 0.2 per cent (East Bohemia) to 33.5 per cent (district of Vyškov near the Moravian metropolis of Brno). The centre of support for this regionally oriented party is the town of Brno and its surroundings (see Figure 14.4).

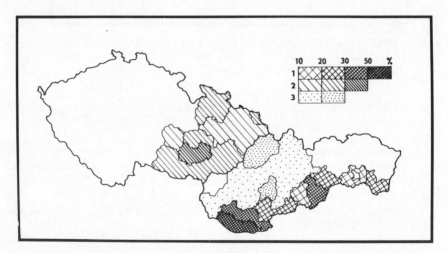

Figure 14.4   Electoral results of 1) Coexistence and Hungarian Christian Democratic Movement, 2) Movement for Self-Governing Democracy – Society for Moravia and Silesia and 3) Slovak National Party

The main issues in the HSD–SMS election programme (and almost the only ones) were the restoration of historical lands. In particular, they wanted the establishment of the Moravian-Silesian Land as a large administrative unit with its capital Brno combined with a considerable degree of self-government. They also wanted a new administrative system that would return the former district offices to most of the former district capitals. Statistically significant higher percentages of HSD–SMS votes were found in towns which in the former (pre-1989) administrative system were the locations of the district offices and which, in the administration reform in the early 1960s, had lost their status. A large number of electors evidently gave their votes to the HSD–SMS in the hope that this would result in benefits for themselves and their place of residence.

HSD-SMS voters were also aroused by the historical awareness of being 'Moravians', understood as part of the Moravian-Silesian Land (abolished in 1949) and, at least by some of them, as part of the 'Moravian nation'. The HSD-SMS support was particularly evident in the present-day districts that are divided by the former historical land border into a Czech part and a Moravian part (see Figure 14.5). This territorial division apparently resulted in a kind of frontier mentality.

The election results of Coexistence are shown in Figure 14.4. Their strongholds are

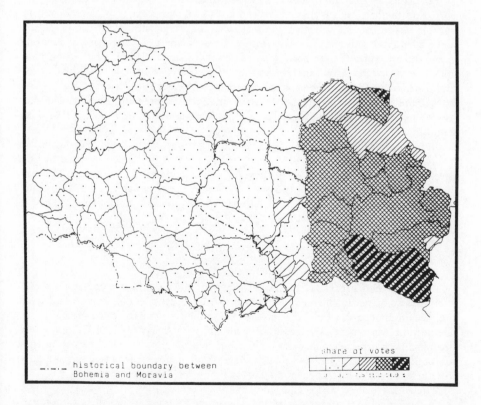

share of votes

_._._ historical boundary between
Bohemia and Moravia

Figure 14.5 Electoral results of the Movement for Self-Governing Democracy – Society for Moravia and Silesia in district Svitavy by communes

situated along the border with Hungary and in some electoral districts, the party obtained more than 50 per cent of all votes. Although Coexistence supported a federal system for the republic and had no separatist ambitions, there is a considerable link between the party and national minority interests. In the case of Coexistence, it represented rather a reaction to potential Slovak nationalism and provided a possibility of setting up a legal means of self-defence.

The Greens

The Green Party represents the 'new politics' in Czechoslovakia. It was the first political party established after the student demonstration of 17 November 1989, that set the 'Velvet Revolution' in motion. First reports about the Greens were published before the revolution was over. However, the very beginnings of the party are obscure and some participation of the former Secret Police, trying to capitalize on the strong ecological awareness of the Czechoslovak population, is generally suspected. After December 1989, the Green Party had to exert a great effort to eliminate the Secret Police influence.

As regards the electoral results, the Greens gained much less support than was anticipated on the basis of pre-election polls. Six seats (3.5 per cent of votes) achieved in the Slovak parliament was their only success. The regional differentiation of the Greens, support indicates the close relation between the devastation of the environment and the votes for the party (Jehlička and Kostelecký, 1991). The Greens won most votes in the most environmentally deteriorated north-western districts of Bohemia. Their lowest support came from south Moravia (the region of great influence of the People's Party and the Moravian autonomist movement), in north Slovakia (stronghold of the Christian Democratic Movement) and in south Slovakia, settled by Hungarians.

In most parts of the country, the Green Party's votes rose with the size of municipality. In the most devastated areas, however, practically no difference existed in the level of support of the Green Party between municipalities of different sizes. In other words, the ecological interest in this area is no longer just an urban phenomenon. Ecological problems are more and more reflected in the political mood of rural areas as well (Jehlička and Kostelecký, 1991).

Other parties

We consider the Christian Democratic Movement and the Alliance of Agrarians and Countryside as newly emerging parties which gained considerable support and have not been examined yet. Opinion polls preceding the elections indicated the Christian Democratic Movement as a favourite in Slovakia but the party gained less support than had been expected. The party political programme emphasised Christian (mainly Catholic) values and Christian morals. The economic part of the programme supported a transition to a market economy stressing the social aspects of reform.

The Alliance of Agrarians and Countryside represented left-wing views, especially from the agricultural cooperative sector. The strongest group within the coalition was the Agrarian Party which had been formed immediately after the November 1989 revolution by managers of some of the larger cooperative farms, fearful of the consequences it would have for the agricultural sector.

For nine parties, support did not reach the 2 per cent threshold. Among these were two coalitions, the Free Bloc and the All-People's Democratic Party and the Association for the Republic–Republican Party of Czechoslovakia. These coalitions contained right-wing parties and ideologies strongly committed to private enterprise and in the case of the latter party, also to the repatriation of foreign workers (Vietnamese, Cuban, Polish) from Czechoslovakia.

Discussion

The Czechoslovak parliamentary elections of 1990 were, in many respects, exceptional. The political spectrum was still somewhat unstructured and provisional. The elections were often considered in the voters' minds to be a referendum on the preference for the old state (the Communist Party) or an open society with a market economy, supported by Civic Forum and almost all the other parties and movements.

In some respects the voting patterns were surprising. After forty years of communism in Czechoslovakia, there were no official cleavages. In spite of this fact, we found in the case of political parties with an historical tradition that the regional patterns in the political orientation of the inhabitants appeared again. These regional loyalties were created even before World War II as a reflection of the then existing cleavages. In the case of the KDU which, like its pre-war predecessor the Czechoslovak People's Party, focused on the Catholic inhabitants, the continuity of regional patterns of political support is not such a surprise. In the regions with the highest percentage of active Catholics, the party preserved its position during the entire era of the communist rule without any great change.

Of much greater interest is the continuity of regions with the greatest support for the communists, because the population in the traditionally pro-Communist regions does not differ significantly from the population of the other regions by any readily measurable social or economic characteristics. It is clear that, in this case, the pro-Communist political orientation in the area to the west of Prague is not a reflection of some contemporary cleavages in society but that there are historical linkages that have become part of the regional identity similarly to the Catholic religion in south Moravia. This hypothesis is supported by the fact that both the Communist Party and the Christian and Democratic Union in the territories of their greatest support are rooted most deeply in the smallest villages where, naturally, traditions play a greater role than in towns.

Unlike the historical parties, Civic Forum did not resurrect any traditions directly. Nevertheless, it is necessary to stress that leaders of Civic Forum derived their politics from the tradition of the pre-war republic, particularly from the thoughts and ideas of T.G. Masaryk, the first president of Czechoslovakia, in office immediately after the state was created after World War I. However, the ideological diversity inside the former protest movement covered by an exceedingly unspecific programme, emphasizing as a matter of fact only the necessity of introducing a parliamentary democracy and a market economy, did not result in a stable electoral basis. In the course of the November 1989 resistance against the communist government, opposition was spreading from Prague to the whole of the country. The voting pattern of Civic Forum resembles the typical distribution of an innovation during the diffusion process. The post-election discord inside Civic Forum, and a relatively fast break-up into several clearly distinguished parties corroborates the fact that the Civic Forum never had (and could not have had) a stable electorate.

Despite a rather different situation in Slovakia, some features of the latest political development are similar to those in the Czech Republic. The electoral winner, the Public Against Violence, has undergone almost the same process of disintegration as the Civic Forum. Movements were a vital phenomenon of the transitional period but a natural differentiation of politics emerged after the election and caused a break-up of movements. This process tends to result eventually in a stable system of political parties and probably also in the creation of relatively stable regions, each with a specific 'political climate'.

Up to early 1992, a conventional party structure developed in each of the republics. Nevertheless, the composition of public support for the respective party groupings is considerably different in both parts of Czechoslovakia. While the strongest successor of the Civic Forum movement, the Civic Democratic Party (ODS), promotes a conservative right-wing policy, a majority of the Public Against Violence supporters followed the leftist and nationally oriented Movement for Democratic Slovakia (HZDS) after the Civic Forum movement had become fragmented.

Besides the ODS, two other relatively important parties emerged from a Civic Forum dead body. One of them, Civic Movement (OH), keeps a loosely organized internal structure, defines itself as a centre party and has not targeted any specific population category. Nevertheless, some important personalities from government or in the parliaments play a key role in getting political support for the party. The second one, Civic Democratic Alliance (ODA), is a liberal right-wing party, which addresses especially the intelligentsia. The political programme is similar to ODS and makes a potential coalition partnership between these two parties probable. The low general support of the ODA but the presence of some well-known personalities in this party further supports this assumption.

Already at the end of 1991, the primarily Czech ODA announced a pre-election coalition for the parliamentary elections in 1992 with Slovak Civic Democratic Union–Public Against Violence (ODU–VPN). As the name suggests, this latter party is one of the successors of Public Against Violence. As a liberal party, ODU–VPN has little support and it is derived particularly from the intelligentsia. The right-wing part of the political spectrum in Slovakia is also occupied by the Democratic Party which closely cooperates with (Czech) Civic Democratic Party (ODS). These cooperations among Czech and Slovak right wing-parties could create a strong backbone for a common state of both nations.

There are more than right-wing movements in Slovakia. A growing coalition of left and nationalist parties is concentrated around the Movement for Democratic Slovakia (HZDS). This ethno-national tendency is further encouraged by considerable support for the Slovak National Party as well as for the Party of the Democratic Left (SDL), the successor party of the Communists. The key role, however, is still played by the Christian Democratic Movement (KDU), the second strongest party in the 1990 elections in Slovakia. This party holds the Slovak prime minister post at the present time. The party balances Slovak politics between promoting either a common state or independent Slovakia as well as between either supporting radical economic reform or a slower process of 'specific Slovak' adaptation to new conditions.

In the Czech republic, the left is also getting stronger with the declines in the average standard of living and rising unemployment. Public opinion polls in 1991–92 show increasing support for Social Democrats. The newly established Social Liberal Union, a coalition of socialists, agrarian workers and greens, wants to get parliamentary seats too. In spite of some recent return of support, the Communist Party will probably play a marginal role only, because no other party will accept them as a coalition partner. Behind the current crystallization of both Czech and Slovak politics towards an internal balance in each republic, it is possible to detect an increasing threat of fundamental disagreement on the future development of the country. Parliamentary elections in the middle of 1992 will give one further answer on the hot issue of the relationship between Czech and Slovak politics and republics. However, it is highly unlikely that this issue will be resolved in one stroke. In what way the tensions between the two nations will be resolved is still highly unpredictable.

Postscript: the parliamentary elections in June 1992

Voters in the 1992 parliamentary elections had to decide about the form of economic transformation and the future of a common state of the Czechs and the Slovaks. The turnout rate was 85 per cent, down about 10 points from 1990, but still much higher than in Poland or Hungary. The growing political diversity of the Czecho-Slovak society was mirrored in the developing structure of political parties before the elections. Only seven parties, from a total number of forty-two which ran for elections, had federal structures and participated in the elections in both republics. None of these parties received significant support in both parts of the country (see Table 14.3).

A strict division of the country into two parts (Czech republic and Slovakia) clearly appeared. The party pushing hardest for a sovereign Slovak state, the Movement for a Democratic Slovakia (HZDS) won more than 33 per cent of the votes for the Federal Assembly and even more for the Slovak National Council. Slovak National Party (SNS) also polled strongly, suggesting that the idea of national sovereignty will have a convincing majority in the republic's assembly. The former Communist Party (Party of the Democratic Left–SDL) polled well in Slovakia, with more than 14 per cent. Therefore, the victors in Slovakia are essentially left-wing, and will not be likely to support rapid economic reform. The Christian Democratic Party (ruling political party before the 1992 elections) experiencing a split of the internal nationalist wing (Slovak Christian Democratic Movement–SKDH) in spring 1992 gained 9 per cent of Slovak votes. KDH together with Hungarian Christian Democratic Movement (MKDH–ESWS–MLS) are the only (Slovak) parliamentary parties supporting both the basic strategy of economic reform and a common state of Czechs and Slovaks.

The Slovak results overshadowed the significant victory of the conservative Civic Democratic Party (ODS – 33 per cent) in the Czech republic. ODS and two other centre-right parties (Christian and Democratic Union and Civic Democratic Alliance) will form a majority in the Czech National Council pursuing rapid economic reform. The Czech left wing consists of Left Block (coalition of Communist Party of Bohemia and Moravia with small Labour Party), Social Democracy and Liberal Social Union will have one third of the seats in the Czech National Council. Two other parties barely crossed the 5 per cent threshold and entered the Czech National Council. The results of the Movement for Self-Governing Democracy – Society for Moravia and Silesia (HSD–SMS) showed decreasing support for the idea of Moravian autonomy. On the other hand, surprisingly high support (6 per cent) for the Republican

Table 14.3   Results of parliamentary elections in Czechoslovakia in June 1992

	Federal		Assembly		National councils	
Party	Chamber of People		Chamber of Nations			
	in CR	in SR	in CR	in SR	Czech	Slovak
1.	33.90	–	33.43	–	29.73	–
2.	–	33.53	–	33.85	–	37.26
3.	–	14.44	–	14.04	–	14.70
4.	14.27	–	14.48	–	14.05	–
5.	–	9.39	–	9.35	–	7.93
6.	–	8.96	–	8.81	–	8.88
7.	7.67	–	6.80	–	6.53	–
8.	0.07	7.37	0.06	7.39	–	7.42
9.	6.48	0.36	6.37	0.34	5.98	0.32
10.	5.98	–	6.08	–	6.28	–
11.	5.84	–	6.06	–	6.52	–
12.	4.98	–	4.08	–	5.93	–
13.	–	4.86	–	8.09	–	4.00
14.	4.23	0.15	4.90	0.15	5.87	0.12
15.	4.39	–	4.74	–	4.59	–
16.		3.96	–	4.04	–	4.03
17.	–	3.95	–	3.66	–	3.31
18.	–	3.45	–	3.24	–	3.05
19.	12.19	9.58	13.00	7.04	14.52	8.98
TOTAL	100.0	100.0	100.0	100.0	100.00	100.00

Notes: CR – Czech Republic, SR – Slovak Republic. Party codes: 1. Civic Democratic Party - Christian Democratic Party (ODS–KDS); 2. Movement for Democratic Slovakia (HZDS); 3. Party of the Democratic Left (SDL); 4. Left Block (Levy blok); 5. Slovak National Party (SNS); 6. Christian Democratic Movement (KDH); 7. Social Democracy (CSSD); 8. Hungarian Christian Democratic Movement-Coexistence-Hungarian People's Party (MKDH–ESWS–MLS); 9. Republican Party (SPR-RSC); 10. Christian and Democratic Union–People's Party (KDU-CSL); 11. Liberal Social Union (LSU); 12. Civic Democratic Party (ODA); 13. Slovak Social Democratic Party (SDSS); 14. Movement for Self-Governing Democracy - Society for Moravia and Silesia (HSD–SMS); 15. Civic Movement (OH); 16. Civic Democratic Party (ODÚ); 17. Democratic Party-Civic Democratic Party (DS–ODS); 18. Slovak Christian Democratic Movement (SKDH); 19. Other parties

Source: Lidové noviny, No.133, 8 June 1992.

party (a extremely right-wing party with the full name of the Association for the Republic – Republican Party of Czechoslovakia) shows hidden ethnic tensions (with the minority of Gypsies) within Czech society.

The federal ballots of two smaller Czech parties (Civic Democratic Alliance and 'Moravians') received less than the 5 per cent threshold of votes and therefore they will participate in national parliaments only. As a curiosity, Slovak Social Democrats, whose support did not reach the threshold for entering of Slovak National Council, will have seats in one of the Federal Assembly chambers. This 'relative' success was caused by the name of Alexander Dubček (Chairman of the Federal Assembly in the 1990–1992 period and a well-known figure of the 1968 Prague Spring) listed on the top of the party ballot for the Chamber of Nations.

Four other parties, which aspired to parliamentary posts, but did not succeed should be discussed. The Civic Movement (OH) with some leading personalities of the 1989 revolution, and afterwards keeping important posts in the Czechoslovak political scene, such as the minister of foreign affairs, prime minister of the Czech republic and chairman of the Czech National Council, will have no member of parliament after the 1992 elections. The same fate as the OH came to two Slovak parties which participated in the Slovak government in 1990–1992: Civic Democratic Union (ODU, the successor of the 'revolutionary' Public Against Violence) and the Democratic Party which ran in coalition with Czech republic victor Civic Democratic Party. The split nationalist wing of the Christian Democratic Movement, i.e. the Slovak Christian Democratic Movement, did not succeed either.

The most important feature of electoral results in the Czech republic is strict right–left polarization and success for well-organized parties (ODS, communists). Liberal-oriented parties, either centre (OH) or centre-right (ODA), with almost no local organizations failed in spite of many well-known and popular personalities on their ballots. On the other hand, the sweeping victory of the left–national block and a total failure of right-wing parties show the political preferences of Slovaks for development in their country. In spite of the polarization of the political scene within the Czech republic, and polarization between Czech republic and Slovakia, the electoral results show the evident stability of party structures in comparison to the 1990 elections. The 'new' significant parties are either direct successors to Civic Forum (ODS, ODA, OH) and/or Public Against Violence (HZDS, ODU), or coalitions of parties well-known from the 1990 elections (LSU, Left block). And thus the parliaments will be formed by political orientations which already participated there during the 1990–1992 period. The only, and rather surprising exception, is a extremely right-wing party, the Association for the Republic–Republican Party of Czechoslovakia, which ran in the 1990 elections, but in June 1992 more then tripled its score.

From the geographical point of view, the electoral results of Czech historical parties fully confirmed the great stability of their voting patterns. All the parties did better in their traditional strongholds and failed in weak spots. An important feature of the 1992 elections is the development of town–countryside polarization in the Czech republic, with the urban population voting predominantly right and rural voters voting mostly left. The capital of Prague where two thirds of the population gave their votes to right-wing parties is a striking case. In spite of the one-sided victory of the left–nationalist block in Slovakia, the traditional geographical pattern is observable: southern regions settled by the Hungarian minority with its specific voting behaviour; eastern Slovakia with higher support for pro-reform and pro-federal central–right parties such as Christian Democratic Movement (KDH), Democratic Party (DS–ODS), and Civic Democratic Union (ODU), as well as for left-wing parties (SDL, SDSS) pursuing the common state, and considerably less support for Slovak National Party, one third of the Slovak average; the Slovak capital of Bratislava with on the one hand the highest concentration of votes for nationalist-oriented parties (SNS, SKDH), and on the other hand significantly supporting liberal center-right wing parties with strong pro-federal orientation (DS–ODS, ODU); western and central parts of the country had average Slovak voting behaviour.

The future of the Czechs and the Slovaks now lies in negotiations between two victors (ODS and HZDS) on a possible governmental coalition on the federal level. Unfortunately, there are considerable disagreements. One of the major quarrels is over the presidential candidature of Václav Havel. He is widely perceived as a guarantor of the common state of the Czechs and the Slovaks. HZDS is against his candidature. Negotiations on the future form of the state and the power structures and policies within them ended in Autumn 1992 with an agreement to split the country into two states on 1 January 1993.

References

Atlas československých dejin, 1965, [The Atlas of Czechoslovak History]. Hlav. věd. redaktor J. Purš., Praha.

Blažek, J., Kostelecký, T., 1991, 'Geografická analýza výsledků parlamentních voleb v roce 1990', [Geographical analysis of parliamentary election results 1990], *Sborník ČGS* **96**, Praha, Academia, No. 1, pp. 1–14.

Broklov, E., 1990, Politický systém ČSR 1918–1938: Pokus o zařazení do evropského kontextu. [Political system of the Czechoslovak Republic, 1918–1938: essay at classification within the European context]. Thesis, Faculty of Philosophy of Charles University 1968–1969, Praha, p. 208.

Historický přehled výsledků voleb do Národního shromáždění v období 1920–1935. [Historical Survey of Results of Elections for the National Assembly in the Period 1920–1935]. Praha, FSÚ 1990, p. 94.

Jehlička, P., Kostelecký, T., 1991, The Greens in Czechoslovakia, Paper presented at the European Conference of Political Research Conference, Colchester, Essex, March, p. 30.

Jehlička, P., Kostelecký, T., Sýkora, L., 1991, 'Oblasti tradiční podpory KSČ', [Regions traditionally supporting the Communist Party], *Respekt* **22**, NTS, p. 6.

Jehlička, P., Sýkora, L., 1991, 'Stabilita regionální podpory tradičních politických stran v českých zemích (1920–1990), [The stability of regional suffrage for traditional parties in the Czech Lands (1920–1990)], *Sborník CGS* **96** (2): 81–95.

Kostelecký, T., Jehlička, P., 1991, Košice versus Bratislava: Dva póly slovenské politiky', [Košice versus Bratislava: two poles of Slovak policy], *Respekt*, 25, NTS, p. 6.

Martis, K.C., Kovacs, Z., Kovacs, D., Peter, S., 1991, An analysis of the spatial aspects of the Hungarian electoral system and the 1990 parliamentary elections. Paper presented at the Conference sponsored by the IGU Commission on the World Political Map, Prague, August.

Wightman, G., 1991, 'The collapse of Communist rule in Czechoslovakia and the June 1990 parliamentary elections', *Parliamentary Affairs* **44** (1): 94–113.

15 The geography of Hungarian parliamentary elections 1990

Zoltán Kovacs

When the National Election Committee announced the results of the first free elections of Hungary since 1947, it meant the end of forty-two years of one party dictatorship. The function of an election in a parliamentary democracy is either to confirm or to replace the political party or coalition in power, as a correction of the existing political structure. It does not apply to the case of Hungary. The 1990 election represented the final step of a long-lasting political transition, a means to find out the distribution of political preferences in society after nearly half a century and to create a new political structure. The aim of this chapter is to investigate what political preferences and cleavages can be recognized within Hungarian society and political culture, after a forty-two years long attempt at depoliticisation and social homogenization.

Historical background

In Hungary the roots of parliamentary democracy go back to 1848, when an anti-Habsburg, anti-feudal uprising took place in the country. Prior to 1848, the parliament was represented by the Estate Assembly and the ratio of those who were eligible to vote was less than 2 per cent of the total population, since the right to vote was extended to adult noblemen only, a mere 154,000 in a country of 10 million total population (Kosáry, 1985). From 1848 to 1945, nine electoral laws still maintained considerable restrictions in various forms (e.g. size of property, level of education, etc). The single criterion of age as the only condition for eligibility to vote did not come into force until as late as 1945.

Until World War I, Hungarian electoral laws were very restrictive not only compared to West European countries but even compared to electoral laws that were then in force in some parts of the Balkans. The most substantial difference between the West European and Hungarian electoral laws was, that while in Western Europe the emphasis was placed on literacy, in Hungary the major criteria was the size of property. Following World War I, a Russian-type proletarian dictatorship succeeded in Hungary for a brief period, under the name of Republic of Soviets/Councils. In this period, 57 per cent of the total population became eligible to vote. Leaving aside all other aspects of that regime, this was a great leap towards a more democratic electoral system. According to this Act, all citizens above the age of 18 acquired the vote. It meant that women, the 18–24 age group, the majority of the industrial and agricultural workers also became eligible to vote. Another important aspect of the law was represented by the fact that elections were to be held by secret ballot. Yet, those who employed persons in order to get profit, the merchants, traders, priests and members of religious orders were all deprived from their vote which indicated the dictatorial nature of this regime (Hajdu, 1985).

Following the fall of the Republic of Soviets, the electoral law in Hungary became more and more restricted due to the growing number of exclusion criteria. By 1922, the circle of eligible voters was restricted to those males over the age of 24, who completed at least four years of primary school and females over 30, who completed six years of primary school education (Pölöskei, 1985). This new Act reduced the number of eligible voters at once by three-quarters of a million. Secret ballot was applied only in Budapest, in its agglomeration and in bigger municipalities. Count István Bethlen, then Prime Minister of Hungary, declared that the secret ballot 'is contrary to the open character of Hungarians'. Despite general expectations, Act XXVI (1925) and Act XIX (1938) further restricted the eligibility to vote. The new law further increased the minimum level of educational attainment of voters and required a minimum period of six years' permanent residency. As a result of the highly restrictive election laws passed during the inter-war period, the number of people eligible to vote was less in 1939 than in 1920 by some 400,000, in spite of the fact that the population of the country increased by 15 per cent in the corresponding period (see Table 15.1).

Table 15.1   The numbers eligible to vote in Hungarian parliamentary elections

Year of elections	Population (thousands)	Number of people eligible to vote (thousands)	Ratio (%)
1920	7,980	3,133	39.3
1922	8,136	2,381	29.3
1926	8,423	2,229	26.5
1931	8,742	2,553	29.2
1935	8,943	3,003	33.6
1939	9,439	2,759	30.4
1945	8,656	5,164	59.7
1966	10,160	7,114	70.0
1990	10,589	7,853	74.1

Since the end of World War II, nine election laws were passed in Hungary but only the first and the last are worth mentioning. Act VIII (1945), passed in a brief period of multi-party democracy, abolished all previous restrictions and reduced the age limit of voters to 20 years. Act III (1983) not only permitted multi-candidate elections but made them compulsory, at a time when such an approach was still unimaginable in many other East European countries.

Political transition and the revival of the multiparty system in Hungary

In February 1989, the ruling Hungarian Socialist Workers' (Communist) Party accepted the principles of multi-party democracy. Within thirteen months of this decision, free elections were held and a complex multi-party political system emerged. Political scientists and historians agree that the roots of the political landslide of 1989 go back till 1956, or at least to 1968, when a new liberal, market-oriented, reform Economic Mechanism was introduced in Hungary, which was the first successful shift in the Eastern bloc away from a redistributive, centrally-directed economy (Hann, 1990). Parallel with the economic liberalization, pressure for a more open society was steady in the 1970s and 1980s. However, more substantial changes could only take place after 1985 when Mikhail Gorbachev came to power in the former Soviet Union. Political groups of various types emerged in 1987 and 1988, and the Hungarian Socialist Workers' Party began roundtable discussion with several of these opposition groups in January 1989, regarding the possibility of amending the Hungarian constitution and establishing a multi-party system. Within a month, the ruling party formally announced its intention to abandon its monopoly of power, which meant the end of communist rule.

Roundtable talks continued throughout 1989, regarding a democratic electoral law and the legalization of political parties. As a result, a law governing the electoral participation of political parties was established in October 1989. This law enumerated four criteria of eligibility for the first free elections. Specifically, a party had to have 1) at least ten members, 2) a recognized leader, 3) a party platform, and 4) a bank account. These extremely generous criteria allowed a proliferation of parties. Indeed, sixty-five parties met the legal registration deadline of 31 January, 1990 for participation in the first round of the elections!

In terms of the post-communist transition and the development of a multi-party system, three major types of regimes emerged in Eastern Europe by 1990. Dominant non-authoritarian party-systems, led by 'national liberation movements' emerged in Poland and Czechoslovakia; dominant authoritarian party systems revived in Romania and Bulgaria; and competitive multi-party systems arose in Hungary and East Germany (Körösényi, 1991). However, the new East German party system was very much influenced by the West German political parties, whereas in Hungary, the new party system developed much more from internal sources.

Considering their origins, the Hungarian political parties can be divided into two main categories. The first is constituted by those parties which had their origins prior to World War II, the so-called 'historic parties' e.g. the Smallholders' Party, Social Democratic Party, Hungarian People's Party, etc. We may also add to this group the two heirs of the former ruling communist party, the reform-oriented Hungarian Socialist Party and the orthodox communist Hungarian Socialist Workers' Party. New parties belong to the second category, which developed out of the dissident movements of the 1980s, e.g. Hungarian Democratic Forum, Alliance of Free Democrats, League of Young Democrats.

The emerging political parties could also be divided into groups along the socialist–liberal–conservative triangle. In the following section, the highlights of the main characteristics of the campaign position of the leading political parties are presented, especially those six parties which won seats in the 1990 elections. The Hungarian Democratic Forum (MDF) was founded in September 1987 around the traditional 'populist' group of intellectuals, whose ideal was a 'third road' (neither communist nor capitalist) towards a genuinely 'Hungarian' future. The party envisioned a slow movement from a socialist economy to a free market economy with the acceptance of mixed forms of ownership. The party promoted itself as a party of traditional 'Hungarian' values and culture. This nationalist and populist tone was manifested in several ways in the party's campaign programme, such as concern for Hungarian minorities in neighbouring countries. The Hungarian Democratic Forum defined itself as a broad political movement in the centre of the traditional European political spectrum before the electoral campaign. However, as a party, the MDF developed towards a centre-right Christian-democratic character after the autumn of 1989.

The Alliance of Free Democrats (SZDSZ) was formed around a dissident group of urban intellectuals in November 1988, but traces its heritage to the 'human rights' opposition to the communist regime which had existed since the mid-1970s. The SZDSZ promoted itself as a progressive modern 'European' party and advocated close ties with the European Community. Their programme was similar to those of the liberal–left parties, emphasizing liberal values, an open society and a liberal social welfare system. The Alliance had a deregulation-oriented libertarian economic programme, which called for a rapid transition (i.e. shock therapy) from socialism to a European-style free market economy.

A peculiar feature of the new Hungarian political scene was that the two main parties grew from two small groups of intellectuals into dominant political parties. The division of the Hungarian intelligentsia into 'urbanist' and 'populist' groups has historical roots and goes back to the 1930s. The 'urbanist' intellectuals of the 1930s received inspiration from the late 19th century liberal traditions and the development of democratic political intitutions in Western Europe and North America. The 'populists' were inspired by nationalism and by the anti-capitalist left as well. Both groups were democratic and opposed the conservative authoritarian regime of Horty in the inter-war period, but in different ways. The political and ideological differences were further strengthened by social factors. The 'urbanist' liberalism was associated with the very influental Jewish urban intelligentsia, whereas the 'populist' ideology was favoured by the Hungarian Christian middle class. Both these political traditions continued during the post-war period. The populist side was especially strong among Hungarian writers and poets, while urbanists turned towards Marxism first, as the only progressive idea against antisemitism and nationalism. Later, from the mid-1970s, they switched back to the original liberal political tradition and became the internal opposition to the communist regime. Thus, the traditional split in Hungarian political thinking re-emerged by the 1980s, in the form of two small but very influental groups, which constituted eventually the basis of the two main political parties.

The Smallholders' Party (FKgP) was originally established in 1930 (though it had a predecessor in the 1920s as well) and was a major party on the political scene until 1948. The smallholders' programme concentrated primarily on the restoration of the 1947 land ownership system, and called for the return of confiscated or nationalised land and property to the original owners. This plank obviously appealed to former rural landholders exclusively. The smallholders, together with the religious Christian Democratic People's Party (KDNP), are generally considered in the centre-right conservative position of the European political spectrum. The KDNP, like most of the Christian Democratic parties in Europe, stood for Christian/Catholic values in the elections and was somewhat aligned with the church's stand on social–moral issues, for example opposition to abortion on demand. The principles of the party appealed to the religious middle-class and rural population.

As a liberal party, the League of Young Democrats (FIDESZ) was formed by radical young intellectuals and students in 1988, and had an explicit concern with the interests of younger age-groups. Their political programme was in accord with most of the platform of the Free Democrats. Therefore, many considered them as a pocket party, or youth organization of the Alliance of Free Democrats (SZDSZ). They advocated non-violent civil disobedience in support of their causes, liberal European values and a free market economy with extensive social welfare provisions.

On the socialist side, the Hungarian Socialist Party (MSZP) is a direct descendant of the formerly ruling Hungarian Socialist Workers' (Communist) Party. The reform wing of the Hungarian Socialist Workers' Party met in party congress in October 1989 and reconstituted and renamed the party as the Hungarian Socialist Party. The orthodox Marxist–Leninist wing of the party kept the name Workers' Party. The socialists claimed that they generated the democratic reform movement in Hungary which ultimately led to the collapse of the communist regime. They campaigned for the protection of workers' rights and jobs and continuation of the social welfare system developed under the communists. Their platform proposed a slow transition to a mixed economy with the protection of 'the traditions of the working class movement'. The Socialist Party was the only left wing party which received enough votes to win parliamentary representation.

Besides the bigger parties, there were a great number of smaller parties which also took part in the elections without any success. Some 'phantom parties' were also formed with the aim of not so much participation in the elections but rather of collecting funds allocated for political campaign purposes. Large numbers of social organizations felt also obliged to register themselves as political parties to enable them to put up candidates for the elections (e.g. Association of Hungarian Humanists, Holy Crown Society, Nature and Society Association etc.). It is interesting to note that the only ethnic minority group which had its own political party were the Gypsies. They even had more than one (Justice Party of New Hungarians and the Social Democratic Party of Gypsies).

Complications arose while several parties had almost identical political programmes and names. For example, four 'Social Democratic' parties and two 'Smallholders' parties were formed. But there were many 'Liberal', 'Democratic' and 'Environmentalist' parties, too. Some of the parties had a regional character intending to represent a certain region only. However, Hungary being a small country, these parties were doomed to failure from the very beginning, lacking national support (e.g. Villagers Association, Christian Coalition of Somogy County, etc.).

As the campaign was very short, it was difficult for the voters to identify which party was on the left and which was on the right. Very often, not even the party programmes gave a proper impression about the parties' political sentiments. Yet, these parties had to go through a selection process in order to form a new parliament.

The Hungarian electoral system and the result of the 1990 parliamentary elections

In drafting the new Hungarian electoral law, not only the functioning electoral systems elswhere in Europe were taken into consideration but also the literature on proportional representation as an equitable theoretical system of democratic parliamentary representation (Johnston, 1979; Balinshi and Young, 1982; Bogdanor, 1984). Thus, the law is a compromise between the concept of strict geographical representation and proportional party representation. From this point of view, the law is most similar to the German electoral system. Nearly half of the MPs are elected by single-member election districts. Therefore, Hungary was divided into single-member districts, 176 in total, on the basis of the number of eligible voters. A candidate is elected in a district if he or she receives a majority of the vote in the first round of the election. The election law requires that over one half of the electorate must vote in the first round of the election for the result to be valid. If no candidate receives a majority in the first round, all candidates receiving at least fifteen per cent of the vote go on to the second round. In the second round, the candidate with the highest number of votes is elected.

Fifty-five per cent of the 386 seats in the Hungarian Parliament are chosen by way of proportional representation. Proportional election occurs by way of two methods, county lists and national lists. In the county list process, each registered political party in each county and the capital selects an enumerated list of candidates in order of their priority of election. The number of county list seats allocated to each county is apportioned by population. Each voter is eligible to vote for one political party list. Thus, an individual voter may cast two votes, one for a district candidate and another for a political party list. Besides county lists, each party selects a national list of candidates in order of priority for election to parliament. The national party list is not directly voted by the electorate but by the 'scrap' (i.e. unused) votes of all the unsuccessful district party candidates and the party county lists. The use of scrap votes is an effort to ensure that all votes count and the parliament reflects the national total vote for the parties.

Before the 1990 parliamentary elections, twenty-eight political parties were able to nominate at least one candidate, nineteen of them could organize at least one county list, and only twelve of the initially registered parties could set up the required number of county lists which enabled them to participate in the national vote pool (the national scrap vote). According to the election law, political parties must receive at least 4 per cent of the total votes to actually receive seats in the Hungarian Parliament. Only six parties out of the sixty-five exceeded the 4 per cent threshold and became parliamentary parties, as is shown in Table 15.2.

In the first round of the elections, the Hungarian Democratic Forum, with just under 25 per cent of the votes emerged as the leading party, closely followed by the liberal Free Democrats with a little over 21 per cent. The 'natural allies' of the Democratic Forum, the Smallholders' Party and the Christian Democratic People's Party won 12 per cent and 6.5 per cent respectively, while the League of Young Democrats attained a remarkable 9 per cent. The only left-wing party which achieved parliamentary representation, the Hungarian Socialist Party, ended up as the country's fourth largest party with nearly 11 per cent of the vote. A further 16 per cent were cast for parties that failed to attain the minimum 4 per cent for parliamentary representation.

The electoral competition and ballot situation in the second round election was unlike the first round. Only five out of the 176 district elections were decided in the first round. However, the number of candidates in each district was greatly reduced because of the 15 per cent first round vote requirement. In most districts, the Democratic Forum and Free Democrats were still on the ballot. In many districts, the Smallholders, Christian Democrat, and Young Democrat candidates did not not make the second round ballot. In this situation 'natural' electoral alliances were formed by the Democratic Forum with the Smallholders and the Christian Democrats. This alliance meant that, if a Democratic Forum candidate was in a competition against other candidates, the supporters of the two smaller centre-right parties were supposed to vote for the

Democratic Forum candidate. This alliance heralded the subsequent centre-right Christian-national coalition government (Martis et.al., 1992).

Table 15.2   The distribution of votes and seats in 1990 Hungarian parliamentary elections

| | National % | Allocation of parliament seats | | | |
		Districts	County	Nat.	Total
Hungarian Democratic Forum (MDF)	24.71	115	40	10	165
Alliance of Free Democrats (SZDSZ)	21.38	34	34	23	91
Smallholders' Party (FKgP)	11.76	11	16	17	44
Hungarian Socialist Party (MSZP)	10.89	1	14	18	33
League of Young Democrats (FIDESZ)	8.94	1	8	12	21
Christian Democratic People's Party (KDNP)	6.46	3	8	10	21
Other parties and candidates	15.86	11	–	–	11
TOTAL	100.00	176	120	90	386

In response to this development, the Free Democrats and the Young Democrats also formed a looser alliance. In this way, the second round became very much a two-horse race, where the Democratic Forum-led coalition secured a convincing majority with 56 per cent of the second round vote. The vote cast for the Democratic Forum candidates alone rose from 25 per cent to over 41 per cent, and they emerged with 165 seats, 42.75 per cent of the parliament. The Free Democrats and Young Democrats attained approximately the same combined result (31 per cent) as in the first round.

In the second round, forty-three candidates won seats in the parliament even though they did not lead after the first round. In the forty-three cases in which second and third place candidates were able to win, forty candidates of the Democratic Forum led centre-right parties were able to displace the liberal frontrunners and in only three cases did liberal parties displace centre-right individuals, which reflects the efficiency of the centre-right alliance (Figure 15.1).

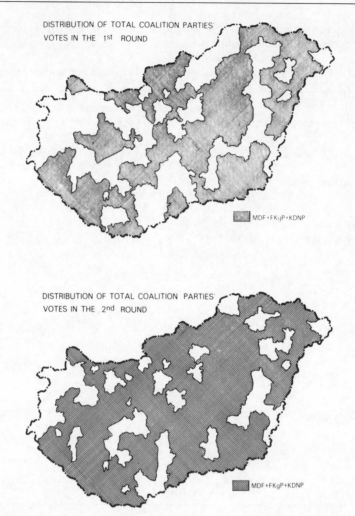

Figure 15.1 Spatial distribution of coalition parties' votes in the first and second rounds of voting in Hungary, March 1990. MDF Hungarian Democratic Forum: FKgP Smallholders' Party: KDNP Christian Democratic Party

Geographical aspects of the 1990 Hungarian parliamentary elections

The first entirely free multi-party elections in Hungary since 1945 were anticipated with great expectations by Hungarians and the world at large. In a nation generally believed to be somewhat 'homogeneous', the vote demonstrated political divisions in Hungarian society with respect to class, education, age, place of residence, and region. In addition, it demonstrated both the ability of most, but reluctance of some, to adopt the parliamentary political system. The results of the election provide, therefore, basic data for political scientists, sociologists, and political geographers to study the divisions and differences in Hungarian society after forty-five years of one-party rule.

Voter participation

The transition to multiparty democracy, culminating in the reforms of 1989 and the elections in the spring of 1990, was acclaimed in the Hungarian and Western media as one of the most significant events of modern Hungarian history. Yet, in spite of the momentous nature of these events, the final participation rate among the voting public was disappointing to those promoting western-style democracy and showed significant disenchantment in a large segment of Hungarian society. The number of eligible voters was 7.8 million, approximately three-quarters of the country's total population. Although this is the highest proportion of eligible voters in the history of Hungarian elections (see Table 15.1), the final participation rate was low even by western standards. In the first round of the election, 64.99 per cent of the potential voters cast votes for the individual district candidates and 63.15 per cent for the party (county) lists. The turnout in the second round fell even further to 45 per cent. This is strikingly low, especially considering the participation rate in other 1990 East European elections (Czechoslovakia 96 per cent, Rumania 86 per cent) or countries in the Mediterranean freed from dictatorships during the 1970s (1974 Greece 80 per cent, 1975 Portugal 92 per cent). In the above examples, free elections were held immediately after anti-communist or anti-fascist revolutions and hence it is speculated that political parties were able to enthuse and mobilize the overwhelming majority of society. However in Hungary, the multiparty elections were the culmination of long-term political manoeuvres and struggles that started with the reform waves of the 1960s. A similar situation of long-term political struggle and change and eventual low voter turnout in the first free election (62 per cent) occured in Poland. Opinion polls in Hungary suggest that, because of the increase in political activity in the years previous to 1990 (e.g. plebiscites, campaigning), a significant segment of the population became disenchanted with politics in general and the 'new' politicians in particular. Forty-two years of communist rule had not only made a portion of the population suspicious of promises and politicians, but also destroyed the infrastructure organization of civil society in many parts of the country.

The participation rate in the 1990 Hungarian elections has noteworthy geographical variations. On the national scale, the participation rate in the western part of the country was much higher than in the eastern counties (Figure 15.2). The explanation of this pattern is partially derived from Hungary's geographical position and human geography. In all seventeen western districts adjacent to the Austrian border, the participation rate was over 70 per cent. By contrast, five districts in the eastern border region had participation rates below 50 per cent, making necessary a repeat of the first round election.

The historical and geographical differences between eastern and western Hungary are well documented (Hofman, 1989; Bernát, 1985). Western Hungary, especially along the Budapest–Vienna corridor, is more urbanized, has a higher education level, and has a more western orientation. Eastern Hungary is rural agricultural and has a lower level of educational attainment. In addition the east has a higher proportion of elderly and Gypsies who generally have a lower political participation level. These variables, plus the pluralistic influence of the western/Austrian broadcast media, which could always be picked up in western Hungary, helped to increase the participation

ELECTION TURNOUT

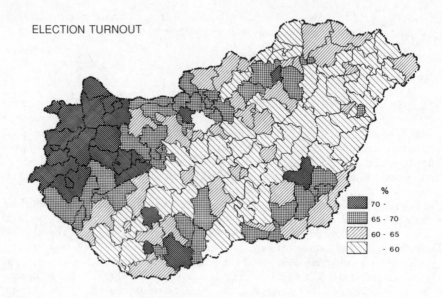

%
■ 70 -
▦ 65 - 70
▨ 60 - 65
◩ - 60

Figure 15.2   Geographic distribution of turnout in the March 1990 parliamentary election in Hungary

rate. Preliminary survey data indicate that the most important variables predicting voting participation were educational background and the urban–rural composition of the district. Urban, university-educated individuals had the highest participation rate, much
higher than the urban working class, or the rural population.

Budapest is by far the largest city in Hungary and the metropolitan region is apportioned thirty-two of the 176 parliamentary districts (nearly one-fifth of all the district
seats and one-fifth of all the voters in the nation). The turnout within Budapest also
had a high geographical variation (Figure 15.3) and reflects the variables mentioned
above. The highest rate, over 80 per cent, was in the western, Buda, side of the city,
which is traditionally the enclave of urban intelligentsia and upper-middle class. The
lowest voter participation was measured in the southern working class areas (Csepel),
where the turnout was barely 60 per cent.

Geography of political party support

There are significant spatial differences in the distribution of political party support in
the spring 1990 Hungarian elections. These geographical variations are clearly shown
in the political party support maps. The cartographic and data observation units are
the 176 single-member electoral districts, which have approximately equal population,
and more or less coincide with the administrative division of the country.

The geographical analysis of the political party support concentrates on the six
major parties that eventually won seats in the Hungarian parliament. The vote for
party candidates in the single-member constituencies is studied for the first round.
Perhaps the strongest relationship concerning political party support is with

ELECTION TURNOUT

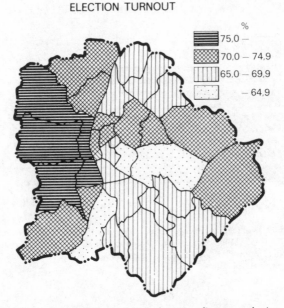

%
75,0 —
70,0 — 74,9
65,0 — 69,9
— 64,9

Figure 15.3   Electoral turnout in Budapest in the March 1990 parliamentary election

settlement, that is, a strong rural/urban dichotomy, or even a Budapest/country town/village trichotomy, in terms of voting behaviour emerges. Figure 15.4 displays the data for each of the top six parties with respect to settlement. For example, the liberal western-oriented Free Democrats (SZDSZ) won most of their votes in Budapest and other towns. On the other end of the scale, the conservative traditional Smallholders' and the Christian Democrats were supported mainly by village people. The peasant-oriented Smallholders' Party for instance gained more than 90 per cent of its vote outside Budapest. The traditional and religious values of these parties, and the question of land restoration, are more relevant to village populations. The distribution of votes cast for the remaining three parties (Democratic Forum, Socialists, and Young Democrats) is somewhat balanced (30–35 per cent) in these three settlement categories.

Hungarian Democratic Forum (MDF)

In the first round, the populist conservative Hungarian Democratic Forum received 24.7 per cent of the vote and emerged as the leading party, closely followed by the Free Democrats. The Democratic Forum had a strong urban middle-class character, but a large portion of the rural intelligentsia and the growing petty bourgeoisie also voted for them. During the campaign, the party's political platform did not resemble a West European style Conservative or Christian Democratic party, but a centrist–populist coalition with a broad political spectrum. The MDF was the only Hungarian political party which was able to create a 'catch-all' character. This became the main source of

PARTY VOTES BY TYPE OF SETTLEMENT

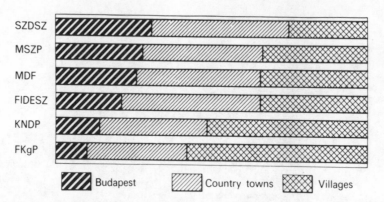

Figure 15.4 Distribution of the party votes by type by type of settlement in the Hungarian parliamentary elections March 1990. SZDSZ Alliance of the Free Democrats: MSZP Hungarian Socialist Party: MDF Hungarian Democratic Forum: FIDESZ Alliance of Young Democrats: KNDP Christian Democratic People's Party: FKg Smallholder's Party

DISTRIBUTION OF DEMOCRATIC FORUM'S VOTES

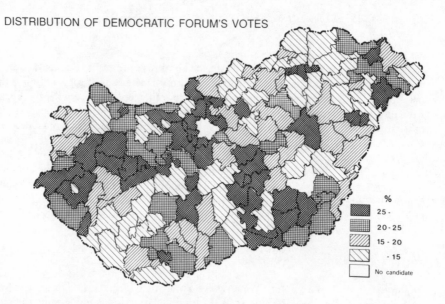

Figure 15.5 Geographic distribution of the Democratic Forum's vote in Hungary in March 1990 elections

its landslide electoral victory. The party could gain in the second round most of the voters of the unsuccessful parties, which meant that the MDF was the second preference of many originally non-MDF voters. Geographically, the MDF did well in all regions, especially in the central and south-eastern parts of the country (Figure 15.5). The Democratic Forum promoted a less radical and slightly etatist economic policy, a 'third road' of development, emphasizing that Hungary should not be 'sold out' to the West European interests. Thus, their programme won great support among ordinary people fearing the financial shock therapy of the economically and politically more liberal Free Democrats.

Alliance of Free Democrats (SZDSZ)

The metropolitan Budapest region and the rather developed and urbanised North West Hungary turned out to be the strongholds of the SZDSZ. It got weaker results in the eastern rural regions (see Figure 15.6). The social basis of the Free Democrats was dominated by urban intellectuals and professionals, that is, by the 'new middle class'. However, the results of Budapest confirm that this party had significant support among the lowest social strata as well. Within Budapest, the Free Democrats won easily in the western districts, where most of the voters belong to the upper stratum, but also in the poorest parts of the city (e.g. Csepel, Soroksár, Ujpest), inhabited mainly by industrial workers. The Free Democratic programme was economically more radical and more aggressively anti-communist than that of other parties. This apparently gained the party some sympathy in the upper as well as the lower strata who were the most disappointed with the former regime. By contrast, the intermediate strata, who could loose a great deal if a more radical shock therapy change occurred, voted for the MDF. In addition, many of the members of the once 800,000 strong Hungarian Socialist Workers' Party, and those employed in the administration and the armed forces also voted for the MDF fearing a possible liberal takeover.

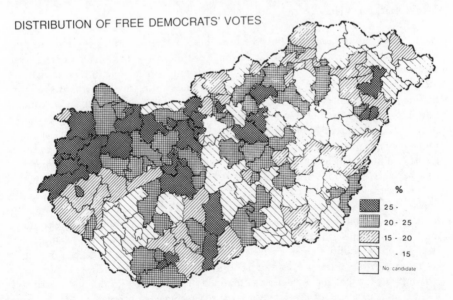

DISTRIBUTION OF FREE DEMOCRATS' VOTES

%
25 -
20 - 25
15 - 20
- 15
No candidate

Figure 15.6 Geographic distribution of Free Democratic Party votes in Hungary in March 1990 elections

DISTRIBUTION OF SMALLHOLDERS PARTY'S VOTES

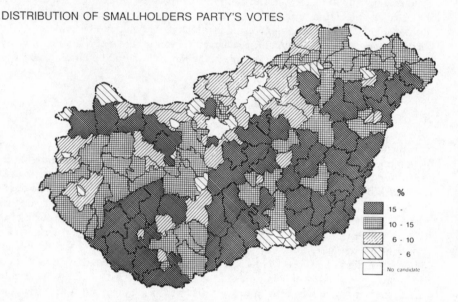

%

15 -

10 - 15

6 - 10

- 6

No candidate

Figure 15.7   Geographic distribution of Smallholders' Party votes in Hungary in March 1990 elections

Smallholders' Party (FKgP)

In the 1945 multi-party elections, the Smallholders' Party won an absolute majority with 57 per cent of the vote. As the leading 'historic party' the Smallholders' leadership envisioned a possible victory or, at least, playing a major role in the new government. The party obtained a disappointing 11.8 per cent of the first round vote. The decline in Smallholders' support is attributed primarily to the almost exclusive concentration on the one issue of restoration of land to previous owners. The party became a sectional party, backed by the poorly educated old-aged groups in the rural areas, by those who agree with the restoration of the 1947 land ownership system. In addition, the once influental urban wing of the party had dissolved. Craftsmen, shopkeepers and civil servants who once constituted the natural voters of the party now supported either the candidates of the Democratic Forum or the small Enterpreneurs' Party (which received 1.9 per cent). As might be expected, the Smallholders' Party strongholds were in rural Hungary. They received their highest percentage on the southern and eastern plains where the agricultural sector still dominates and the FKgP had strong political traditions (see Figure 15.7). On the other hand, Budapest, the bigger towns and the more urbanised western counties turned out to be their weakest regions. The support for the Smallholders' also declined in relationship to the position of agriculture in Hungarian society. Since 1945 the percentage of people employed in agriculture fell very sharply from 48 per cent to 18 per cent.

Hungarian Socialist Party (MSZP)

The Socialists received 10.8 per cent of the first round vote and proved to be the fourth largest party. They tried to put forward a programme of a European-style social democratic party and reminded the population of their role in bringing democracy to Hungary. The vast majority of the electorate, however, viewed the Socialists as the successor of the once-ruling Communist (Hungarian Socialist Workers') Party. The burden of this lineage and the hatred of economic stagnation and the one-party rule of the past, made 90 per cent of the population suspicious of the new Socialist Party. The Socialist vote was the spatially most balanced among the parties (just like in Czechoslovakia), although in Budapest (12.9 per cent) and in the bigger towns they achieved better scores (see Figure 15.8). Their well-known leaders, who took the lion's share of the credit for the abolition of communism, did better than the average. According to preliminary survey data, the Socialists trailed only the Free Democrats in the support received from the urban intelligentsia. Ironically, the largest party declaring socialist and social democratic ideas gained only token support from the working class.

League of Young Democrats (FIDESZ)

The League of Young Democrats as an age-specific political organization had strongest support, as might be expected, from the younger age groups. As a consequence, the FIDESZ found its greatest support in the university and college towns and in the larger urban centres. The resulting geographical pattern of Young Democrat votes consists of insular patches, cities, blank areas, and rural zones (see Figure 15.9). Their results had a slight correlation with the Free Democrats' votes. However, the constituency of the FIDESZ did not have an élite character. Voting data surprisingly also indicate

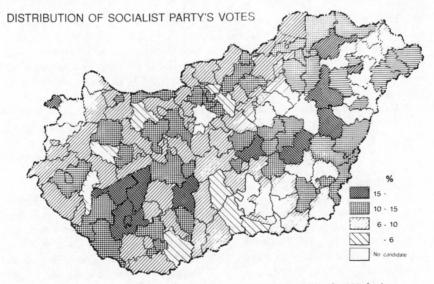

DISTRIBUTION OF SOCIALIST PARTY'S VOTES

%
15 -
10 - 15
6 - 10
- 6
No candidate

Figure 15.8   Geographic distribution of Socialist Party votes in Hungary in March 1990 elections

DISTRIBUTION OF YOUNG DEMOCRATS' VOTES

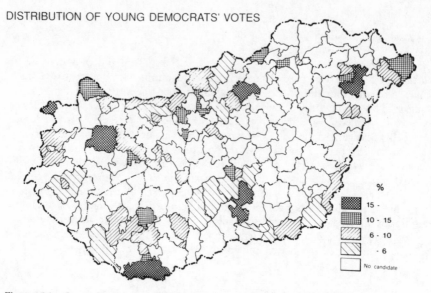

Figure 15.9   Geographic distribution of Young Democratic Party votes in Hungary in March 1990 elections

stronger than average support among elderly and lower income groups. The name of the party appealed to this group who wished to support the 'future of their grandchildren'.

Christian Democratic People's Party (KDNP)

The Christian Democrats received 6.5 per cent of the first round vote. Just like the Christian social parties of the inter-war period, they have their strongholds in northern and western Hungary. Since the KDNP has a close relationship with the Catholic Church, the major religion of Hungary, the party did best in the areas of heavy religious participation and church attendance (see Figure 15.10). In the eastern Protestant region, the party had negligible influence, except for three Greek-Catholic constituencies in the northeast. Similar to the Smallholders', the Christian Democrat voting basis is concentrated in the villages and in the poorly educated, over 50 years age group, with more female than male voters among their electorate.

A new political map of Hungary

The political segmentation of Hungarian society had been obvious for some time, even though it was not highlighted and could not be precisely described in a one-party political system. The 1990 Hungarian parliamentary elections gave the first reliable political map of the country after nearly half a century, even though some of the borderlines are still obscure (Szoboszlai, 1990). The election results had a significant geographical component. This spatial variation is related to a number of variables; urban-rural,

DISTRIBUTION OF CHRISTIAN DEMOCRATS' VOTES

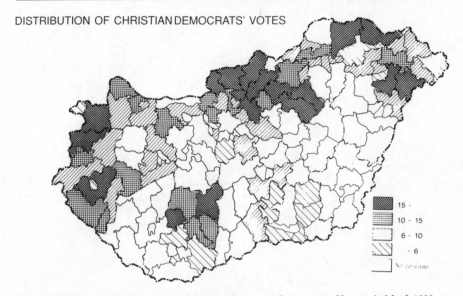

Figure 15.10   Geographic distribution of Christian Democratic Party votes in Hungary in March 1990 elections

class, region, education, occupation, political ideology, age, religion, etc. The new political map of Hungary seems to reveal a more conservative and less politically-motivated Eastern Hungary, and a highly diverse, but nonetheless, more liberal and politically active Western Hungary-Budapest region (Kovács, 1991). The political conservatism of the eastern part of Hungary is well reflected, for example, in the fact, that the surviving fraction of the former communist party (Hungarian Socialist Workers' Party) was able to preserve some of its influence only in this part of the country (see Figure 15.11). Yet, the extent and nature of conservatism varies from one geographic region to the next, closely following the political traditions and the level of economic development. In the area of the Plain for instance, the highest political motivation is still the relation to the land, while in Northern Hungary, Catholic sentiments face a strong communist and socialist ideology.

Comparisons of voting data suggest some stability in the long-term political traditions, voting behaviour and ideological structure, in spite of over four decades of the communist one-party system. For example, ethnic questions always played a significant role in previous Hungarian elections. Nationalism and the question of ethnic minorities also surfaced in the 1990 elections. On the eve of the elections, the worst outbreak of anti-Hungarian violence was reported from Romania. Since the Democratic Forum had always based its appeal on nationalist feelings, the Romanian clashes affected the Hungarian elections by giving a boost to the Democratic Forum in all parts of the country, but especially in eastern Hungary. On the other hand, the Democratic Forum had much less influence in those settlements where the majority of the inhabitants belong to one of the four ethnic groups of the country (Germans, Slovaks, South-Slavs and Romanians) or to Gypsies.

The ideological structure of the Hungarian electorate bear some similarity to the 1945 election. In 1945, for example, the Smallholders' Party, concentrating most of

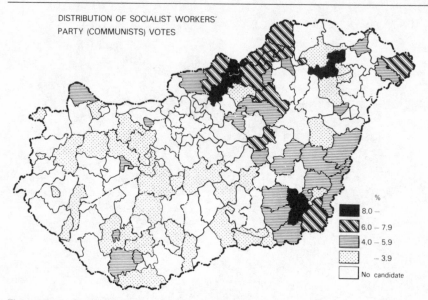

DISTRIBUTION OF SOCIALIST WORKERS'
PARTY (COMMUNISTS) VOTES

%
8.0 —
6.0 – 7.9
4.0 – 5.9
– 3.9
No candidate

Figure 15.11   Geographic distribution of Socialist Workers' Party (formerly Communist Party) votes in Hungary in March 1990 elections

the conservative vote, received slightly over 57 per cent. In the 1990 elections, the centre-right parties obtained virtually the same per centage (56 per cent) (Lomax, 1990). A historical continuity in electoral behaviour is also demonstrated by the strong regional character of the historic parties (FKgP, KDNP).

There are also some basic differences between the emerging Hungarian political party structure and the post-war political system. First of all, the recent elections were dominated by new parties (MDF, SZDSZ, FIDESZ); their proportion of the total vote was 55.3 per cent. Another significant difference was the absolute domination of the right and the failure and fragmentation of the left. The left-wing vote in the 1990 Hungarian election was approximately 24 per cent in the first round. However, the only true left-wing party which won parliamentary seats was the Socialist Party. The remaining left-wing vote was divided among several small parties, three of which barely missed parliamentary allocation (Hungarian Socialist Workers' Party, Hungarian Social Democratic Party, Agrarian Alliance). The result of the elections was very much influenced by the fact, that 35 per cent of those eligible did not cast their vote in the first round. According to Szelényi, people with strong social-democratic values were significantly overrepresented among non-voters (Szelényi, 1991,). Another important feature was that, while in the early post-war years the Hungarian political scene developed towards bipolarization, in 1990 the emergence of a strong liberal centre (SZDSZ, FIDESZ) produced a tripolar structure.

In comparison with the experiences of other East European elections, Hungary seemed to have advanced the furthest in establishing a pluralist multi-party system by 1990. The relative maturity of the party system and the voting behaviour of the citizens indicate that, due to a series of reform movements of the last two decades, Hungary shifted furthest away from the Stalinist model. In some of the East European countries (e.g. USSR, Romania, Bulgaria, Serbia, Albania) though certain changes did take place till 1990, they were not profound enough to transform the Byzantine-type political system. On the other hand, in Czechoslovakia and Poland, political change was accomplished by 1990. But even in these two countries, the party system has not been developed to the extent that it was in Hungary. The political parties in Hungary represented a whole range of political ideas and choice, while Civic Forum in Czechoslovakia and Solidarity in Poland could be considered mass movements, rather than real, 'blue blooded' political parties.

In the near future, the Hungarian political party structure may change substantially, while the basic spatial aspects of ideological/political party support may stay the same. The number of parties will undoubtedly decrease. The restructuring on the left of the political scene is very likely. The many left-wing parties may coalesce behind the Socialists or a wider social democratic coalition to make a larger force in the next election. The Alliance of Free Democrats might be compelled to seek a social democratic character and shift into the political vacuum on the moderate left. The centre right parties may also coalesce around the Hungarian Democratic Forum to establish a grand conservative or western-style Christian Democratic Party. In any event, the 1990 Hungarian parliamentary elections meant a new beginning in the political history of the country, and drew a new political map, which will be the basis for any future comparison.

References

Balinshi, M.L., Young, H.P., 1982, *Fair representation*, Yale University Press, New Haven, CT.

Bernát, T. (ed.) 1985, *An Economic Geography of Hungary* Akadémiai Kiadó, Budapest.

Bogdanor, V., 1984, *What is Proportional Representation?* Martin Robertson, Oxford.

Hajdu, T., 1985, 'Választójog 1918–1919-ben', *História* 7 (5–6): 49–51.

Hann, C.M. (ed.) 1990, *Market Economy and Civil Society in Hungary*, Frank Cass, London.

Hofmann, G.W. (ed.) 1989, *Europe in the 1990's: a geographic analysis*, John Wiley & Sons, New York.

Johnston, R.J., 1979, *Political, Electoral and Spatial Systems*, Oxford University Press, Oxford.

Körösényi, A., 1991, 'Revival of the past or new beginning?: the nature of post-communist politics', *Political Quarterly* 62 (1): 52–74.

Kosáry, D., 1985, 'A polgári parlament megszületése Magyarországon', *História* 7 (5-6): 30–32.

Kovács, Z., 1991, 'Az 1990. évi parlamenti választások politikai földrajzi tapasztalatai', *Földrajzi Értesítô* 40 (1–2): 55–80.

Lomax, B., 1990, 'Endgame in Hungary', *Journal of Communist Studies* 6 (2): 190–193.

Martis, K.C., Kovács, Z., Kovács, D., Péter, S., 1992, 'The geography of the 1990 Hungarian parliamentary elections', *Political Geography* 11 (3): 283–305.

Pölöskei, F., 1985, 'Választójog, parlamentarizmus 1919 után', *História* 7 (5–6): 54–56.

Szelényi, I., Szelényi, S.Z., 1991, 'The vacuum in Hungarian politics: classes and parties', *New Left Review* 117, 121–137.

Szoboszlai, Gy., 1990, 'Politikai tagoltság 1990: a választások tükrében', *Társadalmi Szemle* 45(8–9): 18–31.

Index

Abchazia 92, 101–102
Afghanistan 21, 41, 46
Agency and structure 16–17
Agriculture 38, 53–54, 56–57, 58, 61–67,
    104 169, 171, 180, 200, 205–206,
    248, 255, 263, 268
Albania 2, 58, 64, 66, 67, 121, 272
Albanians (in Yugoslavia) 121–124
Alliance of Free Democrats (SZDSZ)
    258–259, 265, 267, 272
Allies of World War II 2, 158
American foreign policy 54, 60
Andropov, Yuri 32, 44, 49, 76
Anti-geopolitics, 76
Anti-semitism 152, 163
Aral Sea 7, 208–212
Aralsk 209, 210, 211–212
Armenia 92, 97, 101–102, 111
August 1991 attempted Soviet putsch 28, 32,
    90, 100, 102, 105, 107, 192
Austria 17, 45, 46, 79, 116, 127, 130, 223,
    263
Austrian-Hungarian empire 127, 156
Autonomy 4, 32, 33, 35, 43
Axes of public opinion in Soviet Union 192,
    203
Azerbaijan 92, 101, 111, 214

Bakatin, V. 197, 198–200, 203
Balkans 3, 117, 133, 134, 181, 255
Baltic Republics 92, 100–101, 110, 202
Belgrade 59, 61, 117, 120, 123, 129, 130
Berlin 17
    East 18
    Wall 2, 18, 53, 71
    West 18
Bipolar world order 3, 15–21, 23, 26–27
Birlik (Uzbek Popular Front), 104
Blocs (superpower) 4, 5, 17–20, 23, 26, 42,
    44, 46, 74, 199
Bohemia, 137, 143, 237, 243–244, 246, 248,
    251
Borders 1, 19, 21, 41, 52, 56, 78, 141, 149,
    182, 246
    Czech border 246, 248

Disputes 1–61, 80, 93
Hungarian borders 263
Hungarian-Romanian border 141, 148,
    155–156, 162–163
Polish-Romanian 1, 202, 228
Yugoslavian 103, 111, 115, 117, 121–125,
    127, 129, 130
Bourgas (Bulgaria) 167, 170–171, 175, 180,
    182
Brandt, Willy 18
Brezhnev, Leonid 25, 35, 36, 76, 94
Brynkin, V. 211–212
Bucharest 151, 153
Budapest 5, 168, 256, 263, 265, 267, 271
    Elections 264, 267, 268, 269
Bulgaria 2, 6, 7, 11, 12, 31, 43, 58, 64, 66,
    79–80, 121, 122, 133, 186, 257, 272
    Democracy in, 180–184
    Elections 167–169, 171–174
    Environmental issues 169–170, 172,
    175–184
Byelorussia 95, 96, 97, 102, 103

Cantons 126–128, 130
Capitalism 4, 7, 32, 34, 36, 75, 76, 178, 181,
    183
Ceauşescu, Nicholai 2, 145, 151
Central Asia 7, 93, 104, 108, 109, 110, 111,
    196, 208, 209, 210
Central Europe 3, 9, 10, 11, 12, 115, 133,
    168, 169, 171, 174, 176, 235
Chamber of Nations (upper house in
    Czechoslovakia) 236, 253
Chamber of the People (lower house in
    Czechoslovakia) 236
Chernobyl 79, 103
China 33, 34, 43
Christian Democrats
    Czechoslovak 241, 244–245, 248,
    250–251, 253
    Hungarian 258, 260, 265, 270, 273
    Polish 228
    Yugoslavian 117, 119
CIS (Commonwealth of Independent States)
    54, 91–93, 96, 111, 112,189
Citizens' Committees (Poland) 223, 226, 229

Civic Forum 235, 236, 240, 241 244, 249, 250, 253, 273,
Civic Democratic party (ODS) 250, 252–254
Cleavages
Czechoslovakia 249
Hungary 255
Soviet Union 189, 190, 194, 208, 212–213,
CMEA (Council of Mutual Economic Assistance) 20, 35–38, 41–46, 49
Coexistence Party (National Minority Party–Czechoslovakia) 246–248
Cold War 1, 4–6, 15, 18, 25, 31–33, 35, 40, 41, 43, 47, 48, 53, 54, 57–62, 64, 66
Post 71
Second 46, 47, 73
COMECON 9, 169, 171
Communist party 2, 34, 36, 38, 77
Bulgaria 176, 178, 183
Czechoslovakia 226–227, 235–237, 240, 241, 243, 244, 249, 251
Hungary 257, 271
Kazahkstan 104, 209, 214
Romania 150, 158, 160, 162, 173
Soviet Union 99–103,107, 192–193, 197, 198, 200,
Yugoslavia 120–121
Communists
Bulgaria 2, 173, 181
Czechoslovakia 7, 235, 237, 239, 241–244, 250, 253
Hungary 244
Poland 7, 31
Reform Communists in Czechoslovakia 241
Romania 31, 149, 154, 159
Sovereign 99, 103, 104
Soviet Union 7, 99, 102, 106, 107, 192, 193
Yugoslavia 6, 115, 117, 119, 120–122, 127
Competence Act (Local Government Duties and Powers Act in Poland), 222
Confederation 115, 135, 153
Bulgaria 170, 173, 178, 182
Poland 228
Soviet Union 89, 90, 93, 97, 100, 101, 105–108, 110–112, 189–192, 200, 207
Core process 3, 34, 49

Core-periphery 7, 34, 205
Cotton 56, 58, 104, 211
Crimea 95
Croatia 1, 115–117, 119–121, 123–127, 129, 153
CSCE (Conference on Security and Cooperation in Europe) 81
Cuba 20, 22, 59, 60, 249
Culture 3, 9, 11 ,23, 34, 38, 74, 171, 213, 214, 239
Conflict in Romania 147, 149, 150, 156, 158, 159, 161, 162, 163
Gypsies in Czechoslovakia 133, 135, 136, 142
Soviet Union 96, 98, 99, 101, 103, 104, 106, 108, 112
Yugoslavia 117, 122, 124, 125, 127, 129, 130
Czech Republic
Elections 236, 241, 246, 250–253
Gypsies 136–138, 140
Czech National Council 236–237, 239, 251, 253
Czechoslovak Socialist Party 235, 237, 240, 243
Czechoslovakia 2, 3, 4, 5, 6, 7, 8, 9, 11, 12, 18, 20, 27, 43, 58, 63, 64, 66, 77, 78, 79, 80, 159, 168, 179, 257, 263, 269, 273
Demography 135–140
Elections 235–52
June 1992 elections 251–52
Minorities 133–164
Political parties 235–52

Dealignment 25, 74, 83
Democracy 3, 4, 7, 9–13, 100
Bulgaria 167, 169, 173, 175, 176, 180
Czechoslovakia 237, 239–241, 244, 246, 249, 251
Hungary 255–256, 263, 269
Poland 217–220, 222, 224, 227, 234, 235
Romania 154
Soviet Union 189, 190, 212, 214, 215
Yugoslavia 119, 123, 124, 141, 143
Détente 18–22, 23, 26
Dissident Movements 5, 71, 78, 193, 257, 258
Diversion of Siberian rivers 210–211
Dniester 102
Dubcek, Alexander 236, 252

East European revolutions 1, 2, 4–7, 9, 12, 15, 27, 38, 53, 64, 72, 77
    Bulgaria 167, 169, 173,
    Czechoslovakia 235, 236, 249, 253
    Poland 219, 220, 225
    Romania 142, 144, 145, 149, 150, 153, 163
    Soviet Union 189, 213
East-West 2, 18, 21, 25, 33
    Détente 2, 36, 46, 47, 72, 74, 78
    Trade 26, 40
Eastern Europe 1–5, 9, 11, 12, 44, 49, 53, 54, 57–67, 71–75, 77–82, 133, 161, 189, 217, 233, 236, 257
    Environment, 167, 169, 170, 175, 177, 180, 183, 184
    Food aid 31–37
    Gypsies 134
Eco-glasnost 173–75, 179, 180, 182–183
Economic aid 40, 70, 80
EEP (Export Enhancement Program) 65
Electoral apportionment 190
Electoral cleavages 189, 190, 194, 207, 208, 212, 213, 249, 255
Electoral turnout 3, 7
    Czechoslovkia 239, 251,
    Hungary 263, 264
    Poland 228–229
    Soviet Union 189, 193–197, 207, 209
Emigration 26, 64, 66, 105, 146, 150, 160, 161
END (European Nuclear Disarmament) 5, 73, 77, 78
Environmental issues 3, 6, 7, 99, 101, 103, 104, 211, 222, 241, 255
    Bulgaria 167, 168, 169–185
    Security 74, 76, 78–79, 82
Estonia 91, 97, 100, 190
Ethiopia 61
European Community (EEC) 1, 5, 12, 16, 21, 53, 61, 63, 65, 80, 82, 117, 126, 161, 258

Factor analysis 203–204
Fergana Valley 93, 104
Finland 41, 43, 45, 46
Food aid 3, 53–54, 56–62, 64, 66, 67
Food policy 53–57, 63, 66, 67
Food power 62
France 19, 25, 27, 43, 45, 46, 63, 80
Free market 3, 7, 12, 257, 258, 259

GATT (General Agreement on Tariffs and Trade) 54, 66, 67
Genscher, Hans-Dietrich 26, 150
Geopolitical codes 27, 27, 28
Geopolitical divide 72
Geopolitical forces 2
Geopolitical order 15, 16, 17, 19
Geopolitical transition 4, 15, 20, 61
Geopolitics 9, 12, 13, 25, 16, 27–28, 31, 53, 66, 71, 72, 79, 87, 111
Georgia 92, 97, 101, 102, 111, 190, 191, 196
Germans in Romania 6, 145, 146, 149, 150, 153, 154–163
German-Soviet Treaty (1990) 28
Germany 25, 26, 27 41, 271
    East 2, 4, 21, 27, 71, 78, 168, 257
    West 2, 4, 21, 25, 26, 43, 45, 46, 63, 150, 160, 257
Glasnost 33, 39, 75, 78, 113, 168, 172
Gmina (Polish municipality) 221, 228, 232, 233
Gorbachev faction 32, 95, 107, 108, 110, 111, 209, 257
Gorbachev, Mikhail 2, 4, 5, 21, 26–28, 32, 33, 35–38, 49, 76, 77, 89
Grain 36, 37, 41, 43, 45–48, 67
Green Party 7, 168, 174, 175, 179, 180, 189, 240, 248, 251
GSM (Export Credit Guarantee Program) 66
Gypsies 6
    Czechoslovakia 133–144
    Hungary 159, 263, 271
    Romania 145, 149, 152, 154, 158, 161–163
    Yugoslavia 121

Havel, Vaclav 11, 78, 236, 254
HDZ (Democratic Croat Community in Bosnia-Hercegovina) 119, 120, 121, 127, 129
Hegemony 4, 20, 27, 32, 34, 54, 57, 61, 62, 63, 66, 74, 82
Helsinki Watch 18, 146, 149, 151, 153, 154, 158, 161
Historical parties in Czechoslovakia 235, 237, 239, 240, 241, 242, 244, 249, 253
HSD-SMS Party (Movement for Self-Governing Democracy-Society for Moravia and Silesia) 246, 247, 251
Hungarian Democratic Forum (MDF) 265–267, 272

Hungary 2, 3, 4, 6, 7, 12, 18, 20, 26, 27, 58, 63, 64, 66, 67, 79, 116, 117, 133, 136, 147, 149, 151, 152, 154, 155, 156, 157, 160, 162, 163, 168, 174, 248, 251
  Elections 261–272
  Parties 259–260
  Political history 253–257

Iliescu, Ion 151, 152, 163
IMF (International Monetary Fund) 41, 177, 181
Imperial overstretch (Kennedy thesis) 20, 27, 39
INF (Intermediate Nuclear Forces), 77, 78
Ingushia 196, 199
Internal colonization 89, 94, 95, 97, 105, 106
Irredentism 6, 80, 102, 105, 112
Istria 125, 27, 129
Italians 117, 123, 124, 129
Italy 19, 45, 46, 116, 117

Jaruzelski, General 219, 220
Jews 6, 151, 152, 154, 158, 162, 163

Kameno (Bulgaria) 170
Kazakhs 93, 96, 104, 105, 108–111, 201, 208–211
Kazahkstan 7, 108, 209, 210–211
KDU (Christian and Democratic Union) 242, 249, 250
Khrushchev, Nikita 27, 32, 33, 35, 36, 59, 94, 97
Kirgizia 93, 104
Kondratieff phases
  IVA 38, 40
  IVB 49
Kosovo, 121, 122, 125, 127
Krajilna (Bosnia, Croatia and Serbia) 6, 115, 123, 125, 126, 127,129, 130
Kzvl-Orda 208–212

Latvia 92, 97, 100
League of Young Democrats (FIDESZ) 257–258, 260, 269–270
League of Yugoslav Communists 114–15
Leningrad 167, 193, 194, 195, 197, 199, 206, 209, 214

Leninist movements 35, 49, 76
Leninsk 209, 212
Lithuania 92, 97, 100, 103
Local Self-Government Act (Poland) 221
Long peace 18
Loss of strength gradient 17

Macedonia 115, 121–126
  West 125
Magyars 147, 154, 155
Makashov, A. 198, 199, 202, 203, 204
Marshall Plan 5, 63, 70
Marxism-Leninism 9, 38, 75, 259
Marxist parties 9, 36, 163, 258
Mazowiecki, Tadeusz 219, 220, 230, 233
Milosevic, Slobodan 122, 124
Mitteleuropa 1
Moldavia 92, 97, 102, 111, 160, 191
Montenegro 115, 116, 119, 122, 124, 127
Moscow 58, 59, 75, 76, 77, 78, 101, 102, 103, 104, 107, 108, 163, 192, 193, 195, 196, 197, 199, 200, 205, 206, 109, 211, 214
Moslems 95, 97, 104, 111, 119, 120, 121, 122, 123, 124, 126, 127, 130, 212
Movement for Democratic Slovakia (HZDS) 250, 251, 253, 254,

Nagorno-Karabakh 92, 101
National Salvation Front (Romania) 151, 154, 162
Nationalism 2, 4, 6, 12, 80, 122, 130, 145, 151, 152, 153, 161–163, 167, 168, 189, 193
  Ethno-territorial 90, 250, 248, 258, 271
  Soviet Union 89, 90,
NATO 4, 5, 19, 21, 27, 41, 46, 47, 48, 71, 72, 74, 76, 78, 80
NEP (New Economic Policy) 35
Nonoffensive offense (NOD) 73, 76
Nuclear disarmament 110
Nuclear parity 18, 20, 78
Nuclear weapons 18, 19, 71, 72, 73, 74, 75, 76, 79, 103, 110, 111, 173

OECD (Organization for Economic Cooperation and Development) 38, 46 48
Oil and gas 32, 35, 36, 37, 38, 39, 45, 47, 96, 195

Orthodox Christians 119, 122, 129, 196
Ossetia
    North 102, 195, 196
    South 92, 101, 102, 196
Ostpolitik 4, 23, 41
Ottoman Empire 33, 116, 126, 127

Palme Commission (UN Independent
    Commission on Disarmament and
    Security Issues, 1982) 73, 77
Paris Peace Conference (4+2 talks) 2, 27
PDP (Party for Democratic Prosperity) in
    Macedonia 121–122
Peasants 158, 181, 205, 206, 213, 226, 227
    265
Perestroika 33, 39, 49, 50, 75, 77, 172, 183
Persian Gulf 68, 71
PL–480 (Agricultural Trade Development
    and Assistance Act) 56–65
Pluralism, 2, 4, 9, 11, 12, 64 ,115, 117, 119,
    123, 125, 171, 174, 183, 190, 213,
    219, 225, 227, 228, 232, 241, 263,
    272
Poland 2, 3, 4, 5, 7, 12, 20, 26, 27, 43, 53,
    78, 80, 168, 202, 217, 261, 251, 257,
    263, 273
    Elections 224–232, 241, 251
    Food aid 58–61, 64, 67
    Local government restructuring, 218,
        219–225, 233–34
Political groups 1, 2, 3, 15, 16, 263
Political temperature 199–200
Postcommunism 3, 6, 9, 11, 12, 32, 100,
    109, 110, 112, 134, 161, 235
Prague 1, 4, 5, 136, 241, 242, 244, 249, 253
Prague Spring (1968) 142, 236, 253
Proportional Representation (PR) 235, 236,
    259, 260
Public Against Violence 235, 236, 240, 241,
    244, 250 253

Reagan, Ronald 25, 32, 39, 41, 46, 47, 75,
    76, 78,179
Referendum 7, 92, 108, 111, 117, 122, 123,
    126, 129, 154, 189, 192, 195 196,
    197, 200, 203, 208, 241, 249
Refugees 78, 79, 130
    Yugoslavia 130
Regionalism 12, 21, 23, 127, 213
Regulski, Jerzy 218, 219, 231
Resource economy 4, 32, 34, 444–45

Restructuring of economics 79, 171, 177,
    212, 218
Revolution of 1917 34, 39, 190, 204, 205,
    206
Rodnoy Yazyk (mother tongue) 95
Romania 12, 58, 60, 63, 64, 65, 66, 67, 79,
    80, 133, 163, 168, 172, 239, 257, 263,
    271, 272
    Minorities 146–150, 156–163
    Political struggle 145, 151–153, 154–156
Romany (see also gypsy) 6, 133–144
Rousse (Bulgaria)172–173
Rukh (Ukranian front) 102–103
Russia 3, 5, 11, 28, 34, 39, 80, 89, 93,
    105–107, 108, 189, 192, 195–196,
    213, 223
    Elections, 7, 192–194, 195, 197–208
    Nationalism 90–93, 96, 97, 93, 101, 102,
        103, 105, 167, 209
Russian Federation 93, 97, 101, 105, 106,
    110–112, 189, 190, 192, 200, 207
Russians in other Republics 90-92, 93, 94,
    95, 96, 97, 98, 101, 103, 159,
    209–214, 213
Russification 89, 91, 94, 95, 96, 97, 106
Ryzhkov, Nikolai 192, 197, 198, 199, 200,
    203, 204, 208

Sarajevo 126
Sarazhanov, A. 210, 211, 212
SDA (Party of Democratic Action in Bosnia-
    Hercegovina), 210, 126, 127
SDS (Democratic Serb Party in Bosnia-
    Hercegovina) 120, 127, 129
Security 3, 5, 15, 16, 17, 18, 21, 71–80
    Environmental 80–82
Semi-peripheral states 34, 39, 45, 49
Serbia 6, 31, 115, 116, 117, 119, 121, 122,
    123, 124, 126, 127, 272
Siberia 1, 42, 195, 199, 200, 202, 206, 207,
    210
Sinatra doctrine 77
Sistematizare (village destruction in
    Romania) 161
Skopje 122
Slavic populations 92, 93, 95, 96, 97, 101,
    105, 111, 116, 119, 162, 163, 271
Sliyanie (assimilation) 94
Slovak National Council 236, 237, 239, 244,
    246, 251, 252
Slovak National Party 244, 245, 246, 250,
    251, 253

Slovak Peoples' Party (Hlinka Party) 238, 240, 244
Slovakia 31, 133, 168, 237, 239, 244
   Elections and parties 240–252
   Minorities 134–142
   Separatism 244–252
Solvenia 115, 116, 117, 121, 123, 124, 125, 126, 127, 129,130
Smallholders Party (FKgP) 257, 258, 259, 260, 265, 268, 270, 271
Social movements 77, 81, 173, 176, 179, 181, 213
Socialism 10, 31, 36, 39, 75, 76, 79, 141, 159, 258
Socialist Workers Party (Communist Party of Hungary) 256, 257, 259, 267, 269, 271, 272,
Solidarity 7, 60, 167, 168, 223, 227, 228, 233, 273
Soviet Union 1, 2, 3, 4, 5, 6, 7, 9, 10, 20, 21, 25, 27, 28, 31, 32, 33, 34, 35–49, 158, 159, 162, 163, 171, 237, 257
   August 1990 coup 167
   Economy 169, 171
   Environmental issue, 170
   Ethnic groups, 89, 113, 149
   Exports, 33, 35, 36, 37, 41, 43, 44, 45, 47 48
   Imports, 33, 35, 36, 37, 39, 42, 43 44, 45, 48
   International relations, 53, 57, 60, 61, 71, 72, 73, 74, 75, 76, 77, 78, 79, 80
   Politics 189–191, 196, 204, 208, 212–215, 272
   Productivity, 38
Stalinist movements 32, 33, 35, 36, 38, 39, 49, 75, 94, 159, 163, 272
Structures of post-war Eastern Europe 2, 3, 4, 9, 12, 16, 17, 18, 21, 26, 49, 66, 71, 73, 79, 81, 90, 99, 103, 106, 107, 110, 112, 122, 123, 169, 170, 190–91, 193, 194, 197, 205, 209, 212, 213, 220, 221, 232, 236, 255, 271, 272, 273
Stucturation 12, 15, 16
Sverdlovsk 197, 199
Szekler Hungarians 147, 148, 155, 158, 159, 160, 163

Tadjikistan 93, 104
Tatars 93, 95, 105, 106

TEA (Targeted Export Assistance) 65
Third World 4, 18, 21, 31, 32, 34, 36, 7, 40, 41, 43, 49, 62, 67, 214
Tito, Josef Broz 2, 6, 58, 59, 61, 117, 119, 124
Titular groups and languages 5, 89, 90, 91, 92, 93, 97–107, 112
Trade Act of 1974 (Jackson-Vanik Act) 64, 66
Transcaucasia 92, 101
Transylvania 146, 147, 149, 151, 153, 154, 155, 156, 157, 158, 159, 160, 162, 163
Trianon Peace Settlement (1920) 156–157
Tuleyev, A. 198, 199, 200, 201, 202 203, 204
Turkmenistan 93, 104

United States 36, 76, 78, 80, 82, 168
   Food aid 58, 60, 61, 64, 65, 66
   Soviet relations 23, 25
Ukraine 11, 92, 95, 96, 97, 102, 103, 108, 109, 110, 111, 191
Unemployment, 7, 12, 143, 154, 170, 177, 182, 212, 250
Uneven development, 213, 221
Unitary system in Soviet Union 107
Ural 1, 155, 195, 199, 202, 206
Uzbekistan 93, 104, 214

Vatra Romaneasca (Romanian hearth) 151, 152, 153
Velvet Revolution (1989) 2, 142, 235, 248

VMRO (Revolutionary Nationalist Macedonian Organization) 121–22
Voivodship (electoral district in Poland) 220, 221, 222, 223, 232,

Walesa, Lech 219, 230–231
Warsaw, 5, 223, 228
Warsaw Pact 9, 27, 40, 60, 71, 77, 78
WEIS (World Events Intention Survey) 42, 46–48
West European Union, 80
Western Europe 9, 11, 41, 47, 49, 61, 63, 71, 77, 79, 80, 81, 161, 255, 258
   Gypsies 134, 149
Women 74, 138, 139, 140, 141, 142, 143, 158, 178, 209, 225, 228, 255

Candidates 210, 225
World economy 32, 33, 34, 35, 37, 39, 41,
    49, 213
World-system 4, 32, 33, 213

Xenophobia 162

Yeltsin, Boris 192, 193, 195, 196, 197, 198,
    199, 200, 203, 208
Yugoslavia 3, 5, 6, 31, 45, 46, 53, 58, 59, 60,
    61, 64, 66, 72, 79, 80, 81, 130, 136

Civil War 121–25
Elections, 118–123
Political history 116–118
Separation into Republics, 124–130
Yugoslav Constitution (1974) 124

Zagreb 117, 119, 120
Zhirinovsky, V. 198, 199, 202, 203, 204, 208
Zhivkov 6, 168, 171, 173, 174, 179, 182
Zwischeneuropa (in between Europe) 12